Mental Health in Ireland
Policy, Practice & Law

Mental Health in Ireland

Policy, Practice & Law

Edited by

AGNES HIGGINS **and** SHARI MCDAID

GILL & MACMILLAN

Gill & Macmillan
Hume Avenue
Park West
Dublin 12
www.gillmacmillan.ie

The opinions expressed by contributing authors are not necessarily those of the editors
or the publisher.

978 07171 5980 2

Print origination by Síofra Murphy
Printed by GraphyCems, Spain
Index by Adam Pozner

*The paper used in this book comes from the wood pulp of managed forests. For every tree felled, at
least one tree is planted, thereby renewing natural resources.*

A CIP catalogue record is available for this book from the British Library.

110005406

To Lisa McGowan, who struggled in life and whose death challenges us all to do better.

Acknowledgements

It is our pleasure to acknowledge the many people whose encouragement and enthusiasm for a book of this nature gave us confidence to embark on the project in the first place. The book is a product of collaborative efforts by a number of different people and we are grateful to all the contributing authors for sharing their ideas and for staying with us throughout the process. We would like to thank all those who read drafts of the chapters and who, through their comments, strengthened the thoughts expressed therein. We would like to acknowledge Ivor Browne and Eddie Molloy who generously gave of their time to write the forewords for the book, and to Ciara Leavy for patiently checking references. Marion O'Brien, Catherine Gough and Nora Mahony at Gill & Macmillan also deserve mention for having faith in us to complete the project within the time frame and worked diligently with us to bring it to completion. We are deeply indebted to the many service users and family members who in the course of our work courageously spoke about their experience, touched our lives and shaped our thinking. Finally, a big thank you goes to the two men in our lives, James P. O'Neill and Edmund McDaid, who remained calmly silent and tolerant of the many late nights of writing and editing and kept us fed.

Agnes Higgins and Shari McDaid

Foreword
Eddie Molloy, PhD

The domain of mental health is more riddled with controversy and dispute than any other area within the wider health system. As the authors set out in their introduction, many fundamental questions remain unresolved: Is mental illness a problem of the mind or of the brain? Should we even use the term 'illness' in this context? Where do the protagonists stand on the matter of medication? Does a personal narrative add to the scientific evidence base? How do we judge the capacity of a distressed individual to make decisions or address the risk inherent in these decisions?

If an individual were deeply conflicted about his identity, troubled about dark deeds in the past (like locking people up unnecessarily) and anxious about his future, that person would undoubtedly need the assistance of the mental health services.

For all forms of emotional or mental distress ranging from small worries to psychotic breakdowns, the single most efficacious and indispensable response is to listen with respect to the person in difficulty, whether or not medication or even involuntary admission to a secure place is deemed necessary. Creating a context in which the person feels genuinely respected as a person is the most essential determinant of good outcomes. Without this element, the effect of all other therapies, cognitive, chemical or other that might be applied will be blunted, neutralised or even detrimental.

In keeping with what works best for the troubled individual, there is a pressing need for mutually respectful and sustained dialogue among the diverse actors in the mental health care system – people who are in distress and their families, professional carers, researchers, lawyers, GPs and others – who have a part to play. It is in this context that Agnes Higgins and Shari McDaid have done a great service to all involved in producing this book.

While the authors' own perspectives naturally dominate in the choice of material, a 'broad church' is represented in the papers. Also they set a tone that is appreciative of other views in order to 'generate further discussion, to provoke further debate and facilitate the reader's reflection on their own role and contributions to the mental health system'.

The book 'does not offer answers'; rather it covers a range of viewpoints and ends each chapter with a 'set of reflective questions to prompt further discussion and debate'. In a sense what Agnes and Shari have done is to create a 'space' in which needed, mutually respectful engagement may take place.

Not only is there breadth of perspective in this book but there is also depth. The authors do not shrink from raising the philosophical questions that inevitably underpin the differences in causation, treatment, power, risk, capacity and other matters that arise every day for carers and service users alike.

These philosophical questions are messy to deal with and practitioners often lose patience quickly whenever they are raised. However, there is no avoiding sustained, patient discussion on these deeper issues if the parties involved are to advance towards a consensus that serves the best interests of the person in distress. *Mental Health in Ireland* represents a significant contribution to these vital deliberations among those directly involved in the mental health services.

This is not a specialist book, however. Although each of the authors' contributions represents a scholarly treatment of the subject matter, the content will be accessible to the general reader. This is important because in so far as it reaches a wide readership, the book will contribute to further diluting the stigma surrounding mental health problems and breaching the associated taboo on discussing it.

Both Agnes and Shari are very busy people, but because of their dedication to relieving the emotional and mental distress experienced by so many people in our society they have worked long hours to produce this book. For this I express gratitude on behalf of the many people who will ultimately benefit from their endeavour.

Eddie Molloy, PhD
Chairman, Mental Health Reform

Foreword

Ivor Browne

When the medical profession took over the management of the mentally ill, they instituted a range of so-called 'treatments' – bleedings, purgings, beatings, dropping people into freezing water, swinging chairs and so on – that one can only look at now as torture. Seeking to distinguish contemporary practice from the barbarism of the past, many in the profession found refuge in a reductionist, mechanistic conception of the human being that separated out the biological brain from the rest of the functioning body and analysed mental illness in terms of a malfunction in the brain.

In many ways, the profession of psychiatry still struggles with the shadow of this legacy today. The colonisation of psychiatry by this reductionist thinking continues to hinder the profession's development. Psychiatry is woefully out of date, bound up in a germ theory of disease that has long outlived its relevance. The psychiatrist's current arsenal consists mostly of psycho-active medications that act on the brain as if it were an independent organism, administered on a long-term basis, while too often there is little in the way of a trusting, therapeutic relationship with the aim of addressing the underlying causes of breakdown. Psychiatrists' desire to align themselves with medicine is shown in the labels they choose for their treatments – 'antidepressants', 'antipsychotics' – which sound like medical treatments used for physical illnesses: antibiotics and anticonvulsants. The outcomes are poor, with many people led into a state of chronic sickness.

As is shown in this volume, psychiatrists and other professional groups working in the realm of 'psychiatry' or human suffering are challenged on many fronts. The process of deinstitutionalisation, begun during the early days of my career in the mental health services, is now reaching its conclusion. Professionals are now called upon to go beyond deinstitutionalisation, to consider their role in supporting people back into education, work and a life within the community. Where in the past it was enough to reduce a person's psychotic symptoms to a manageable level, now those receiving treatment are beginning to demand professional care that actually helps them and their family members to recover and be part of their community, as opposed to merely reside in the community. Where in the past, psychiatrists were perhaps the 'only game in town', today people can choose from a host of practitioners, alternative forms of psychotherapy and other body therapies.

For many years I have seen people in my practice who have been through the mental health services and sought my help, people who wanted to be treated as a whole person and find the therapeutic support to escape chronic illness.

This book captures many of the challenges that have grown around psychiatry as a profession in the past 50 years: the critique of medicalisation, the rise of a collective advocacy voice from people who have received psychiatric treatment, the development of peer-provided services and the extension of human rights to people in inpatient units. Mapping these issues within an Irish context will be useful for anyone who seeks to understand their role in the therapeutic process, and the challenges facing practitioners in the next phase of humanising the mental health services. The book has a wealth of information drawing together policy, research and valuable unorthodox literature to give the reader some critical perspectives on the past, present and possible future directions. The profession has an opportunity to be at the forefront of the change to a more holistic approach, facilitating human beings to learn how to take responsibility for their own health. If this volume sparks a movement in that direction and opens debate and action by any individual who works in, or alongside, the psychiatric profession, Agnes and Shari will have made a valuable contribution to mental health care in Ireland.

Ivor Browne
Professor emeritus of psychiatry, UCD

Contributor Profiles

Agnes Higgins (RPN, RGN, RNT, BNS, MSc, PhD) is a Professor in Mental Health Nursing at the School of Nursing and Midwifery, Trinity College Dublin, where she teaches on both the undergraduate and postgraduate mental health programmes. She has worked in the areas of mental health practice, palliative care, general nursing and education for over thirty years. Agnes is committed to a philosophy of recovery in mental health care and endeavours to develop and support excellence in research and education that embodies the ethic of recovery-focused practice. She has published widely in the area of recovery, sexualities, and motherhood. Her particular research expertise is in qualitative methodologies, mixed methods and action research.

Shari McDaid (BA, MA (SocSci), PhD) is the Director of Mental Health Reform and has worked in social policy in Ireland for over ten years, specialising in mental health. She completed her PhD in equality studies at the School of Social Justice, University College Dublin on the topic of user involvement in mental health services and has written numerous policy publications for the National Disability Authority, Amnesty International Ireland, Shine: supporting people affected by mental ill health, and Mental Health Reform.

Damien Brennan (RPN, RNT, GDipDevS, MEqualS, MEd, PhD) is Assistant Professor at the School of Nursing and Midwifery, Trinity College Dublin. He trained and worked as a psychiatric nurse in Ireland and completed his PhD at the Department of Sociology, Trinity College. His research details and critiques mental hospital use in Ireland. Dr Brennan rejects the idea of an epidemic of 'insanity', arguing that social forces, along with the actions of the individuals, families and professional groups, drove the excessive utilisation of mental hospitals in Ireland.

Líam Mac Gabhann (BSc, MSc, DNursSci) is a psychiatric nurse, a medical sociologist, an activist in the mental health arena and a lecturer in the School of Nursing and Human Sciences at Dublin City University. His research focuses on transforming dialogues in mental health communities, generally centring on people reconciling their own experiences, perceptions and practices with other people/groups associated with mental health and using different approaches to improve these at individual, group, organisational and community level. Approaches include cooperative learning, participative action and open dialogue.

Paddy McGowan is currently employed as a lecturer with DCU School of Nursing as an expert by experience. He recovered from 'schizophrenia' with the support of other survivors and professionals and can speak authoritatively and humanely 'from the inside out'. Paddy was involved in organising the first Voices conference in Derry in November 1999 and was the founder and first CEO of the Irish Advocacy Network, which was heavily involved in developing peer advocacy training alongside staff awareness training in user empowerment.

Liz Brosnan (PhD) recently completed a doctorate in sociology on mental health service-user involvement, examining the inherent tensions for service-users, service-providers and movement actors in involvement practices and policies. She was a core member of the first user-led research project in Ireland, 'Pathways', and has been active in user-led research and in the national survivor/service-user movement in Ireland since 2000. She has contributed a service-user perspective on many national advisory committees, including Amnesty International Ireland's recent mental health campaign. She has many interests beyond mental health politics, which help maintain sanity.

Mike Watts (BA, MSc, PhD) Mike and his wife Fran are ex-service-users who recovered from diagnoses such as schizophrenia and bipolar through participation in GROW. As part of his recovery, Mike became involved in many community-based activities such as traditional music and Toastmasters and studied psychology and family therapy, recently completing a doctorate in recovery. He worked for GROW for 30 years and is currently involved in research and the delivery of recovery workshops to professionals. Mike has been a service-user representative on the Mental Health Commission, for the NESF and for Amnesty.

Rebecca Murphy (BA, MSc) is a PhD candidate in the School of Nursing and Midwifery, Trinity College Dublin. She has a BA and an MSc from University College Dublin. She has been involved in healthcare research since 2007, most recently working on maternity service evaluations with refugee mothers in Australia. Her PhD work builds on this experience, exploring the mental health care experiences of African forced migrants in Ireland. Her interests are in participatory research, mental health and the integration of ethnic minority populations.

Gerry Leavey (MA, PhD) is the Director of the Bamford Centre for Mental Health and Wellbeing at the University of Ulster. Professor Leavey holds an MA and

PhD from the University of London. Prior to returning to Northern Ireland he held several senior posts in Mental Health NHS Trusts in London. He continues to collaborate extensively with colleagues in the Department of Mental Health Sciences at University College London. He has published widely on ethnicity, culture, religion and faith-based organisations. His current research focuses on access to, and acceptability of mental health services. His study on the religious beliefs of ex-combatants of the conflict in Northern Ireland was published as a co-authored book in 2013 by Palgrave.

Shane Butler (PhD) is Associate Professor at the School of Social Work and Social Policy, Trinity College Dublin, where his main teaching and research activities are focused on mental health and addictions. Prior to working in TCD, he worked as a mental health social worker with the Eastern Health Board. He is the author of *Alcohol, Drugs and Health Promotion in Modern Ireland* (Institute of Public Administration, 2002) and *Benign Anarchy: Alcoholics Anonymous in Ireland* (Irish Academic Press, 2010). He is a Fellow of Trinity College Dublin.

Darius Whelan (PhD) is a lecturer in law at the Faculty of Law, University College Cork. His research interests include mental health law and Internet regulation. His book, *Mental Health Law and Practice*, was published by Round Hall in 2009. He is President of the Irish Mental Health Lawyers Association, the members of which represent patients admitted to approved centres under the Mental Health Act 2001.

Michael Brennan (PhD, RPN, RNT, MEd, Dip in Addiction Studies, Dip Social Studies) is an Assistant Professor in mental health nursing at the School of Nursing and Midwifery, Trinity College Dublin. He is a registered psychiatric nurse and nurse tutor. His PhD focused on the pathways to mental health care of people with mental health problems within the Irish criminal justice system. His specialist areas of teaching are primary mental health care, forensic and prison mental health care, and his research interests include criminal law and criminology, transformative/mixed-method theories and discrimination and marginalisation, equality issues for mental health service users, forensic mental health issues, and service-needs analysis for mentally disordered offenders.

Brendan Kennelly is a lecturer in economics and the director of the MSc (Health Economics) programme at NUI Galway. His main research interest is health economics, particularly mental health and suicide. He also does research in economics education. He has published papers on these and other topics in journals such as Public Choice, Health Policy, Social Science and Medicine, and the Journal of Economic Education.

Mary Keys (PhD) is a lecturer in the School of Law at the National University of Ireland, Galway specialising in mental health law. She was awarded a PhD by Cardiff University Law School on the topic of mental health law and human rights. She is a founder member of the Centre for Disability Law and Policy at NUI Galway and has published in the area of human rights, mental health and mental capacity law. A member of the Mental Health Commission, she is committed to the dissemination of useful legal information to people who use services and frontline staff.

Jo Murphy-Lawless (PhD) is a sociologist who has worked with and written about issues of risk and ethics in the health services in the context of late modernity. She lectures in the School of Nursing and Midwifery, Trinity College Dublin. She is widely published in her area of expertise, which includes women's health, poverty and social exclusion, health care delivery and the uses and problems of risk in scientific discourses.

Michael Nash is an Assistant Professor in the School of Nursing and Midwifery, Trinity College Dublin. He trained and worked as a psychiatric nurse in the UK. His research interests are in the area of the physical health, working therapeutically with risk in mental and civic engagement and social inclusion.

Marina Bowe (MRCPsych) is a Consultant General Adult Psychiatrist. She has worked as a Consultant in rehabilitation, inpatient and community psychiatry. She has delivered training on community psychiatric services, recovery and positive risk management in the context of practice development and change management. She is first author on the book *Home not Hospital*, which describes the evolution of Ireland's first home treatment team over twenty years as told by service users, carers and staff. Marina's interest is in the delivery of recovery-focused, individualised services.

David Healy (MD) is Professor of Psychiatry at Cardiff University and a former Secretary of the British Association for Psychopharmacology. He is a founder member of RxISK.org – the only global adverse event reporting website. He is the author of books including *Pharmageddon, Let Them Eat Prozac, The Antidepressant Era* and *Mania*.

Contents

Section 3: Emerging Issues and Implications for the Future

SECTION 1: CONTEXT FOR MENTAL HEALTH SERVICE DELIVERY IN 21ST-CENTURY IRELAND

1

Introduction: struggle and contestation in the field of mental health

Shari McDaid and Agnes Higgins

The mental health field is a space of contestation, struggle and resistance. Depending on epistemological and ontological perspectives, people struggle with how to talk about the phenomenon of interest – is it 'mental illness' as a biologically based though socially triggered life-long condition, 'mental and emotional distress' as a legitimate reaction to traumatic events and stressful situations, 'spiritual crisis' as a mystical experience involving an altered state of consciousness, or some yet unlabelled category that is simply an indication of the diverse ways that human beings experience their emotions and environment?

People disagree about how to respond to these phenomena with the following questions often taking centre stage: Is there a place for pharmacology in supporting people through their experience, and if so, how big a place? Are psychological interventions just another form of professional control and colonisation? Should the spiritual be acknowledged, and if so, how? And whose responsibility is it to address the social and economic determinants of mental health that can hinder recovery?

People argue about the level at which the conversation about mental health should take place. Is it a national conversation involving all communities and organisations including statutory, voluntary and business groups, or is it a local conversation between primary, secondary and tertiary service providers? Depending on their own positions within the system, others debate about who should be involved in the conversation and how the conversation should unfold. Should the clinical encounter primarily include the expert mental health professional directing the discussion with the service user who takes a passive role? Or should the conversation occur as a dialogue between the mental health professional and the person with self-experience? And should relatives be included in the conversation, and if so, how can the issue of service-user confidentiality be addressed?

People contest whose version of 'the mental' is true, with one side asserting the validity of diagnoses and medical conceptualisations, another countering with a critique of diagnostic systems, and others still demanding alternative, service-user-defined understandings. In defending one's position on 'truth' and proffering evidence to support each truth, there are heated debates over knowledge production: What constitutes valid knowledge and evidence? What methodologies should be used to produce evidence, and what is the best way to evaluate the quality of evidence produced?

Within all of these debates, various voices, institutions and personal and political agendas come to the fore as people seek to take power over the field. Psychiatrists, having gained authority over mental health care, now sit in the dominant position in the legal, managerial and clinical structures of service delivery. In a domain where psychiatric nurses have been allied with the power of psychiatry for generations, challenging power relations are emerging, with professionals including psychologists, social workers and occupational therapists who were once almost invisible now demanding an equal role in decision-making. At the same time, service users are beginning to resist professional authority and are seeking their own empowerment, as are family members. Likewise, advocates and lawyers are adjunct protagonists in the power game, confronting psychiatric authority on behalf of service users.

All of these struggles lead to a field of practice that is highly contested, with each monologue of truth representing itself as the authentic discourse that represents a logical march of progress in knowledge development and treatment, when in reality there are no certainties and no universal answers.

While this book is not a replay of these debates, they do form the backdrop for the text, and no doubt have influenced many of the authors. The idea for this book arose out of a recognition that there was a gap in the literature on mental health in Ireland. While major shifts had occurred in policy, law and practice in the past 50 years, no text appeared to explore or critically reflect on the overall implications and consequences of these developments within the Irish context. A number of factors have shaped mental health in Ireland from 1945 onwards, including economics, new technologies of treatment, global health policy, human rights law and the rise of the service user/survivor movement. A key instigator of deinstitutionalisation was the high cost of maintaining people in large-scale, segregated psychiatric hospitals. This economic equation facilitated the transformation to community-based mental health services.

The wave of deinstitutionalisation was also nudged forward by global health policy, particularly the World Health Organisation (see Commission of Inquiry on Mental Illness 1966). Alongside the cost motive and international policy, a general public abhorrence for asylum living was supported by the passing of the European Convention on Human Rights (1950), which eventually led to the Mental Health Act, 2001. More recently, the rise of the service-user/survivor movement in the 1980s elsewhere and from the late 1990s in Ireland has also influenced mental health policy. All of these factors feature in the chapters that follow. Equally, no text had yet grappled with recent landmark changes in law and policy, such as the significant implications of the UN Convention on the Rights of Persons with Disabilities (2006) and the impact of the 2006 Irish mental health policy *A Vision for Change*. This text seeks to chart these 20th- and early 21st-century developments and critically analyse their influence.

There was also a need for an up-to-date text that gathered together some of the critical voices within Ireland, to air the developing perspective of people with self-experience alongside that of mental health professionals and academic analysts. While we hope the text is more a dialogue giving space to alternative viewpoints than a monologue, we have purposively privileged certain voices and perspectives in recognition of the previous omission of the self-experience voice from Irish literature. And we have also sought to acknowledge the perspective of family members while recognising that this is a relatively undocumented voice. Where contemporary discussion has failed to address the inaccessibility of mental health services for some minority groups for whom the complexity of their situation is challenging to service configuration, we have sought to name and describe their positions with a view to recognising it in future policy.

Many of the chapters situate themselves within current debates about knowledge production and the ownership of knowledge. The service-user/survivor movement has posed a profound challenge to mental health expertise by positing that a knowledgeable perspective is that of the person with self-experience. This perspective is most challenging when considering how to implement the recovery ethos, but it also raises questions about the way services incorporate the perspective of relatives and the basis upon which services are judged to be both of good quality and value for money. The question of knowledge production also reflects wider trends evident in the disability sphere and more generally in the social sciences. It accords with the mid-20th-century call of disabled people to have 'nothing about us without us' and is congruent with a democratising trend reflected in feminism and other social movements. Mental health has not escaped these wider democratising influences, and the chapters that follow on recovery (Chapter 5), empowerment (Chapter 6) and peer support (Chapter 7) show how people in Ireland are re-shaping these themes towards Irish perspectives.

*

As editors, we have both personal and professional perspectives on mental health. Shari brings experience of living with a mental health issue for many years, while Agnes, like so many others, has family members who have experienced severe emotional distress and mental health challenges. Agnes also has practitioner and academic experience, while Shari has been a policy advisor and campaigner for reform. There is no doubt that our personal backgrounds have influenced our choice of topics and authors, yet we did seek contributors with expertise across a range of mental-health-related disciplines and subject areas. This volume is not exhaustive, and we are aware that there are other topics that could have been included. Our collaborating authors have produced chapters that, while unique in terms of content, contribution to knowledge and writing style, offer a synergy in their intention. The overall aim of the book was to draw together published and grey literature in the field of mental health in Ireland, identify current practice and arrangements, and critically analyse trends in mental health policy, law and service delivery. Our intention was to give each author the space and scope to convey their views in a manner that would allow the reader to gain an insight into the current state of mental health service delivery, while simultaneously resisting polarising positions.

Being mindful that the book will be used by lecturers, researchers and students from a number of disciplines, each chapter ends with a set of reflective questions to prompt further discussion and debate. In addition, each chapter contains potential research questions that should be of interest to researchers, service users, practitioners and funders.

CONTEXT FOR MENTAL HEALTH SERVICE DELIVERY IN 21ST-CENTURY IRELAND

The text begins with the two key developments that arose in the mid-20th century: deinstitutionalisation and medicalisation.

Deinstitutionalisation began in the 1950s and featured as the major theme in mental health service reform during the second half of the 20th century. In 1958 Ireland had the highest proportion of people in psychiatric hospitals of anywhere in the world. In Chapter 2, Damien Brennan explains the particular Irish roots of institutionalisation arising from British administrative decisions about the resolution of a host of 19th-century Irish social problems. He describes how the legal, physical and managerial structures of the asylum system came into being and alludes to a system of categorisation of 'insanity' that was the precursor to our current widely used diagnostic framework. Having charted the rise of institutionalisation, Brennan then outlines the process of deinstitutionalisation in the latter half of the 20th century while also discussing particular factors that allowed institutionalisation to persist in Ireland. Importantly, Brennan highlights how the managerial structures of the institution transferred into the community, with psychiatrists and psychiatric nurses maintaining supervisory power over those who ended up residing in community-based mental health service accommodation. He refers to these residences as the 'multi-locational total institution'.

One of the points that Brennan makes is how the institutional arrangement and increasing use of a system of categorisation of insanity facilitated the rise of medical control over the response to mental distress. In Chapter 3, Líam Mac Gabhann describes how the medical profession organised itself to have authority over people's disturbing mental experiences and worked to maintain that authority so that the legacy of that campaign continues to have a strong influence on practice to this day. Citing Bracken and Thomas, he summarises the consequences of this medicalisation in terms of the internalisation of mental distress (excluding social and cultural factors), the development of a technical framework for intervention that excludes non-medical supports, and the mandating of psychiatry with a unique role in overseeing coercion and forced treatment. Mac Gabhann also identifies the important role that psychiatry has been assigned in contemporary society in monitoring fitness/unfitness to work, thereby performing a necessary function for the state in the administration of welfare. Mac Gabhann goes on to discuss how in Ireland, these developments influenced the practice of nursing, showing how nurses benefited from medicalisation by being allied with psychiatrists, while struggling to establish their own distinctive position. Mac Gabhann also draws attention to the prevailing attitude in Ireland of deference to authority which underpinned reticence on the part of family members and service users to question the medical profession.

Shari McDaid (Chapter 4) shows how the persistence of these two trends led to reinstitutionalisation in the community and the widespread social exclusion of mental health service users. While mental health policy in the 20th century expressed optimism about the potential for community living, hidden within its recommendations were the structures that would underpin segregation of people with long-term mental health difficulties into living what she calls 'shadow lives' in the community. McDaid draws on Irish research to foreground the perspective of mental health service users that challenges the prevailing positive discourse around deinstitutionalisation. She also argues that Ireland's mental health policy on social inclusion remains largely unfulfilled.

EMERGING DEVELOPMENTS IN RESPONSE TO MENTAL DISTRESS

The second section of the book charts a path through a range of key issues facing the mental health services today. In some cases these represent new opportunities to reshape Ireland's response to mental/emotional distress: the promotion of a new 'recovery' ethos for mental health service delivery, the rise of the voice of people with self-experience of mental health services and the growth of peer support represent three such opportunities. Other chapters outline significant challenges that have yet to be addressed, such as the lack of involvement of relatives and other supporters in the process of mental health treatment, the struggle of ethnic minorities to have their needs and values recognised in an Irish society that has not yet come to terms with its cultural diversity; the inaccessibility of mental health services to people with alcohol problems; and the failure of Irish law to protect the human rights of those who come in contact with the criminal justice system.

Agnes Higgins and Paddy McGowan (Chapter 5) discuss the development of the recovery ethos as a paradigm shift in the conceptualisation of both the cause and treatment of mental distress. Combining Higgins' professional background with McGowan's self-experience, they describe the roots of the recovery ethos in two contrasting perspectives: a liberatory challenge by ex-service-users and survivors, and research evidence that provided a clinical challenge to prognostic pessimism. They emphasise that ultimately the definition of the meaning of recovery lies in the hands of the individuals who will shape their own 'journey of discovery' through mental/emotional distress. Their view of recovery poses an enormous challenge for the structure of mental health service delivery and for those practitioners who must develop new ways of working and relating to people as they embrace different explanatory models of mental distress within a post-modern discourse.

Liz Brosnan (Chapter 6), coming from an insider peer position, provides an in-depth analysis of the service-user/survivor challenge to the medical model through a critical history of this movement in Ireland. Drawing on the concepts of empowerment and new social movements, and her own and other Irish research, she traces the rise of the service-user/survivor voice here. She differentiates between advocacy from the inside through the development of an Irish peer advocacy service, consumer panels and a national service user advisory committee (the National Service User Executive), and what she terms 'advocacy from the outside' through collective peer advocacy groups. She concludes by drawing the reader's attention to the continuing tensions within the movement surrounding ideology, insider versus outsider positioning, representativeness and funding.

Higgins and McGowan identify peer support as a key component of a recovery-oriented mental health service. In Chapter 7, Mike Watts takes up this theme and explores the potential contribution that peer support and mutual help can make to a transformed mental health practice, and argues that the experiential knowledge which underpins peer support is equally as valuable as expert knowledge. Watts posits that equality and reciprocity are defining features of peer support. Drawing on his own research and international evidence he identifies the healing benefits of peer support in people's recovery journeys. He also describes emerging peer support networks in Ireland and reviews Irish policy on peer support, critiquing professional attitudes towards it and the lack of implementation of this approach in the Irish context.

Relatives of people with mental and emotional distress also struggle to be part of the conversation. While the position of users of services has dramatically changed in the past 20 years, the role of their primary supporters at home has not, and there has been little research on this topic in Ireland. Generally the subject is examined in terms of the 'burden' on relatives of an individual's mental distress. As we (McDaid and Higgins) describe in Chapter 8, relatives come from a historical position of having been seen as the 'cause' of 'mental illness' and consequently have struggled to be acknowledged as valued participants in the discussion about their family member's treatment. Though they are named in Ireland's mental health policy, their role has yet to be clearly articulated in a way that translates into widespread, inclusive practice. Similarly, the issues of children of people with mental health difficulties are largely unaddressed. Since relatives often provide emotional, financial and practical support and are frequently relied upon to initiate emergency, involuntary mental health treatment under the law, they find themselves in the paradoxical position of being both necessary to and excluded from the mental health system.

Three other groups struggle to be included in mental health policy and practice: ethnic minorities, people with co-occurring problematic substance/alcohol misuse, and people involved in the criminal justice system. In Chapter 9, Rebecca Murphy and Gerry Leavey shine a light on the position of ethnic minorities, including asylum seekers and members of the Traveller community, in relation to the mental health system. They point out that the changing demographic profile of Irish society and its increasing ethnic diversity has not been met with a corresponding development of health and social care policies and practices. Two of the challenges they identify are the different explanatory models of mental distress across cultural groups and the lack of cultural competence among mental health practitioners. They conclude that more information is needed on the lives of ethnic minorities in Ireland in order to fully understand the interplay between their socioeconomic positions in Irish society and their experiences of mental/emotional distress as these relate to access to services and differences in care.

Shane Butler (Chapter 10) highlights the ambivalent treatment of alcohol misuse in Irish mental health policy. Similar to McDaid, Butler navigates a critical history of Irish mental health policy on drinking problems and highlights how it has 'flip-flopped' over their conceptualisation and the approach to their practical management. One of the distinctions he draws is the difference between how public- and private-sector psychiatry have responded to alcohol abuse, arising from different funding arrangements. Since people with mental health difficulties often have addiction difficulties as well, Butler questions the wisdom of separating addiction and mental health services as recommended in *A Vision for Change*.

A group that is doubly marginalised as a result of crossing between the boundaries of two different government departments (Health and Justice) are those who have a mental health difficulty and come in contact with the criminal justice system. In Chapter 11, Darius Whelan and Michael Brennan help to unpack this interface through an introduction to the provisions in the Criminal Law (Insanity) Act 2006. By describing current mental health service provision within the criminal justice system, they assist the reader in understanding the interaction between these two spheres. Whelan and Brennan discuss the relevance of human rights law for people involved in both systems by reviewing a number of key legal cases. They conclude by pointing out that there is an urgent need for improvement in joined-up thinking and service provision to protect individuals' human rights.

EMERGING ISSUES AND IMPLICATIONS FOR THE FUTURE

The third section of the book takes a look at issues that have been present in the background but are now taking on new significance in contemporary debates about economics, practice, policy and law. These are controversial topics without clear pathways or resolutions at the current moment. Nevertheless, they are issues that all people involved in mental health services – from practitioners to users to family members – will confront as they navigate their way through to recovery.

Given the importance of economics as a driver for mental health practice, Brendan Kennelly (Chapter 12) introduces key concepts in relation to the economics of mental health and describes different types of economic evaluation. He explores the two-way relationship between mental health difficulties and the economy, firstly in terms of the costs of service provision and other direct costs to families and service users, and secondly in terms of indirect costs to the economy through the lost contribution of people with a mental health difficulty to society. Kennelly refers to a range of challenges that make conducting economic research about mental health difficult, not least the challenges in converting into economic figures the high personal cost of mental distress to the individual and their family. In the context of Ireland, he decries the lack of population evidence and mental health service financial information that could inform policymaking.

In Chapter 13, Mary Keys discusses the relationship of the law to people deemed to have a 'mental disorder' and considers Ireland's human rights obligations under the UN Convention on the Rights of Persons with Disabilities and the European Convention on Human Rights. The core purpose of the UN Convention is to ensure the full and equal enjoyment of all human rights by all people with disabilities in all aspects of life. Keys discusses the critical area of legal capacity from the perspective of both Conventions in order to identify the areas for law reform. She examines elements of Irish law for their compliance with human rights standards and notes the recommendations for change from service users, families and the NGO sector. Consent to admission and treatment, as a fundamental element of the right to autonomy and self-determination, is addressed with particular attention given to the safeguards for people who have impaired capacity and are admitted as 'voluntary patients'. Non-consensual interventions such as seclusion and restraint are examined, taking into account commentary from national and international monitoring bodies. Keys concludes with a focus on the future, considering the recently-published Department of Health Interim Report on the Review of the Mental Health Act 2001 and the potential for legal tools like advance directives to enable self-determination.

Like every other branch of medicine and indeed, the social services in general, psychiatry has permitted itself to be absorbed in recent decades by the growing imperative to order its work in relation to perceived risk. In Chapter 14, Michael Nash, Jo Murphy-Lawless and Marina Bowe explore from whence this imperative has arisen and the stark issues that lie behind it. They review the source of the pressure to generate formal risk assessment schemes and ask what distinguishes top-down risk schedules from the risks borne by individuals subjected to and made vulnerable by the vagaries of neoliberal health systems. They go on to consider some recognised risk assessment tools and critique the current HSE risk management policy toolkit in the context of an institutional environment that is risk averse. Pointing to the future, they ask whether the notion of 'positive risk' as it relates to the recovery ethos can help with the ongoing challenges for mental health services in relation to risk management.

One of the biggest areas of contestation, worldwide, is the use of pharmacological interventions to address mental and emotional distress. The level of disquiet and critique of the use of pharmaceuticals is shown in the number of texts that have been published in recent years such as Peter Breggin's *Toxic Psychiatry* (1993), Joanna Moncrieff's *The Myth of the Chemical Cure* (2008/2009), Robert Whitaker's *Anatomy of an Epidemic* (2010), Irving Kirsch's *The Emperor's New Drugs: Exploding the antidepressant myth* (2009), and Richard Bentall's *Doctoring the Mind: Why psychiatric treatment fails* (2009). However, unlike these authors who critique the evidence base that supports the use of pharmaceuticals, in Chapter 15 David Healy analyses the industrial structure that underpins their marketing, describing it as 'a perfect market' of the 'perfect product' to the 'perfect consumer'. In so doing, he highlights how the development of the randomised controlled trial (RCT) impacted the wider discursive framework so that the RCT became the gold standard by which all other evidence is judged. He concludes by suggesting some ways that the market for drugs could be rebalanced.

In the final chapter (Chapter 16), we (Higgins, McDaid and McGowan) reflect on the current state of affairs of mental health in Ireland in the context of all of the preceding chapters. While no one can accurately predict future trends and service configuration, they discuss some of the factors that are likely to influence policy, practice and law, including changing demographics, health technologies, economics and funding arrangements, restructuring the health service system, international law and policy, and discourse on health and wellbeing in general.

In conclusion, we hope that this text will help people interested in the field of mental health to navigate its terrain and discover their own route through the territory. We do not offer answers; rather, we have tried to gather together the issues and perspectives that are shaping and will shape how mental health is and will be enacted in policy, practice and law in Ireland. We aim to generate further discussion, to provoke further debate and to facilitate the reader's reflection on their own role and contribution to Ireland's mental health system.

REFERENCES

Bentall R (2009/2010) Doctoring the Mind: Why psychiatric treatment fails. London: Penguin Books

Breggin P (1993) Toxic Psychiatry. London: Fontana

Commission of Inquiry on Mental Illness (1966) Commission of Inquiry on Mental Illness 1966 Report. Dublin: Stationery Office

Council of Europe (1950) European Convention on Human Rights

Government of Ireland (2001) Mental Health Act. Dublin: Stationery Office

Kirsch I (2009) The Emperor's New Drugs: Exploding the antidepressant myth. London: The Bodley Head

Moncrieff J (2008/2009) The Myth of the Chemical Cure: A critique of psychiatric drug treatment. Basingstoke, Hants.: Palgrave/MacMillan

United Nations (2006) Convention on the Rights of Persons with Disabilities and Optional Protocol

Whitaker R (2010) Anatomy of an Epidemic: Magic Bullets, Psychiatric Drugs, and the Astonishing Rise of Mental Illness in America. New York: Crown Publishers Random House

2

Mental hospital institutionalisation and deinstitutionalisation in Ireland

Damien Brennan

INTRODUCTION

During the 1950s the level of mental hospital usage in Ireland was the highest internationally with a rate of 710.34 beds per 100,000 (Brennan 2014). For almost two centuries the expressed function of these buildings was the provision of institution-based care for those who were categorised as 'insane', 'mentally ill' or having 'mental health problems' as it is now described. However, they also developed into locations of substantive social and economic importance to the communities in which they were situated. This chapter firstly explores the factors that underpinned institutionalisation within the Irish asylum/mental hospital system, followed by a consideration of their demise and contemporary legacy. A core observation made is that the spectacular growth of Irish institutions for the mentally ill had little, or indeed nothing, to do with the mental state of the individuals who were institutionalised. It is also demonstrated that, similar to institutional expansion, deinstitutionalisation was driven by social, cultural, political, legal and economic factors, rather than an improvement in the mental state of the Irish population.

WHY DID IRELAND HAVE SUCH HIGH LEVELS OF INSTITUTIONALISATION?

A seminal driver of Irish asylum/mental hospital expansion and legacy was the *Report of the Select Committee to Consider the State of the Lunatic Poor in Ireland* (1817). Prior to the publication of this document there was no centralised state-backed system for the institutional care of the mentally ill in Ireland. '... in 1817, a Committee of the House of Commons gave it as their opinion, that the only mode of effectual relief would be found in the formation of District Asylums exclusively appropriated to the reception of the Insane' (Inspector of Lunatic Asylums 1846:5). The 1817 report was followed almost immediately with the passing of an Act in 1817, which, along with amendments made in 1820 and a further act, the Lunatic Act in Ireland 1821, provided a legal and administrative framework which underpinned the development of a national asylum system in Ireland. These Acts informed the work of Commissioners for the Erection of Lunatic Asylums, who oversaw the construction of new district asylums in Armagh, Ballinasloe, Belfast, Carlow, Clonmel, Derry, Limerick, Maryborough and Waterford. These new asylums, along with Dublin's Richmond Asylum and the Cork Asylum, constituted the national public asylum system in Ireland.

While the 1817 report was published some two centuries ago, it created institutional structures, systems and power dynamics that continue to have a direct impact on the nature of mental health service delivery today. Colonisation, with direct rule of Ireland from Westminster, was the political milieu in which this report was published. This political dynamic removed the planning and control of localised social interventions from the local context. The outcome of the 1817 report was a centralised and well funded bureaucratic administration, which oversaw rapid asylum construction and utilisation. Extensive policies and protocols were developed for the running of the national asylum system as a whole and of individual institutions, which further embedded these asylums at the political, economic and societal levels.

Once constructed, asylums were embraced by the Irish as locations of social intervention for a host of social problems. Poverty was widespread and chronic in 19th-century Ireland, and during the great famine of the 1840s it became catastrophic. The public asylum system provided a local form of intervention which could be used by families during crises. Individuals, families and communities became familiar with the workings of the asylums as sites of social intervention and engaged directly with the committal process. This resulted in an on-going 'supply of patients' to the asylums, which further secured the success of these institutions as built and bureaucratic entities. While there was no proactive programme of patient recruitment, a push–pull dynamic developed between families seeking intervention and asylums in need of patients.

Admission to an asylum was predicated on the existence of two key features, a categorisation system that distinguished the 'sane' from the 'insane' and a committal process, which was usually underpinned by legislation. In the pre-colonial era, Brehon Law set out rights, responsibilities and protections of the 'insane' within a community context, categorising people as 'idiots, fools and lunatics' (Robins 1986:14). Systems of categorisation became more developed with the construction of asylums. In his first report the Irish Inspector of Lunatics categorised patients as 'Idiot, Epileptic and Mania' (Inspector of Lunatic Asylums 1846:30). In the report for 1879 the inspectors set out the 'Supposed

Causes of Mental Disease of Patients in Asylums' under three categories: 'Moral Causes, Physical Causes and Hereditary' (Inspectors of Lunatic Asylums 1880: 65). In essence, during the period of asylum expansion, diagnostic criteria changed, became all-encompassing and were applied inconsistently. This vague concept of insanity served to rationalise, justify and facilitate admission to an asylum as a response to a wide range of social problems. 'Moral causes' included categories of 'Poverty and Reverse of Fortune; Grief, Fear and Anxiety; Domestic Quarrels and Afflictions; Religious Excitement; Study and Mental Excitement, Ill-treatment; Pride; Anger; and Love, Jealousy and Seduction' (Inspectors of Lunatic Asylums 1880:65). This was compounded further in Ireland by the fact that admission to asylums operated in a confused legal quagmire up until 1838. This changed with the passing of the 1838 Dangerous Lunatics Act that placed admission within a judicial context, which was to become the predominant route of admission during Irish asylum expansion.

The 1838 Dangerous Lunatics Act provided for the detention of a 'dangerous lunatic' if two magistrates formed the view that the 'lunatic' was *likely* to commit a criminal offence. However, this legislation did not set out criteria for insanity, and the magistrates were not initially obliged to seek medical advice concerning the mental state of the person before them. If judged to be a 'dangerous lunatic' the person could be committed to prison and then transferred to a district asylum. There were few checks and balances to prevent the misuse of this legislation, and the ensuing high rate of admission generated increased demand for further accommodation within asylums, which was provided for through the building of new institutions and the expansion of those institutions already in existence. Concern regarding the misuse of this legalisation was expressed by the Lord Chancellor who pointed out that 'Friends of a Lunatic (could) induce him to commit some trifling Act – e.g. breaking a Window, or striking some Person,– and then take him before Magistrates, and procure his Committal as a dangerous Lunatic to Prison, from whence in the course of Time he is transferred to a Lunatic Asylum; and this Plan prevents those Checks against improper Admissions to the Asylum' (Select Committee of the House of Lords Appointed to Consider the State of the Lunatic Poor in Ireland 1843: xiii).

As asylums increased in size they became economically very important to local communities in terms of the consumption of local goods and services. They also became one of the largest sources of direct employment within their communities. Two groups had particular success in securing employment: medics and attendants/nurses. While Irish asylums operated under the control of lay 'moral' managers in the early 19th century, by the 1850s the medical profession had moved to gain a monopoly over all key positions of power including inspection (up to two inspectors could be appointed at any one time), management and clinical control. A large cohort of compliant attendants, who later became known as psychiatric nurses, operated at a lower level within the asylum/mental hospital hierarchy. The *General Rules and Regulations for the Management of District Lunatic Asylums in Ireland* (Lord Lieutenant 1885) sets out the relationship between these professional groups clearly: attendants/nurses had responsibility for patient care and the smooth operation of the institution, under the strict direction of their superior medical colleagues. Medical control and nurse compliance has been remarkably robust in surviving as a core characteristic of mental health service delivery from 1850 to date.

From its commencement in 1817 the national asylum system in Ireland had a pattern of continuous growth until 1922 when Ireland was partitioned into what was to become Northern Ireland, which remained in the UK, and the larger Republic of Ireland in the South. An important point to note is that during this phase of asylum expansion the overall population in Ireland was in decline, almost halving from 8,175,124 in 1841 to 4,390,219 in 1911 (Vaughan 1978), which was driven by the famine of the 1840s and long-term high rates of emigration. As such there was a strong inverse relationship between the level of asylum residence and the overall population trend at this time. This resulted in a rapid increase in rates of institutional residency per 100,000 of population, increasing from 88.43 in 1851, to 561.59 in 1911. The number of people resident in mental hospitals continued to increase in the post-partition Irish Republic, reaching a high of 21,720 in 1956. At this point the Irish rate of mental hospital utilisation per 100,000 was the highest in the world at 710.34, followed by the USSR at 617.58 and the USA at 511.38 (Brennan 2014). This marks the highest institutional usage in Ireland's history and is the point of departure from which deinstitutionalisation needs to be understood.

TURNING POINT IN INSTITUTIONALISATION AND THE EMERGENCE OF DEINSTITUTIONALISATION

The declining pattern of institutional residency which commenced from 1956 onwards continued at a steady rate, reducing to a level of 4,522 persons in institutional settings at the commencement of the 21st century (Brennan 2014). Significantly, the population of the Republic of Ireland experienced a slow and steady upward growth from 1962 onwards. Hence an inverse relationship between the institutional residency of the 'mentally ill' and overall population occurred, resulting in a substantive decline in the rate of institutional residency per 100,000, falling from 749.35 in 1956 to 119.33 in 2000. Like the rise of institutional confinement, this demise had little to do with the mental state of those committed; rather, it was driven by the combined impact of legal, social, cultural and economic changes, along with new clinical innovations which re-focused practice away from the institutional setting.

The Dangerous Lunatics Acts of 1838 and 1867 provided the legislative framework that underpinned asylum expansion, both before and after partition.

The Mental Treatment Act of 1945 replaced this outdated legislation and changed the control of admission from a judicial to a medical process. This served to further consolidate the medical dominance of mental hospitals as doctors now had direct control over admission and discharge, along with a monopoly on mental hospital management, inspection and clinical decision-making. Three principal modes of admission to mental hospitals were provided for: voluntary, temporary and admission for 'persons of unsound mind'.

'Voluntary admission' involved an application being made by the person seeking admission themselves. However 72 hours' notice was required if the person wished to be discharged, during which the patient's doctor could move to make arrangements for involuntary detention if they were of the view that the person was not fit to leave. 'Temporary admission' was the admission of a person against their will. A spouse or adult relative made an application by signing a temporary admission form, which was also to be signed by a medical practitioner (usually the patient's general practitioner), or two practitioners in the case of a private patient. The person could then be moved to a mental hospital where they were examined by a medical doctor, who could then make an order for involuntary admission. Temporary admission could last up to six months after which there was a mandatory review of the patient's case; this could be repeated up to three times, thus providing for a possible committal of up to two years' duration. However, a practice of discharge and immediate re-admission could be used after two years as a means for securing a new temporary admission, resulting in the long-term detention of the person under these provisions. Admission as a 'person of unsound mind' was also provided for under the 1945 Act. Similar to a temporary admission, application is usually made by a spouse or relative (or a Garda) and a medical practitioner. The patient was then taken to the mental hospital where a medical doctor examined them and made a decision on making an order for admission. A person of unsound mind could be detained until they were medically discharged, which provided the possibility of long-term committal. Most patients who were resident in mental hospitals prior to 1945 were re-categorised as persons of unsound mind, which facilitated the continuation of their long-term institutionalisation. On 31 December 1949 there were 17,332 persons of unsound mind resident in District and Auxiliary Mental Hospitals, compared with 886 temporary and 250 voluntary patients (Inspector of Mental Hospitals 1949:46). The 1945 Act provided patients with some safeguards that had not existed previously; for example, the patient had a right to a second medical opinion, had the right to know all information relating to the committal, and could make an objection to the Inspector of Mental Hospitals or the President of the High Court.

In 1945 there were 19,538 persons resident in institutions for the mentally ill in the Republic of Ireland, which steadily increased to reach a high of 21,720 in 1956. However, the proportion of patients admitted involuntarily steadily decreased and voluntary admission became the predominant form of admission. By 2001 83 per cent of patients were voluntary (Walsh and Daly 2002:31). This increase in voluntary admission, coupled with the provision for mandatory six-month reviews of temporary patients, appear to have been contributing factors in the decline of long-term institutional residency from the late 1950s to the present day. Interacting with this legislation was the tightening of criteria on which admissions were based, with the introduction of internationally standardised diagnostic systems.

Classification systems remained vague, all-encapsulating and internationally inconsistent until the mid-20th century. This was to change when the World Health Organization (WHO) included a section on mental illness in the sixth edition of the International Classification of Diseases (ICD) in 1948, which was followed by the publication of the first edition of the Diagnostic and Statistical Manual (DSM) by the American Psychiatric Association in 1952. These classification systems resulted in a more uniform approach to the diagnosis and treatment of mental illness internationally. However, even with this more scientific approach, the conceptualisation of mental illness has continued to shift and change, a classic example being the diagnosis and then de-diagnosis of homosexuality as a mental disorder. A similar categorisation process is evident with the increased use of psychiatric diagnosis for childhood behavioural issues in more contemporary times, such as Attention Deficit Hyperactivity Disorder. The international standardisation of diagnostic criteria interfaced with the provisions contained in the Mental Treatment Act of 1945 to create a practice in which more refined diagnostic criteria were utilised within a more constrained legal system for admissions. This would appear to be a causal factor that stimulated the declining use of Irish mental hospitals from the mid-1950s onwards.

Parallel with the tightening of the legal and diagnostic systems for mental illness was the development of new forms of clinical practice during the mid-20th century. Psychopharmacology (prescribed drugs), and to a lesser extent ECT (electroconvulsive therapy), became the leading forms of clinical intervention. Most patients in Irish mental hospitals received at least one of these treatments. This had the effect of refocusing medical practice away from long-term institutionalised care and towards patient treatment, which acted as an additional catalyst to reducing levels of residency from the late 1950s onwards. Psychological interventions, such as psychoanalysis, behavioural and cognitive therapy also developed during this era, but in Ireland these forms of treatment were only used sporadically and were not rolled out nationally.

The emergence of new clinical innovations re-consolidated bio-medical power within mental health service delivery during the mid-20th century. An academic critique of this bio-medical power emerged internationally, notably in the work of Laing (1960, 1964), Foucault (1967, 1973, 1977), Szasz (1972) and Illich (1976, 1977). Within this 'anti-psychiatry' school of thought, the diagnosis of 'mental illness' is considered as a form of social control, enacted by psychiatrists whose main concern is to maintain professional power and occupational security. A core feature of this movement was an activist-style alliance between academics, former mental hospital patients and non-governmental voluntary organisations. However, this movement had limited penetration in Ireland, where most voluntary organisations working in the area of mental health were organised and controlled by the staff of mental hospitals, predominantly psychiatrists and psychiatric nurses. For example, the work of the Mental Health Association and Schizophrenia Ireland complemented rather than challenged existing mental health services. While these organisations did very honourable work in raising awareness of mental illness and in advocating for better services, they did not challenge the conceptualisation of mental illness itself or the professional power structures that controlled interventions. In reality, the radical aspect of the 'anti-psychiatry' movement had a very limited impact in Ireland. Indeed, the emergence of academic and political critiques of mental hospital institutionalisation in the 1960s was subsequent to the commencement of mental hospital decline in Ireland.

The social policy approach of institution utilisation, which was articulated in 1817, continued to be the key mental health policy post partition up until 1966 when new proposals were published in the *Report of the Commission of Inquiry on Mental Illness*. This report expressed concerns at the continued excessive use and expense of mental hospitals in Ireland. In a radical departure from the asylums/mental hospital social policy that had endured for 150 years, this report recommended the development of community mental health services and the relocation of residential care to small units. This was the first Irish proposal that advocated deinstitutionalisation and it harmonised with similar polices being pursued across the western world at this time. While there were some innovative attempts to develop community services, particularly in West Dublin, the radical changes articulated in the 1966 Report were not acted on nationally in any substantive manner, and residential treatment within the large mental hospitals continued to be the predominant service available for the 'mentally ill'. Subsequent to the 1966 report patient numbers in public asylums continued to decline, which was but a continuation of the trend established in 1956; in practice the report failed to usher in a new post-institutional service.

A new government policy was articulated in *The Psychiatric Services – Planning for the Future* (Department of Health 1984), which like the 1966 report, recommended a reduced reliance on mental hospitals and called for the development of community-based services. This report was much more robust in setting out the administrative and managerial structures required for deinstitutionalisation. In particular it stipulated that service provision should reflect population size and should be delivered within distinct geographical areas. While this report did reorientate mental health services towards community interventions, it failed to call for the actual closure and sale of mental hospitals. Furthermore, during the early 1980s Ireland was in a deep economic recession with chronically high levels of unemployment. This stimulated political unease at potential job losses as a consequence of mental hospitals' closure. Professional groups, most notably psychiatrists and psychiatric nurses, also had a vested interest in continuing to practice within the physical buildings that offered them occupational security. The outcome was a reluctance to scale down residential facilities. This resulted in uneven levels of bed availability and utilisation, with oversupply in the rural areas where the old, large 19th-century asylums were located, and radically lower levels in the rapidly expanding suburban areas that did not have a legacy of large asylum buildings. The Inspector of Mental Health Services noted in 2004 that the 'rate of generation of new long stay patients is influenced by a number of factors. It is decreased in those areas that are well provided with 24-hour staffed community residences and increased in areas that continue to admit to remaining long stay wards' (Inspector of Mental Health Services 2004:111). Even where new community services were developed, these were managed directly under the administrative structures that had governed the old mental hospitals. As such, the doctor–nurse–patient power inequalities that characterised the old institutions were transferred to residences in the community setting. The result was multi-locational total institutions, where patient care was prescribed by medics and implemented by nurses, with patients having little control over decision-making, clinical treatment or their environment in a residential setting.

The provisions of the 1945 Mental Treatment Act fell well short of Ireland's obligations under the *Council of Europe Recommendations for the Legal Protection for Persons Suffering from Mental Disorders Placed as Involuntary Patients* (Council of Europe 1983) and the UN *Principles for the Protection of Persons with Mental Illness and the Improvement of Mental Health Care* (United Nations General Assembly 1991). After a protracted drafting process, new legislation was enacted in the 2001 Mental Health Act. This Act established a Mental Health Commission and set out new regulations governing admission and discharge. Under this legislation involuntary admission can occur:

> Because of the illness, dementia or disability: there is a serious likelihood of the person concerned causing immediate and serious harm to himself or herself or other persons.
> Or
> Because of the illness, dementia or disability: The judgement of the person concerned is so impaired that failure to admit the person to an approved centre would be likely to lead to a serious deterioration of his or her condition or would prevent the administration of appropriate treatment and reception, detention and treatment of the person is likely to benefit or alleviate the condition of that person to a material extent. (Mental Health Commission 2005: Section 2.2:1)

In operational terms, admission under the 2001 Mental Health Act is similar to that of the 1945 Mental Treatment Act. A relative or (other suitable person), a medical practitioner and a consultant psychiatrist of the inpatient service must sign a form, and the patient must be made aware of their rights at the time of admission. However the protections under the 2001 act are much greater than those set out in the 1945 legislation. For example, the patient is admitted for only 21 days in the first instance. Furthermore, the admission order must be sent to the Mental Health Commission for review by a Mental Health Tribunal within 21 days. A legal representative is assigned to the patient by the Mental Health Commission, and the admitted person must be examined and interviewed by a consultant chosen from their panel of consultants. All documentation relevant to the person's case is sent to a Mental Health Tribunal, which comprises a consultant psychiatrist, a barrister or solicitor and a lay person (other than a barrister, solicitor, consultant psychiatrist, registered medical practitioner or registered nurse). This tribunal either affirms or revokes admission or renewal orders. While this is very progressive legislation, it was enacted at a time when the actual level of involuntary admission to institutions was at its lowest point in over 150 years. As such, while this legislation marks the end of wide-scale institutional usage, it was not a causal factor in deinstitutionalisation, which had commenced in the mid-1950s.

THE LEGACY OF MENTAL HOSPITAL INSTITUTIONALISATION IN IRELAND

The drive towards community services was articulated once more in the Government policy document *A Vision for Change: Report of the Expert Group on Mental Health Policy* (Department of Health and Children 2006). Key recommendations within this report closely resemble those set out previously in 1966 and 1984:

> Mental health services should be organised nationally in catchments ... Well-trained, fully staffed, community-based multidisciplinary CMHTs (Community Mental Health Teams) should be put in place for all mental health services and ... offer multidisciplinary home-based and assertive outreach care, and a comprehensive range of medical, psychological and social therapies relevant to the needs of services users and their families. (Department of Health and Children 2006:9)

However *A Vision for Change* went much further than the earlier reports as it also recommended that 'A plan to bring about the closure of all mental hospitals should be drawn up and implemented' (Department of Health and Children 2006:9). Effectively this report was the first to call for the actual closure of the asylums/mental hospitals that were originally created as a result of the 1817 *Report on the Lunatic Poor in Ireland*. However, since mental hospital residency was in continuous decline from 1956 onwards, in effect, the policies of 1966, 1984 and 2006 provided a commentary on this fact rather than leading this change. Furthermore the Celtic Tiger economy created almost full employment in Ireland from 1997–2007, which eroded the political resistance to job losses in mental hospitals.

A second distinguishing feature of *A Vision for Change* was its stipulation that the 'involvement of service users and their carers should be a feature of every aspect of service development and delivery' (Department of Health and Children 2006:9). This explicitly challenged the top-down power arrangement that had characterised mental health service delivery for nearly two centuries. However, a reproduction of the mad/sane dialectic that typified the asylum is embedded in this service user model. A person becomes a 'service user' through the act of diagnosis and hence acceptance of the existence of one's 'mental illness' is a requirement for participation in planning structures. Service users continue to be constructed as somehow separate to the general public, which reinforces the divide between the sane and insane. While *A Vision for Change* was a milestone in advocating the final closure of mental hospitals, the authors of this document were predominately drawn from the professional groups that had developed their practice and power within the mental hospital system. A persistent feature of this policy, and the 2001 Mental Health Act, is the maintenance and reproduction of the position of these professionals groups, albeit beyond the walls of the institution. Medical doctors still retain overall responsibility for service delivery and inspection. The participation of service users in service development and delivery is facilitated and accommodated by professionals who continue to control both the consultation process itself and overall service delivery. This would appear to be an obstacle to the planning of services that meet the mental health needs of the Irish public, rather than a subset of those categorised as being 'mentally ill'.

The expansion and demise of the Irish asylum/mental hospital was spectacular by international standards. The evidence overwhelmingly suggests that this institutional usage was not driven by bio-medical factors within the individual patient, but resulted from the combined forces of law, policy, economic circumstances, bureaucratic power, professional monopolies and the actions of families who actively participated in the admission process. In spite of this, the legacy of a bio-medical model towards mental health problems remains the corner stone of contemporary Irish mental health services. Doctors and nurses continue to be key professionals employed in this service, and psychopharmacology continues to be the principal form of intervention, now delivered in a host of community as well as institutional settings. A counterpoint to the bio-medical model has been evident in the sporadic and comparatively limited introduction of non physical approaches such as 'cognitive-behavioural therapy', 'mindfulness' and currently the 'recovery model'. In reality, these approaches are predominantly led by members of the professional groups that had formally developed practice within institutional mental hospital settings. Indeed, these alternative forms of intervention have created new markets for professional practice, which professionals very much need, having lost their anchor clients – the patients within the asylums/mental hospitals.

The mental hospital system was by far the largest form of institutional intervention ever to have existed in the Republic of Ireland. Interestingly, these institutions were one of the few places that were fully state run, rather than being a Church/State partnership. While there has been apparent public shock at the neglect and abuse experienced within church-run institutions, such as industrial schools (institutions for children with problematic social circumstance) (O'Sullivan and O'Donnell 2012) and Magdalene laundries (institutions for women with problematic social circumstance including pregnancy outside marriage), the state-run public mental hospital system has escaped such scrutiny to date. Furthermore, when industrial schools and Magdalene laundries were eventually closed, the religious orders running them were not placed in charge of child welfare and sexual health programmes. In contrast, the very professional bodies, particularly of psychiatrists and psychiatric nurses, who directly oversaw and enacted the most enduring and wide-scale Irish programme of institutionalisation, have now secured the most predominant positions of control within contemporary Irish mental health services.

*

REFLECTIVE QUESTIONS FOR DISCUSSION AND DEBATE: PRACTICE

- Was there an epidemic of mental illness in Ireland from 1800–2000?
- What were the key drivers of high mental hospital usage in Ireland?
- Why did mental hospital usage decline in Ireland?
- Who controls contemporary mental health services in Ireland?

REFLECTIVE STATEMENTS FOR DISCUSSION AND DEBATE: RESEARCH

- Is homelessness in Ireland linked to deinstitutionalisation?
- What groups are diagnosed by professionals in contemporary Ireland?

REFERENCES

Brennan D (2014) Irish Insanity 1800–2000. Oxon: Routledge

Commission of Inquiry on Mental Illness (1966) Commission of Inquiry on Mental Illness Report. Dublin: Stationery Office

Council of Europe (1983) Council of Europe Recommendations for the Legal Protection for Persons Suffering from Mental Disorders Placed as Involuntary Patients. Strasbourg: Council of Europe

Dangerous Lunatics Act (1838). Dublin: HMSO. (Note: this Act is also referred to as the Criminal Lunatics (Ireland) Act (1 and 2 Vic. C. 56) in some publications)

Dangerous Lunatics Act (1867). Dublin: HMSO. (Note: this Act is also referred to as the Lunacy Act (Ireland) in some publications)

Department of Health (1984) Psychiatric Services – Planning for the Future. Dublin: Stationery Office

Department of Health and Children (2006) A Vision for Change: Report of the Expert Group on Mental Health Policy. Dublin: Stationery Office

Foucault M (1967) Madness and Civilization: A History of Insanity in the Age of Reason. London: Tavistock

Foucault M (1973) The Birth of the Clinic. London: Tavistock

Foucault M (1977) Discipline and Punish: The Birth of the Prison. London, Allen Lane

Government of Ireland (1945) Mental Treatment Act. Dublin: Stationery Office

Government of Ireland (2001) Mental Health Act. Dublin: Stationery Office

Illich I (1976) Limits to Medicine, Medical Nemesis: The Expropriation of Health. London: Marion Boyars

Illich I (1977) Disabling Professions. London: Marion Boyars

Inspector of Lunatic Asylums (1846) Report on the District, Local and Private Lunatic Asylums in Ireland 1845. Dublin: HMSO

Inspector of Lunatic Asylums (1880) 29th Report on the District, Criminal and Private Lunatic Asylums in Ireland. Dublin: HMSO

Inspector of Mental Health Services (2004) Mental Health Commission Annual Report 2004: Including the Report of the Inspector of Mental Health Services. Dublin: Mental Health Commission

Inspector of Mental Hospitals (1949) Report of the Inspector of Mental Hospitals for the Year 1949. Dublin: Stationery Office (Note: no publication date is indicated in this report other than the date provided in the title)

Laing R D (1960) The Divided Self. London: Tavistock

Laing R D and Esterson A (1964) Sanity, Madness and the Family. London: Tavistock

Lord Lieutenant and Council of Ireland (1885) General Rules and Regulations for the Management of District Lunatic Asylums in Ireland. Dublin: The Queen's Printing Office

Mental Health Commission (2005) Reference Guide to the Mental Health Act 2001. Dublin: Mental Health Commission

O'Sullivan E and O'Donnell I (eds.) (2012) Coercive confinement in Ireland: patients, prisoners and penitents. Manchester: Manchester University Press

Robins J (1986) Fools and Mad: A History of the Insane in Ireland. Dublin: Institute of Public Administration

Select Committee to Consider the State of the Lunatic Poor in Ireland (1817) Report of the Select Committee to Consider the State of the Lunatic Poor in Ireland. Dublin: Parliamentary Papers

Szasz T (1972) The Myth of Mental Illness. St Albans: Granada

United Nations General Assembly (1991) UN Principles for the Protection of Persons with Mental Illness and the Improvement of Mental Health Care. New York: United Nations

Vaughan W E and Fitzpatrick A J (1978) Irish historical statistics: population, 1821–1971. Dublin: Royal Irish Academy

Walsh D and Daly A (2002) Irish Psychiatric Hospitals and Units Census 2001. Dublin: Health Research Board

3
Medicalisation and professionalisation of mental health service delivery

Líam Mac Gabhann

How people view mental health, mental health problems and the way care services are provided is affected by personal and societal perspectives and changing social processes. There are similarities between nations and cultures and there are idiosyncrasies specific to each. If one considers the delivery of mental health services in Ireland today, depending on one's perspective, several questions might arise. Why is care so dependent on diagnosis and pharmacological treatment? Why do psychiatrists and mental health nurses[i] dominate care delivery? Why is so much power invested in psychiatry to determine the meaning and trajectory of people's lives? Why, amidst an espoused 'recovery' discourse, do traditional institutional norms still hold sway? These questions themselves reflect assumptions and are not necessarily everyone's experience. Much has been written that seeks to address such questions from a variety of theoretical perspectives. Rather than trying to answer these and other questions with some definitive truths, if that were even possible, this chapter offers a critical commentary to illuminate how we might have come to the present state of play in mental health service delivery in Ireland, with a particular focus on the relative roles of psychiatrists and mental health nurses.

A critical social theory framework will provide the medium for this critique and reveal key milestones in the evolution of mental health care in Ireland. The title of this chapter suggests a position already taken in relation to mental health care. While acknowledging that any critique is subject to the biases of both the author and the reader, the author asks that the reader first suspend their judgement in relation to the title and only after reading the critique consider if this title is justified.

The author has been a psychiatric nurse for over 25 years, and is a complementary therapy practitioner, a medical sociologist and an activist in the mental health arena, all of which influences the critical lens through which he perceives the evolution of mental health care.

The chapter will first provide a historical context for the advent of psychiatric care in Ireland, followed by a theoretical reflection on the societal positioning of mental illness. By examining the evolution of psychiatric care in mental health policy and practice alongside the evolving role of psychiatric nurses and their relationship to medicine, it will become evident why mental health care has continued to be viewed through a medical lens. This chapter includes a wider exploration of the role of society in the development of psychiatric care and the positioning of medicine as the gatekeeper and determinant of that care. Finally an epilogue will consider how new social movements are shaking the foundations of institutional psychiatric care and the long-held psychiatric dominance that have maintained the status quo.

CRITICAL SOCIAL THEORY

Critical social theory looks beneath the surface of a social phenomenon or taken-for-granted organisational structures, examining the genesis of knowledge claims and distorted and exploitative power relations, seeking to make sense of any given status quo. As such, it is a useful medium for exploring the complexities of mental health care. Porter offers a definition of critical theory as a discipline that:

> Entails looking beneath the surface of knowledge and reason (Kant) in order to see how that knowledge and reason is distorted in an unequal and exploitative society (Marx) and in doing so, to point the way to less distorted forms of knowledge and reason (Hegel). (Porter 1998:131)

The perspectives of two critical theorists, Paulo Freire and Jürgen Habermas, are more commonly utilised in nursing literature than others (Porter 1994, Freshwater 2000, Meyer 2001, Fontana 2004) and in the theorisation of health encounters (Mishler 1984, Scambler 1987). Habermas's (1987) theory of 'communicative action' offers a perspective on the medicalisation and professionalisation of health care and provides a critical framework for exploring health and illness (Scambler 1987, Porter 1994, Hyde and Roche-Reid 2004, Hodge 2007, Mac Gabhann 2010, Pilgrim and Rogers 2010).

Porter (1998) explains Habermas's theory of communicative action as being about a public sphere where people communicate through rational debate, where consensus rather than power prevails, and where culture, social integration and personality (in the sense of competency to express one's own identity) are reproduced. The theory of communicative action supports the primacy of communication as a means of maintaining a balance of power between participants in order to avoid exploitation of knowledge by one group in society above that of others. Habermas (1987) argues that two forms of rational action, purposeful and value, influence how we communicate. Purposeful rational action can be seen as the most efficient way of attaining certain ends. It involves applying scientific and/or technical means to demonstrate this efficiency as opposed to any ethical considerations promoted by the prevailing 'system'. Value-rational action can be determined by values, ethical concerns and some form of, for example, religious, aesthetic or other behaviours, regardless of their prospect of success. Value-rational action usually represents lifeworlds, which are any communities that share taken-for-granted background assumptions, convictions and relations that function as resources for what goes into communicative action. For Habermas, both value- and purposeful rational action are necessary for communicative action. Unfortunately, what happens more frequently is that the system uses purposeful rational action to colonise lifeworlds and assimilate them, so that the values of the system are overriden. Later in this chapter the theory of communicative action will be employed as an explanatory model for how today's mental health service delivery remains fundamentally a psychiatric model subject in part due to the professionalisation strategies of psychiatrists and psychiatric nurses, albeit sanctioned and legislated for by the state.

CONTEXTUALISING 'MENTAL ILLNESS' AND PSYCHIATRIC CARE

The development of psychiatric care in Ireland is inextricably linked to developments in England at least up until Irish independence, though Ireland evolved none the less with its own idiosyncrasies. Asylums and the rise of the institution are discussed in another chapter (see Brennan, Chapter 2). In this chapter, the psychiatric institution will be discussed in so far as it provides a historical milestone for the encroachment of 'medicine' into the lives of people deemed unsuitable for mainstream society and segregated into asylums (Foucault 1965/2003).

The Lunacy Act 1845 (England) perhaps provided the first policy diktat relating to the identification and treatment of the 'mad' in society (Pilgrim and Rogers 1994). There are competing analyses of the purpose of the programme of building asylums that ensued to house the mad. Jones (1960) argued that the reform movement was behind the project to provide housing and moral treatment to those who were unable to function according to social etiquette. Others, such as Scull (1977), were more inclined towards the argument that asylums provided capitalism with a mechanism to segregate unproductive citizens from the working population; those in the asylums were more often the poor and disenfranchised, and were not necessarily deemed insane. Foucault (1965/2003) saw the institutions as a repository and a solution devised for segregating social deviants from society in order to maintain prescribed social norms. Any of these arguments provide a sense that within society there was an important 'us' and 'them' and the housing of 'them' in asylums provided a walled distinction between the two. These institutions expanded over the 18th and 19th centuries.

It was not until after the Medical Registration Act 1858 that medicine in general began to infiltrate the institutional populations. The General Medical Council was subsequently formed and became a powerful lobby group for the now registered medical practitioners. This convenient unity enabled doctors to usurp their unregistered competitors. It also gave support to doctors in pressurising the government and institutions for more power over the provision of health services. An example of this pressure and its success is a prolonged diplomatic campaign in the 19th century in which physicians and surgeons slowly wrested responsibility for hospital admission from subscribers working for the voluntary hospitals, done under the auspices of humanitarian intervention (Scambler, 1997). Over time this campaign ensured that only registered doctors were employed by friendly societies and under the rules of the Poor Laws. Slowly they became the practitioners of choice employed by the growing middle class and supported by the state. The social status of doctors was increased by association with the middle classes and later, following a successful dispute with the British Army, the rank of officer was automatically conferred on enlisted doctors. Competition for patients amongst the middle classes necessitated creative marketing and the institutional population provided a readymade group. In keeping with this general trend among medical professionals, as Scull (1982) argued, from the middle of the 19th century 'mad doctors' manoeuvred themselves to secure positions providing medical observation and care over those in the institutions, slowly replacing lay asylum superintendents with medical superintendents. The process of the medicalisation of asylum inmates was further enabled by the 1867 Lunacy Act, which provided a means to segregate the criminally insane from criminals and other social deviants by the judiciary incarcerating them in purpose-built institutions under the care of medicine (Powell 1998).

CONSTRUCTING 'MENTAL ILLNESS'

Having wrested control of 'lunatic' asylums from lay administrators, medical superintendents then had a large population in their charge. The asylums provided a captive melting pot of human activity to be observed, classified and deemed 'mentally ill' by the expanding branch of medicine known as psychiatry. A professional strategy then emerged where medicine went about developing a classification system that asserted that 'madness' was a biological condition (Scull 1979). The origin of this biomedical classification system is generally accepted as having evolved from the initial observations of Emil Kraepelin in 1887. He described the medical condition 'dementia praecox', an early deteriorating condition of the brain that led to a sustained state of madness. Other conditions he described were 'manic depression' and 'paranoia'. Later, in around 1912, Eugen Bleuler renamed 'dementia praecox' 'schizophrenia' (Pilgrim 2005, Tummey and Turner 2008). These were the early pioneers who constructed the psychiatric diagnostic model; those who came after perpetuated and expanded the field of psychiatry that today grounds its assumptions in psychiatric diagnoses (Bentall 2003). Although the initial classifications were purported to be based on 'physical' or observable biological symptoms of brain dysfunction, they were generally not physically observable or indeed related to obvious biological function (Tummey and Turner 2008). None the less, psychiatrists laid claim to this emerging biomedical model. The elaborations of this model have been demonstrated in the two classification systems: the WHO *International Classifications of Diseases [ICD]*; and the American Psychiatric Association's *Diagnosis and Statistical Manual of Mental Disorders [DSM]* and their subsequent editions (Pilgrim 2005).

Bracken and Thomas (2001) argue that psychiatry was very much rooted in the European Enlightenment project. Following Foucault's interpretation, they argue that a societal preoccupation with 'reason' and 'unreason' as polarised positions, fulfilled through the practice of empirical scientific endeavour and a focus on the 'individual', enabled psychiatry to prosper as it aligned itself with medicine and offered a functionalist role to exclude the unreasonable through diagnosis and segregation. They identify three pertinent consequences for the concomitant relationship of psychiatry to this modernist era: madness as internal, a technical explanatory framework for madness, and coercion and psychiatry.

Firstly, madness becomes an internal psychic phenomenon separate from any external context, and emotional distress and psychoses are defined in terms of a disordered individual experience. Social and cultural factors are secondary at best, perhaps not surprisingly so, considering that most clinical encounters occur within an institutional psychiatric setting, with or without walls.

Secondly, in keeping with Enlightenment promises that human suffering would be overcome through the advancement of rationality and science, psychiatry develops as a technology to address mental distress. As Bracken and Thomas argued,

> Psychiatry sought to replace spiritual, moral, political, and folk understandings of madness with the technological framework of psychopathology and neuroscience ... (Bracken and Thomas 2001:724)

The emerging paradigm of madness as caused by neurological dysfunction and cured by pharmacological intervention has held sway to this day. The DSM classification system provides a technical idiom for defining over 300 'mental illnesses'.

Thirdly, mandated through legislation and ascribed roles by the state in the involuntary detention and treatment of individuals defined as having a 'mental disorder', psychiatry is in a powerful position and has continually asserted its power in a quest to fulfil its promise to control madness through medical science. Although inextricably linked to social exclusion, incarceration and enforced treatments, the psychiatrist's role as a technical expertise was taken as a socially accepted given (Bracken and Thomas 2001).

Although sociological critique might argue that the Enlightenment period has come to an end and the notion of any singular objective truth is no longer accepted, political positioning by psychiatry enables certain truths to be given precedence (Rorty 1989). Psychiatry still prevails in mental health service delivery, and as Crowe (2000) argued, still provides the social mechanism by which normality is constructed within a technical rational viewpoint as defined by ever-increasing DSM classifications of life experiences.

PSYCHIATRY: THE GUARDIAN OF NORMALITY

As an established medical discipline, psychiatry has an important gatekeeping role in society by determining who is fit and unfit for productive social endeavour. Medicine has a long history of providing this function to the state. Parsons' (1951) concept of the 'Sick Role' provided a theoretical framework to describe the process by which people deemed sick were considered deviant, as they were unable to perform normal social roles. According to the theory, the primary function of the sick role is to control the disruptive effect of illness in society with the aim that those deemed sick were to be returned to optimum function as soon as possible. There are four expectations relating to the sick role: (1) the sick person is exempt from performing normal social roles; (2) the sick person is exempt from responsibility for his own state; (3) the sick person must be motivated to get well as soon as possible; and (4) the sick person must seek technically competent help and cooperate with medical experts (Morgan et al. 1985). Psychiatrists were the professionals who policed this role in relation to people deemed to have a 'mental illness'. Importantly, as a profession they were given autonomy in how they interpreted and dealt with the sick role for such people in so far as they were legally responsible for providing certification for sick leave. Although Parsons' formulation from the 1950s appears dated, the legacy of professional gatekeeping and state accommodation has been perpetuated in social, employment and health legislation in Ireland and his four core expectations remain contemporary. Irish welfare law requires that for a person to be sick and excused from work or even from a state of unemployment the permission of a 'medical practitioner' is required, as it is for a person who wishes to return to work following a period of absence due to sickness. Interestingly, other health care practitioners do not have this power and consequently it is specifically medical practitioners, including psychiatrists, who can deem a person sick or well in the eyes of the state.

As is described in Chapter 2, the Mental Treatment Act 1945 saw the wresting of power from the judiciary and the transfer to psychiatrists of the responsibility for determining the progress of individuals deemed mentally ill (Powell 1998). Successive legislation in Ireland, e.g. Mental Health Act 2001 (Government of Ireland 2001), and health policy direction (Department of Health 1984; Department of Health and Children 2006) has ensured that the role of the psychiatrist is by law and policy the most powerful among the mental health professions, and in practice, psychiatrists are ultimately responsible for clinical care, despite the parallel aspirations for multidisciplinary teams working articulated in the successive government mental health policies. Although progressive policy (Department of Health and Children 2006) has sought to reframe how people with mental health problems are perceived and care provided, arguably towards a more biopsychosocial model, as long as psychiatry with its dominant role remains grounded in its historical medical assumptions, policy aspirations may remain in conflict with the status quo.

THE RISE OF PSYCHIATRIC NURSING AND ITS SYMBIOTIC RELATIONSHIP WITH PSYCHIATRY

Without dismissing the various mental health/psychiatric professionals involved in psychiatric care, psychiatric nurses have a pivotal role alongside psychiatrists in the medicalisation and professionalisation of mental health care. They too emerged from the asylums alongside psychiatrists and psychiatric patients.[ii] During the asylum era, psychiatric nurses evolved from keepers and attendants. They were managed by lay and medical superintendents and their role was to assist the doctors in their work, principally by looking after the patient's physical body, being a mediator between patient and doctor, and ensuring a safe environment. Everything about their role was either dictated or provided by the discipline of medicine via training or prescribed ritual. 1919 saw the enactment of legislation that provided for individuals to register as 'mental' (later 'psychiatric') nurses in Ireland (Nurses Registration (Ireland) Act 1919). This could perhaps be viewed as a sign that they were seeking to take control of their own work and develop their own professional identity. Alternatively, this could be viewed as the imposition of an ascribed state role, in that the state was embroiled in post-war health reforms and wanted an account of the available nursing workforce. Up until 1945, 'mental nurses' were still employed in large institutions, which were essentially self-contained communities that also provided produce to local communities. These nurses, although under strict hierarchical supervision, could diversify in particular aspects of running the institution. However they still neither controlled their own work nor set their own terms of reference. The

1945 Mental Treatment Act formalised the title of 'psychiatric nurse', fostering a close titular relationship to the 'psychiatrist' (Powell 1998).

Elsewhere, particularly in the US, nurse academics were seeking to establish a separate body of knowledge and separation from the diktats of medicine. Vocationalism, the Catholic Church and institutional medical care ensured that some of this scholarly activity did not affect Irish mental health care until much later (Healy 1991). Finally Ireland too responded to the WHO (1956) report on psychiatric nursing regarding skills, competencies and educational requirements (1956). In 1960 a specific psychiatric nursing syllabus was introduced, arguably indicating that nursing could now forge elements of its own destiny (Sheridan, 2000). However, a cursory examination of a contemporary psychiatric student nursing text such as the *Handbook for Psychiatric Nurses* (Ackner 1964) shows that it still bound any nursing activity to the diktats of psychiatry. One example is how the guidance instructs that nurses be responsible for observing the activities and behaviours of patients and reporting back to the doctor for further instruction, an indication of a functional role of nurses in extending the gaze and authority of psychiatry.

As psychiatric nursing engaged in its own process of professionalisation, ostensibly through the development of applied nursing models, an argument could be made that the symbiotic relationship between psychiatric nurses and psychiatry would eventually split. The specialisation of knowledge application to nursing practice is summed up by Pashley and Henry (1990:46) who term nurses in the nineties as 'professionals of care' rather than 'handmaidens of cure'.

NURSING MODELS

In considering the role of the Irish mental health nurse today, it might be useful to reflect upon nursing models over time. Starting with the sometimes perceived founder of nursing, Nightingale (1859) defined a concept of nursing practice as a vocation that would be dedicated to the service of patients, handmaiden to the doctor, punctual, obedient, good tempered and loyal to all rules (cited in Morrall 1998:35). This conception is a long way off from Pashley's and Henry's view, which more closely resembles the ideas of Peplau. Peplau's (1952) theory/model of interpersonal relations nursing grew out of the American Enlightenment. As the 'mother of psychiatric nursing', it was Peplau who identified the location of nursing therapy within the nurse–patient relationship, a prevailing message and one which still resonates with and influences mental health nursing in Ireland today.

However, nursing models themselves are subject to the influence of prevailing discourse. Prior (1991) identified three evolving discourses in psychiatry: (a) the psychoanalytical discourse, in which cause was located in the psyche and care in therapy; (b) asylum care in North West Europe, in which rather than locating mental illness in the psyche or mind, there was a preoccupation with physical observations and machinations, and in which the prevailing ideology was that mental illness was located in the body, more specifically the brain; and (c) in the later part of the 20th century, he argues that there was a shift in focus from the physical body to personal behaviour. In this latter discourse, mental illness was akin to maladaptive behaviour, and the role of therapy was to correct behaviour, to normalise it. Relating these discourses to nursing models, one could say that Peplau's theory is aligned with the first discourse (a) because of her focus on the psychotherapeutic relationship. The Activity of Daily Living (ADL) model (Roper et al. 1985) that focussed on people's deficits in daily activities, and the self-care model of Orem (1985) that focussed on people regulating their abilities to manage their daily lives, both fit partially with Prior's 'physical location' discourse (b) and partially into the 'behavioural location' discourse (c). If this analysis is correct then psychiatric nursing may have continued to align itself with psychiatry over time.

Later, Prior posited another influential discourse on the evolving role of the 'Lay Expert' in health care (Prior 2003). We can see the idea of expertise by experience in Barker et al.'s (1999) 'Tidal Model' of nursing where the whole model is based on the service user's narrative and how nurses and others can help them achieve their goals.

DEINSTITUTIONALISATION, COMMUNITY CARE AND CRISIS OF MEDICAL DOMINANCE

As inpatient custodial care shifted into the community towards the end of the 20th century, the mechanisms by which psychiatrists and psychiatric nurses maintained their control over mental health care needed to change, as there were then many other variables involved in care provision, not least the involvement of other professionals.

The 1950s saw the beginning of deinstitutionalisation from large psychiatric hospitals. There are three common, not necessarily commensurable, arguments put forward for this transition: the pharmacological revolution; economic determinism; and a shift in psychiatric discourse (Pilgrim and Rogers 2010).

Advances in the development of psychotropic drugs for managing symptoms and behaviour provided an opportunity to consider that the mentally ill could now safely live in the community and without the protection of walled institutions for them and society. Pharmacological interventions were seen as the panacea for addressing mental illness, remaining to this day the bedrock of psychiatric treatment and a continued preoccupation of psychiatric nursing discourse (Lakeman and Cutcliff 2009).

Not necessarily aligned but equally relevant was the shift in economic focus by the welfare state on the economic costs of the asylums (Commission of Inquiry

1966; Scull 1977). The costs of segregative control mechanisms, the loss of unpaid labour and the increasing costs of labour rendered large institutional provision no longer cost effective; the maintenance of ex-patients on welfare payments and the development of alternative community care seemed to be a more viable state policy. However, Scull argued that the inhumanity of the asylum was simply replaced by the negligence of the community (Pilgrim and Rogers 2010).

Pilgrim's and Rogers' (2010) third argument focuses on the changing psychiatric discourse, where the focus of care was on acute problems, particularly relevant to the concurrent advances in pharmacology that aspired, perhaps for the first time, to 'cure'. On the one hand there was a proliferation of diagnoses, experiences of recovery and a realisation that many conditions could be safely treated in the community, such as anxiety and depression. Furthermore, there were service users who were less responsive to intervention in the community, and who became the focus of acute care in an evolving building programme of community mental health centres and acute psychiatric units adjacent to district general hospitals. Although the 1950s saw the emergence of this discourse, the bricks-and-mortar changes were slow in terms of the exodus from institutions to community units, and it was at least the late 1980s before they became commonplace in the UK and Ireland (Pilgrim and Rogers 2010; Department of Health 1984).

It is notable that evolving community care structures, though without containment walls, were no less encapsulated within an institutional setting. The development of acute psychiatric units, psychiatric day hospitals, psychiatric day centres, psychiatric hostels and sheltered working environments continued to contain patients within a 'mental health bubble', managed as they were by the same devolved structures, professions and cultures as those of the asylums. These 'institutions without walls' are an example of how community care has simply shifted the institution into the community and reinstitutionalised care provision according to the same practices, cultures and values of the asylum (Baruch and Treacher 1978, Lelliot and Quirk 2004, Pilgrim and Rogers 2010).

Prior (1991) in his analysis of how psychiatric care and professional roles were organised over time suggests that deinstitutionalisation represented another shift in the way that 'mental illness' was interpreted and psychiatric care was organised. He saw the previous medical dominance as moving towards a more socio-medical organisation of mental illness with responsibility shared between medicine and social services. The social aspects relevant to people's mental health such as family and social networks were seen as the domain of social services and related professionals, and the meaning and treatment of 'madness' remaining in the domain of psychiatrists and psychiatric nurses. Whilst this analysis suggests a dilution of the global domination of mental illness by psychiatrists and mental health nurses it still locates the power of diagnosis, treatment and acute management within the remit of these two professional groups.

The mental health policy document *Planning for the Future* (Department of Health 1984) shows the continued dominance of the medical profession within community care. Powell (1998) argues that this document was basically a medical report, dividing the country (through sectorisation) and segments of the community (through specialist services across the lifespan and interest areas, e.g. addiction) between individual psychiatric consultants who would have a team of health and social care professionals working for them in the community. Psychiatrists would still maintain bases and wards in either dissolving institutions and/or purpose-built wings of general hospitals, the latter being an attempt to normalise mental illness and healthcare or improve the stature of 'psychiatry', depending on which way one wants to argue. A slow incremental development of more community-based care ensued with some targets met and others lost. One of the aspirations of *Planning for the Future* was that nurses would prepare patients in institutions to be able to reintegrate into normal society (Sheridan 2000). This opened up the area of rehabilitation as a speciality for nursing, albeit rehabilitation operating within the larger or smaller community institutions, as opposed to being involved in mainstream social reintegration, recovery or relapse prevention. The latter concepts which emerged later within Irish policy are more attuned to the 'community care provision' envisaged in *Planning for the Future* than the idea of rehabilitation. Subsequent policy documents and legislation continue to support the psychiatric dominance, despite evolving discourses. The control of emerging structures, specialist services and the interpretation of madness remains firmly in the hands of psychiatry (Department of Health and Children 2001, 2006).

THE POTENTIAL FOR EXTRACTING 'NURSING' FROM PSYCHIATRIC CARE

Armstrong (1995) in his analysis of shifts in how medicine as a whole moved from dominating 'hospital medicine' to community medicine argued that a new form of medicine, 'surveillance medicine', provided a framework by which health and illness was located in the normal population, with everyone in the population located somewhere on the health and illness continuum. Within surveillance medicine everyone was in a state of potential illness and medicine continued to be the state-sanctioned body to police this continuum. Adopting Prior's analysis alongside Armstrong's, a critical position offers the hypothesis that the control and dominance by medicine of mental health care in the asylum has been replicated and enhanced through the colonisation of normality using mental health and illness constructs.

The colonisation of the community by medicine brought with it a developing partnership between medicine and the social sciences (Armstrong 1995). The move into the community led to a focus within psychiatry on community life and the family and gave rise to a discourse that recognised the role of the social. However, this was a not a familiar arena for psychiatry given that it was more used to working within asylum walls and focusing on the individual corporal disease. In fact, the emergence of psychosocial discourse and competing theories for explaining mental illness almost came into vogue. The Stress Vulnerability Theory (Zubin and Spring 1977) of mental illness located it in the lived experience of individuals and their vulnerability and in ability to cope with life's stress. This model brought endless possibilities in terms of effective therapies to cope with mental illness, and offered nursing and other professional groups an opportunity to engage in therapeutic interventions central to service user engagement (Gamble and Brennan 2006) as opposed to proliferating medical treatment.

In relation to the continued professionalisation of mental health nursing, another historical milestone provided further opportunity for nurses to disentangle themselves from the onwards trajectory of a medical/psychiatric model of care. In 1998 a commission on nursing was set up to examine the future role of nursing in Ireland (Government of Ireland 1998). The commission covered everything from pre-registration training to postgraduate education and from clinical career pathways to professional regulation. It had grown out of a longstanding and entrenched conflict during the 1990s between nurses and the state about pay and conditions. Initially one might think that the deliberations of the commission on nursing had no influence on nursing in Ireland. Nursing unions were so unimpressed that they called a national strike that lasted for nine days until a pay deal was reached and confirmation was given of their future involvement in any partnership programmes with the government for the public services. For only the second time in history, the report was a catalyst for placing nursing in a leadership role relating to negotiating its own destiny. For the first time, it established nursing, including mental health nursing, as a degree-qualified profession. The report and subsequent actions also brought about a tiered approach to mental health nursing with the potential to enable increased autonomy and responsibility for the organisation of nursing care and partnership in multidisciplinary care through the development of Clinical Nurse Specialists and Advanced Nurse Practitioner roles.

Although these changes offered nurses the chance to distinguish themselves from the wider medical authority, there is little evidence to suggest that despite a broadening of their role, mental health nurses have become any less ensconced in the psychiatric discourse since that time (see for example Health Service Executive 2012).

THE POWER OF THREE: THE PERSISTENCE OF BIO-POWER

Nurses' roles have evolved to become increasingly autonomous; psychiatrists have continued to be mandated by the state for policing 'madness'; and patients are still beholden to psychiatry for ascribing meaning to their experiences, subject to psychiatrists' judgements in relation to their treatment and monitored through the lens of surveillance. With roots in the birth of asylum care and the construction of the idea of mental illness, a seemingly perpetual, entangled power relationship between patient, psychiatric nurse and psychiatrist has emerged and persists in modern mental health care in the community, despite an imagined freedom to choose another path. At certain times, the professional trajectories of psychiatrists and mental health nurses offered opportunities for them to part ways, yet something still holds this symbiotic relationship together. Some look to power and power dynamics to make sense of why these entanglements persist. There is a strong affiliation between the two disciplines and the 'patient' that is enabled by the services operating within a mental health bubble that holds on to persistent asylum cultures and psychiatric discourse in the 21st century (Clarke 1998, Nolan 2000, Barker and Stevenson 2000, Casey and Long 2003, Barker 2003, Perron et al. 2005, Roberts 2005).

Using Foucault's theory of bio-power (Foucault 1995), Perron et al. (2005) put forward a paradoxical argument that whilst nurses have felt disempowered and oppressed by working within a psychiatric paradigm (Jewell, 1994) and subservient to the omnipotent psychiatrist (Fulton 1997), they have concomitantly been empowered by this association. The combined effect of social exclusion and subjectification by a polemical dogma of 'psychiatry' is seen by some to have brought about the construction of 'psychiatric identities' for individuals in receipt of mental health treatment (Roberts 2005). The psychiatric identity is one where the meaning of people's experiences is provided by categorisation as forms of mental illness by healthcare professionals. Categorisation in itself is not sufficient; people need to be trained and socialised into the role through the orchestration of bio-power (Foucault 1995). Bio-power operates from two poles, at the individual level through anatomo-politics and at population level through bio-politics. Anatomo-politics aims to produce technologies that exert a hold over individuals' bodies. Various disciplines or processes are introduced to the individual to be internalised. These include depersonalisation through removal of familiar personal objects, succumbing to perpetual monitoring and correcting behaviour accordingly and the instigation of strict timetabled routines. Through this process, the individual undergoes a socialisation process where they are required to assimilate the identity prescribed and recurrently reinforced through interactions with nurses and doctors. Bio-politics enables the management of groups of individuals by enshrining its discourse in social policy and regulating the population accordingly. In this way psychiatric identities are both sanctioned and pre-programmed in individuals who are unable to self-regulate according to social expectation (Perron et al. 2005). For Perron et al. (2005), contrary to the idea that psychiatry imposes disempowering positions on mental health nurses (as nurses themselves articulate), they can and do exercise substantial power as anatomo-political managers and agents of bio-politics.

COLONISATION OF THE LIFEWORLD

This chapter has discussed some of the influential concepts, policy and historical milestones in the evolution of psychiatric medicine and nursing, not least the construction of the idea of mental illness in the first place. Considered from Porter's (1998) perspective on Habermas there is a clear indication that purposeful rationality has completely overridden value rationality at two levels. Two lifeworlds: that of people who experience mental distress, and that of psychiatric nursing, which over time has developed its own identity, ethics, values and relations, have joined up in a relationship with psychiatric power. Over time the lifeworlds of both psychiatric nursing and individuals in receipt of psychiatric care have been dominated by purposeful rationality in the form of a technological, medicalising discourse, becoming 'colonised' and assimilated into the psychiatric system in the process. This is a historical legacy and one that continues to influence the ongoing trajectory of mental health care.

CONCLUSION

Mental health care in Ireland entered the 21st century with the promise of and aspirations to a new discourse: 'recovery' (see Higgins and McGowan, Chapter 5). By 2006 mental health professionals, service users and family members were envisaged within policy as equal partners in determining how care that would be radically different from the past would be defined, how needs would be assessed and services designed and delivered (Department of Health and Children 2006). By adopting the principle of recovery, the *Vision for Change* report directly confronted medical colonisation and provided once again an opportunity for value-rational action to prevail through the development of recovery orientated services and a role for practitioners that by any definition could not be subjugated by purposeful rationality. At this juncture it remains to be seen whether the tide has indeed turned and we are moving into a post-colonial era of recovery-orientated mental health care.

Finally, the medicalisation and professionalisation of mental health care could have been explored through another lens, however the perspective taken has allowed me to uncover the assumptions within the system.

The focus has been on the three main actors: patients, psychiatrists and psychiatric nurses. Other professional groups and families could have been included. Their exclusion was not an attempt to disguise their involvement in the emerging process of care. Instead, the focus purely on the inextricable relationship of the three main actors in this process of colonisation was chosen in an attempt to render the process clear.

Habermas (1987) argued that one of the most likely ways that colonisation could be reversed or at least challenged to the extent that purposeful and value-rational action could take on a balanced interaction once again, was through the evolution and action of New Social Movements (NSMs) (see Brosnan, Chapter 6). The survivor and service-user movements can be described and understood as NSMs, and over the last 10 years in Ireland have been sanctioned by the state and recognised in society as a force for change in mental health education, research and service development (Lakeman et al. 2007, Walsh and Mac Gabhann 2011). Perhaps it will be the strength of these NSM activities that will overturn the medical colonisation of madness.

REFERENCES

Ackner B (1964) Handbook for Psychiatric Nurses. London: Baillière, Tindall and Cassell

Armstrong D (1995) The rise of surveillance medicine. Sociology of Health and Illness 17 (3) 393-404

Barker P, Jackson S, Stevenson C (1999) What are psychiatric nurses needed for? Developing a theory of essential nursing practice. Journal of Psychiatric and Mental Health Nursing 6 (4) 273-282

Barker P, Stevenson C (2000) The Construction of Power and Authority in Psychiatry. Oxford: Butterworth Heinman

Barker P (2003) The Tidal Model: Psychiatric colonization, recovery and the paradigm shift in mental health care. International Journal of Mental Health Nursing 12:96-102

Baruch G, Treacher A (1978) Psychiatry Observed. London: Routledge and Kegan Paul

Bentall R (2003) Madness Explained: Psychosis and Human Nature. London: Penguin

Bracken P, Thomas P (2001) Postpsychiatry: a new direction for mental health. British Medical Journal 322:724-727

Casey B, Long A (2003) Meanings of madness: a literature review. Journal of Psychiatric and Mental Health Nursing 10:89-99

Clarke L (1998) Schizophrenia: all in the mind or locked in the brain? Journal of Advanced Nursing 28 (2) 398-404

Commission of Inquiry on Mental Illness (1966) Report of the Commission of Inquiry on Mental Illness. Dublin: Government Publications Office

Crowe M (2000) Constructing normality: a discourse analysis of the DSM-IV. Journal of Psychiatric and Mental Health Nursing 7:69-77

Department of Health (1984) The Psychiatric Services – Planning for the Future Study group on the development of the Psychiatric Services. Dublin: Stationery Office

Department of Health and Children (2006) A Vision for Change: Report of the Expert Group on Mental health Policy. Dublin: Stationery Office

Fontana J S (2004) A Methodology for Critical Science in Nursing Advances in Nursing Science 27 (2) 93-101

Foucault M (1965) Madness and Civilization. New York: Random House

Foucault M (1995) Discipline and Punish. New York: Random House

Foucault M (2003) (republished 1965 edition) Madness and Civilization. London: Routledge Classics

Freire P (1970) Pedagogy of the Oppressed. London: Penguin

Freshwater D (2000) Transformatory Learning in Nurse Education: A reflexive action research study. Southsea, Hants: Nursing Praxis International

Fulton Y (1997) Nurses' views on empowerment: a critical social theory perspective. Journal of Advanced Nursing 26:529-536

Gamble C, Brennan G (2006) Working with Serious Mental Illness: A Manual For Clinical Practice. London: Elsevier

Government of Ireland (1998) Report of The Commission on Nursing: A blueprint for the future. Dublin: Stationery Office

Government of Ireland (2001) Mental Health Act. Dublin: Stationery Office

Habermas J (1987) The Theory of Communicative Action, Volume 2, Lifeworld and System: A Critique of Functionalist Reason. Cambridge: Polity Press

Health Service Executive (2012) A Vision for Psychiatric/Mental Health Nursing: A shared journey for mental health care in Ireland. Dublin: Health Service Executive

Healy D (1991) Irish Psychiatry in the Twentieth Century in Berrios G, Freeman H (1991) (eds.) 150 Years of British Psychiatry Vol 2: The Aftermath. London: Athlone Press

Hyde A, Roche-Reid B (2004) Midwifery practice and the crisis of modernity: implications for the role of the midwife. Social Science and Medicine 58:2613-2623

Hodge S (2007) Competence, Identity and Intersubjectivity: Applying Habermas's Theory of Communicative Action to Service User Involvement in Mental Health Policy Making. Social Theory and Health 3:165-182 (August 2005)

Jewell M L (1994) Partnership in learning: education as liberation. Nursing and Health Care 15 (7) 360-364

Jones K (1960) Mental Health and Social Policy, 1845-1959. London: Routledge and Keegan Paul

Lakeman R, McGowan P, Walsh J (2007) Service users, authority, power and protest: a call for renewed activism. Mental Health Practice 11:12-16

Lakeman R, Cutcliff J (2009) Misplaced epistemological certainty and pharmaco-centrism in mental health nursing. Journal of Psychiatric and Mental Health Nursing 16:199-205

Lelliot P, Quirk A (2004) What is Life Like on Acute Psychiatric Wards? Current Opinion in Psychiatry 17 (4) 297-310

Mac Gabhann L, McGowan P, Walsh J, O'Reilly O (2010) Leading change in public mental health services through collaboration, participative action, co-operative learning and open dialogue. The International Journal of Leadership in Public Services 6 (supplement) (September) 6 (3) 38-50

Meyer J (2001) Lay Participation in Care in a Hospital Setting: An action research study. Portsmouth, UK: Nursing Praxis International

Morgan M, Calnan M, Manning M (1985) Sociological Approaches to Health and Medicine. London: Routledge

Orem D E (1985) Nursing: Concepts of Practice. New York: McGraw

Parsons T (1951) The sick role and the role of the physician reconsidered. Milbank Memorial Fund Quarterly: Health and Society 53:257-78

Pashley G, Henry C (1990) Carving out the nursing nineties. Nursing Times 86: 45-46

Peplau H E (1952) Interpersonal Relations in Nursing. New York: Putnam

Perron A, Fluet C, Holmes D (2005) Agents of care and agents of the state: bio-power and nursing practice. Journal of Advanced Nursing 50 (5) 536-544

Pilgrim D, Rogers A (1994) A Sociology of Mental Health and Illness. Buckingham: Open University Press

Pilgrim D (2005) Key Concepts in Mental Health. London: Sage Publications

Pilgrim D, Rogers A (2010) (4th Ed) A Sociology of Mental Health and Illness. Buckingham: Open University Press

Porter S (1994) New nursing: the road to freedom? Journal of Advanced Nursing, 20:269-274

Porter S (1998) Social Theory and Nursing Practice. Basingstoke: Palgrave

Powell F (1998) Mental health policy in the Republic of Ireland: backwards into the future in Cambell J, Manktelow R (1998) (eds.) Mental Health Social Work in Ireland: Comparative Issues in Policy and Practice. Aldershot: Ashgate

Prior L (1991) Mind, Body and Behaviour: Theorisations of Madness and the Organisation of Therapy. Sociology 25 (3) 403-421

Prior L (2003) Belief, knowledge and expertise: the emergence of the lay expert in medical sociology. Sociology of Health and Illness 25:41-57

Roberts M (2005) The production of the psychiatric subject: power, knowledge and Michel Foucault. Nursing Philosophy 6:33-42

Roper N, Logan W W, Tierney A J (1985) The Elements of Nursing. Edinburgh: Churchill Livingstone

Scambler G (1987) Habermas and the power of medical expertise in Scambler G (1987) (ed.) Sociological Theory and Medical Sociology London: Tavistock

Scambler G (1997) Sociology as Applied to Medicine (4th ed). London: W B Saunders

Sheridan A (2000) Psychiatric Nursing in Robins J (2000) (ed.) Nursing and Midwifery in Ireland in the Twentieth Century. Dublin: An Bord Altranais

Scull A (1977) Decarceration: Community Treatment and the Deviant – A Radical View. Englewood Cliffs, NJ: Prentice Hall

Scull A (1982) (2nd Ed) Museums of Madness. London: Penguin

Tummey R, Turner T (2008) Critical Issues in Mental Health. UK: Palgrave Macmillan

Walsh J, Mac Gabhann L (2011) Practice, Education, Research Expert by Experience. Dublin: Dublin City University

World Health Organization (1956) Expert Committee on Psychiatric Nursing First Report. Geneva: World Health Organization

Zubin J, Spring B (1977) in Gamble C, Brennan G (2000) Working with serious mental illness: A manual for clinical practice (ed.). London: Bailliere Tindall

NOTES

[i] In this chapter the terms 'psychiatric nurse' and 'mental health nurse' are both used; 'psychiatric nurse' in a historical context and 'mental health nurse' to refer to contemporary practice.

[ii] 'Patient' has been used purposefully in this text, as opposed to, for example, 'service user' or 'consumer'. This fits with the discourses being critiqued and the central premise of colonisation that very much places the person in care as patient.

4

Shadow lives: social exclusion and discrimination in the mental health context

Shari McDaid

Recently there has been a greater recognition that mental health professionals have a role to play in promoting the social inclusion of users of mental health services. Bracken and Thomas (2005) have argued that the profession of psychiatry is heavily implicated in the history of social exclusion of people with a diagnosis of mental illness because the profession played a key role in legitimizing their incarceration and exclusion from modern society (Bracken and Thomas 2005). However, according to Slade (2009), the shift towards recovery-oriented mental health services provides an opportunity for mental health professionals to be part of the solution to social exclusion rather than part of the problem. Slade suggests that a focus on mental health treatment alone cannot help individuals to recover; mental health professionals must reorientate their work towards helping service users to remain within their communities, develop valued social roles and regain a positive identity. In their seminal book *Social Inclusion and Recovery: A model for mental health practice*, Repper and Perkins (2003) made promoting social inclusion one of the core competencies for recovery-focused mental health practice, and more recently, this perspective is beginning to surface even within mainstream psychiatry. The Royal College of Psychiatry in the UK has published a text advocating that social inclusion be a concern of psychiatrists and other mental health professionals (Boardman et al. 2010).

In Ireland, social inclusion features as a goal in the government's mental health policy *A Vision for Change* (Department of Health and Children 2006) and both the Mental Health Commission (Higgins 2008) and the NGO coalition Mental Health Reform (McDaid 2013) have identified social inclusion as an essential component of a recovery-oriented mental health service. People with self-experience of a mental health condition in Ireland have also described reconnection with community life as an important part of their recovery. In his exploration of recovery among users of GROW peer support groups, Watts (2012:187) found that becoming involved in education, work or leisure activities enabled individuals to experience 'becoming empowered through social involvement' and to 're-author' new stories of their own belonging. It is evident, then, that in both international and Irish discourse on mental health there is increasing discussion about the issues of social exclusion and inclusion.

This chapter considers the transition to community-based services from the lens of social exclusion/inclusion, asking questions about the consequences of the closure of psychiatric hospitals for the social and economic lives of mental health service users in the community. The chapter begins with a brief discussion of the concept of social exclusion. This is followed by a critical review of mental health policy since 1966 that evaluates how it underpinned the segregation and marginalisation of mental health service users. The reality of service-users' social and economic lives in the community is revealed through Irish research. The chapter concludes with a critical analysis of A Vision for Change and its implementation to date.

SOCIAL EXCLUSION AS A MEANS OF UNDERSTANDING MENTAL HEALTH INEQUALITY

Before embarking on a discussion about mental health and social exclusion in Ireland, it will be useful to establish a working definition of the term 'social exclusion'. A widely cited definition is that of Levitas et al. (2007:9) who state:

> Social exclusion is a complex and multi-dimensional process. It involves the lack or denial of resources, rights, goods and services, and the inability to participate in the normal relationships and activities, available to the majority of people in society, whether in economic, social, cultural, or political arenas. It affects both the quality of life of individuals and the equity and cohesion of society as a whole.

Social exclusion enables a wider focus for discussions of disadvantage than the concept of poverty (Hudson and Williams 2001), one which allows the mental health dimension of inequality to come into view. The concept of social exclusion also moves away from a concern with enduring, stable statuses such as class, to a recognition that disadvantage occurs as a result of dynamic processes that can change in their effects over time. Such a dynamic conception can account for the interplay between a person's mental health status and various social processes such as labelling, stigma/prejudice and discrimination, homelessness and exclusion from work. The National Economic and Social Forum (NESF 2007:10) highlights how processes of social exclusion are thus both dynamic and multifaceted.

In 2007, the NESF wrote that 'those who experience enduring mental ill-health are among the most socially excluded in Irish society …' (2007:11). There are many indicators of this socially excluded status. People with a mental health disability in Ireland are nine times more likely to be outside the labour force than those without a disability (Watson et al. 2012:19). They have a much higher rate of unemployment than the general working age population, at more than 40% (CSO 2012:15), and upwards of 20,000 people with a mental health disability were living on Disability Allowance in 2009.[i] Many who experience mental health issues stop their education earlier than people without a mental health disability (CSO 2009:75).

The question that arises, then, is how this socially excluded status has developed alongside the modern policy of community care. The history of the mental health services in Ireland in the latter 20th and early 21st centuries has been presented as a progressive trajectory from archaic institutionalisation to a modern, community-based mental health system (see Department of Health 2011 and Walsh and Daly 2004). But a careful reading of the evidence shows a more nuanced and complex story than a move away from outdated institutions to modern services. The other history of so-called deinstitutionalisation in Ireland could equally be read as a story of reinstitutionalisation, segregation and marginalisation of people who have come into contact with the mental health services.

MODERN MENTAL HEALTH POLICY FOR A MODERN IRELAND

The 1960s represented a dynamic period in the history of the Irish state. The government undertook a number of modernising initiatives, most notably with regard to the economy and education. An increasing focus on social issues was also evident in the publication of reports on topics such as reformatories and industrial schools (Committee on Reformatory and Industrial Schools 1970) and the Traveller community (Commission on Itinerancy 1963). It is within this context that the Commission of Inquiry on Mental Illness arose in 1966 to evaluate the then current state of affairs for people in psychiatric hospitals.

The Commission's report was in part a response to a shocking statistic: in 1961, Ireland had more people in psychiatric hospitals per capita than any other country in the world (Commission of Inquiry on Mental Illness 1966:24). This disturbing fact was an embarrassment to a government that sought to be modern.

The Commission's response was to set out an ambitious programme of reform that reflected the optimistic spirit of the time. In its own words 'an era of hope ha[d] arrived' in relation to 'mental illness' because they believed that ECT, insulin therapy and other drug treatments were enabling people to recover and to be discharged into the community (p.15).

By 1984 the atmosphere in Ireland had already dramatically changed. Optimism about Ireland's future had given way to economic crisis and discouragement (Brown 2004). In this context and on foot of the Commission of Inquiry report, the government produced a more measured mental health policy, *Planning for the Future* (Department of Health 1984). Rather than an aspirational declaration for mental health reform, the new policy was much more of a technical document setting out the bureaucratic organisation of mental health services in the community. Gone were the inspiring statements of expectation for a new era in mental health. Nevertheless, *Planning for the Future* remained rooted in a level of optimism about the potential for psychiatric treatments to improve the lives of people with a mental health diagnosis; it continued to attribute the new 'community-oriented approach' to the development of new drug treatments and even stated that psychiatric services can 'treat and cure many forms of mental illness [sic]' (Department of Health 1984:5). Equally important, it drew a link between the new treatments and more positive attitudes of staff towards users of services, postulating that staff were beginning to view the 'mentally ill' as having medical problems that responded to medical interventions and treatment.

Planning for the Future received some criticism at the time for failing to reflect alternative understandings of mental health. Butler stated that *Planning for the Future* represented little more than 'a *medical* report; that is, it is based on an implicit assumption that the planning of the psychiatric services is merely a matter of assessing the prevalence of mental illness and establishing the structures which best facilitate the delivery of modern, scientific treatment methods' (Butler 1987:48).

More importantly for this discussion, both the Commission of Inquiry and *Planning for the Future* reports set out a programme of restructuring that envisaged that deinstitutionalisation could be accomplished through the transfer of services into the community. Thus the Commission of Inquiry strongly advocated for the development of a range of hostels, day hospitals and day centres specifically for people with mental health conditions, while also promoting the development of 'sheltered employment' and 'industrial therapy' (Commission of Inquiry 1966:62 and 45-46). *Planning for the Future* also underpinned a substantial increase in the number of Health-Service-run, segregated community residences for users of mental health services (Department of Health 1984:Chapter 9). The seeds of segregation in the community were thus sown.

Both the Commission of Inquiry report and *Planning for the Future* portray the development of an array of specialist community-based mental health services as a progressive initiative, but it is worth noting that both also acknowledge some risks in these plans. In relation to people who will require long-stay residential care, the Commission cautions that 'It is essential that the long-stay hospital should be developed as a centre for treatment and not merely as a centre for custodial care; its aim must be to rehabilitate and to restore to the community as many patients as possible; for those who cannot be restored to the community, the aim must be to save them from a vegetative existence and to enable them to lead lives as full and happy as their disabilities permit' (Commission of Inquiry 1966:41). While this comment largely reflects a determination that large psychiatric hospitals not maintain a custodial style of care, the Commission also sounds a note of caution in relation to community services, that 'there is a danger that community care can become a catch-cry and that mentally ill patients may merely exchange neglect in a hospital for neglect in the community' (p.55). *Planning for the Future* also acknowledged that people in community residences who do not work might become isolated (Department of Health 1984:68). Nevertheless, ironically, the solution proffered in such instances was for residents to attend mental health day centres.

THE DEVELOPMENT OF SERVICES SINCE 1984

The common story told about the history of mental health services since these two reports were published is one of steady progress towards deinstitutionalisation and community-based care (see for example Department of Health and Children 2001:145). The actual progress made up until 2002 was documented in a report prepared by Daly and Walsh (2004). They highlighted the dramatic reduction in the numbers of people in hospital, falling from 21,000 in 1958 to around 4,000 in 2001. They attributed this reduction in the first instance to the death of older patients in hospitals and a much slower rate of admission of new individuals into long-stay, hospital-based care. They also cited the development of community residences as a factor and strongly advocated the continuation of this policy in order to end the practice of housing individuals in psychiatric hospitals (p.84).

Ten years after the publication of the health strategy *Quality and Fairness: A Health System for You* (Department of Health and Children 2001), the Department of Health produced a briefing document for the incoming Minister of Health that described the long-term progress in transforming the mental health services (Department of Health 2011). Its snapshot of the prior decade focused on the reduction in usage of inpatient facilities in four respects:

- A 33.5% reduction in the number of people resident in inpatient facilities
- Shorter length of stay in inpatient units
- A 19% reduction in the number of admission to inpatient units, and
- A reduction in the number of re-admissions.

The Department stated that these trends were in line with an approach to mental health services that is 'patient-centred, flexible, community based and where the need for hospital admission is greatly reduced' (p.168).

So too, there was a steady development of community residences throughout the period as shown in Table 4.1:

Table 4.1: Growth in mental health service community residences 1992–2003

Year	No. of Hostels	No. of Places	Places per 100K of Population
1992	343	2441	68
1993	361	2556	73
1994	368	2685	77
1995	377*	2666	72
1996	385	2904	78
1997	391	2878	75
1998	386	2871	79
1999	398	2923	79
2000	[Missing report]		
2001	406	3077	83
2002	411	3146	85
2003	418	3210	82

Source: Inspector of Mental Hospitals Annual Reports 1992–2003.

*Note that from 1995, figures for community residences no longer include figures for rehabilitation units as in previous reports.

It is clear, then, that successive governments and those involved in monitoring government policy have viewed the gradual closure of psychiatric hospitals and reduction in inpatient numbers as evidence of the fulfilment of a policy of deinstitutionalisation first articulated in 1966. Yet such trends indicate deinstitutionalisation only in terms of the location of individuals receiving care. What of the nature of that care? The statistics do not say very much about the lives of the individuals using the mental health services over the long term. For deinstitutionalisation to be meaningful, it must include not only freedom from physical walls of containment but also genuine opportunities to live a fulfilling life as an integrated member of a community. There is a difference between residing in a community setting and living as part of the community. To assess which of these was happening, it is worth looking away from statistics about the location of individuals to information about the quality of their lives.

REINSTITUTIONALISATION IN IRELAND

Some initial hints about the quality of life of individuals residing in community residences began to appear in successive reports of the Inspector of Mental Hospitals from the mid-1990s onwards. While initially the Inspector looked upon these developments favourably, stating in 1992 that he was 'happy to report the continuous growth in community services,' (Inspector of Mental Hospitals 1992:4) he simultaneously expressed concern that staff in these facilities might not have an adequate understanding of rehabilitation appropriate for community care (p.5). By 1997, the Inspector commented about an 'over-provision' of support to individuals in community residences that was preventing them from developing their own capacities (Inspector of Mental Hospitals 1997:4). By 2002, the Inspector was reporting that in community residences, '[t]oo often, for example, little effort is made by staff to encourage patients living in a group home to manage the day-to-day affairs of the home, such as opening independent bank and rent accounts' (Inspector of Mental Hospitals 2002:16). Finally, by 2003, in the last report of the then Inspector he concluded that many community residences were operating as 'mini-institutions':

> The Inspectorate had been struck by how little rehabilitation took place in community residences and how their management was oriented towards continuing, rather than decreasing dependency. Many were over-staffed, patients were not encouraged to take on the management of these, their homes, did not take charge of domestic matters ... It was little wonder then that some community residences or hotels are referred to as 'mini institutions' in the community. (Inspector of Mental Hospitals 2003:10-11)

The initial signs for deinstitutionalisation did not look promising.

Other evidence further supports this alternative history. Firstly, while many people were being discharged from psychiatric hospitals, re-admission rates rose and continued to remain stubbornly high throughout the period. Thus even in the early 21st century, a steady 65–70% of admissions to psychiatric units were re-admissions, indicating that many individuals were ending up back in hospital as a normal part of their care. It is also worth considering whether other forms of institutionalisation for people with mental health distress were rising during this period. Elsewhere in Europe, it has been argued that an era of 'reinstitutionalisation' has occurred in which the reduction in psychiatric beds has been offset by other forms of institutionalisation including increased use of forensic beds and a rise in the prison population (Priebe et al. 2005). In Ireland,

Kelly (2007) has highlighted the fulfilment of 'Penrose's Law' here: the reduction in numbers of psychiatric beds has correlated strongly with an increase in the prison population, though he points out that the increase in absolute numbers of prisoners is much lower than the decrease in psychiatric inpatients. Another study found that a six-month prevalence of psychosis in the remand prison population in Ireland was higher than international norms (Curtin et al. 2009). These facts raise questions about whether the closure of psychiatric beds in Ireland has resulted in a genuine movement of service users into the community, or to some extent, a transfer of people with the most severe mental distress into the prison system.

Other evidence began to emerge that showed the nature of the life in community residences was institutional rather than integrated into the mainstream activities of the community. In the early 1990s, research into the lives of 38 individuals transferred from psychiatric hospitals to community residences showed that they participated in their local community significantly less than the norm: the level of residents' participation in 'non-arranged' activities was very low and 'very few were involved in community activities.' None of the mental health service residents had a daily visitor compared to 23% of ordinary residents of the same area (Leanne and Sapouna 1998). Another study of 87 people discharged from long-stay psychiatric hospitals between 2000 and 2001 found there was no significant increase in ex-patients' [sic] level of activity, interest or community skills after five years of living in the community (McInerney et al. 2010). The authors caution that 'there is a risk of these community residences becoming institutions in the community' (p.472).

Things had not significantly improved even towards the middle of the 2000s when a national study into community residences was conducted between 2004 and 2006. To begin with, many of the residents were regularly attending mental health day services, even those identified as having low support needs (Tedstone Doherty et al. 2007). Only a small number of residents participated in community activities, and only 5% were in open employment. Sadly, the residents articulated their desire to increase their independence in the most basic of ways: '[T]hey would like more independence in terms of being able to cook and eat when and what they liked and to spend their money as they pleased' (p.110). By and large this study found a highly institutional mode of living, with 'the residences, even the medium and low support residences, [being] quite restrictive in what the residents were allowed and did not differ significantly in this regard to the large institutions' (p.121). Furthermore, not only were residents' lives highly restricted, but they were also closely monitored and lacked privacy:

> For example, the comings and goings of the residents were often monitored; residents did not have their own door key and could not lock their bedroom doors. (Tedstone Doherty et al. 2007:121)

Such reports put paid to any idea that individuals living in mental health service-staffed accommodation were living deinstitutionalised lives. Their lives in the residences were still highly institutional, while their lives outside of the residences were largely confined to mental-health-service-related activities.

SHADOW LIVES: SOCIAL EXCLUSION IN IRELAND

But what about people with experience of mental/emotional distress living outside community residences?

Qualitative evidence gives a glimpse of the nature of their social exclusion. A small-scale study of attendees to a vocational training programme in Dublin, conducted in 2000, found that they were living isolated, lonely lives (Bruce 2000). Over half of participants did not socialise regularly and almost two-thirds were not involved in any clubs or organisations. As in the earlier study on community residents, much of their social activity revolved around mental-health-related supports. In terms of the types of leisure activities that people typically undertake, almost half of the group seldom or never went to a pub with others, almost three quarters seldom or never went to a restaurant with others and almost all seldom or never went to sporting events with others. In fact, the majority of these individuals' leisure activities were solitary.

Two reports by people who use mental health services about their day activities further underscored the poor quality of life they were living in the community. The *Pathways* participatory research reports represented the first time that in the Irish context, users of services themselves were involved in researching their own situation (Brosnan et al. 2002; Wynne et al. 2004). The picture painted in both reports is one of ongoing boredom and being trapped in mental health day services with little opportunity for integration in the community.

In the report on East Galway, almost two-thirds of the participants were long-term unemployed and nearly two-thirds said they did not get any help in returning to work (Wynne et al. 2004:64). Boredom featured in day activities, with 54% of trainees at training centres saying they were bored either occasionally or generally. Similarly, 40% of participants who attended day centres found boredom to be a problem at the centres.

While these studies were small-scale, their participants are not unusual. There were 7,301 individuals diagnosed with a mental health disability in day services in 2008 (Health Service Executive 2012) and while many day services operated person-centred activation services, users of services for people with all types of disabilities, including people with a mental health disability, continued to report experiencing boredom. A review by the Health Service Executive (HSE) found that '... training and support in day services vary from clearly planned programmes to situations where people spend time with nothing to do or doing repetitive activities, which they see as of little use or value' (p.49).

The issue of marginalisation goes beyond quality of life indicators, however; what is at issue is as much about human rights as about happiness. A groundbreaking report conducted by Dublin City University for Amnesty International Ireland reconceptualised the problem in terms of prejudice and discrimination (Mac Gabhann et al. 2010). The study revealed for the first time the prejudice and discrimination experienced by individuals with a mental health diagnosis in Ireland. The 300 participants who volunteered for the study reported being treated unfairly in every domain of social life including by friends, neighbours, family, health service staff and the police, and in housing, education, work, public transport and welfare. The evidence of prejudice and discrimination in the area of employment was particularly compelling: 36% of participants had experienced unfair treatment in finding a job and 43% in keeping a job. Their qualitative feedback provided a picture of the nature of this unfair treatment:

> I did an interview which went very well and I got the job, I was asked what was the nature of my disability and when I told her it was schizophrenia she never got in touch with me after that.

While another participant said:

> I can't get a job, I've tried and tried and tried. And you can get interviews, you fill in the application form, you send it away and you get to an interview and everything is going grand in the interview and there might be a gap in your employment record or whatever. They'll say well where have you been? And I'll say well I was in a psychiatric hospital and you can see the look and it's all downhill afterwards and you never hear from them again. (Mac Gabhann et al. 2010:26)

These experiences arose despite the existence of equality legislation in Ireland that prohibits discrimination on the grounds of a mental health disability in employment.

These personal views are corroborated by successive national surveys showing that the general public has more negative attitudes towards people with a mental health condition than any other disability category. In the most recent survey conducted by the National Disability Authority, people were less comfortable working with or living near someone with a 'mental health difficulty' than someone with any other type of disability. Only 56% of the general public thought that people with a 'mental health difficulty' should have the same right to have a sexual relationship as anyone else (National Disability Authority 2012).

Many people with experience of mental/emotional distress were living isolated, marginalised lives within communities in Ireland during a period when national policy was one of deinstitutionalisation. What has emerged, then, is a system that can lead to segregation and institutionalisation of mental health service users within local communities where they may experience prejudice and discrimination.

THE EQUALITY AND SOCIAL INCLUSION AGENDA IN *A VISION FOR CHANGE*

2006 was the year in which social justice issues featured in mental health policy for the first time (Department of Health and Children 2006). An entire chapter of *A Vision for Change* is devoted to addressing social inclusion in recognition that policy on mental health must extend not only to medical and psychological treatments, but also to how mental health problems impact on the socioeconomic status of individuals diagnosed. For the first time in government policy, there was a statement asserting that people with experience of mental/ emotional distress should have equal rights to housing, education, employment and an adequate income. The policy underscores the need to address 'stigma' but also discusses the problem of 'discrimination'. Here for the first time the issue of stigma is referred to not only as a hindrance to moving mental health services into communities, but as a 'cause of social exclusion and one of the greatest barriers to social inclusion', that is, as an issue to be addressed for its own sake because of how it affects the lives of people with a mental health diagnosis. Significantly, the policy recognises that prejudice and discrimination can cause more harm than mental or emotional distress itself.

The Expert Group that wrote the report also adopted a new philosophy of mental health embodied in the recovery ethos and a commitment that the 'recovery' principle should be the 'cornerstone' of the mental health policy (p.15). Since the recovery ethos itself includes social inclusion, this recommendation by the Expert Group set up an expectation that all mental health services should be involved in fostering social inclusion of their service users as well as improving their mental health.

At the same time, *A Vision for Change* has much that harks back to *Planning for the Future*. While the recommendations on social inclusion are relatively vague, the bulk of the policy details how various types of community mental health services already envisaged in *Planning for the Future* should be further developed. In contrast, Amnesty International Ireland has criticised the lack of specificity of the cross-departmental, non-mental health service recommendations in *A Vision for Change* and recommended a detailed implementation plan for these recommendations (Amnesty International Ireland 2010:37). The imbalance between highly specific mental health service recommendations and relatively vague social inclusion recommendations has facilitated a continued focus more on bed closure rather than on social inclusion, citizenship and socioeconomic rights. Little specific funding has been allocated for the social inclusion recommendations in the report. Equally, it was only the Health Service Executive that was called upon to produce an implementation plan, not the government as a whole. It is not surprising, then, that successive reports by the Independent Monitoring Group for A Vision for Change found little evidence of implementation by government departments other than Health.

The Departments for Housing and Criminal Justice have been the exceptions. The Department of Environment and Local Government established a mental health sub-group for the development of the housing strategy for people with disabilities and in 2011 its *National Housing Strategy for People with Disabilities* included a chapter dedicated to people with a mental health disability (Department of Environment, Community and Local Government 2012). The housing strategy acknowledges that having secure accommodation is an important support to recovery from a mental health difficulty (p.99). The commitments in the strategy are focussed on ensuring that people in HSE mental health service accommodation have the supports necessary and are facilitated to transition into community housing. The strategy also contains actions to ensure that people with a mental health disability have equitable access to housing options offered by local authorities. Elsewhere the Department of Justice, Equality and Law Reform established a working group that produced a Memorandum of Understanding on co-working between An Garda Síochána and the mental health services, though the impact of this Memorandum on the ground is yet unknown (HSE/ An Garda Síochána 2011).

More recently the Department of Health has part-funded a national 'stigma reduction' programme, the See Change initiative (www.seechange. ie). See Change is a partnership project between more than 80 organisations that aims to 'bring about positive change in public attitudes and behaviour' towards people with a mental health condition. The project uses community events and social media to engage the general public. A significant feature of the project is that it features people with self-experience of mental/emotional distress speaking publicly about their experience. For example the 'Make a Ripple' social media campaign enables individuals to post their personal stories about mental/emotional distress online. As part of the See Change initiative, Amnesty International Ireland produced a ground-breaking national media campaign focused on combating discrimination against people with a mental health diagnosis and featuring people with self-experience. The See Change partnership has been successful at engaging a broad spectrum of community organisations to raise awareness about mental health and challenge negative attitudes. During the first two years of the programme, attitudes towards people with a mental health diagnosis generally improved somewhat, though negative attitudes towards people with a diagnosis of schizophrenia persisted (see www. seechange.ie/research/).

Despite the relative lack of Government policy focus on social inclusion and mental health, there is a range of programmes and local initiatives that aim to support individuals to access education and employment. The National Learning Network (NLN) provides training and education programmes in a supportive environment where individuals can gain new skills and achieve recognised qualifications, experience peer and staff support and move towards engaging in work (McDaid and Kelleher 2013). In terms of service user-led initiatives, the Gateway project in Rathmines, Dublin is a member-led community development project for people with experience of mental/emotional distress (see http://www.rpcp.ie/gateway.html). The project aims to support people to identify their own goals and integrate into the social, cultural, education and working life of the local community. Gateway provides an empowering space by engaging members in the management of the project. In West Cork, the Home Focus project employs a Peer Support Worker and helps individuals who would otherwise be isolated in rural communities to connect with the range of social inclusion resources in the area. An evaluation of the project found that participants had improved social engagement, linked in with community groups and support organisations, improved independent living skills, and that some achieved improvements in employment and training outcomes (Sapouna 2008).

While *A Vision for Change* promised something in terms of improving the socioeconomic status and social inclusion of people with a mental health condition, over the first eight years of its implementation little changed. Positive initiatives to improve the social inclusion of people with mental/emotional distress were largely locally driven or led by individual organisations such as Amnesty or NLN, apart from the See Change partnership. Overall today, people with experience of mental or emotional distress are as likely to be unemployed, isolated, impoverished, stigmatised and discriminated against in Irish society, as they were when *A Vision for Change* was published in 2006.

CONCLUSION

In 1966 there was great reason to be hopeful about the situation for people with a diagnosed mental health condition. New treatments were supposedly improving mental health outcomes, and a commitment to closing down the old-fashioned, decrepit psychiatric hospitals anticipated a new, more inclusive life in the community for people who would previously have been institutionalised. In practice what occurred in the later 20th and early 21st centuries was for too many people involved with the mental health services a process of re-institutionalisation and social exclusion in Irish communities. And while many may have preferred living outside the walls of an 'asylum', their voices show that they were far from satisfied with their lives.

The views of users of mental health services themselves, articulated through their own research and that of non-peer researchers, show how they have ended up living under the close scrutiny and disempowering supervision of mental health service staff in segregated settings throughout Ireland. So too, in their daily lives have people attending mental health services been too often segregated into mental health-specific programmes that left them bored and unfulfilled. It may be that they have in some measure chosen to remain in these places of relative safety, given the unforgiving, prejudiced and discriminatory world they face. But the reality for some has been one of a lifetime on benefits, living on the fringes of local communities, deterred and hindered from participating in social and economic life. The deinstitutionalisation of people from psychiatric hospitals cannot be said, then, to be an unmitigated success for modern mental health policy. Rather, if some benefited, many were left to lead shadow lives in a world that was not ready for their full participation as equals. In that sense, the social inclusion goal of government's mental health policy remains to be fulfilled.

*

REFLECTIVE QUESTIONS FOR DISCUSSION AND DEBATE: PRACTICE

- What role do you think changing expectations of mental health care have played in the development of mental health policy in Ireland since 1945?
- What responsibility do government departments and agencies outside of the Department of Health have for fostering recovery by individuals with poor mental health?
- What role should mental health professionals play in promoting social inclusion and challenging prejudice and discrimination?

REFLECTIVE QUESTIONS FOR DISCUSSION AND DEBATE: RESEARCH

- Explore the distinctions between stigma, prejudice and discrimination against people with experience of mental/emotional distress.
- To what extent are people with a history of a mental health diagnosis socially excluded in Ireland today?
- To what extent do people with a history of contact with mental health services participate in local activities such as voting, health screening, volunteering and attending community groups?

- Given that most people with long-term mental health difficulties now live in the community, what might be the extent and nature of their need for advocacy in relation to issues of social exclusion?

REFERENCES

Amnesty International Ireland (2010) The Missing Link: Coordinated Government Action on Mental Health. Dublin: Amnesty International Ireland

Boardman J, Currie A, Killaspy H and Mezey G (eds.) (2010) Social Inclusion and Mental Health. London: The Royal College of Psychiatrists

Bracken P, Thomas P (2005) Postpsychiatry: Mental health in a postmodern world (International perspectives in philosophy and psychiatry). Oxford: Oxford University Press

Brosnan L, Collins S, Dempsey H, Dermody F, Maguire L, Maria, Morrin N (2002) Pathways Report: Experiences of Mental Health Services from a User-Led Perspective. Galway: The Western Health Board/Schizophrenia Ireland

Brown T (2004) Ireland: A Social and Cultural History 1922-2002. London: Harper Perennial

Bruce A (2000) Social Inclusion & Mental Illness: Needs identification and service provision. Dublin: Schizophrenia Ireland

Butler S (1987) 'The Psychiatric Services – Planning for the Future: A critique'. Administration 35 (1) 47–68

Central Statistics Office (2009) National Disability Survey 2006: Volume 2. Dublin: Stationery Office

Central Statistics Office (2012) Census Profile 8 – Our Bill of Health – Health, Disability and Carers in Ireland. Dublin: Stationery Office

Commission of Inquiry on Mental Illness (1966) Commission of Inquiry on Mental Illness 1966 Report. Dublin: Stationery Office

Commission on Itinerancy (1963) Report of the Commission on Itinerancy. Dublin: Stationery Office

Committee on Reformatory and Industrial Schools (1970) Reformatory and Industrial Schools Systems, Report. Dublin: Stationery Office

Curtin K, Monks S, Wright B, Duffy D, Linehan S and Kennedy H G (2009) 'Psychiatric morbidity in male remand and sentenced committals to Irish prisons'. Irish Journal of Psychological Medicine 26 (4) 169-173

Department of Environment, Community and Local Government (2012) National Housing Strategy for People with a Disability 2011-2016. Dublin: Department of Environment, Community and Local Government

Department of Health (1984) The Psychiatric Services – Planning for the Future: Report of a Study Group on the Development of the Psychiatric Services. Dublin: Stationery Office

Department of Health and Children (2001) Quality and Fairness: A Health System for You: Health Strategy. Dublin: Stationery Office

Department of Health and Children (2006) A Vision for Change: Report of the Expert Group on Mental Health Policy. Dublin: Stationery Office

Department of Health (2011) Brief for New Minister: Mental Health available at http://www.dohc.ie/publications/pdf/briefings_2011.pdf?direct=1 downloaded 30 September 2012

Health Service Executive (2012) New Directions: Review of HSE Day Services and Implementation Plan 2012-2016: Working Group Report, February 2012. Naas, Co. Kildare: Health Service Executive

Health Service Executive/An Garda Síochána (2011) 'Memorandum of Understanding between An Garda Síochána and the HSE on Removal to or Return of a person to an Approved Centre in accordance with Section 13 and Section 27, and the Removal of a person to an Approved Centre in accordance with Section 12, of the Mental Health Act 2001' available at http://www.lenus.ie/hse/bitstream/10147/116376/1/MemoofUnderstandbetweenHSE%26Garda.pdf

Higgins A (2008) A Recovery Approach within the Irish Mental Health Services: A Framework for Development. Dublin: Mental Health Commission

Hudson R, Williams A M (2001) Re-shaping Europe: The challenge of new divisions within a homogenized political-economic space in J Fink, G Lewis, J Clarke (eds.) Rethinking European Welfare. London: Sage, pp.33-64

Inspector of Mental Hospitals (1992, 1997, 2002 and 2003) Report of the Inspector of Mental Hospitals. Dublin: Stationery Office

Kelly B (2007) Penrose's Law in Ireland: An ecological analysis of psychiatric inpatients and prisoners. Irish Medical Journal 100 (2) 373-4

Leanne M, Sapouna L (1998) Deinstitutionalisation in the Republic of Ireland: a case for re-definition? in Jim Campbell and Roger Manktelow (eds.) Mental Health Social Work in Ireland: Comparative issues in policy and practice, Aldershot: Ashgate, pp.101-120

Levitas R, Pantazis C, Fahmy E, Gordon D, Lloyd E, Patsio E (2007) The Multi-Dimensional Analysis of Social Exclusion. Bristol: Department of Sociology and Social Policy, Townsend Centre for the International Study of Poverty and Bristol Institute for Public Affairs, University of Bristol

Mac Gabhann L, Lakeman R, McGowan P, Parkinson M, Redmond M, Sibitz I, Stevenson C, Walsh J (2010) Hear My Voice: The experience of discrimination by people with mental health problems. Dublin: Amnesty International Ireland

McDaid S (2013) Recovery ... what you should expect from a good quality mental health service. Dublin: Mental Health Reform

McDaid S, Kelleher C (2013) Final Report to the National Learning Network: Research into the value of Rehabilitative and Vocational Training and Support Services for People with Mental Health Issues. Unpublished report prepared for the National Learning Network

McInerney S J, Finnerty S, Avalos G, Walsh E (2010) 'Better off in the Community? A 5-year follow up study of long term psychiatric patients discharged into the community'. Social Psychiatry and Psychiatric Epidemiology 45:469-473.

National Disability Authority (2012) National Survey of Public Attitudes to Disability in Ireland 2011 available at http://www.nda.ie/website/nda/cntmgmtnew.nsf/0/90F8D23334D786A880257987004FCF51?OpenDocument downloaded 22 July 2012

National Economic and Social Forum (2007) Mental Health & Social Inclusion, Report 36, October 2007. Dublin: National Economic & Social Development Office

Priebe S, Badesconyi A, Fioritti A, Hansson L, Kilian R, Torres-Gonzales F, Turner T, Wiersma D (2005) Reinstitutionalisation in Mental Health Care: Comparison of data on service provision in six European countries. British Medical Journal 330:123-126

Repper J, Perkins R (2003) Social Inclusion and Recovery: A model for mental health practice. Edinburgh: Ballière Tindall

Sapouna L (2008) Having Choices: An evaluation of the Home Focus Project in West Cork. Kildare: Health Service Executive

Slade M (2009) Personal Recovery and Mental Illness: A Guide for Mental Health Professionals. Cambridge: Cambridge University Press

Tedstone Doherty D, Walsh D, Moran R (2007) Happy Living Here... A Survey and Evaluation of Community Residential Mental Health Services in Ireland. Dublin: Mental Health Commission

Walsh D, Daly A (2004) Mental Illness in Ireland 1750-2002: Reflections on the Rise and Fall of Institutional Care. Dublin: Health Research Board

Watts M (2012) Recovery from 'mental illness' as a re-enchantment with life: a narrative study. Unpublished PhD thesis: Trinity College Dublin

Watson D, Kingston G, McGinnity F (2012) Disability in the Irish Labour Market: Evidence from the QNHS equality module 2010. Dublin: Equality Authority/Economic and Social Research Institute

Wynne J, Egan C, Collins S, Maguire L, Morris J, Campbell M, Connolly P, Maher J, Lohan G, Flynn A (2004) East Galway Pathways Report: Experiences of the East Galway Mental Health Services from Service Users' Perspectives. Galway: The Western Health Board

NOTES

[i] Calculation based on Department of Social Protection (2010) Value for Money Review of the Disability Allowance Scheme available at http://www.welfare.ie/EN/Policy/CorporatePublications/Finance/exp_rev/Documents/DAReviewFinal.pdf downloaded 22 July 2012, p.54.

5

Recovery and the recovery ethos: challenges and possibilities

Agnes Higgins and Paddy McGowan

INTRODUCTION

The concept of recovery and recovery-oriented practice is an emerging paradigm within Irish mental health policy, practice and research, with a growing body of advocates considering recovery as a viable alternative to the traditional paternalistic and biopsychiatric driven service that has dominated Irish mental health services. As an empowering discourse, recovery has significant implications for service users, family, carers, practitioners, policymakers and funders. This chapter traces the development and debates around recovery, and charts the current state of practice within an Irish context, with specific emphasis on the challenges and possibilities that the recovery movement presents.

BACKGROUND TO RECOVERY AND THE RECOVERY MOVEMENT WITHIN IRELAND

The concept of recovery from illness is not new, in so far as it has been a feature of treatment and aspiration for those with physical illness and is frequently defined as a return to the pre-morbid or pre-illness state (Higgins and McBennett 2007). The application of the concept of recovery within mental health, and more specifically to people with 'severe' mental distress is more recent, and owes its origins to two different but interrelated sources: the service-user/survivor movement marked by its political and social justice goals and research that challenged the 'chronicity discourse' that has pervaded mental health since the beginning of institutional care (Davidson and Roe 2007).

Powerful autobiographical accounts by activists like Deegan (1996), Coleman (1999) and others challenged the presumed chronicity discourse that surrounded people with a diagnosis of 'severe' mental health problems and showed that they can recover and lead fulfilling and meaningful lives. These first-person accounts highlight the role of hope, personal responsibility, self-determination, ownership of experience, meaning and choice in each person's unique journey of recovery. In addition, these 'discourses of resistance' call for the recognition of civil and human rights for those who experience mental distress. They also advocate actively for a radical shift in how mental health practitioners frame and respond to people's experience of distress urging a greater distribution of power between the institution of psychiatry and people using the services.

The second strand supporting the recovery movement is research that challenges clinicians prognostic pessimism by demonstrating a broad heterogeneity in outcome for 'serious mental illness'. Ever since the *International Pilot Study of Schizophrenia* (WHO 1973), this and a number of other studies have demonstrated the potential of people diagnosed with 'serious mental illness' to recover their ability to resume personal, social and vocational activities (Harding et al. 1987, Harrison et al. 2001).

Subsequently, the voices of policymakers and health professionals joined in calling for and setting out policy to support the development of recovery-oriented mental health services within their respective countries. Slade et al. (2008) notes that countries such as the US, New Zealand, the UK and Australia have policy documents or guiding frameworks that identify recovery as a central pillar of their mental health service developments.

In 2005, prompted by the service-user representative voice, the Mental Health Commission (MHC) in Ireland published a discussion paper on *A Recovery Model in Mental Health Services* (Mental Health Commission 2005). The content of this document was based on an extensive literature review and consultation with key stakeholders. It was also in line with the Commission's strategic priorities, in particular, the promotion of high standards and good practice in the delivery of mental health services. Simultaneously, an Expert Group, again with service-user representation, was convened by the then Minister of State at the Department of Health and Children with special responsibility for mental health, Mr Tim O'Malley, TD, and tasked with developing a mental health policy that would transform the mental health services. In keeping with international trends, in 2006, with the publication of *A Vision for Change: Report of the Expert Group on Mental Health Policy*, recovery became a core part of Irish mental health policy (Department of Health and Children 2006).

While recognising that recovery does 'not necessarily imply cure' in the traditional sense of absence of symptoms, and that it is more about the individual's ability to 'live a productive and meaningful life despite vulnerabilities' (Department of Health and Children 2006:13), the Expert Group clearly considered recovery to belong within a relational-, strengths- and human-rights-based paradigm of care, when they stated that:

> A recovery approach should inform every level of the service provision so service users learn to understand and cope with their mental health difficulties, build on their strengths and resourcefulness, establish supportive networks, and pursue dreams and goals that are important to them and to which they are entitled as citizens. (Department of Health and Children 2006:5)

Subsequently, following a wide consultation process with service users, families, carers and practitioners, the MHC set out a *Quality Framework for Mental Health Services* which enshrines recovery as one of the standards of care for mental health services in Ireland (standard 3.5) (Mental Health Commission 2007a). Over time, other groups and individuals have added their voices and calls for recovery-oriented mental health services. Representative bodies like Mental Health Reform (MHR), the National Service Users Executive (NSUE); service-user-led organisations such as GROW (www.grow.ie), the Irish Advocacy Network (www.irishadvocacynetwork.com), Mad Pride Ireland (www.madprideireland.ie), Mindfreedom (www.mindfreedomireland.com) and, most recently, the Irish Critical Voices Network (www.criticalvoicesnetwork.com) have called for a shift in services towards the recovery paradigm.

RECOVERY: AN EXPLORATION OF MEANING AND TYPES

The word 'recovery' as used within the mental health context has multiple meanings, arising from different epistemological and theoretical perspectives. The concept of recovery is spoken of as a movement, a philosophy, a set of values or principles, a paradigm and a policy. The terms 'clinical recovery', 'functional recovery', and 'personal recovery' are also used. Clinical recovery frequently refers to a reduction or elimination of 'clinical symptoms' and is defined and measured by health professionals using objective criteria or tools developed by researchers or clinicians (McDaid 2013). Similarly, within rehabilitation contexts, the traditional view of functional recovery is synonymous with maximising people's skills in order that they may fulfil social and related roles, such as skills needed to work, pursue education, form relationships and live independently. Again these skills are objectively defined and assessed by the 'expert' using standardised assessment measures, rather than being evaluated by the individual concerned.

People coming from a traditional psychiatric perspective might argue that clinical recovery is a subset of personal recovery, or that clinical and functional recovery must take place before personal recovery can begin. From the perspective of people who experience mental distress, the division appears irrelevant, as recovery for them is an individual process of 'growth and development' that is unique to the person, with no two people taking identical paths (MHC 2005). Importantly, in the writings of the MHC there is recognition that recovery is not something that professionals do to service users but rather a personal process that belongs to the service user. As such, recovery or personal recovery is conceptualised as 'a journey of discovery' where the person develops 'personal resourcefulness ... control, a positive sense of self ... and rediscovers their voice and a belief in their ability to live a meaningful life, despite the presence of challenges' (MHC 2005, Higgins 2008:7). There is also recognition that recovery is not linear but a complex process characterised by achievements and setbacks. Similarly, in their publication titled *Recovery: What you should expect from a good quality mental health service* (McDaid 2013), MHR advocates for this view of recovery, describing recovery as an:

> individual process of discovering one's own strengths, values, meaning and aspirations; a self determined journey that can take place inside and outside the mental health system, through personal development, through partnership relationships with professionals, through peer support or through community support. It is a process of reconnecting with life that can happen for some with the continuation of symptoms while for others, a reduction in symptoms is important. (McDaid 2013:8)

This view of personal recovery poses a significant challenge to traditional conceptions of clinical recovery and functional recovery; namely the elimination of symptoms or the maximisation of people's skills. In contrast, both the MHC and MHR support the view that personal recovery can take place in the absence of symptom reduction or elimination. In addition, the MHC states that personal recovery 'is best defined by the individual within the context of their personal wishes, dreams and capabilities' (Higgins 2008:7). Thus, there is an acknowledgment that the person experiencing a mental health problem is an 'expert' in their own lives and as such sets the criteria for their own recovery.

The MHC's description of recovery also incorporates the importance of 'meaningful participation in community life' (Higgins 2008:10) and puts the spotlight and emphasis on the need to challenge inequalities by addressing social, economic and attitudinal barriers that prevent people from being included and leading socially integrated lives. Again, this view of recovery, which is located within the context of a social model of disability, reflects a different conception to that of 'functional recovery', where the person rather than society is viewed as 'defective' and in need of an intervention that is designed, delivered and evaluated by the 'expert' practitioner.

IRISH RESEARCH EVIDENCE TO SUPPORT THE RECOVERY PARADIGM

In the world of evidence-based practice, hierarchies of knowledge and Cochrane reviews, it is understandable that one of the major critiques of recovery is the lack of empirical evidence on what the recovery process entails and the absence of evidence that demonstrates that investment (financial and human) in transforming services will have significant impact on outcomes (Mental Health Commission, 2007b). A number of studies and meta-syntheses of studies exist within an international context that describe people's recovery journeys (Spaniol et al. 2002, Brown and Kandirikirira 2007), and since the publication of *A Vision for Change* and the MHC documents, two in-depth qualitative research studies involving people with experience of mental distress have been produced in Ireland (Kartalova-O'Doherty and Tedstone Doherty 2010, Watts 2012). Echoing much of the international recovery literature, both studies conceptualise people's recovery as individual personal journeys that frequently involve triumphs and setbacks. In addition, both studies reveal in different ways that people are recovering not just from 'mental illness', but from the social, political, cultural and economic consequences of the 'illness'. This may include the consequences to self and relationships of being labelled 'mentally ill', losing rights and voice, suffering the harmful effects of treatments and disempowering practices within mental health services, and experiencing stigma and discrimination in wider society.

Kartalova-O'Doherty's study involving 32 participants, highlights that vital to people's recovery journey is hope, acceptance, validation by others, being listened to and an ongoing involvement in the community. On the other hand, factors such as being given a diagnosis of chronic mental illness with no hope for recovery, being treated like a disease rather than a person, not being treated with dignity or respect by professionals, having to endure treatments' side effects, handing over control of one's life to service providers, carers or medication, and accepting the identity of a 'passive patient' all worked against the will to recover (Kartalova-O'Doherty and Tedstone Doherty 2010, Kartalova-O'Doherty et al. 2012).

Watts' (2012) study involving 26 participants who were attending GROW (mental health peer support) groups also identified various social and interpersonal processes people found useful in enabling their recovery. Participants described GROW as acting like a 'social womb' where they were empowered to choose to absorb tensions rather than avoid them and enabled to develop qualities such as hope, courage, strength, self-belief and a positive sense of identity and belonging. It was also a place where they began a process of re-authoring the negative professional and cultural stories or scripts they had absorbed about themselves as a 'mentally ill person'. Collectively, they reported the positive effects of experiencing belonging and friendship, being encouraged to tell their story, take responsibility, make choices and decisions, as well as the healing effect of developing reciprocal supportive relationships both within and beyond GROW. A significant aspect of people's recovery was finding niches in the community such as education, work, leisure activities or volunteering. Not only did involvement in these activities enable meaningful participation but also a re-authoring of identity beyond that of a 'person with mental illness'. While these studies help to describe the concept of recovery, there is yet to be research in Ireland that assesses the cost-effectiveness of this approach.

RECOVERY-ORIENTED APPROACH TO MENTAL HEALTH SERVICES

Although a recovery-oriented approach was identified within *A Vision for Change* as the 'cornerstone' of Irish mental health policy (Department of Health and Children 2006:15), there was little exploration of the meaning of a recovery-oriented approach, bar an acknowledgment that the principles and values of recovery mark a substantial shift in how services are developed, delivered and evaluated.

Two years after the publication of *A Vision for Change*, the MHC published *A Recovery Approach within the Irish Mental Health Service: A Framework for Development'* (Higgins 2008). This document was intended to assist services and practitioners in incorporating recovery into their philosophy, mission and practice. To this end, the document makes clear that developing a recovery-oriented service is not simply about relabeling current practices or adopting the language of recovery, but requires a significant paradigm shift in how people conceptualise 'mental illness' and distress, as well as how people living with mental distress and 'illness' are understood and supported. Within this document, recovery is seen as a transformational ideology that challenges ideas and beliefs about the cause and treatment of 'mental illness', as well as asking for a deep analysis of the way services are organised and implemented, including a critique of how power is distributed and shared within services and within the practitioner-service user dyad.

Within the document the MHC set out eight core principles and values that should guide services in the development of recovery-oriented practice (Table 5.1).

Table 5.1 Core principles underpinning a recovery approach

Having optimism and hope about recovery	Believing in the person's capacity to recover and develop personal resourcefulness irrespective of medical diagnosis or symptoms. Developing hope-inspiring relationships that acknowledge the common humanity of the practitioner, service user and family member.
Valuing the person's voice and personal meaning	Locating the person's own narrative explanation, fears, hopes and wishes at the heart of the therapeutic process.
Respecting personhood and uniqueness	Viewing the person as having rights to the same pleasures, passions and dreams as the rest of society and treating the person as an active participant in their own care with a right to self-determination.
Mobilising the person's own resources	Developing a culture of partnership and respectful dialogue that emphasises strengths rather than deficits, pathology or symptoms.
Supporting partnerships between peer networks and mental health services	Incorporating peer support and self help as an integral part of recovery journey as opposed to an optional extra.
Respecting expertise by experience	Involving people with self-experience in decision-making at all levels, including service planning, development and evaluation of services.
Enabling meaningful participation and inclusion	Challenging wider social, economic and attitudinal barriers to social integration, such as stigma, access to education, housing, work and friendships.
Respecting and embracing multiple perspectives	Embracing social, psychological, biological and spiritual perspectives, including the person's perspective.

(Higgins 2008)

In setting out these principles the MHC endorses a radical shift in mental health services and envisions a truly inclusive service where the person's right to self-determination and inclusion is respected and where their voice is central to the recovery process. There is also a call for practitioners to recast the professional narrative as a more empowering and hopeful narrative and embrace the concept of people's right to failure. The MHC also emphasises the person's right to engage in normative life pursuits consistent with their goals, values and preferences, and practitioners' roles in advocating for social change and the removal of barriers to the person's participation in friendships, relationships, sport, education and employment. More importantly and fundamentally, the role and dominance of professional expertise and the biomedical model as the primary focus of care is questioned in the following manner:

> The recovery approach respects and embraces the contribution of all perspectives ... However the recovery approach challenges the privileging of one theoretical perspective as the primary explanation for, and the treatment of, mental distress; and the privileging of professional interpretations and expertise over expertise by experience and personal meaning. The biomedical model and medical treatments may have an important place for some people in the recovery process, but as an invited guest, rather than the overarching paradigm. (Higgins 2008:11)

In articulating this view, the MHC acknowledges the socially constructed nature of mental distress and the limitations of categorising 'human suffering' or 'problems of living' using a language of symptoms, diagnosis and syndromes (Szasz 1961, Barker and Buchannan 2005). As such, they set a strong challenge to traditional psychiatry or what Crowe and Taylor (2006:61) describe as the 'disease-based maintenance approach'. While not denying a role for medication and other medical interventions, the MHC document asks psychiatry as a whole to critique current ideas and practices in a desire to 'open the field to different ways of understanding, framing and responding to [people's] experiences' (Bracken and Thomas 2010:227). They are clear this is not about abandoning knowledge of the physical or psychological sciences or moving away from evidence-based practice, but about having a real commitment to critiquing the values, beliefs and practices that underpin the current biomedical model and what is considered 'expertise' or 'truth' in mental health. It is also a call for the development of services that are truly multidisciplinary and provide a range of therapies and approaches.

There is also recognition, within the MHC document, that for many people the medical or illness-based model is oppressive as it does not speak to their distress. Within the current system, this group of people is often labelled as 'anti-psychiatry' or 'lacking in insight' and 'non-compliant', and in some cases forced to accept treatment on what Crowe and Taylor (2006:60) refer to as 'the deluded basis that they are too ill to recognise their need for treatment ... *ipso facto*, compliance is brought about by breaking the person's will or medicating resistance'. While no doubt very challenging for practitioners, a recovery approach is about creating a space where people experiencing mental distress can take ownership of their experience and the meaning of that experience, as opposed to being defined by others though a language of psychopathology. In the words of Bracken and colleagues, practitioners are encouraged to foster 'a healthy scepticism for biological reductionism, tolerance for the tangled nature of relationships and meanings and the ability to negotiate these issues in a way that empowers service users and their carers' (Bracken et al. 2012:433).

Many of the principles outlined by the MHC are endorsed by MHR in its documents (MHR 2012, McDaid 2013). Drawing on international and national literature, and more importantly, on findings from a public consultation held during 2011/2012, MHR identifies components or building blocks for a recovery-oriented service. In elaborating on the five components, MHR calls on practitioners to truly engage in dialogue with service users and families so that understandings, solutions, and plans are co-constructed, and a consensus reality of what is real is continually produced. Similar to other documents on recovery, underscoring the MHR document is an emphasis on the human rights, citizenship and democratising agenda that recovery entails. In keeping with the human rights theme and the centrality of choice and self-determination within recovery, MHR also calls for services to develop a range of treatment and therapy options, arguing that 'in the absence of choices between alternative types of treatment, people are essentially denied their right to make decisions over their own mental health care' (McDaid 2013:11).

TRANSFORMING SERVICES TO A RECOVERY PARADIGM

Walsh et al. (2008:251) rightly point out that although the shift from traditional psychiatry or 'biopsychiatry' to recovery can be achieved on paper with a 'few deft strokes of a pen', actualising the shift within an organisation is far more challenging. The MHC and MHR both identify the importance of national leadership, as well as a number of important cultural and structural changes within organisations to support the development of recovery-oriented services (Table 5.2).

Table 5.2: Requirements to support development of recovery-oriented services

National and local leadership
Service mission statements, policies and procedures that reflect recovery values and demonstrate organisational commitment
Service-user- and practitioner-led education to promote values-based as well as evidence-based practice
Person-centred and empowering practices that support social inclusion, positive risk-taking and self-determination
Spaces for dialogue between service users, family/carers and practitioners to enable shared understandings of challenges and solutions
Employment of service users in delivery and evaluation of services
Engagement with peer-led organisations and the wider community
Provision of resources to ensure access to a range of therapies
Involvement of all stakeholders in evaluation and research

(Higgins 2008, McDaid 2013).

The Sainsbury Centre (2009) in the UK set out a framework or methodology for service transformation based on ten key organisational challenges (Table 5.3). While many of the challenges are similar to and support the views expressed by the MHC and MHR, the proposal to establish a 'Recovery Education Centre' to drive the programme of change is an exciting possibility. The focus of such a centre would be to educate people with lived experience of mental distress to become 'peer workers' and to gain skills and tools to promote recovery. In addition, it would aim to re-orientate mental health services towards viewing interventions and supports through an educational rather than a therapeutic lens.

Table 5.3: Implementing recovery: A new framework for organisational change

Changing the nature of day-to-day interactions and the quality of experience

Delivering comprehensive, service-user-led education and training programmes

Establishing a 'Recovery Education Centre' to drive the programmes forward

Ensuring organisational commitment, creating the 'culture'

Increasing 'personalisation' and choice

Changing the way we approach risk assessment and management

Redefining service user involvement

Transforming the workforce

Supporting staff in their recovery journey

Increasing opportunities for building a life 'beyond illness'

(Sainsbury Centre for Mental Health 2009)

Other Irish documents have identified recovery-oriented practices at the level of engagement with service users that are required if services are to achieve the desired paradigm shift. These include wellness recovery-oriented individual planning, recovery-oriented prescribing practices, the presence of peer advocates within services and a partnership approach towards positive risk-taking (Department of Health and Children 2006, MHR 2012, MHC 2012a, Health Service Executive (undated)).

REALITIES OF THE IRISH CONTEXT: PROGRESS TO DATE

Although the language of recovery entered the lexicon of Irish policy in 2006, prior to this, a number of practitioners, mainly within nursing, championed the Tidal Model within services in the Mayo, Dublin and Cork regions (www.tidal-model.com/Mayo). Tidal is one of the first recovery models, developed from practice-based research in the mid-1990s in England (Barker and Buchanan, 2005). The model acknowledges that psychosocial distress can be viewed through different theoretical lenses and asserts the centrality of lived experience, personal biography, mutual understanding and hope in the caring process; thus, the Tidal philosophy is congruent with the values underpinning recovery as currently defined within Irish policy. Since the publication of *A Vision for Change*, although sparse, a number of other initiatives have developed primarily driven by local champions and mainly funded by the public–private partnership organisation Genio.

Some services are adopting an organisational or system-wide approach to achieving the cultural and practice changes required. In their document *Moving West Cork Mental Health Services in a Recovery Direction* (Independent Monitoring Group Appendix 2012), the West Cork mental health services clearly set a vision for a service that is guided by a commitment to service-user involvement, a recovery philosophy, community-orientation and the importance of integrated partnership working. The methodology informing this development is the framework set out by the Centre for Mental Health UK (formally the Sainsbury Centre for Mental Health) and based on the ten key challenges outlined in Table 5.3. Although a 'work-in-progress', the West Cork mental health service is the one service that has been repeatedly commended in reports from the Independent Monitoring Group (IMG) for *A Vision for Change* for their work in moving the service away from the more traditional 'medical-model' approach (IMG 2012). The Mayo mental health services are leading the Advancing Recovery in Ireland (ARI) project, which involves seven sites nationally and also uses the methodology developed by the Centre for Mental Health UK. A number of services are also participating in the 'open dialogue' or 'trialogue' initiative through the Irish Mental Health Trialogue Network (www.trialogue.co). The focus of this community initiative is on creating a neutral space where service users, family members, practitioners and communities can come together to develop shared understandings of mental health issues with a view to transforming thinking and developing better services and healthy communities.

Although modest, there is evidence of educational programmes where service users, carers and practitioners come together to learn new ways of thinking and working. Since 2007, tripartite teams of service users, carers and practitioners from around the country have been participating in the Cooperative Learning and Leadership Programme, a collaboration between DCU and the HSE. This programme focuses on helping the groups involved to develop leadership and change management skills for use within their own services. Tripartite education on self-management and self-help approaches such as Wellness Recovery Action Planning (WRAP) are becoming more widely available (Higgins et al. 2010) and used within the Mental Health Service (IMG 2012). During 2012 and 2013, the Nursing Practice Development Unit of the HSE and the Irish Institute of Mental Health Nursing sponsored a training programme in facilitating voice-hearer support groups. On foot of this training, Hearing Voices Support Groups have been established in Dublin and there are firm plans for establishing groups within other areas (www.iimhn.com). A peer- and clinician-led informational programme (EOLAS) for people who experienced psychosis and their families is being rolled out in Kildare and other mental health services in the Dublin area. This Genio-funded project was developed in collaboration with service users and family members and preliminary evaluation indicates positive outcomes for both groups (Higgins et al. 2012).

A web-based mental health recovery profiling and outcome measurement tool (Recovery Context Inventory or RCI) has been developed by staff within EVE (a service within the HSE) in collaboration with key stakeholders (O'Brien et al. 2012). The RCI is currently being rolled out in a number of mental health services as part of the Genio-funded ARI project. The Recovery Star, another planning tool developed by Dickens et al. (2012) in the UK, is being used in a number of services throughout the country (MHR 2012).

Since the development of the Irish Advocacy Network, peer advocates are becoming increasingly involved in inpatient units and have been included in local management groups, policy groups, recruitment panels and research groups. Paid peer workers are also part of a number of initiatives designed to advance the implementation of a recovery ethos within the services. For example, peer workers are included within the ARI initiative in Mayo, the EOLAS project and the reorientation of the West Cork mental health services. There is also evidence that services users are having greater input into the education and training of mental health nurses (Sheridan and Collins 2012, Higgins et al. 2011) and psychiatrists (Refocus Carers Subgroup 2013)

Another initiative that embodies the recovery paradigm and represents the changing understandings of and responses to psychosocial distress is the Cork Slí Eile Housing project. Slí Eile is a supportive, non-medical housing project for people who experience mental health difficulties, which is based on recovery principles and Glaser's choice theory. Following a case study analysis, Farrell (2013) concluded that in the current economic climate, the Slí Eile approach represents excellent value for money.

RECOVERY: AN UNFULFILLED PROMISE FACING MOUNTING CHALLENGES

More than eight years has passed since publication of A Vision for Change and although momentum is slowly developing mainly due to local leadership and recovery champions as opposed to national leadership, overall progress has been slow and inconsistent. Annual reports from the IMG and the Inspectorate of Mental Health Services have consistently reported little evidence of a systematic approach to implementation or the embedding of recovery within HSE structures and processes. While noting that 'the initial scepticism that greeted recovery is slowly being eroded and replaced with practical concerns around implementation and debates around meaning' (IMG 2012:84), the IMG also notes the continuing dominance of the medical model, the absence of recovery plans, multidisciplinary teams, poorly developed recovery competencies in service delivery, the inconsistency of service user involvement and the minimal involvement of family members. The need for a more humane, person-focused service that acknowledges people's right to information, involvement and respect is still te consistent message within service-users' and family feedback (De Burca et al. 2010, National Service Users Executive 2011, MHR 2012, MHC 2012 b, c).

A key concern of advocacy groups is that as the concept of recovery becomes incorporated into the language of mental health practitioners, the civil and human rights dimension will become overshadowed by debates about symptom reduction, clinical recovery, diagnosis and functional recovery. Similarly, there is a concern that the social inclusion agenda for marginalised groups, such as those living with an intellectual disability, homeless people, the travelling community, asylum seekers and the prison populations may become sidelined in the current climate of dwindling human resources and depleting budgets.

Barker describes the remarkable capacity of psychiatry to 'shrug off its many critics, whether philosophical, scientific, social or political' (Barker 2003:97). Hence, there is real danger in the current climate of economic cutbacks, recruitment embargos and the public service moratorium that people will simply 'shrug off' the recovery agenda, or simply adopt and assimilate the language of recovery without deconstructing the current disease, deficit and paternalistic paradigm.

In setting out their recommendations on recovery, the IMG (2012) notes the urgent need for leadership, a national implementation framework, education, and properly staffed multidisciplinary community mental health teams and rehabilitation and recovery teams. MHR (2012) also draw attention to the need to embed recovery principles into legal frameworks so that the person's human rights are fully protected and the principles of choice and partnership realised. Without this, conflict is inevitable for practitioners who try to walk a tight rope between a government policy that espouses recovery and a legal framework that sanctions compulsory treatment. In addition, Amnesty International (2010) calls for robust key performance indicators, such as the percentage of patients in receipt of an individual care and recovery programme which incorporated a self-management plan and the percentage of those in receipt of psychological therapies.

We are now eight years into the A Vision for Change policy and it is reasonable to say that the development of recovery-oriented services remains an unfulfilled promise. Without leadership at a national level, legal reform, multidisciplinary resources and incentives to implement recovery-oriented practice, recovery may simply become another word change rather than a set of core values and principles that fundamentally changes the way we think about, and engage with, people experiencing mental distress.

*

REFLECTIVE QUESTIONS FOR DISCUSSION AND DEBATE: PRACTICE

• Does the recovery movement need to be rescued from the increasing professionalisation and colonisation by mental health practitioners?
• Is recovery just another way of putting the onus on service users to take responsibility for their own health, while ignoring the structural and social inequalities that contribute to people's psychosocial distress?
• What legal and clinical issues are in conflict with the recovery ethos?

REFLECTIVE STATEMENTS FOR DISCUSSION AND DEBATE: RESEARCH

• Comparative studies between recovery- and non-recovery-oriented services are not feasible because of practical, ethical and methodological challenges.
• Studies designed to explore recovery and recovery outcomes need to be service-user led.
• Research into recovery needs to disaggregate participants as the current evidence assumes too much homogeneity among participants.

REFERENCES

Amnesty International Ireland (2010) Accountability in the delivery of A Vision for Change – a performance assessment framework for mental health services. Dublin: Amnesty International

Barker P, Buchanan-Barker P (2005) The Tidal Model: A guide for mental health professionals. London: Brunner-Routledge

Barker P (2003) The Tidal Model: Psychiatric colonization, recovery and the paradigm shift in mental health care. International Journal of Mental Health Nursing 12:96-102

Bracken P, Thomas P, Timimi S, Asen E, Behr G et al. (2012) Psychiatry beyond the current paradigm. British Journal of Psychiatry 201:430-434

Bracken P, Thomas P (2010) From Szasz to Foucault: On the role of critical psychiatry. Philosophy. Psychiatry and Psychology 17 (3) 219-228

Brown W, Kandirikirira K (2007) Recovering mental health in Scotland – Report on narrative investigation of mental health recovery. Glasgow: Scottish Recovery Network

Coleman R (1999) Recovery: An Alien Concept. Gloucester: Hansell Publishing

Crowe K, Taylor K (2006) The Recovery Approach: The desired service user empowerment process (Chapter 4) in Knowledge in Mental Health: Reclaiming the social. Sapouna L and Herman P. New York: Nova Science Publishers Inc.

Davidson L, Roe D (2007) Recovery from versus recovery in serious mental illness: One strategy for lessening confusion plaguing recovery. Journal of Mental Health 16 (4) 459-470

De Burca S, Armstrong C, Brosnan P (2010) Community mental health teams: Determinants of effectiveness in an Irish context. Limerick: Health Systems Research Centre

Deegan P E (1996) Recovery as a journey of the heart. Psychiatric Rehabilitation Journal 19 (3) 91-97

Department of Health and Children (2006) A Vision for Change: Report of the Expert Group on Mental Health Policy. Dublin: Stationery Office

Dickens G, Weleminsky J, Onifade Y, Sugarman P (2012) Recovery star: validating user recovery. The Psychiatrist Online 36:45-50.

Farrell A (2013) Supporting recovery in mental health through community living: A case study of Slí Eile Critical Social Thinking: Policy and Practice. 5:1-28 http://www.ucc.ie/en/appsoc/researchconference/conf/cstj/cstjournalvolume 52013/section1/AoifeFarrell.pdf accessed 13 August 2013

Harrison G, Hopper K, Craig T, Laska E, Siegel C et al. (2001) Recovery from Schizophrenia, a 15 and 25 year international follow up study. The British Journal of Psychiatry 178:506-517.

Harding C M, Brooks G, Ashikage T, Strauss J S, Brier A (1987) The Vermont longitudinal study of persons with severe mental illness II: long-term outcome of subjects who retrospectively met DSM-III criteria for schizophrenia. American Journal of Psychiatry 144:727-735

Health Service Executive (undated) Guidance document: Risk management in Mental Health Services. Available at http://www.hse.ie/eng/services/publications/services/mentalhealth/riskmanagementinmentalhealth.pdf

Higgins A (2008) A recovery approach within the Irish Mental Health service: A framework for development. Dublin: Mental Health Commission

Higgins A, Breen M, Boyd F, Heavey D, Sharek D, McBennett P (2012) An evaluation of a peer and clinician led psychoeducation programme for people diagnosed with severe mental health difficulties. Dublin: School of Nursing and Midwifery Trinity College Dublin

Higgins A, Callaghan P, de Vries J, Keogh B, Morrissey J, Nash M, Ryan D, Gijbels H (2010) Evaluation of Mental Health Recovery and Wellness Recovery Action Plan (WRAP) education programme on participants' knowledge, attitude and skills of mental health recovery. Dublin: Irish Mental Health Recovery Education Consortium

Higgins A, Maguire G, Watts M, Creaner M, McCann E, Rani S, Alexander J (2011) Service user involvement in mental health practitioner education in Ireland. Journal of Psychiatric and Mental Health Nursing 18 (6) 519-25

Higgins A, McBennett P (2007) The petals of recovery in a mental health context. British Journal of Nursing 16 (14) 852-856

Independent Monitoring Group (2012) Sixth Annual Report on Implementation: 2011 available at www.dohc.ie/publications/vision_for_change

Kartalova-O'Doherty Y, Tedstone Doherty D (2010) Reconnecting with life: personal experiences of recovering from mental health problems in Ireland. HRB Series 8. Dublin: Health Research Board

Kartalova-O'Doherty Y, Stevenson C, Higgins A (2012) Reconnecting with life: a grounded theory study of mental health recovery in Ireland. Journal of Mental Health 21(2) 136–144

McDaid S (2013) Recovery: What you should expect from a good quality mental health service. Dublin: Mental Health Reform

Mental Health Commission (2005) A Vision for a recovery model in Irish Mental Health Services: Discussion Paper. Dublin: Mental Health Commission

Mental Health Commission (2012a) Guidance document on individual care planning: Mental Health Services. Dublin: Mental Health Commission

Mental Health Commission (2012b) Inspector of Mental Health National Overview Report. Available at www.mhcirl.ie/Inspectorate_of_Mental_Health_Services/National_Overview_Reports

Mental Health Commission (2012c) Your views of mental health inpatient services. Dublin: Mental Health Commission

Mental Health Commission (2007a) Quality framework – Mental health services in Ireland. Dublin: Mental Health Commission

Mental Health Commission (2007b) A Vision for a recovery model in Irish Mental Health Service; A qualitative analysis of submissions to the Mental Health Commission. Dublin: Mental Health Commission

Mental Health Reform (2012) Promoting Improved Mental Health Services: Guiding a Vision for Change-Manifesto. Dublin: Mental Health Reform

National Service Users Executive (2011) Second Opinions 2010 available at http://www.nsue.ie/documents/

O'Brien T, Webb M, Stynes G (2012) The Recovery Context Inventory: an innovative response to mapping mental health recovery. Irish Association of Suicidology Newsletter 8 (2) 1-2 available at www.eve.ie

Refocus Carers Subgroup (2013) Who cares? Listening to the needs and experiences of carers of people with mental illness available at www.irishpsychiatry.ie/Libraries/External_Affairs/REFOCUS_Who_cares_POST_Council_19_March_2013_2_FINAL.sflb.ashx

Sainsbury Centre for Mental Health (2009) Implementing recovery: A new framework for organisational change: Position paper available at www.centreformentalhealth.org.uk/pdfs/implementing_recovery_paper.pdf

Sheridan A, Collins E (2012) Supporting Recovery: Using a collaborative learning approach: Student nurses and service users working and learning available at www.mhcirl.ie/Training_Development/NMHSC_Symp12/Posters_Abstr.pdf

Slade M, Amering M, Oades L (2008) Recovery: an international perspective. Epidemiologia e Psichiatria Sociale 17 (2) S 128-137

Spaniol L, Wewiorski N, Gagne C, Anthony W (2002) The process of recovery from schizophrenia. International Review of Psychiatry 14:327-336

Szasz T (1961) The Myth of mental illness: Foundations of a theory of personal conduct. New York: Hoeber-Harper

Watts M (2012) Recovery from 'mental illness' as a re-enchantment with life: a narrative study. Unpublished PhD thesis: Trinity College Dublin

Walsh J, Stevenson C, Cutcliffe J, Zinck K (2008) Creating a space for recovery-focused psychiatric nursing care. Nursing Inquiry 15 (3) 251-259

World Health Organization (1973) The international pilot study of schizophrenia. Geneva: World Health Organization

6

Empowerment and the emergence of an Irish user/survivor movement

Liz Brosnan

INTRODUCTION

This chapter presents a brief history of the Irish mental health service-user/survivor movement. It also outlines how and why the user/survivor movement can be understood as a health social movement responding to the position of service users vis-à-vis the mental health services (MHS), and considers the significance of empowerment and peer advocacy as ways of understanding the movement's emancipatory struggle. It is written from the 'insider' perspective of someone who has experienced both service use and long-term activism in the user/survivor movement in Ireland.

Irish service-users' experience of the MHS, consistent with the international literature, is often described as oppressive, given the MHS' emphasis on medication as the sole treatment available (Brosnan et al. 2002, Coles et al. 2013, Wynne 2004). Until very recently, Irish MHS had exceptionally high rates of institutionalised residents in mental hospitals, in contrast with international trends (Sapouna 2006; Brennan 2014). The predominant ethos within Irish MHS continues to be an approach that ignores or minimises the social conditions contributing to, or exacerbating, psychosocial distress. Service users have various experiences of professional practice, but all too frequently they report that their treatment is disempowering and disabling. In addition, there remains a pervasive stigma associated with being a mental health service-user which has wider social consequences for housing, employment and general well-being (Mac Gabhann et al. 2010). My own recently completed research on the user/survivor movement in Ireland found that contestation of bio-psychiatry and naming taken-for-granted practice as human rights failures were important issues for the user/survivor-movement activists interviewed (Brosnan 2013). This research also found tensions between the agendas and strategies for involvement with MHS within the Irish user/survivor movement itself. In order to make sense of the user/survivor movement in Ireland, it will be helpful to discuss two theoretical ideas: empowerment and the user/survivor movement as a health social movement.

EMPOWERMENT

Empowerment is a prevalent yet imprecise concept: empowering service users is often proposed as a response to the powerless position of service users within MHS and society generally. Conceptualisations of empowerment derive from two broad strands of thought: collectivist social action and individual consumerism (Masterson and Owen 2006). The idea of empowerment, proposed in the 1960s in the USA and in the 1970s in the UK, included social action and group unity in the development of a collective 'voice'. In the US, the first critical voices of the service-user[i] movement drew heavily on ideas about power, oppression, and collective action from black civil rights and women's movements (Chamberlin 1977). However, the concept of empowerment was subsumed into the political rhetoric of neoliberal consumerism in the 1980s and 1990s under Reagan in the US and Thatcher in the UK, in which patient choice became equated with empowerment as part of the package of privatisation, competitive tendering and the creation of a market for health services. Under this conceptualisation, empowerment is based on individualist notions of self- care and self-responsibility, perspectives that represent a shift away from collective social action (Masterson and Owen 2006).

Community empowerment occurs as people 'organise themselves around a common critical characteristic. Since the meaning of empowerment is, among other things, the overcoming of difficult experiences of isolation and alienation, it can be realised only in a stable and ongoing connection with others' (Sadan 2004:108). Furthermore, McDaid argues that empowerment requires collective action in the public political sphere where decisions about law, policy and funding are made (McDaid 2010).

Professionals seeking to engage in empowering practice must give space to service users to find their own voice; otherwise, such well-meaning practice can become oppressive. And while it is critical that professionals not work with service users in ways that reinforce oppressive practice, one of the major difficulties is that empowering practice itself can be construed as patronising, disrespectful and tokenistic unless it genuinely seeks to reflexively redress the power imbalances that service users experience vis-à-vis the MHS (Carey 2009, Wilson and Beresford 2000).

Users/survivors increasingly appear in professional and academic literature to explain what they understand by the term empowerment. I will deal briefly with two writers: Judy Chamberlin from the US and Peter Beresford from the UK. Chamberlin and Schene (1997) reported on the deliberations of a group of

American service users who developed a working definition of empowerment. They identified 15 different elements of empowerment important to service users, listed in the table below.

Table 6.1: 15 Elements of a working definition of empowerment (Chamberlin and Schene 1997:44)

1. Having decision-making power
2. Having access to information and resources
3. Having a range of options from which to make choices (not just yes/no, either/or)
4. Assertiveness
5. A feeling that the individual can make a difference (being hopeful)
6. Learning to think critically; unlearning the conditioning; seeing things differently, e.g.   a. Learning to redefine who we are (speaking in our own voice)   b. Learning to redefine what we can do   c. Learning to redefine our relationships to institutionalised power
7. Learning about and expressing anger
8. Not feeling alone: feeling part of a group
9. Understanding that people have rights
10. Effecting change in one's life and one's community
11. Learning skills (e.g. communication) that the individual defines as important
12. Changing others' perceptions of one's competency and capacity to act
13. Coming out of the closet
14. Growth and change that is never ending and self-initiated
15. Increasing one's positive self-image and overcoming stigma

Peter Beresford (2010) cuts through the confusion that arises in the literature on empowerment and the different meanings attached to it. Given that experiences within the MHS often add to the feelings of powerlessness that accompany psychosocial distress, he states that empowerment at the political and social levels require change at a personal level. In his view, 'if political change is to occur, and be truly inclusive and democratic, then all of us need to be involved in the process and a process of growth and development will also need to take place within each of us' (Beresford 2010:36). One response to the experience of disempowering MHS across the international user/survivor movement (in the US, Canada, Australia and New Zealand in particular), has been the development of peer-controlled MHS. These put service users in control of the running of the service so that the professional is 'on tap rather than on top' (Slade et al. 2012:2). As a result, peer-run services, including crisis centres, have become common features of the international user/survivor landscape (Doughty and Tse 2011, Solomon 2004), with peer-support services much more prevalent (Shaw 2013).

Within mainstream MHS, however, much of the empowerment rhetoric focuses on the individual or psychological understanding of empowerment, thereby deflecting attention away from injustice and oppression, if not directly enabling it. Such rhetoric ignores the concerns of user/survivor activists about the social impact of objectifying discourses of psychiatry and brain malfunction theories. McDaid (2010:210) points out: 'while not overtly blaming people with mental health problems for their own powerlessness, such discourse nevertheless has orientated itself from a position that saw the solution to this powerlessness to be through improvements in the individual's self-confidence and self capability rather than in action to target power relations'. An example of this is the rhetoric about training centres empowering service users to gain employment. While many service users spend long periods on training programmes designed to increase self-confidence and skills, there is no substantial improvement in their ability to combat the stigma and discrimination they experience in relation to job seeking, as well as in other aspects of their lives (McDaid 2010).

McDaid also problematises linking empowerment to service user involvement. She reviews the practical difficulties in terms of the achievements, or lack thereof, by the user/survivor movement in the UK. For the past two decades, much of the energy of the service-user movement there has focused on seeking to increase their influence within the MHS. Greater participation at decision-making level within the services has been a goal of the movement, with participation on advisory/planning committees and in consultations being sought. However, the failure of this approach has been articulated by individuals within the UK movement who note that during the same period, service-users' status in wider society did not improve (Campbell 2005, Wallcraft et al. 2003). In contrast to policy-focused and/or professionally controlled user groups, Beresford (2010) explains the importance of user-run organisations where service users can resist the overwhelming pressures to comply with the MHS' agendas and discourse. Other writers also speak of the risk of the 'capture' of marginalised and less powerful groups in structures set up to hear their voices (Gaventa and Cornwall

2008), for instance the risk of co-option and appropriation of their ideas. The appropriation of the term 'recovery' by professionals to refer to practice that is fundamentally the same coercive or patronising experience for service users is an example of core challenges for the service-user/survivor movement are the issues of power, powerlessness and empowerment in relation to their position vis-à-vis MHS and service-user (Brosnan 2012).

HEALTH SOCIAL MOVEMENTS

Brown and Zavestoski (2004:679) define health social movements (HSMs) as 'collective challenges to medical policy, public health policy and politics, belief systems, research and practice which include an array of formal and informal organisations, supporters, networks of cooperation and media.' HSMs challenge political power, professional authority and personal and collective identity across three broad domains. The type being considered here is embodied health movements (EHMs). EHMs address the individualised experience of disease, disability or illness by challenging science on aetiology, diagnosis, treatment and prevention. EHMs include 'contested illnesses' that are either unexplained by current medical knowledge or have environmental explanations that are often disputed (Brown and Zavestoski 2004:685). EHMs have three unique features:

- they introduce the biological body to social movement studies, especially with regard to the lived experience of people with the condition/disease,
- they typically challenge existing medical/scientific knowledge and practice and,
- they often involve activists collaborating with scientists and health professionals in pursuing treatment, prevention, research and expanded funding (Brown et al. 2004:50).

Some members of EHMs criticise the dominant science, but instead of engaging to develop alternative science (with or without professional allies), they reject scientific explanations. Brown et al. (2004) characterise elements of the mental health user/survivor movement as an example of an EHM because 'they resist traditional psychiatry, eschew reform approaches and oppose the very idea that they have (or have had) mental illness' (Brown et al. 2004:53).

The embodied nature of EHMs develops from a personal awareness and understanding of an 'illness experience' which represents a cognitive, moral and emotional connection with other people with the same illness (Brown et al. 2004:55). An important feature of EHMs is a 'politicised collective illness identity', which develops by switching the focus from a personal experience to a wider social analysis that considers structural inequalities and the uneven distribution of social power as responsible for the causes and/or triggers of ill-health. A politicised collective illness identity transforms health issues from a personal trouble into a social problem (Brown et al. 2004:61). Although the term 'illness' is used by Brown and his colleagues in writing about EHMs, the politics of the mental health movement is unlike any other area of health in the way that it involves rejecting 'mental illness' terminology and contesting the very language used to describe and categorise the human condition.

Exemplifying a politicised collective identity, participants in my research articulated their very strong opposition to prevalent mental health practice, in many cases naming taken-for-granted practices such as the over-use of medication, ECT and forced or coercive treatment as human rights failures and placing them on the agenda for reform of MHS. This collective political understanding of the positioning of service users vis-à-vis the MHS was one characteristic that motivated participants to engage with service-user involvement but also contributed to the frustrations and tensions that collaboration with the MHS posed for participants.

Brown et al. (2004) explain the diversity within health movements in terms of a continuum of strategies and agendas that social movement organisations (SMOs) pursue. At one end of the continuum are advocacy-oriented SMOs, i.e. groups that work within the existing system and biomedical model, use tactics such as education rather than direct, disruptive action, and tend not to push for lay knowledge to be inserted into expert knowledge systems. Activist-oriented groups, on the other hand, engage in direct action, challenge current scientific and medical paradigms, and work largely outside the system (Brown et al. 2004:51). The following short description of user SMOs in Ireland reveals that both strategies are present in the Irish user/survivor movement. Some groups have sought to influence or improve the situation for service users within the MHS by engaging within health service structures, while others reject the current system as unhelpful, and even abusive, preferring to advocate from the outside.

BACKGROUND CONTEXT OF THE IRISH USER/ SURVIVOR MOVEMENT

The service user/survivor movement developed later in Ireland than in many other countries. Beresford (2010) notes that the policy of service-user involvement in MHS was in place internationally from the 1970s. Irish MHS have been slower to adopt service user involvement as a core principle of good practice because of the late development of a coherent, broad-based user/survivor movement, and the endemic resistance to change of an institutionalised, medically controlled service model (Brennan 2012, Sapouna 2006). Speed (2002) conducted an analysis of documents from the Irish Department of Health and public mental health agencies[ii] in the 1980s and 1990s. He noted that there were no user-run

SMOs active at that period and argued that there was no challenge to psychiatric hegemony because of the lack of an organised user movement (Speed 2002:77). Since Speed's analysis a user/survivor movement in Ireland has emerged and several user/survivor-run SMOs have been established. In addition, the government's updated policy for MHS, *A Vision for Change* (Department of Health and Children 2006), emphasised service user involvement at all levels of the MHS. Peer-run services were recognised, including the need for 'mainstream funding and integration' of user-run services (Department of Health and Children 2006:27). Peer-run MHS have not yet emerged in Ireland, although peer advocacy has become well established. Indeed the beginnings of a user movement in Ireland can be traced to the emergence of the Irish Advocacy Network (IAN) in 1999.

IRISH ADVOCACY NETWORK

IAN has become a prominent service-user presence in the mental health field in Ireland. An island-wide, peer-run organisation, IAN has secured Health Service Executive (HSE) contracts to provide independent peer advocacy services at approved centres (i.e. licensed centres to detain people under the Mental Health Act 2001) in all but one of the 26 counties of the Republic.[iii] In Northern Ireland, IAN employs peer advocates who are integrated into community mental health teams. A manifesto for the Network, by founder member Paddy McGowan [not dated], outlines the process of struggle for users/survivors to forge a common identity to resist their unequal position within society and within the MHS. McGowan had been involved with the UK peer advocacy movement (UKAN) which started in 1991. McGowan [not dated] articulates a vision to develop a critical mass of empowered service users who would use peer advocacy skills and training to demand respect, dignity and control over how they are treated.

Advocacy and peer advocacy

IAN's strategy was to develop a national, peer-run advocacy service. According to the WHO (2003, p.2), the principle elements of advocacy are: awareness-raising, information, education, training, mutual help, counselling, mediating, defending and denouncing. In the Irish context, a key concern of the user/survivor movement had been the risk that peer advocacy – that is, advocacy by people with self-experience of the mental health services – would be sidelined. In 2003, the National Disability Authority (NDA) reported on the state of advocacy in Ireland. Their principle focus was on Irish legislation regarding advocacy, examining how systems (e.g. the health care system) might facilitate or hinder advocacy, and what model of advocacy might best serve the needs of particular disability groups. The study reports on consultations with different advocacy groups, including

IAN. Representatives from IAN were concerned that the distinctive focus of peer advocacy would be lost or diluted if an overall mandate to develop advocacy was granted to a state body, such as Comhairle, because 'those who in the past oppressed and ignored those with mental health difficulties in Ireland would be the very ones shaping advocacy' (NDA 2003, Chapter 4).

The unique feature of the service provided by IAN is the user-led element of peer advocacy, rather than advocacy by professionals with legal, mental health or other qualifications. Peer advocates have themselves experienced distress and/or used MHS, and this experience means that they have a unique understanding of what service users are going through, and consequently can be more empathetic and offer more validation of the idea that recovery is possible (Brandon 1995, Irish Advocacy Network 2013, Repper and Carter 2011, Shaw 2013). Peer advocacy honours peer-to-peer relationships and seeks to reduce stigma and promote more empowered independent voices within the service user community (Irish Advocacy Network 2013).

Peer advocacy is based on supporting self-advocacy. Self-advocacy seeks to involve individuals who share common experiences of oppression in self-advocacy support groups in order to empower them to engage with, and change, the structures that oppress them. Gosling (2010) describes in some detail how peer advocacy work and promoting self-advocacy can shift the balance of power and powerlessness in individuals' relationships with themselves, their peers and services. Gosling's (2010) work is an interesting read on the challenges of users maintaining independence from providers' agendas.

IAN also recognises the fundamental importance of self-determination as a basis for advocacy. The founder members of IAN understood how individual autonomy, self- confidence and self-respect can be eroded by experiences of mental distress and encounters with MHS. Therefore, a core principle of the organisation's code of practice is that advocates only work with people who self-refer. Despite many requests from concerned others, advocates will not work on behalf of someone who does not engage freely with them, because this is regarded as replicating a disempowering dynamic all too frequently experienced in dealing with professionals. Additionally, peer advocates will not engage in negotiations with service providers without the service user present, operating under the principle of 'nothing about us without us', as drawn from the disability movement. Through their practice, peer advocates strive to encourage self-advocacy and autonomy, supporting service users to develop their own voice and volition.

IAN's stated goals for peer advocacy are:
- to help achieve basic human rights, which those with mental health difficulties have been refused
- to afford those with mental health difficulties the same respect as other citizens
- to secure freedom and liberty for those with mental health difficulties

- to enable those with mental health difficulties to become equal citizens (NDA 2003, Chapter 4)

Development of IAN

McGowan's [n.d.] account details the events surrounding the founding conference in Derry in 1999, where 270 survivors from all over the island gathered together to tell their stories. At this and a subsequent conference in 2003 in Ballybofey, Co. Donegal, user-only space was created for the first two days to give service users an opportunity to share their stories, and professionals were only invited to attend for the third day. This was the first forum of its kind in Ireland, where service users claimed their own public space to articulate their discontent with the MHS and share a vision of how they might address these shortcomings. Emerging out of this conference, twelve people from both Northern and Southern Ireland formed a committee to develop an island-wide peer advocacy organisation. After the Derry conference, Paddy McGowan, with other IAN members, attended numerous meetings across the country with officials from the Department of Health and Children and Health Boards lobbying for peer advocacy within the MHS. Their lobbying reached open ears, as the then Minister of Health and Children, Micheál Martin, had a wider agenda of greater citizen involvement in health services, within which peer advocacy fitted well. The lack of service-user involvement in mental health was out of step with the citizen involvement agenda emerging at that time, and therefore the case for peer advocacy was favourably received by senior policymakers. Peer advocacy filled a need to demonstrate that there were progressive developments occurring, despite the overall failure to achieve reform of institutionalised mental health services.

In 2002, IAN secured funding from Micheál Martin, Minister for Health and Children, for a peer advocacy development programme. The first five employees worked to establish and prove the value of peer advocacy and service-user involvement in assisting the modernisation of Irish MHS. In the intervening years, IAN has grown to employ 21 peer advocates, who now offer an independent peer advocacy service, with weekly visits to inpatient units throughout the country. IAN's service is very valuable for individuals in that it offers a trusted advocate to assist service users in taking their concerns to professionals, especially when they are involuntarily detained. It is important to note, however, that there are limitations in the service. For example, individuals do not usually have a choice of advocate. The consolidation of IAN was also helped by the recognition of the right of service users to an advocate in *A Vision for Change*, the latest government policy for MHS (Department of Health and Children 2006:25). Members of IAN were invited onto the expert group that produced this policy, and had an influential role in crafting Chapter 3, which deals with partnership with service users (Sapouna 2012).

Apart from providing advocacy support, IAN has been engaged in documenting the state of MHS. Members of IAN (on a voluntary basis) commenced a service audit for the Southern Health Board in 2001. Since then IAN has continued to conduct audits of different MHS, highlighting service-users' need to be listened to, to feel respected and to enjoy adequate living conditions within the services on which they depend.[iv] Other user-led research in which IAN has been involved included the evaluation of projects for the Mental Health Commission, and assisting the Inspector of MHS to gather information on service-user involvement and service-users' experiences of the services themselves. IAN has also provided training to mental health professionals on service-user perspectives, most recently training members of Mental Health Tribunals for the Mental Health Commission. IAN advocates also became involved in local, regional and national planning of mental health services and in numerous local innovation projects as representatives on planning and project committees.

Training in self- and peer advocacy, co-developed by Mind Yourself in Derry and IAN, has been provided to hundreds of service users across the country over the past 14 years. Recently this training has shifted to become a collaborative project with the School of Nursing and Midwifery at Dublin City University. Peer advocacy training is significant in the development of IAN because it created a pool of peer advocate volunteers, some of whom were later employed by IAN as advocates.

Local advocacy groups emerged over the years as a result of peer advocacy training, most notably in Kerry, Dublin, the Midlands and Mayo. However, due to the wide range of other demands on IAN advocates' time, the necessary resources to maintain and support the development of volunteer networks were not available, and as a result advocacy groups emerged and folded without the support that might have made them viable.

Nevertheless, IAN has forged a strong position in the Irish user movement because of its position as an organisation with advocates on the ground across the country. Its countrywide, frontline advocacy work gives IAN a very strong claim to speak about the concerns of local service users.

Yet IAN's focus as a service provider to the HSE over the preceding decade has not been without its drawbacks. IAN's relationship with the HSE as its primary funder and contractor has constrained its lobbying or campaigning voice within the mental health field and in broader society. Members of IAN who were interviewed for my research confirmed that the insider strategy the organisation has adopted to develop peer advocacy within the MHS has constrained their freedom to air any strong criticisms they may have about how the MHS fails to meet service-users' needs. Concern for the plight of people within the system, and a desire to provide peer-run services that work for change, albeit with very little power to affect change, are features not just of the Irish user/survivor movement, but of large sections of the international movement. Health social movement theorists point out that many activists personally depend on the very health system that they seek to reform, be it for themselves or a loved one (Brown et al. 2004). Advocacy groups must also make a difficult choice between wanting to address individual cases of injustice and seeking systemic change (Flynn 2011).

CONSUMER PANELS

User involvement at a local/regional level developed sporadically in Ireland on foot of the Department of Health's 2001 Health Strategy that recommended the establishment of consumer panels across the country, particularly for those with a 'mental illness' (Department of Health 2001:81). The definition of the service user in this document (and all subsequent health policy documents) is wide, and includes any potential future user of health and social care services. Consumer panels, comprised of service users, carers and professionals working in mental health non-government organisations (NGOs), are directed by a rationale that public participation can support management to address some of the structural and cultural obstacles to providing client-centred care (Carey 2009, Cowden and Singh 2007). While never implemented across the board, local consumer panels developed in some services throughout the 2000s, driven by a combination of local activism and individual professionals' leadership. Their relationships with the MHS vary from place to place, but they generally have meetings with local senior management to provide consumer feedback on services. There is also considerable variability as to the amount of support they receive, including variable access to meetings with senior management, and with some areas having a small account with funds provided from the MHS to cover members' travel expenses, whereas other areas receive no such support.

USER INVOLVEMENT AND THE NATIONAL SERVICE USERS EXECUTIVE

An officially sanctioned voice for service users and carers – the National Service Users Executive (NSUE) – emerged as a result of a specific recommendation in government policy (Department of Health and Children 2006, Chapter Three). NSUE was established with support from the HSE in 2006 to represent the service-user voice as a publicly funded advisory body to the HSE and the Mental Health Commission. It operated at national level in the first instance and later supported the development of regional consumer panels.

During the process to establish the NSUE, it was decided that this representative body would include carers as well as service users in a ratio of three service users to one carer. Members are elected onto the NSUE from a body of voters consisting of self-selected members. It was planned to elect members onto the NSUE to represent the four regions of the HSE on a four-year rotation, with one election per year; two elections were held, in 2009 and 2010. Establishing a proportional, representational electoral system may not have been the wisest move in terms of developing a strong grassroots service-user movement, given the isolated and marginalised position of service users generally in society. The process of representational democracy can foster a culture of powerful elites, compared to participatory democracy that values each voice equally and seeks to provide equal opportunity to participate in important decisions about policy and direction (Beresford 2010, Young 2000). As a result, the NSUE is not sufficiently accessible to local service users, who are removed from the operations of their imposed representative body (Lakeman et al. 2007). The amalgamation of the service-user and carer voices has not helped. For several reasons, including potentially conflicting perspectives, both user and carer voices risk dilution by their merger (Brosnan 2012).

Heenan (2009:459) claimed that the establishment of the NSUE was a move forward in terms of developing the service-user perspective on the MHS, by ensuring that service users are: 'at the epicentre of developments, using their insights and knowledge to shape the direction of policy and practice'. She was comparing the NSUE with the situation in Northern Ireland, where there has been relatively little movement in terms of establishing a corporate mechanism for service-user representation. However, there is emerging disquiet within the service-user movement – based on many discussions within the 'Expert by Experience' Advisory Group (EEAG) forum (see below) – that the NSUE has failed to live up to the expectations that it would adequately represent the user/survivor voice in Ireland. The NSUE produced four reports based on annual surveys of its members, reporting each year that the majority were 'happy with their local mental health service', and felt their local services 'promote Recovery' (NSUE 2012). The methodology of the annual surveys has been criticised by Crummey (2013) (personal communication). For at least two surveys more than 80% of the respondents were attendees at either day care or training centres, although this cohort only represents about a third of total service users. In addition, there was no minimum eligibility criteria used to determine whether a questionnaire was deemed valid or spoiled based on its level of completeness. According to Crummey, up to 15% of them were spoiled because the services being used were not identified, but such questionnaires were included in the results regardless. Such criticisms indicate that the results of these surveys are unlikely to be representative of service-users' views generally, as basic research protocols were not adhered to in collating the data they provided. However, on the basis of these surveys, the NSUE established annual awards for the 'best-performing' MHS. At the time of writing, the NSUE's funding from the HSE has been suspended and its future is uncertain.

ADVOCACY FROM THE OUTSIDE

Other, more radical voices, such as Mad Pride Ireland, Mind Freedom Ireland and the Critical Voices Network have emerged over the past decade to create spaces of resistance to psychiatric hegemony (Sapouna 2012). The first two survivor-run organisations are small in number but are very active nonetheless and have significant links with their international counterparts. The international Mad Pride movement challenges negative views of mental and emotional distress, and Mind Freedom was established internationally as the voice of the movement against human rights violations in the psychiatric system. Both Irish groups have been involved in symbolic resistance and lobbying about the disproportionate and harmful effects of ECT and psychotropic medication. Members of Mind Freedom contributed to the Oireachtas Joint Committee on Health and Children's review of the pharmaceutical industry (O'Donovan 2009). They facilitate personal accounts of resistance to, and recovery from, encounters with MHS (Maddock and Maddock 2006). Members make extensive use of social media and also engage with the mainstream media to get their message into TV, radio and print journalism. Mad Pride Ireland initiated a strong media campaign to highlight the stigma of mental health, organising a series of very widely reported Family Fun Days in the Park (McCarthy 2008). The Critical Voices Network is a shared space for professionals, academics and service users who are disaffected with the current ethos of MHS, and who advocate for a vision of non-coercive, recovery-orientated services with a central role for service-user perspectives (Sapouna 2012).

Another Irish peer group was the Women Together Network, formed in 2004 to meet the needs of women with mental health difficulties. A peer support network, it emphasised creative expression for members and raised awareness of the additional challenges experienced by women. The network faltered with the axing of Combat Poverty Agency's funding in 2008, as many of the women involved were on very low incomes.

Advisory group to Amnesty International

Another recent development in the user/survivor movement was the establishment in 2008 of an 'Expert by Experience' Advisory Group (EEAG) to Amnesty International Ireland (AI) to advise on their mental health campaign. AI has been campaigning on mental health in Ireland since 2003, with a focus on successive governments' failures to support the human rights of mental health service users. The EEAG worked with AI to ensure that the objectives, projects and literature developed for their latest campaign reflected robust user perspectives. Members of the EEAG were drawn from across the spectrum of the user/survivor community, including user-members of most SMOs such as IAN, NSUE, Mad Pride Ireland, Suicide or Survive, Women Together

Network, GROW and SHINE. However, members participated on the group as individuals rather than representing their organisation. The group met with AI campaign staff several times a year over five years to advise and shape the direction of the campaign (see http://www.amnesty.ie/mentalhealth). As a result, EEAG members developed as a cohesive group with a strong collective identity, plus considerable skills in policy analysis and human-rights-based approaches to mental health, informed by the UN Convention on the Rights of Persons with Disabilities. Although AI has wound down its prominent campaign on mental health, there remains a determined commitment among most EEAG members not to let the accumulated skills and knowledge dissipate, as this group has the potential to become a strong independent lobby for service users in Ireland. Areas of concern identified by the group are the capacity legislation recently published by the Oireachtas, and the review of the Mental Health Act 2001. There has been minimal government-led service-user involvement or consultation with the user/survivor movement on both these important issues for service users. The EEAG is well placed to contribute to these debates, given their knowledge of human-rights-based approaches, as collectively they have the most experience as mental health peer activists of any group in Ireland.

CONCLUSION

Both empowerment and health social movement theory have been threads running throughout this chapter, which describes the role of the user/survivor movement in relation to MHS and the wider policy environment. Peer advocacy, with IAN as the national peer advocacy provider, was discussed as the most developed form of service-user involvement in an Irish context. User involvement emerged as official policy in 2006, but apart from peer advocacy, involvement practices on the ground have been ad hoc and at the discretion of pioneering service providers within the MHS. The NSUE has been a disempowering experience for those involved, partly because it did not have an independent status or the power to speak publicly. Likewise, IAN has been constrained; despite its commitment to advocate for change for individuals it has been unable to be publicly vocal about the need for change. In contrast, although the EEAG has been an internal advisory group for Amnesty's campaign, Amnesty has given EEAG members an opportunity to see how public campaigning works and to speak publicly as the voice of the campaign. Perhaps this will provide a basis for the EEAG to become a separate, more empowering organisation in the future.

The Irish user/survivor movement has responded to discontent with MHS in three divergent ways: by establishing peer advocacy services; by responding to invitations to consult on the MHS' terms; or by rejecting outright the current system as inadequate or damaging. These strategies have had mixed results in achieving empowerment. The peer advocacy service has increased the power of individuals to contest their conditions in the hospital environment, but while the NSUE and consumer panels have increased user involvement in planning services, the NSUE has been criticised for not being representative of the wider user/survivor voice. At a political level, a large user/survivor organisation geared towards collective advocacy in the public sphere has yet to develop, though there is the potential for the EEAG to become this voice.

Future developments within the movement are likely to continue to be shaped by the inherent tension between insider and outsider strategies, and between contesting the current paradigm of bio-psychiatry and its disempowering practices and collaboration with it in order to seek reform of the current MHS. The risk for the user/survivor movement remains that without independently funded, sufficiently robust user-controlled organisations with strong links to active local service-user groups, influencing the professionally dominated policy environment of MHS will remain a daunting challenge.

*

REFLECTIVE QUESTIONS FOR DISCUSSION AND DEBATE: PRACTICE

- Why is the term 'user/survivor' used throughout this chapter? Why are labels significant?
- Why is 'empowerment' a disputed term, especially in relation to professional efforts to empower service users?
- How does the peer advocacy movement show potential to improve the situation of service users?
- Can the user/survivor movement ever be independent of the MHS, especially given their current funding relationships?

REFLECTIVE QUESTIONS FOR DISCUSSION AND DEBATE: RESEARCH

- There is a need to understand the constraints on developing peer-led crisis services in Ireland. Are these constraints just due to the fact that we are a small country, or are there other forces at work?
- What models of empowerment practice (between professionals and service users) are reported in the literature and can these be implemented in the Irish MHS?
- What user-/survivor-developed models of MHS delivery are documented in the literature (including 'grey' literature), and can any of these be piloted in your area?

- What form of service-user activity might be occurring in your local area, and can these groups be supported in ways that ensure the service users remain in control of their own agenda?

REFERENCES

Beresford P (2010) Public partnerships, governance and user involvement: a service user perspective. International Journal of Consumer Studies 34:495-502

Beresford P (2013) Experiential Knowledge and the Reconception of Madness in Coles S Keenan S, Diamond B (eds.) Madness, Contested Power and Practice. Ross-on-Wye: PCC Books 181-196

Brandon D (1995) Peer Support and Advocacy – international comparisons and developments in Jack R (ed.) Empowerment in Community Care. London: Chapman and Hall 108-133

Brennan D (2014) Irish Insanity 1800-2000. Oxon: Routledge

Brennan D (2012) The Rise and Fall of Irish Asylum Utilisation: A Theoretical exploration in Prior P M (ed.) Asylums, Mental Health Care and the Irish: Historical studies 1800-2010. Dublin: Irish Academic Press

Brosnan L (2013) Service-User Involvement in Irish Mental Health Services: A Sociological Analysis of Inherent Tensions for Service Users, Service-Providers and Social Movement Actors. Unpublished PhD thesis: University of Limerick

Brosnan L (2012) Power and Participation: An Examination of the Dynamics of Mental Health Service-User Involvement in Ireland. Studies in Social Justice 6:45-66

Brosnan L, Collins S, Dempsey H, Dermody F, Maguire L, Maria, Morrin N (2002) Pathways Report: Experiences of Mental Health Services from a User-Led Perspective. Galway: The Western Health Board/Schizophrenia Ireland

Brown P and Zavestoski S (2004) Social movements in Health: an introduction. Sociology of Health and Illness 26:679-694

Brown P, Zavestoski S, McCormick S, Mayer B, Morello-Frosch R and Gasior Altman R (2004) Embodied health movements: new approaches to social movements in Health. Sociology of Health and Illness 26:50-80

Campbell P (2005) From Little Acorns – The Mental Health Service User Movement in Bell A and Lindley P (eds.) Beyond the Water Towers: The Unfinished Revolution in MHS 1985-2005. London: Sainsbury Centre for Mental Health 73-82

Carey M (2009) Critical Commentary: Happy Shopper? The Problem with Service User and Carer Participation. British Journal of Social Work 39:179-188

Chamberlin J (1977)[1988] On Our Own: Patient Controlled Alternatives to the Mental Health System. London: MIND

Chamberlin J, Schene A (1997) A Working Definition of Empowerment. Psychiatric Rehabilitation Journal 20:43-47

Coles S, Keenan S, Diamond B (eds.) (2013) Madness Contested: Power and Practice. Ross-on-Wye: PCC Books

Comhairle (2003) The Jigsaw of Advocacy available at http://www.citizens informationboard.ie/downloads/Jigsaw_Advocacy.pdf

Cowden S, Singh G (2007) The 'User': Friend foe or fetish? A critical exploration of user involvement in health and social care. Critical Social Policy 27:5-23

Department of Health and Children (2006) A Vision for Change: Report of the Expert Group on Mental Health Policy. Dublin: Stationery Office

Department of Health and Children (2001) Quality and Fairness: A Health System for You: Health Strategy. Dublin: Stationery Office

Doughty C, Tse S (2011) Can Consumer-Led MHS be Equally Effective? An Integrative Review of CLMH Services in High-Income Countries Community. Mental Health Journal 47:252-266

Flynn E (2011) Making Human Rights Meaningful for People with Disabilities: Recognising a Right to Advocacy in International Human Rights Law. SSRN eLibrary.

Gaventa J, Cornwall A (2008) Power and Knowledge in Reason P, Bradbury H (eds.) The Sage Handbook of Action Research, Participative Inquiry and Practice. London: Thousand Oaks 172-189

Gosling J (2010) The Ethos of Involvement as the Route to Recovery in Weinstein J (ed.) Mental Health Service User Involvement and Recovery. London: Jessica Kingsley Publishers

Heenan D (2009) Mental Health Policy in Northern Ireland: The Nature and Extent of User Involvement. Social Policy and Society 8:451-462

Irish Advocacy Network Ltd (2013) Annual Report 2012. Dublin: Irish Advocacy Network

Lakeman R, Walsh J, McGowan P (2007) Service Users Authority Power and Protest: A Call for Renewed Activism. Mental Health Practice 11:12-16

Mac Gabhann L, Lakeman R, McGowan P, Parkinson M, Redmond M, Sibitz I, Stevenson C, Walsh J (2010) Hear My Voice: the Experience of Discrimination of People with Mental Health Difficulties in Ireland. Dublin: Amnesty Ireland/ Dublin City University

Maddock M, Maddock J (2006) Soul Survivor: A Personal Encounter with Psychiatry. Sheffield: Asylum.

Masterson S, Owen S (2006) Mental health service users' social and individual empowerment: Using theories of power to elucidate far reaching strategies. Journal of Mental Health 15:19-34

McCarthy J (2008) Mad Pride Ireland. MindFreedom: 49

McDaid S (2010) Redefining Empowerment in Mental Health: an Analysis using Hannah Arendt's Power Concept. Journal of Power 3:209-225

McGowan P (not dated) 'The Time is Right' available at http://www. irishadvocacynetwork.com/About%20the%20Irish%20Advocacy%20 Network%20Ltdhtm: [accessed 21-02-2013]

National Disability Authority (2003) Exploring Advocacy available at [http:// www.nda.ie/cntmgmtNewnsf/0/666A6A86EBA5B64180256D9E005EAF8D? OpenDocument#41]

National Service Users Executive (2012) Second Opinions 2011. Dublin: National Service User Executive Available at http://www.nsue.ie/documents/

O'Donovan O (2009) Pharmaceuticals, progress and psychiatric contention in early twenty-first century Ireland in Ging D, Cronin M, Kirby P (eds.) Transforming Ireland: Challenges, Critiques, Resources. Manchester: Manchester University Press 139-154

Repper J, Carter T (2011) A review of the literature on peer support in MHS. Journal of Mental Health 20:392-411

Sadan E (2004) [1997] Empowerment and Community Planning: Theory and Practice of People-Focused Social Solutions. Tel Aviv: Hakibbutz Hameuchad Publishers [in Hebrew]

Sapouna L (2006) Tracing Evidence of Institutionalisation in the Process of De-institutionalisation; the Irish Case in Sapouna L and Herrmann P (eds.) Knowledge in Mental Health; Reclaiming the Social. New York: Nova Science 85-99

Sapouna L (2012) Foucault, Michel (2001) Madness and Civilization: A History of Insanity. Community Development Journal 47:612-617

Shaw B (2013) Peer Support in Coles S, Keenan S and Diamond B (eds.) Madness Contested Power and Practice. Ross-on-Wye: PCC Books 293-306

Slade M, Adams N, O'Hagan M (2012) Recovery: Past progress and future challenges. International Review of Psychiatry 24:1-2

Solomon P (2004) Peer Support/Peer Provided Services: Underlying Processes Benefits and Critical Ingredients. Psychiatric Rehabilitation Journal 27:392-401

Speed E (2002) Irish Mental Health Social Movements: A Consideration of Movement Habitus. Irish Journal of Sociology 11:62-80

Tomes N (2006) The Patient as a Policy Factor: A Historical Case Study of the Consumer/Survivor Movement in Mental Health. Health Affairs 25:720-729

Wallcraft J, Read J, Sweeney A (2003) On Our Own Terms: Users and Survivors of Mental Health Services Working Together for Support and Change. London: User Survey Steering Group, Sainsbury Centre for Mental Health

Wilson A, Beresford P (2000) 'Anti-Oppressive Practice': Emancipation or Appropriation. British Journal of Social Work 30:553-573

World Health Organisation (2003) Advocacy for Mental Health (Mental Health Policy and Service Guidance Package). Geneva: World Health Organisation

Wynne J, Egan C, Collins S, Maguire L, Morris J, Campbell M, Connolly P, Maher J, Lohan G, Flynn A-M (2004) East Galway Pathways Report: Experiences of the East Galway Mental Health Services from Service Users' Perspective. Galway: Western Health Board

Young, I M (2000) Inclusion and Democracy. Oxford: Oxford University Press

NOTES

[i] The term 'consumer' instead of 'service-user' is commonly used in the rest of the English-speaking world apart from the UK and Ireland, but for the sake of consistency I will use the contested term 'service-user'.

ii Planning for the Future, Report of a Study Group on the Development of the Psychiatric Service (1984); Shaping a Healthier Future: A Strategy for Effective Healthcare in the 1990s (1994); Guidelines for Good Practice and Quality Assurance in Mental Health Services (1998).

iii Steer, a user/carer-run organisation, provides advocacy services in County Donegal.

iv Some of the audits the Irish Advocacy Network have conducted: Focusing Minds Southern Health Board Mental Health Service System Audit report (2001); Midland Health Board Mental Health Service System Audit report (2002); North Western Health Board Service System Review, Appendix 3 Sainsbury Centre for Mental Health Report (2004); 'What We Heard' Report from consultation process for the Expert Group on Mental Health Policy, Department of Health and Children, Dublin (2005); South Eastern Health Board Service User Consultation Report (2005); Northern Area Health Board, Sector 6 Service User Consultation Report (2005).

7

Peer support and mutual help as a means to recovery

Mike Watts

INTRODUCTION

The current mental health system is constructed as a hierarchy rather than a community network composed of equal parts. It is a hierarchy that tends to ignore the experience of one part of the system (the 'mentally ill'[i] person) and to favour the beliefs and views of another (the scientific expert). The medically constructed model of 'mental illness' supports this hierarchy by locating the primary site of mental illness in the brain, with malfunction of the brain as the primary cause of 'symptoms'.

Pert (1998) questions the assumption that control must necessarily be hierarchical:

> A network is different from a hierarchical structure that has a ruling 'station' at the top and a descending series of positions that play increasingly subsidiary roles. In a network, theoretically you can enter at any nodal point and quickly get to any other point; all locations are equal as far as the potential to 'rule' or direct the flow of information. (Pert 1998:184)

The idea of mutual help, where experiential knowledge is considered to be equally as valuable as expert knowledge thus fundamentally challenges the hierarchical organisation of mental health services which rely exclusively on a form of professional expertise. This chapter explores the concept of mutual help; its origins, definition and the central role it can play in both personal recovery and systems transformation. International and Irish research findings on the effectiveness of mutual help are explored as well as current developments in the area of mutual help and peer support within the Irish context.

MUTUAL HELP: A UNIVERSAL PRINCIPLE

According to Patent (1995:5), mutual help through peer support is a 'universal principle involved in all levels of successfully living together'. Hamilton (2008) suggests that sacred texts from which most cultures have evolved contain a reference to the centrality of mutual help in the successful organisation of society. Common to Christianity, Judaism and Islam is the commandment to 'love your neighbour as yourself' (Isaiah 8:20). The idea of mutuality (e.g. equality and brotherhood) has also been at the centre of secular revolutions and of communist philosophy, which saw any form of inequality contained within traditional hierarchies as evidence of a deep-rooted social evil (Marx and Engels 1848).

Biologists Maturana and Varela (1998) suggest that mutual help may operate at a much more basic level than the consciously social. In their view, all living cells 'language' or communicate with one another to bring about a constant state of healthy equilibrium through a self-regulating negative feedback loop, a process known as autopoiesus. Irish psychiatrist Ivor Browne (2008:246) identifies five different levels within which this principle operates: the cell, the individual creature, a collection of similar creatures (such as local or national communities), an aggregate of species and finally within the biosphere. The idea of the human being as an example of an autopoetic system that is itself part of a wider system has huge relevance and implications for the structure and practice of mental health services.

Within Irish society the idea of mutuality has been at the centre of social organisation throughout history. Robins (1986:14) recounts how in pre-Christian times the Brehon Laws were designed to protect the human rights and dignity of each individual and were painstakingly developed through a process of mutual help. All new laws had to be agreed by a representative cross-section of the community, not by an appointed hierarchy. There was a deeply embedded notion of the equality of all people, with men and women, young and old, learned and unschooled all being consulted about the new laws. In more modern times the idea of 'meitheal', where people would come together, especially in rural communities, to help each other with specific tasks such as saving the hay, killing the pig, or harvesting the turf lay at the centre of Ireland's rural community.

THE HELPER PRINCIPLE AND RISE OF MUTUAL HELP

While the idea of mutual help can trace its roots at least as far back as biblical times, Riessman first drew attention to its potentially central role in recovery from mental illness in 1965 with the publication of 'The Helper Therapy Principle' (Riessman 1965). Riessman coined the term 'Helper Therapy' or 'The Helper Principle' after observing various self-help groups and concluding that 'the act of helping another helps the helper more than the person helped'

(Riessman 1965:28). By the early 1970s this principle was being noted in many premier psychiatry journals as more researchers found that helping others was beneficial to the helper in a variety of contexts (Rogeness and Badner: 1973).

'Mutual help' as we know it today began to become a feature of western society through the establishment of Alcoholics Anonymous (AA) in the United States in 1935. AA itself grew directly out of the Oxford Group, a revolutionary social movement started in the aftermath of the Great War by Lutheran Minister Frank Buchman. The Oxford Group aimed to foster world peace and individual well-being and was firmly grounded in the concept of 'a reciprocity of human weakness and the potential for positive change through mutual help' (Watts 2012:33).

AA is currently described as the father of mutual help, and has become a model for many other twelve-step programmes. Post estimates that:

> Close to 350 anonymous twelve step programmes exist in the United States, thus many millions of Americans know about the twelfth step (a call to mutual help) through a self-help organisation. (Post 2008:2)

Katz suggests that in the two decades since Riessman's recognition of mutual help as an important therapeutic and human resource there were 'some half million separate self help groups in North America embracing several million member-participants' (Katz 1981:129). GROW, Ireland's largest and longest-established mutual help group working in the area of recovery from emotional distress was itself one of many offshoots of AA, beginning in Australia in 1957 and coming to Ireland in 1969.

DEFINING MUTUAL HELP AND PEER SUPPORT

Because of the number and variety of mutual help groups, arriving at an all-encompassing definition of mutual help is difficult, a difficulty further compounded by the interchangeability of the terms 'self-help' and 'mutual help'.

Katz and Bender (1976) created the following general definition which is still widely accepted and cited:

> Self help groups are voluntary, small group structures for mutual aid and the accomplishment of a special purpose. They are usually formed by peers who have come together for mutual assistance in satisfying a common need, overcoming a common handicap or life-disrupting problem and bringing about desired social and/or personal change. The initiators and members of such groups perceive that their needs are not, or cannot, be met by or through existing social institutions. Self help groups emphasise face to face social interactions and the assumption of personal responsibility

by members. They often provide material assistance, as well as emotional support. They are frequently 'cause' oriented, and promulgate an ideology of values through which members may attain an enhanced sense of personal identity. (Katz 1981:135-136 citing Katz and Bender 1976)

Katz later appended this definition by making the following observations:

> Personal participation is an extremely important ingredient; bureaucratisation is antithetical to mutual help. The members agree and engage in some actions and typically the groups start from a position of powerlessness. Finally the groups fulfil needs for a reference group, a point of connection and identification of others, a base for activity and a source of ego reinforcement. (Katz 1981:137)

Two defining features of mutual help lie in the notions of equality and reciprocity. Each member of the group is valued equally whatever their level of education, and the guiding principle for decision-making is one of shared values. Unlike in the mental health system, where leadership is hierarchical, in mutual help groups it is reciprocal, with every member able to give and to receive leadership.

While mutual help is a feature of many spheres of life, the term 'peer support' has been specifically defined as 'any organised support provided by and for people with mental health problems' (Mental Health Commission of Canada 2009:1). Mead defines peer support as:

> a system of giving and receiving help founded on key principles of respect, shared responsibility and mutual agreement about what is helpful.... It is about understanding another's situation empathically through shared experience of emotional and psychological pain. It is not based on psychiatric models and diagnostic criteria. (Mead 2004:1)

Peer support initiatives include:

> programs, networks, agencies or services that provide peer support. They can be funded or unfunded; use volunteers, paid staff or both; operate out of psychiatric consumer/survivor run organisations OR other agencies; delivered by a group of peers OR by an individual peer in a team of professionals; a primary activity of the initiative OR a secondary benefit, such as in a consumer/survivor business; or 'part of an indigenous healing ritual'. (O'Hagan et al. 2010:42)

While mutual help or peer support groups differ widely in terms of membership, member training and frequency of meetings, the common feature lies in group members' shared experience of a problem, the emotional and spiritual support provided and the empowering generation of hope for the future.

WHAT DOES RESEARCH SAY ABOUT MUTUAL HELP? INTERNATIONAL EVIDENCE

Christensen and Jacobson (1994) reviewed studies comparing the value and effectiveness of para-professional (non-professional) help with much more expensive, professionally delivered types of help. The studies consistently showed very little difference in outcome between the two types of help, suggesting that non-professionals could provide equivalent outcomes to professionals.

Davidson et al. (1999) reviewed the history and potential effectiveness of peer support among persons with severe mental illness. They described three primary forms of peer support that had been developed to date by and for this population, and examined the existing empirical evidence for the feasibility, effectiveness, and utilisation of each of these approaches in contributing to the recovery of individuals with mental health problems. These three forms are (1) naturally occurring mutual support groups, (2) consumer-run services, and (3) the employment of consumers as providers within clinical and rehabilitative settings. They found promising results for the benefits of mutual support groups, but concluded that this finding was 'tentative' given the dearth of systematic studies available at that time. What evidence existed seemed to indicate that mutual support groups could reduce hospital stays, support individuals' social integration and improve their quality of life (Davidson et al. 1999:169-172). The authors also considered that consumer-run services and the use of consumers as providers promised to broaden the access of individuals with mental health problems to peer support. However, they did caution about the limited evidence available to demonstrate the feasibility of consumer-run services (Davidson et al. 1999:172).

Pistrang et al. (2008) reviewed 12 empirical studies which asked whether participation in mutual help groups by people with mental health problems led to improved psychological and social functioning. They reported 'limited but promising evidence that mutual help groups benefit people with chronic mental illness, depression/anxiety and bereavement' (Pistrang et al. 2008:210). Seven of the studies reported positive changes for those attending support groups. The strongest findings came from two randomised controlled trials showing that the outcomes of mutual help groups were equivalent to those of substantially more costly professional interventions. O'Hagan et al. (2010) also noted an emerging body of evidence showing that peer-led projects demonstrate the following positive outcomes: fewer hospitalisations; less symptom distress; improvement in social support and improvement in quality of life. The authors again concluded that more high-quality research is needed to evaluate the effectiveness of mutual help groups across the spectrum of mental health problems.

As well as reporting on empirical studies, some commentators have developed theoretical explanations for the contribution that mutual help makes to recovery from emotional distress. Rappaport (2000), commenting on mutual help within GROW, suggested that mutual help fosters recovery by providing a community narrative based on personal value, one that is strong enough to counter the powerfully negative professional and social narratives that cast the 'emotionally distressed' as second-class citizens with lifelong scripts of illness, unreliability and disease. Through mutual help, people are empowered to leave their old identities behind and emerge as independent individuals embedded within and supported by ongoing mutually respectful relationships. Likewise, Mead et al. (2004) argue that persons labelled with psychiatric disability have become 'victims of social and cultural ostracism and consequently have developed a sense of self that reinforces the patient identity.' In their view, the way to recovery lies through education and training provided through peer support. Mead's ideas would appear to be reinforced by Stein et al. (1987), who examined the social support networks of people attending GROW. They found that where these support networks were primarily provided by mental health professionals, those being supported came to believe that they were intrinsically inferior to all other human beings.

MUTUAL HELP: RECENT IRISH RESEARCH

Qualitative research exploring the value of mutual help in recovery is rare within an Irish context. A recently completed narrative study (Watts 2012) based on reflective interviews with 26 long-term members of GROW in Ireland identified many processes and outcomes of mutual help that appear to be an integral part of an ongoing journey of healing. Its objectives were to explore:

- the recovery experiences of a cohort of GROW leaders;
- how various types of help facilitated, aided or impeded recovery; and
- the role that mutual relationships such as friendship, reciprocity and leadership played in recovery.

Inclusion criteria for the participant comprised:

- a minimum of three years involvement in GROW;
- involvement in GROW leadership at a formal level;
- a diagnosis of 'mental illness', and either prescription of medication or hospitalisation; and
- personal confidence in own recovery from mental illness.

The findings showed that recovery was a non-linear but progressive journey beginning in mental illness. Mental illness itself was described not as a symptom of a chemical imbalance within the brain, but as an ongoing process of becoming trapped and isolated within a 'Place of Terror'. This Place of Terror involved a number of levels of being, including feelings and thoughts, which were visibly related to real and unresolved traumatic and terrifying life events. Notably, many participants reported that hospitals, medication and encounters with professional help often added to their sense of terror instead of facilitating recovery. An important minority of participants, however, did recount incidents where different forms of professional help were experienced positively, identifying relational qualities such as warmth, personal interest and compassion as key to a therapeutic or healing relationship. Through participation in mutual help, described by research participants as 'A Time of Healing', people experienced epiphanic 'body stories' of hope, human warmth and a sense of being valued for themselves. These in turn helped them to nurture positive thoughts and new ways of dealing with both self and others. The power of people's first encounter with mutual help was reflected in the language used to describe its effect:

> I felt I had been lifted. (Frances)
> I felt I had got hope and hope had never occurred to me before. (Mags)
> I felt so comfortable inside that room. (Jess)
> To meet these people who seemed to understand me was amazing. (Nan)
> (Watts 2012:132)

Listening to others and having others bear witness to their own suffering and their own value, being called to active participation in reciprocal activities involved in leadership and friendship, and learning to take progressive but legitimate risks were all processes that occurred when, as one participant put it, 'I left my small self and joined a bigger self' (Watts 2012:129) – and recovery began. In this study, recovery was further reinforced when people became re-involved in society, which had transformed into 'an opportunity to become'. Participants' reports of re-joining society through work, education or leisure primarily highlighted a realisation of their essential equality with or sameness as others. They now experienced society as a place of mutual relationships and brotherhood instead of pathogenic difference, alienation and exclusion.

Some of the findings of this research serve to dramatically challenge current views about mental illness and the nature of recovery. For instance, while ten of the participants had been diagnosed with 'lifelong' forms of mental illness such as schizophrenia or bi-polar disorder, only four of these were still taking psychiatric medication at the time of the research. Participants' descriptions of healing through mutual help highlighted the role of spiritual qualities such as hope, warmth, encouragement, compassion and belonging as key elements in recovery. The small units of mutual help that comprise GROW in Ireland were described as 'spiritual wombs' which provided all the members of the group with the spiritual nutrients necessary for recovery.

IRISH POLICY ON MUTUAL HELP

At the heart of the mental health policy document *A Vision for Change* (Department of Health and Children 2006) lies a commitment to the recovery principle, which itself incorporates a strong valuing of mutual help and peer support. For example, Judi Chamberlin's landmark 1977 book *On Our Own* explained how service users could set up their own, peer-run mental health services. She later described mutual support as the key element in her own recovery journey (Chamberlin 2008).

While the psychiatric establishment espouses a bio-psychosocial model of mental health difficulties, in practice the dominant approach to treatment is chemical. The narrowness of view that relies primarily on chemical treatments tends to ignore the value of peer support.

One way to gauge whether the recognition of mutual help has gained ground over the years as a valuable resource for mental health and recovery lies in a comparison of the contents of the two official Irish policy documents on mental health: *The Psychiatric Services: Planning for the Future: Report of a Study Group on the Development of the Psychiatric Services* (Department of Health and Children 1984) and *A Vision for Change: Report of the Expert Group on Mental Health Policy* (Department of Health and Children 2006).

Planning for the Future (Department of Health and Children 1984) heralded the end of institution-based mental health services and instigated a radical move towards the notion of community care. However within this document there is no mention of the value of mutual help or the value of 'expertise' through experience. Its contents are almost exclusively professionally oriented, having been compiled by seeking 'the views and experiences of those who now provide the service' (Department of Health and Children 1984:9). While the document introduces the idea of rehabilitation with reference to a population that hitherto were regarded as chronically sick and in need of ongoing institutional care, rehabilitation nonetheless remained the exclusive responsibility of the professional with psychiatrists, general practitioners and nurses being the chief professional actors. Like mutual help, the idea of recovery appears to be totally absent. Rehabilitation (is defined as 'returning skills to a person impaired by mental illness and providing training in new skills' (Department of Health and Children 1984:71).

By contrast, *A Vision for Change* (Department of Health and Children 2006) makes frequent mention of the potential value of mutual help and continually emphasises the need to include service users (and carers) as active agents in their own recovery. At the heart of this document is the aspiration to transform our mental health system from one that over-emphasises the biological cause of mental illness to one where 'a recovery approach should be adopted as a cornerstone of this policy' (Department of Health and Children 2006:15).

A *Vision for Change* goes on to quote international evidence (Solomon and Draine 2001) suggesting that peer-led interventions can bring about 'improvement in symptoms, an increase in social networks and quality of life, reduced mental health service use, higher satisfaction with health, improved daily functioning and improved illness management' (Department of Health and Children 2006:26). Such services also benefit peer providers by bringing about fewer hospitalisations and greater opportunities to practice their own recovery, build their own support system and engage in professional growth. Finally the report notes that the development of peer-led services leads to 'cost savings through decreased hospitalisations and reduced use of mental health services, a reduction in negative attitudes towards services, improved relationships with service users, improved mental health outcomes and having the needs of those alienated from services addressed' (Department of Health and Children 2006:27, citing Solomon and Draine 2001).

Despite this policy support, there has been little significant development of peer-run services since publication of *A Vision for Change*. While the report notes that 'there is a lack of peer support for this group of service-users' (people with enduring mental health problems) within the mental health system (Department of Health and Children 2006:108), the 6th Annual Report of the Independent Monitoring Group (IMG 2012) reported that the implementation of *A Vision for Change* has been slow and inconsistent. Disappointingly the only reference to mutual help as an important resource reads:

> The IMG is aware of the long history of the voluntary sector in Irish mental health services. The IMG wishes to acknowledge the valuable work being done by the voluntary sector and recommends the proactive partnership already formed should be developed further to enhance full implementation of AVFC. (IMG 2012:96)

While the government pledged substantial extra funds on an annual and incremental basis (Department of Health and Children 2006:4), these were largely earmarked for the provision of multidisciplinary teams and more professional-led services. While the government provided an extra €35,000,000 in 2012 to help implement *A Vision for Change*, budgets for mutual help organisations such as GROW have been systematically reduced by 20% since 2009, and in one of its operational areas by 35%. It therefore appears that the policy commitment to mutual help has not been followed up with action or resources for implementation.

MUTUAL HELP: AN UNREALISED POTENTIAL WITHIN THE IRISH MENTAL HEALTH SYSTEM

In a 1987 World Health Organisation study that compared four mutual help groups involved in recovery from mental illness, (GROW, Recovery Inc., Schizophrenics Anonymous and Emotions Anonymous), Turner and Jablensky (1987) urged all governments to make these resources available to people experiencing mental health problems. Despite this, mutual help in the area of recovery from 'emotional distress' remains a largely under-developed resource.

Ireland currently has a number of well-established mutual help groups aimed at service users or family members such as Alcoholics Anonymous, Al Anon, Al Ateen, Gamblers Anonymous, Narcotics Anonymous, Sex Addicts Anonymous, GROW, Recovery Inc., Bodywhys, Out and About, Console, Clubhouse and Patientwise. While these groups traditionally operate through regular face-to-face meetings, a number of online support groups are also emerging (www.selfhelpgroups.org). Despite the existence of groups for a number of mental health problems, their availability and numbers are inconsistent throughout the country, with some groups being well represented nationwide and others focused mainly within larger cities. For instance, current figures show that AA runs 249 weekly meetings in Dublin alone (as well as 50 Al Anon meetings) while the GROW website advertises just nine.

Ironically, those who become mentally ill and who seek help from the hierarchical, professionally driven mental health system still tend to be denied the healing experience of mutual help and of being able to help someone else because they are cast in the role of passive receivers of others' expert knowledge. In addition, people who receive a medical diagnosis of mental illness, experience the side-effects of treatment and know the processes involved in recovery have been routinely ignored by professionals, funding bodies and policymakers, and their knowledge was not considered to be valid sources for evidence.

Furthermore, research suggests that professionals are not always positive toward self-help groups. In an attempt to gauge professional attitudes towards mutual help in Ireland, UCC-based psychologists Dunne and Fitzpatrick (1999) conducted a postal survey of 255 mental health professionals from two health boards using a semi-structured questionnaire. They obtained a response rate of 35%, a result which suggests their findings must be interpreted with some caution. While respondents did acknowledge a role for mutual help in providing support to patients and their families, information on mental illness and mental health to the general public, and lobbying for services relevant to the needs of their members, respondents also revealed a major concern that the 'philosophy and programme of a group should not conflict with established models of mental health' (Dunne and Fitzpatrick 1999:84). These findings were in broad agreement with the results of a similar survey carried out in New Zealand by

Pamela Clarke (1992) who found that professionals' support for mutual help groups was in inverse relationship to their knowledge of those groups.

Salem et al. (1988) advocated for a changing role for mental health professionals which highlights the central role of mutual help. In their view, instead of being the primary helpers, mental health professionals should:

> help people find niches in society which are based on mutual rather than unidirectional relationships instead of trying to be the sole providers of help themselves. (Salem et al. 1988:407)

The challenge for a mental health system would therefore seem to be to find valid ways that the experience and knowledge of all concerned can be seen to be of value whether a person has been cast in the role of expert by training or expert by experience. GROW's manifesto clearly suggests that the primary helpers in recovery must be:

> friendly human beings who know from experience how to recover ... all other helpers, including doctors, are necessarily subordinate, good in their place, but harmful when they do not make way for that vital activation through mutual help. (GROW in Ireland 1994:48)

NEW IRISH DEVELOPMENTS IN MUTUAL HELP

Despite the continued trend to channel the bulk of new mental health service funding into professional types of help and to systematically cut the budgets of well established and proven effective mutual help organisations such as GROW, there are a number of recent developments which suggest that mutual help groups are gaining in status and becoming more central to mental health services in other countries, and gradually increasing within Ireland. Crucial to these developments may be the availability of funding through bodies such as Genio (a public–private partnership) and the National Lottery. Significant among these initiatives is the promotion in Ireland of the Hearing Voices Network, an England-based organisation being actively promoted in Ireland by Jacqui Dillon. Jacqui is a service user herself and a mental health professional who experienced severe childhood abuse and who began hearing voices at the age of five. The general approach of the network is shared with other groups around the world, which are often grouped as the Hearing Voices Movement. Currently, there are over 40 groups in the network across Britain. In these groups, which are exclusive to individuals who hear voices, voice-hearers are afforded the opportunity to share their experiences, coping mechanisms and explanatory frameworks in a non-medical setting. Since its inception the network has developed considerably as an organisation, and now publishes newsletters, guides to the voice-hearing experience and workbooks where individuals can record and explore their own experiences with voice hearing. In Ireland, the expansion of the Hearing Voices Network has come about as a result of funding from the Irish Institute of Mental Health Nursing and Nursing Practice Development Units. In addition, there are a number of support groups emerging in the area of bereavement through suicide such as Console, It's a Wonderful Life, Angel Whispers, Suicide Ireland and Living Links that have been established both nationally and locally.

CONCLUSION

Mutual help is a relationship that is key to healthy living at many different levels of life, including recovery from mental illness/emotional distress and the well being of individuals and of society. Our current mental health system has historically been constructed as a hierarchy in which one view (that of professional experts holding the increasingly challenged paternalistic medical model) has dominated and effectively silenced the voice of service users. Effects of this have been to cast service users in the role of 'cacogenic other', to deny them access to mutual help and full humanity or citizenship, and to create a sense that their distress has neither meaning nor value.

Since the rise of the recovery movement in the 1960s and the acknowledged therapeutic contribution that being able to help another makes, small pockets of mutual help have been formed around the world. Policymakers are beginning to take note, and in Ireland the government's mental health policy *A Vision for Change* (Department of Health and Children 2006) advocates for the recognition of the value of the experience of service users and their families, and the positive benefits of peer support alongside professional help. Mutual help is now embracing a new phase where all the different voices are being allowed to be heard. We are coming together as human beings, called to tackle the shared challenge represented by recovery from mental illness/emotional distress.

*

REFLECTIVE QUESTIONS FOR DISCUSSION AND DEBATE: PRACTICE

- If mutual help is 'the' key ingredient in recovery, how will this affect the role of the mental health practitioner?
- While every person involved in the mental health system has a label (mental health professional, carer or service user), behind each label is a person with their own experiences of life. How can mental health professionals know what parts of their life are appropriate to share within a professional relationship?

- How can mental health professionals find or create resources within their local community that might help people on a recovery journey from serious mental illness? What role might mutual help play in this journey?
- What aspects of mutual help have been valuable to you in life? How can you make these resources available to those with whom you work/meet?

REFLECTIVE STATEMENTS FOR DISCUSSION AND DEBATE: RESEARCH

- How would you design a research project based on the experiences of people diagnosed with a severe and enduring mental illness who have successfully and safely dispensed with psychiatric drugs through involvement in mutual help? What would the implications for services of such research be?
- How would you design research that would explore the impact of participating in a mutual help group on the worldviews and professional practices of mental health professionals.

REFERENCES

Browne I (2008) Music and Madness. Cork: Atrium

Chamberlin J (1977) On Our Own: Patient-controlled alternatives to the mental health system. New York: Hawthorn

Chamberlin J (2008) 'Developing a recovery vision' downloaded 13/2/12 from http://voices-of-recovery-schizophrenia.blogspot.com/2008/01/judi-chamberlin-developing-recovery.html

Christensen A, Jacobson N S (1994) Who (or What) Can do Psychotherapy?: The Status and Challenge of Non-professional Therapies. Psychological Science 5 (1) 8-14

Clarke P (1992) Mutual-Help Groups and Mental Health Professionals: Barriers and Implications for Co-operative Relations. Unpublished Master's thesis: University of Auckland

Davidson L, Chinman M, Kloos B, Weingarten R, Stayner Kraemer Tebes (1999) Peer Support Among Individuals with Severe Mental Illness: A Review of the Evidence. Clinical Psychology: Science and Practice 6 (2) Summer 165 -187

Department of Health (1984) Psychiatric Services – Planning for the Future: Report of a Study Group on the Development of the Psychiatric Services. Dublin: Stationery Office

Department of Health and Children (2006) A Vision for Change: Report of the Expert Group on Mental Health Policy. Dublin: Stationery Office

Dunne E A, Fitzpatrick A C (1999) The views of professionals on the role of self-help groups in the mental health area. Irish Journal of Psychiatric Medicine 164 (3) 84-89

Finn L (2001) Mutual Help Groups and Psychological Wellbeing: a Study of GROW A Community Mental Health Organisation. Unpublished PhD thesis: Curtin University Perth

GROW in Ireland (1994) GROW in Ireland: A Celebration and a Vision of Innovations in Community Mental Health. Kilkenny: GROW in Ireland

Hamilton C (2008) Buddhism. St Petersburg, FL: Red and Black Books

Independent Monitoring Group (2012) A Vision for Change – the Report of the Expert Group on Mental Health Policy: Sixth annual report on implementation 2011 available at http://www.dohc.ie/publications/vision_for_change_6th/hse_nat_reg/final_6th_annual_report

Katz A H (1981) Self-help and mutual aid: an emerging social movement? Annual review of sociology 7:129-155

Katz A H, Bender E (1976) The strength in us: self help groups in the modern world. New York: Franklin-Watts

Marx K, Engels F (1848) The Communist Manifesto. London: The Communist League

Maturana H R, Varela F J (1998) The Tree of Knowledge: The biological roots of human understanding. Boston: Random House

Mead S, Hilton H, Curtis L (2004) Peer Support: A Theoretical Perspective Unpublished Report www.peerzone.info/sites/default/files/resource_materials/Peer%20

O'Hagan M, Cyr C, McKee H, Priest R (2010) Making the case for peer support: Report to the Mental Health Commission of Canada Mental Health Peer Support Project Committee. Calgary: Mental Health Commission of Canada

Patent A M (1995) You Can Have it All: A Simple Guide to a Joyful and Abundant Life. New York: Pocket Books

Pert C B (1998) Molecules of Emotion. London: Simon and Schuster

Pistrang N, Barker C, Humphreys K (2008) Mutual Help Groups for Mental Health Problems: A review of Evidence. American Journal of Community Psychology 42:110-121

Post S G (2008) The Joy of Giving: Why altruism and generosity make us healthier and happier-and how we can all give more. Psychology Today 3 (September): 43-44

Rappaport J (1998) The Art of Social Change: Community Narratives as Resources for Individual and Collective Identity in Addressing Community Problems: Psychological Research and Intervention (Arriaga A B, Oskamp S, eds.) Thousand Oaks, CA: Sage

Rappaport J (2000) Community Narratives: Tales of Terror and Joy. American Journal of Community Psychology 28 (1) 1-24

Riessman F (1965) The Helper Therapy Principle. Social Work 10 (2) 27-32

Robins J (1986) Fools and Mad: History of the Insane in Ireland. Dublin: Institute of Public Administration

Rogeness G A, Badner R A (1973) Teenage helper: A role in community mental health. American Journal of Psychiatry 130:933-936

Salem D A, Seidman E (1988) Community Treatment of the Mentally Ill: The Promise of Mutual Help Organisations. Social Work September/October: 403-408

Shannon P J, Morrison D L (1990) Who Goes to GROW? Australian and New Zealand Journal of Psychiatry 24:96-102

Solomon P, Draine J (2001) The State of Knowledge of the Effectiveness of Consumer Provided Services. Psychiatric Rehabilitation Journal 25 (1) 20-27

Stein C H (1987) Social Networks, Social Support and Psychological Adjustment Among Participants in a Mutual Help Organisation for the Mentally Ill. Unpublished PhD thesis: University of Illinois at Urbana-Champaign

Turner-Crowson J, Jablensky A (1987) WHO Survey on Self Help Groups and Mental Disorder. Geneva: World Health Organisation

Watts M (2012) Recovery from 'mental illness' as a re-enchantment with life: a narrative study. Unpublished PhD thesis: Trinity College Dublin

NOTES

[i] The term 'mental illness' or 'mentally ill person' is a term that illustrates the dominance of the medical view that 'mental illness' is caused by a chemical imbalance within the brain and therefore belongs in the realm of medicine. Because many people within the recovery movement believe that 'mental illness' is the result of unresolved emotional distress the term 'emotional distress' will be used throughout this chapter.

8

The paradoxical role of families in mental health

Shari McDaid and Agnes Higgins

INTRODUCTION

Family members who provide support to their relative with mental or emotional distress occupy a paradoxical position within the mental health system. On the one hand, family members, particularly those who provide ongoing support, housing and financial assistance for their relative, view themselves as having a valuable role in supporting their relative's recovery. In addition, research and policy literature suggests that the support of family members and other close friends can be pivotal in people's recovery journeys. On the other hand, family members are often marginalised by the mental health system, finding themselves on the outside of discussions about medical diagnoses, treatment and recovery. Ironically, they can themselves become users of services as a result of the emotional, social and economic pressures of their caring role.

This chapter will consider the changing role of 'carers', or what is sometimes referred to as 'family supporters', in Ireland in the late 20th and early 21st centuries. The impact of a relative's mental/emotional distress on the family will be discussed. A critical analysis of developments in Irish policy and law and discussion of the experience of family supporters in Ireland based on Irish research will highlight the contradictory position that family supporters have held inside and outside the Irish mental health system. The chapter will conclude by identifying some current innovations in the involvement of family supporters and recommendations that may enhance family members' visibility within mental health service delivery. The term 'family' as used in this chapter is intended to cover all types of close relationships including family, civil partners, non-married partners, friends and others who provide ongoing support, except mental health professionals.

FAMILY CARERS/SUPPORTERS: WHO ARE THEY?

Traditionally, the focus of government policy developments and supports has been on the person experiencing mental distress. Consequently, the needs and rights of family carers – or what will also be referred to as 'family supporters' – have not been in the foreground. Little Irish data has been gathered or research undertaken to describe their experience, and information on those who provide care/support is sparse. In the Irish Census (2011) 187,112 people identified themselves as carers (4.1% of the population), with over 10,500 of these being under 19 years of age. While there is no specific evidence on the total number of people providing support for individuals with ongoing mental distress in Ireland, the same census showed a total of 96,000 individuals having a mental health disability, many of whom would be likely to receive support from a family member (Central Statistics Office 2012). The Health Research Board in Ireland does not collect statistics on the number of service users who have children, so the exact number of children within Ireland who potentially are taking on a supporter role is unknown; however, research elsewhere suggests that between 20% and 35% of adult service users are parents and that a percentage of these children are engaging in caring functions (Maybery et al. 2009).

ROLE OF THE FAMILY AND THE MENTAL HEALTH SERVICES: AN UNEASY RELATIONSHIP

Gambel and Brennan (2006) assert that 'families have been as much burdened by the mental health system as by the illness' (p. 179), as all too often they were seen as part of the problem if not the cause of the person's mental health problem. In the 1940s and '50s the theory of the 'schizophrenogenic mother' put forward by Fromm-Reichmann (1948), and the double-bind theory of Bateson et al. (1956) became influential and had the effect of positioning mothers as part cause of schizophrenia rather than as positive contributors to recovery. There were a number of ideas embodied within these theories that sent a powerful message about mothers, namely, mental health problems were connected to maternal rejection or hostility and/or maternal domination or over-protection (Gosdin 2001). While both theories were later discredited, they had the effect of engendering hostility among professionals who held parents, and particularly mothers, as 'morally' culpable for their child's distress. Indeed, social commentators at the time often blamed mothers for any troubles children had with social adjustment, and also for any problems the society might have had with 'maladjusted or delinquent children' (Gosdin 2001). Later the focus of research moved on to examining marital relationships between mothers and fathers with Lidtz and colleagues in the mid-'60s postulating that interactions and distortion in parental relationships were the cause of schizophrenia.

Consequently, for years, the idea of family members contributing to care or being involved in supporting a family member was treated as a 'taboo' (Gosdin 2001).

In the 1970s consideration of the family moved to an exploration of the family environment as a whole, with theories postulating that any member of a family, or all the members of a family together, might somehow create the conditions of stress that produced 'schizophrenia' in a family member. This work focused on what was unhelpfully described as 'High Expressed Emotion' or patterns of over-involvement, criticism and lack of emotional warmth within the family that could exacerbate a loved one's mental distress and increase relapse rates (Leff and Vaughn 1981). While it is important to note that problematic family relationship styles may reflect the low self-esteem of family members, this theory helped to open the door to family involvement, as practitioners began to consider families as resources and allies in 'relapse prevention'.

Keogh (1998) notes that:

> The theoretical work on expressed emotion and subsequent development of social interventions for families represented a significant shift in attitude for mental health professionals. Families were viewed more positively and were actively recruited into the treatment of the patient. The potential value of the family in preventing relapse and thus rehospitalisation was also a vital part in the success of many new community programmes, whose effectiveness was often judged very simply in terms of readmission rates and days in hospital. (Keogh 1998:19)

FAMILY EXPERIENCES: 'FAMILY BURDEN'

While there are positive and rewarding aspects of caring, exploring the experience of family members has been largely motivated by an interest in the potential for 'family burden' (Platt 1985, Schene 1990, Keogh 1998, Drapalski and Dixon 2011) to have arisen from the impact of deinstitutionalisation (Keogh 1998). The idea that community-based mental health services might impose a 'burden' on families features in Irish mental health policy as far back as 1984. The government's mental health policy *Planning for the Future* referred to evidence that the transfer of mental health services from institutions into the community could result in a significant 'burden' on the relatives of some individuals with a mental health difficulty (Department of Health 1984:12).

The term 'burden' is defined by Platt (1985) as: 'The presence of problems, difficulties or adverse events which affected the life (lives) of the psychiatric patient's [sic] significant others' (p.383). Two distinct facets of burden are identified in the literature: objective and subjective burden (Drapalski and Dixon: 2011). Objective burden generally refers to observable negative impacts on the family as a result of the person's mental distress (Drapalski and Dixon 2011:188) such as financial strain, disruption of family relationships and routines, constraints in social, leisure and work activities, and isolation and decreased social networking due to the prejudiced attitudes of others. Subjective burden refers to 'internal' impacts on the family in the form of psychological distress and associated feelings (Schene et al. 1998:610), such as chronic stress, feelings of loss and grief, depression, anxiety, stigma and embarrassment in social situations.

Notwithstanding the emotional, social and economic impacts on family members caused by a relative's mental distress, the persistent emphasis on family burden positions family members as the victims and service users as the cause of their burden. It is important to acknowledge a critical lens through which family burden may be considered. Many, including service users, might reject the 'family burden' concept, favouring a more systemic and interdependent approach that acknowledges the potential reciprocal relationship between the person experiencing distress and their wider family. The positioning of people experiencing mental distress on the dependent or 'taking' end of the dependence–independence continuum not only minimises the person's positive contribution to the family system, but ignores the positive and reciprocal aspect of family caring relationships. Nevertheless, research conducted from the perspective of family members indicates that some experience both objective and subjective negative consequences from their relative's engagement with mental health services. Such impacts are likely to be the result of a complex interplay of factors including society's negative attitudes towards mental distress, the social welfare system's failure to adequately compensate carers economically, a lack of relatives' rights and gaps in mental health services for them.

The challenges of supporting a person experiencing mental distress and the associated 'burden' are not exclusive to the parents. Kartalova-O'Doherty et al.'s (2006) exploratory study found that the family members, and grandparents particularly, were concerned for those children whose parent had a mental health condition. Some children whose parent experiences mental distress not only assume age-inappropriate responsibilities (emotional and practical), such as caring for younger siblings and preparing meals, but also may become hyper-vigilant, assuming responsibility for parental safety and mental well-being (Riebschleger 2004, Houlihan et al. 2013a). Somers (1998), in an Irish study examining 37 service users with a diagnosis of schizophrenia and their children, found that the children experienced emotional distress, sadness and upset when their parent was unwell. Six of the children were responsible for suggesting to their parent that he/she may be unwell and should see a doctor, and four were responsible for reminding their parent to take medication. Children, irrespective of age, may also struggle to make sense of their parent's distress, may feel guilt that they in some way caused or worsened their parent's distress, or worry about being separated due to hospitalisation. Children also suffer from stigma and can become isolated from their peers because of feelings of fear and shame (Brown 2000; Handley et al. 2001).

The impact of mental/emotional distress on family members is not necessarily uniform either within the family or across different types of families. Kartalova-O'Doherty and Tedstone Doherty (2009) found some gender differences in family members' relationship with the individual with mental/emotional distress and with mental health services. In their small-scale study, a significantly higher proportion of those who were caring for their relative at home were female (p.261). While more than half of the male carers were satisfied with mental health services, 81.5% of female carers were dissatisfied with the services their relative was receiving. Male carers had better relationships with their relative, while more than half of the female carers found the relationship with the person in mental health treatment was 'mutually intrusive'. Kartalova-O'Doherty and Tedstone Doherty conclude that female family members may experience more burden than male family members, but acknowledge that the results in their study may reflect the fact that more of the female carers were living with the relative.

Burden can also be influenced by social class. Kartalova-O'Doherty and Tedstone Doherty (2009) found that carers of a higher socioeconomic status had a lower burden than those of lower status. Family members in a higher socioeconomic group were more satisfied with the level of support for their relatives and were also more positive about community supports (p.268). These results suggest that in addressing the impacts of mental/emotional distress on families, policy should take account of the different levels of impact based on social class and gender. Although the concept of 'family burden' largely arose out of research into the experience of family members of people with a diagnosis of schizophrenia, and some studies suggest that this diagnosis is associated with higher level of burden, Keogh's research, which was conducted in Ireland, found no significant difference in the experience of burden across diagnosis (Keogh 1998). Rather, the key issue appeared to be negative experiences at the initial stage of coming in contact with the mental health services, a finding also noted by Kartalova-O'Doherty and Tedstone Doherty (2009).

FAMILY SUPPORTERS IN IRISH MENTAL HEALTH LAW AND POLICY

The law has had a significant influence on the role of family members in mental health treatment in Ireland, both enabling and inhibiting their participation. The 1945 Mental Treatment Act began a process of reducing the role that family members played in admission procedures. Previously it was relatively easy for a family member to have their relative admitted to a psychiatric hospital indefinitely for any reason, regardless of whether they had a defined mental disorder, due to the vagueness of criteria for admission and the lack of a rigorous admission and discharge system. However, under the 1945 Act, a system of admission based on psychiatric assessment, along with increased use of internationally recognised diagnostic categories within these assessments, led to a more medically-controlled process for admission (see Brennan, Chapter 2). Though family members still had a role to play under the law in initiating admission, it became harder for them to have a relative admitted arbitrarily.

The 2001 Mental Health Act continued the statutory basis for family members' role in admission, providing that a spouse or relative can make an application for admission of an adult under the Act (Section 9(1)). However, Ralston notes that apart from this role, the 2001 Act is 'virtually silent' on the role of families in the treatment of their adult relative (Ralston 2013:13). The Act does not provide for an active role for families in their relative's treatment, neither a right to information, nor a right to involvement in discharge planning – nor does the Act create any statutory duty on mental health services to assess the support needs of family members. Ironically, Ralston notes that the 2001 Act does not provide a family member the right to attend the review (tribunal) hearing for their relative's detention even when they had initiated that detention (p.13). Ralston concludes that '… [i]t is evident from the 2001 Act that the best interests of the health service user are paramount with due regard to be given thereafter to the interests of other persons including family members …' (p.15).

Nevertheless, the Act makes one provision that could have had a positive impact on family members. The 2001 Act created the role of 'Authorised Officer' as someone independent of both the family and An Garda Síochána who could make an application for the person to be admitted to hospital. This role had the potential to relieve family members of the responsibility for initiating the admission process, minimise the trauma experienced by families as a result of being involved and reduce the possibility that the admission process would damage trust between the person admitted and the family member. However, unfortunately there has been little implementation of Authorised Officer positions across the mental health services and not surprisingly, in 2012 only 8% of admissions were initiated by an Authorised Officer compared to 57% initiated by a spouse or relative (Mental Health Commission 2012:35). It is clear that family members still play the predominant role in initiating involuntary admission of their relative, a situation that is problematic for maintaining good family relationships.

In terms of mental health policy, the two principle government documents *Planning for the Future* (Department of Health 1984) and *A Vision for Change* (Department of Health and Children 2006) mark important moments in defining a role for the family in modern mental health service delivery. Both envisage a substantial role for family members in the process of mental health support. As part of its programme for deinstitutionalisation and the development of community-based mental health services in Ireland, *Planning for the Future* contained a separate section on support for families (paras. 3.6-3.10). The study group who wrote the report highlighted evidence of burden on family members in the context of deinstitutionalisation, stating:

> The main burden of caring for a mentally ill person [sic] in the community, particularly a chronic psychotic patient [sic] living at home, may fall on the patient's family and the cost to the family, in terms of emotional stress, can be considerable. (para. 3.7)

It is clear that *Planning for the Future* recognised the potential for a policy of community-based mental health service provision to have an impact on family members and consequently sought to establish practices to address this impact. The study group emphasised the need for mental health services to 'accept some responsibility for the welfare of the family...' and set out some of the practices that services should consider when engaging with families, including education, advice and guidance and respite provision (para. 3.7). The study group went so far as to say that family members should be considered as part of the community mental health team (para. 3.8), particularly for individuals experiencing psychosis, and made the following specific recommendations on how mental health teams should engage with family members, including that teams have a role and commitment to:

- supporting family members of service users who live in the family home
- assigning a link person (a community mental health nurse) on the team to the family
- considering a role for the family in assessment and care planning
- providing respite care, and support to families in the event of a crisis (para. 3.10).

In 2006 the role of families was expressed in very similar ways in *A Vision for Change*, but for the first time in Irish government policy, it was counter-balanced by the role of service users. During the years since 1984, the rise of the service-user movement in Ireland resulted in increased pressure to have service users be recognised and involved in the decisions about their own treatment. *A Vision for Change* thus devotes considerable discussion to setting out the importance of involving service users in the mental health services. The policy recommends that both service users and carers be involved in every level of mental health service delivery, from the individual level of planning care to being members of management teams at local and national level. The document also reiterates the recommendations of *Planning for the Future* that mental health teams should support and engage with families as part of mental health service provision

(Recommendation 3.6). However, in relative terms, the document has less to say about the role of family members than about service users.

Following on from *A Vision for Change*, the Mental Health Commission produced a standard and a Code of Practice that included guidance on family involvement. The Commission's *Quality Framework* for mental health services sets standards for the involvement of family members in mental health treatment (Mental Health Commission 2007a). Standard 6.1 states that: 'Families, parents and carers are empowered as team members receiving information, advice and support as appropriate.' Yet the standard contains only three criteria about the role of families as supporters, and the first criterion is more concerned with ensuring that communication with family members be based on the service user's wishes than with meeting the needs of family members themselves. Only two criteria concern the needs of family members themselves: criteria 6.1.1 on the provision of information, and criteria 6.1.2 on the provision of support to the family and access to the individual's key worker. Thus while the standard reflects an intention to provide for family members' needs and a partnership role, the criteria are relatively narrow in their scope. The more recent National Carers' Strategy (Department of Health 2012) also sets out a series of actions to ensure that carers are recognised and respected as key care partners and included in decisions relating to the person that they are caring for. The strategy also recognises the need for carers to be supported through the provision of adequate information, training, services and supports.

The Mental Health Commission's *Code of Practice on Admission, Transfer and Discharge to and from an Approved Centre* (Mental Health Commission 2009) expresses an intention that family members should have 'active involvement' in their relative's treatment, where appropriate (para. 1.4); however this intention is unequally balanced with a more absolute requirement to respect the privacy of the individual service user (para. 5.1). Throughout the Code encouragement is given to mental health service providers to engage with family members in the areas of admission, transfer and discharge. In particularly, the Code recommends that 'every effort should be made to identify the support needs of the family/ carer, where appropriate, prior to discharge.' (para. 39.3), and recommends that keyworkers serve as a point of contact with family members (para. 20.4). However the Code's guidance is always constrained by the requirement to respect the relative's right to confidentiality. The Code's impact on practice is also limited by its non-binding status; it represents guidance to service providers but not a statutory requirement.

With reference to service-users' rights to confidentiality, practitioners are also working within other legal and professional frameworks. Although the term 'confidential' does not appear in the Irish Constitution, the courts have ruled that privacy is a core personal right and the right to confidentiality stems from that right, with a common-law duty to preserve professional confidence existing. Practitioners are also bound by codes of practice that emphasise client confidentiality, which emanate from their professional bodies such as the Medical Council or the Nursing and Midwifery Board of Ireland, and many may be bound by a confidentiality clause in their work contract. While an obligation of confidence can be breached if 'in the interest of: the law; the patient; other individuals and society', the principle of confidentiality holds an honoured place within the health professional-patients relationship (Dooley and McCarthy 2012:67).

These various policy documents, standards, codes and legal frameworks show that a disjuncture has developed between policy, law and practice over the past years. While mental health policy and other policy have consistently recognised that family members play a valued role in providing support for their relative with mental/emotional distress, the law has hindered such involvement by failing to provide a statutory basis for it, instead underpinning only the service-user's right to confidentiality. In this way, while policy, guidance and standards have highlighted the responsibilities of mental health services to support families, the law has served to make them invisible.

FAMILY SUPPORTERS' VIEWS ON THE MENTAL HEALTH SERVICES

While the amount of Irish research evidence into the experience of family members is small, some studies have shed light on their perspectives. Indicative of the neglect in research is that a search of the *Irish Journal of Psychological Medicine* for the purpose of this chapter found only one article on the family, dated 1991.

What evidence exists seems to indicate gaps in the supports available to family members. Despite consistent policy since 1984 advocating support and engagement with family supporters, and one survey which suggests that by the early 1990s, 86% of psychiatrists who responded were using family therapy in their practice (Sheerin 1991), there is a significant deficit in the formal supports currently available to families/supporters of people experiencing mental distress and accessing Irish mental health services. The majority of the 38 family participants in Kartalova-O'Doherty's and Tedstone Doherty's (2009) family support study reported having to rely on informal supports such as other relatives, friends and neighbours, and information resources such as books or television.

This lack of acknowledgment and involvement has led to widespread dissatisfaction with mental health services among family supporters. In the consultation undertaken for *A Vision for Change*, carers reported particular dissatisfaction with discharge planning, as family members received inadequate notice that their relative was being discharged (Department of Health and Children 2006). So too, while accepting the need to respect service-users' privacy, family supporters have expressed concern about the way that client confidentiality operates to withhold information from family members (Mental Health Commission 2005:85). A 2002 European survey *Breaking the silence* carried out by EUFAMI among family representatives of five European countries, including Ireland, reported that between 22% and 44% of the carers were dissatisfied or very dissatisfied with the quality of care provided for their family member and for themselves (de Haan et al. 2002). Most Irish carers were in the range between rather unsatisfied and rather satisfied, and most of their dissatisfaction related to wanting more information and advice on how to handle specific problems that arose while supporting their relative (de Haan et al. 2002). Another Irish study also found dissatisfaction with mental health service support, with a perceived lack of uniformity of services and supports provided to families across different catchment areas and between public and private sectors. The initial encounter with mental health services was often perceived to be the most dissatisfactory, with lack of information being a key issue: '[m]ost participants commented that there had been a lack of understanding, practical advice, or appropriate response at the time of their first contact for help' (Kartalova-O'Doherty et al. 2006). Family supporters who were most dissatisfied were those who reported 'a lack of open and trusting communication with psychiatrists' (Kartalova-O'Doherty and Tedstone Doherty 2009:266), experienced a lack of partnership between themselves and service providers, and reported an absence of services and supports in the community. In addition, dissatisfied participants also reported experiencing a clash between practitioners' desire to maintain the person's right to confidentiality regarding diagnosis and treatment, and the family need to understand how best to support and help their relative. Similarly, the 21 family members consulted by Higgins et al. (2012) spoke of a lack of information on how to cope with or respond to their family member, and a lack of involvement and support when family members were in crisis. Family members in the consultation part of this project also expressed anger and frustration at their marginalisation by the mental health system and considered that they were 'abandoned', 'left out' and 'lost' by the services (Higgins et al. 2012:9).

Despite *A Vision for Change* directing mental health service providers to be mindful of the presence of children whose parent has a mental health problem and to adopt supportive and child-friendly approaches to service provision, evidence of systematic practices or policies to support these children are notable by their absence from the Mental Health Commission Annual Reports (MHC 2007b, 2008 and 2012). Research involving Irish children reported that they had little experience of receiving help from any agency to deal with their parents' mental health condition and often experienced reluctance from others to discuss issues with them or involve them in any way (Somers 1998:135). This lack of emphasis on child- and family-focused practices within Irish mental health services was also highlighted in studies involving psychiatrists (O'Shea 2004) and mental health nurses (Houlihan et al. 2013 a, b) with both groups expressing concern about the quality of support and information offered to children.

LOOKING TO THE FUTURE: INNOVATIONS IN THE ROLE OF FAMILY SUPPORTERS IN IRELAND

Family supporters comprise a heterogeneous group, and as such their needs for support will depend on their individual personal, social and economic circumstances and the needs of those for whom they are caring. The needs of adult family members/supporters differ significantly from the needs of children or young adults with caring/support responsibilities. In addition, family members/ supporters from ethnic minority groups or other marginalised group may have additional needs or approach mental health support in culturally different ways.

Consultations and research with family supporters has identified a number of improvements that could be made to mental health service delivery in relation to family engagement. The Mental Health Commission's (2007a) consultation with family supporters in preparation for its *Quality Framework* identified the following key areas for improvement or development:

- factual information about what services are available, how they work and how to access help in a crisis
- a complaints mechanism for family members
- counselling and psychotherapy to help family supporters to handle their own stress and anxiety
- access for family supporters to a helpline or other support in a crisis
- access for family supporters to respite services
- access for service users to housing so that they are not forced to remain in the family home
- listening to and respecting the views of family supporters
- a keyworker or liaison for family members

In addition, the coalition Mental Health Reform (2012:10) seeks:

- a dedicated consultation with family members/significant others and the voluntary mental health sector to develop a mental health carer framework;
- provision in legislation for the role of carers and a duty on mental health services to assess carers' support needs; and
- assessment of the needs of the children of adult service-users where appropriate.

These recommendations are supported by a body of international research indicating that family support/information programmes not only improve family members' understanding of mental health issues but also reduce subjective burden, increase their sense of empowerment and improve their wellbeing and ability to cope (Dixon et al. 2004, Lucksted et al. 2004, Pickett-Schenk et al. 2006, 2008). They are also consistent with those of Kartalova-O'Doherty, Tedstone Doherty and Walsh (2006) who advocate for the introduction of a keyworker and report that family supporters who were most satisfied with the mental health services were those provided with family counselling and who had access to family support groups. Counselling was reported as being very helpful in enabling family members to establish unintrusive relationships with their relative and in helping relatives to hand over control and responsibility to the person for their own rehabilitation and recovery. Satisfied participants also felt they were accepted as partners in the mental health service and were provided with information about mental health issues, treatments and recovery.

There are a number of carer support/information groups being run by agencies such as Shine, Bodywhys, and Mental Health Ireland. For example, the Advanced Nurse Practitioner (ANP) in Recovery and Rehabilitation in East Galway works in partnership with the SHINE office in the West, where they facilitate a monthly Relatives' Support Group meeting. This group is seen as an integral part of the local CMHT service and is used to promote the overall recovery of the family unit through meeting and sharing with others with similar experiences. At a wider community level the County Galway Vocational Educational Committee has provided funding to support a variety of self-care and stress-management initiatives for families. Evaluation data from these initiatives suggest that they are welcomed by family members and are a major source of informational and emotional support (Cleary et al. 2013). Similarly, a family-focused education programme (EOLAS) is being piloted in a number of services in the eastern region (Higgins et al. 2013). Other recovery initiatives that include family members are the Trialogues, the Cooperative Learning and Leadership Programme and the Wellness Recovery Action Planning education programmes (see Higgins and McGowan Chapter 5). In terms of information provision advising carers how to be involved in their relatives' recovery, a booklet titled *The Journey Together* was published in 2007 as a joint initiative between the National Service Users Executive, the Irish Advocacy Network, Shine and HSE Mental Health. While these are all welcome responses to the needs of families, there is an inconsistency in developments across services and regions, resulting in minimal innovation in the area of family involvement within mainstream mental health services. Not surprisingly, therefore, the Implementation Monitoring Group (IMG) for *A Vision for Change* recently noted that 'In respect of family members it would appear that more often than not the specific need of members are not identified and acknowledged in the care planning process' (IMG 2012:43).

CONCLUSION

Family members/supporters are an important part of the environment for mental health recovery. When family members have a good understanding of mental health and ways of coping, they can play a positive role in supporting recovery. However, family members have struggled to be recognised within Irish mental health policy, practice, research and law. Contradictory positions on the role of 'carer' or family supporter have appeared in Irish mental health law and policy since 1945 in which the role of the family has sometimes been promoted and at other times neglected or made invisible. Supporters also have their own needs for mental health, economic and social support. Yet there is relatively little research about the experience of family supporters in Ireland compared with the quantity of research both about and by service users. And in practice, many family members have felt excluded from the process of mental health support due to the growing emphasis on the individual service-user's human rights and professional commitments to patient confidentiality. One of the key questions for mental health practitioners in the future will be how to rebalance the respective roles of family supporters and individuals with mental/emotional distress so that everyone who is affected can recover.

*

REFLECTIVE QUESTIONS FOR DISCUSSION AND DEBATE: PRACTICE

- Would involving family members in mental health services only serve to further marginalise the service-user's voice?
- Does research that explores family members' experiences using the construct of 'burden' perpetuate a negative stereotype of people who experience mental/emotional distress?

REFLECTIVE STATEMENTS FOR DISCUSSION AND DEBATE: RESEARCH

- There is a need for studies to evaluate the effectiveness and cost-effectiveness of interventions to support family carers of people with mental distress.
- The needs and experiences of children who take on caring responsibilities require more in-depth exploration.

REFERENCES

Brown M J, Roberts D P (2000) Growing up with a Schizophrenic Mother. Jefferson, NC: McFarland and Company Inc.

Central Statistics Office (2012) Profile 8: Our Bill of Health. Dublin: Stationery Office

Cleary A, Walsh F, Dowling M (2013) The lived experience of family caregivers of a relative experiencing ongoing symptoms of a major mental illness. 13th Annual Interdisciplinary Research Conference. Transforming healthcare through research and education. School of Nursing and Midwifery, Trinity College Dublin. 7 November

de Haan L, Kramer L, van Raay B, Weir M, Gardner J, Akselson S, Ladinser E, McDaid S, Hernandez-Dols S, Wouters L (2002) 'Priorities and Satisfaction on the Help Needed and Provided in a First Episode of Psychosis: A survey in five European family associations'. European Psychiatry 17:425-433

Department of Health (1984) The Psychiatric Services – Planning for the Future: Report of a Study Group on the Development of the Psychiatric Service. Dublin: Stationery Office

Department of Health and Children (2006) A Vision for Change: Report of the Expert Group on Mental Health Policy. Dublin: Stationery Office

Department of Health (2012) National Carers' Strategy: Recognised, Supported, Empowered Dublin: Stationery Office

Dooley D, McCarthy J (2012) Nursing Ethics: Irish cases and concerns. Dublin: Gill and Macmillan

Drapin A L, Dixon L B (2011) 'Programmes to support family members and caregivers' in Graham Thornicroft, George Szmukler, Kim T. Mueser and Robert E. Drake (eds.) The Oxford Textbook of Community Mental Health, Oxford: Oxford University Press 188-194

Fromm-Reichmann F (1948) Notes on the development of treatment of schizophrenics by psychoanalysis and psychotherapy. Psychiatry 11:263-273

Gamble C, Brennan G, (eds.) (2006) 'Working with Families & Informal Carers' in Working with Serious Mental Illness: A Manual for Clinical Practice (2nd ed). Edinburgh: Elsevier

Gosden R (2001) Punishing the Patient: How Psychiatrists Misunderstand and Mistreat Schizophrenia. Melbourne: Scribe Publications Pty Ltd

Government of Ireland (1945) Mental Treatment Act. Dublin: Stationery Office

Government of Ireland (2001) Mental Health Act. Dublin: Stationery Office

Handley C, Farrell G A, Josephs A, Hanke A, Hazeldon M (2001) The Tasmanian Children's Project: The needs of children with a parent/carer with a mental illness. Australian and New Zealand Journal of Mental Health Nursing 10 (4) 221-228

Higgins A, Breen M, Boyd F, Heavey D, Sharek D, McBennett P (2012) An evaluation of a peer and clinician led psychoeducation programme for people diagnosed with severe mental health difficulties Final Report. Dublin: Dublin School of Nursing and Midwifery Trinity College

Houlihan D, Sharek D, Higgins A (2013a) Supporting children whose parent has a mental health problem: An assessment of the education, knowledge, confidence and practices of registered psychiatric nurses in Ireland. Journal of Psychiatric and Mental Health Nursing 20 (4) 287-295

Houlihan D, Sharek D, Higgins A (2013b) Psychiatric nurses' attitudes towards children visiting their parent in a mental health ward. Irish Journal of Psychological Medicine, Available on CJO 2013 doi:10.1017/ipm.2013.50 [ePub ahead of print]

Independent Monitoring Group (2012) Sixth Annual Report on Implementation: 2011 available at www.dohc.ie/publications/vision_for_change

Kartalova-O'Doherty Y, Tedstone Doherty D, Walsh D (2006) Family Support Study: A study of experiences, needs and support requirements of families with enduring mental illness in Ireland. Dublin: Health Research Board

Kartalova-O'Doherty Y, Tedstone Doherty D (2009) Satisfied Carers of Persons with Mental Illness: Who and why? International Journal of Social Psychiatry 55:257-271

Keogh F (1998) Family Burden and Mental Illness in Ireland: a thesis submitted in partial fulfilment of the requirements of Trinity College Dublin for the degree of Doctor of Philosophy. Dublin: Trinity College Dublin

Leff J P, Vaughn C E (1981) The role of maintenance therapy and relatives' expressed emotion in relapse of schizophrenia: A two-year follow-up. British Journal of Psychiatry 139:102-104

Maybery D, Reupert A, Kent P, Goodyear M, Crase L (2009) Prevalence of parental mental illness in Australian families. Psychiatric Bulletin 33:22-26

Mental Health Commission (2005) Quality in Mental Health – Your Views: Report on Stakeholder Consultation on Quality in Mental Health Services. Dublin: Mental Health Commission

Mental Health Commission (2007a) Quality Framework for Mental Health Services in Ireland. Dublin: Mental Health Commission

Mental Health Commission (2007b) Annual Report 2007 including the Report of the Inspector of Mental Health Service. Dublin: Mental Health Commission

Mental Health Commission (2008) Annual Report 2008 including the Report of the Inspector of Mental Health Services. Dublin: Mental Health Commission

Mental Health Commission (2012) Annual Report 2012 including the Report of the Inspector of Mental Health Services. Dublin: Mental Health Commission

Mental Health Commission (2009) Mental Health Commission's Code of Practice on Admission, Transfer and Discharge to and from an Approved Centre. Dublin: Mental Health Commission

Mental Health Reform (2012) Guiding A Vision for Change – Manifesto. Dublin: Mental Health Reform

O'Shea R, Sheerin D, Canavan D, Russell V (2004) Attitudes to visits by children to parents hospitalized with acute psychiatric illness. Irish Journal of Psychological Medicine 21 (2) 43-47

Platt S (1985) Measuring the burden of psychiatric illness on the family: An evaluation of some rating scales, Psychological Medicine 15 (2) 383-393

Ralston J (2013) Mental Health Support: The role of the family/carers/significant others in Irish and international law. Mental Health Reform: unpublished report: 13

Riebschleger J (2004) Good days and bad days: The experiences of children of a parent with a psychiatric disability. Psychiatric Rehabilitation Journal 28 (1) 25-31

Sheerin F (1991) Psychiatrists and family therapy: Impressions at the interface of ideology and practice. Irish Journal of Psychological Medicine 8 (2) 138-143

Schene A H (1990) Objective and subjective dimensions of family burden. Social Psychiatry and Psychiatric Epidemiology 25:285-297

Schene A H, van Wijngaarden B, Koeter M W J (1998) Family Caregiving in Schizophrenia: Domains and distress. Schizophrenia Bulletin 24 (4) 609-618

Somers V (1998) Schizophrenia: The impact of parental illness on children. Unpublished MLitt thesis: Trinity College Dublin

9

Mental health needs of minority ethnic communities in Ireland: contexts and controversies

Rebecca Murphy and Gerry Leavey

INTRODUCTION

For decades, if not centuries, Ireland was a net exporter of mostly young unmarried migrants and today it is home to a considerable diversity of people from black and ethnic minority (BME) communities. While many migrants sought a new home in Ireland because of the employment and economic opportunities that the now-deflated Celtic Tiger promised, many others found themselves on this island seeking sanctuary from war, civil unrest and torture. The speed at which this expansion has occurred has not been matched by a commensurate response in the development of health and social care policies designed to anticipate the difficulties faced by BME communities or to accommodate their needs within the relevant public services.

We know from epidemiological evidence in other countries that people from migrant and minority ethnic communities tend to be more vulnerable to 'mental illness', but the circumstances, contexts and factors associated with migration are highly varied as are the factors which shape a positive settlement. While of course it is true that significant historical, social and economic differences exist between Western states we can still discern an epidemiological patterning in BME mental health problems. We can also identify commonalities across different national health services that determine a similarity of access, experience, engagement and institutional response. Ireland should be able to take advantage of the experiences and knowledge gained in other Western settings.

This chapter seeks to draw on the evidence on mental illness and minority ethnic and migrant communities in other Western states in order to suggest how Irish mental health services could respond appropriately to BME communities. We review the evidence on inequalities of access, treatment and outcomes in the provision of mental health services, sifting through perspectives in which structural or discriminatory practices contrast with cultural problems and the difficulties of cultural competency. We then suggest ways in which Ireland might learn from them, improving the well-being of migrant and BME communities and providing mental health and social care services that are appropriate, accessible and produce beneficial outcomes.

ETHNIC MINORITIES IN IRELAND: DEMOGRAPHICS AND POLICY

The ethnic composition of Ireland has been transformed over a short period of time. While the minority Traveller Community has been a long-term feature of Irish society, the proportion of 'non-nationals' living in Ireland has more than doubled from 5.8% of the population in 2006 to 12% of the population in 2011, with a diversity of people from over 199 different nations (Central Statistics Office 2012). The ethnic profile of non-nationals includes a large percentage (9.3%) of those who identify as 'any other white background' reflecting the significant number of people living in Ireland from the UK, Polish and other former Eastern-Bloc countries. The remaining ethnicities include Chinese (0.4%), non-Chinese Asian (1.5%) and African (1.3%). Ireland's indigenous ethnic minority, Irish Travellers, make up 0.6 % of the population. It must be noted, however, that the construction of the ethnic categories cited in the Census is strongly contested, due to arguably inappropriate and crude parameters of the options included.

Ireland is party to the UN Convention on Economic, Social and Cultural Rights and as such is required to uphold the right of all individuals to 'culturally appropriate' health services, as outlined in the UN Committee's General Comment 14 (United Nations 2000). How best to provide appropriate services for the newly arrived communities has provoked interest from Irish academics and clinicians at both local and national levels. Such efforts, however, have arguably achieved little more than identifying the areas of concern for BME communities in Ireland, compiling sets of recommendations and outlining priority areas for action.

In 2009, the College of Psychiatry of Ireland published a position paper on the mental health needs of asylum seekers and refugees (Nwachukwu et al. 2009). The College's three recommendations focused on developing consultant-led multidisciplinary teams, training in the transcultural aspects of psychiatry and the preparation of psychiatric reports for asylum seekers. The paper also acknowledged the potentially negative mental health effects of the Irish asylum seeking process and reaffirmed the Irish Psychiatric Association's recommendation that:

> Health services and mental health services should be systematically informed and trained for the reality that culturally sensitive mental health

care is now a requirement of modern Ireland. The extra needs of non-national communities should be widely and properly provisioned for. (Nwachukwu 2009:3)

The Irish government's mental health policy, *A Vision for Change*, also acknowledged an ethnic and cultural dimension to mental distress, stating, 'Mental Health Services should be provided in a culturally sensitive manner' (Department of Health and Children 2006:41). The policy recommended the resourcing of mental health services to enable them to become 'culturally sensitive', which would include the provision of interpreters. No further elaboration was made as to what a 'culturally sensitive' service would involve, what the content or format of training would or should be, how it should be rolled out, or if it was to be mandatory or voluntary. Our limited evidence suggests that the *Vision for Change* recommendations have not been acted upon.

In 2007, a more comprehensive initiative for the whole public health service was developed: the National Intercultural Strategy 2007-2012 (NIHS) (Health Service Executive 2008). The strategy identified the need to make generic health services more appropriate and accessible to BME communities in Ireland. It set out four priority areas for development:

- information, language and communication
- service delivery and access to services
- changing the organization, and
- working in partnership with ethnic minority communities

Due to the starkly different economic situation since the strategy's introduction in 2007, the emphasis of the National Intercultural Health Strategy (NIHS) Committee's work quickly shifted to implementing quick and cost-effective recommendations including the translation of core health-related information into the major languages spoken in Ireland (Nurse 2009) (none of which are specific to mental health services), good practice guidelines for working with interpreters and a HSE intercultural guide. The timeframe for the NIHS has now expired and few of its recommendations have been implemented. At the time of writing, there are no evident plans for an extension of the Strategy. However, the HSE's National Service Plan 2012 'adopted' three of the NIHS's recommendations (Health Service Executive 2012) including the roll-out of a national database to increase staff access to relevant translated materials, the extension of an 'ethnic identifier' to record health information on BME groups, and lastly, to improve the accessibility, data and staff support needed to ensure ongoing culturally competent service delivery. To the best of our knowledge, successful implementation of these recommendations has not occurred in 2012.

THE PREVALENCE OF MENTAL HEALTH PROBLEMS AMONG BLACK AND MINORITY ETHNIC COMMUNITIES

In Ireland, with the exception of annual inpatient statistics which arguably offer little insight into the composition of BME admissions (Daly and Walsh 2012), there are limited national mental health data disaggregated by country of birth, ethnicity or immigration status, especially in relation to outpatient services. The few studies that do offer a glimpse of what may be happening in mental health services are limited to local services, include heterogeneous samples and are mostly restricted to a quantitative focus (Clare 2002, Feeney et al. 2002, Foley-Nolan et al. 2002, Kelly et al. 2008, Kennedy et al. 2002, Linehan et al. 2002). By contrast, internationally, there is extensive data on such issues. Evidence gathered elsewhere shows that BME communities are often considered to have a higher susceptibility to developing mental health difficulties and are often diagnosed with more enduring mental health difficulties and at a higher rate when compared to the native populations. Higher rates of schizophrenia among migrants were first noted by Ödegaard in his study of migrant Norwegians to the USA (Ödegaard 1932). Since then consistent evidence from the UK and elsewhere indicates greater incidence of psychosis among 'African Caribbeans' compared to white British people (Boydell et al. 2001, Goater et al. 1999, Harrison et al. 1988, King et al. 1994), an issue which has dominated psychiatric epidemiology for many years (Bhugra 2004, Littlewood and Lipsedge 1997). A recent meta-analysis found a mean weighted relative risk of schizophrenia among first-generation migrants of 2.7% (95% CI 2.3-3.2); and even higher rates were found in the second generation (Kirmayer et al. 2011).

Refugees and asylum seekers

Fazel et al.'s 2005 meta-analysis estimates that about one in ten adult refugees in Western countries has diagnosable Post Traumatic Stress Disorder (PTSD), about one in 20 fulfil a diagnosis for major depression and about one in 25 could fulfil a diagnosis of generalised anxiety disorder, with a high probability of co-morbidity (Fazel et al. 2005). The few relevant Irish studies surmise that Irish rates are in keeping with other international studies (Kelly et al. 2008, Kennedy et al. 2002).

The Irish Traveller Community

There is limited research in Ireland on the mental health needs of members of the Irish Traveller community. The *All-Ireland Traveller Health Study – Our Geels 2010* (Kelleher et al. 2010) found that there are seven times more instances of suicide among Traveller men than in the general population. This study also gave an indication of the self-reported psychological needs of Irish Travellers;

62.7% of Irish Traveller women said that their mental health was not good for one or more days in the last 30 days compared to 19.9% of female medical-card-holders from the broader population. Among Irish Traveller men, 59.4% said that their mental health was not good for one or more days in the last 30 days compared to 13.5% of male medical-card-holders from the broader population.

REASONS BEHIND INCREASED RATES

It has been argued that different types of migration (e.g. asylum seekers and economic migrants) may be too neatly dichotomised, suggesting quite different antecedent experiences and thus, a differential vulnerability to mental distress. While people accorded refugee or asylum-seeking status are generally recognised to have suffered a traumatic experience in their homeland, the more prosaic experiences of so-called 'economic migrants' are less examined and understood (Leavey et al. 2007). Of course, while adverse events may make people vulnerable, the settlement experiences of migrants may also determine outcomes, and in this respect we can consider access to housing, health and welfare services, education and the opportunity to work (Lakeman et al. 2008). In particular, in the case of asylum seekers, the protracted asylum-seeking process has gained increasing attention in recent years for its detrimental impact on asylum seekers' mental health (Nwachukwu et al. 2009). However, in addition to the often-limited access to these socio-structural opportunities, migrants, whether economic or forced, may face hostility and rejection on racial grounds by local populations (Lakeman et al. 2008, McGinnity et al. 2006, Sanders and Whyte 2006). Recent research suggests the protective effects of ethnic density which hint at problems of low social capital may shed some light on why some ethnic minority populations appear more vulnerable to a range of mental disorders compared to others in apparently similar circumstances (Das-Munshi et al. 2012, Weich et al. 2004, Wilson et al. 2010).

ETHNIC MINORITIES' MENTAL HEALTH NEEDS: EXPLANATORY MODELS OF MENTAL ILLNESS

Beliefs within different ethnic minorities about the causes of mental health difficulties can influence a wide range of clinically relevant variables, such as coping, help-seeking behaviour, compliance, therapeutic relationships and treatment satisfaction (Ghane et al. 2012). The explanatory models of mental/ emotional distress may vary considerably between and within cultures (Kleinman 1987, Littlewood and Lipsedge 1997). Thus, causal explanations of mental health difficulties that lie outside normative medical explanations may lead to delays in getting access to appropriate psychiatric help. When they do, there is also evidence of poor engagement with services and relatively poor outcomes

(McCabe and Priebe 2004). While there is evidence that stigma concerning mental health difficulties may be more prevalent among BME communities compared to white Western populations (Knifton 2012), the factors that lay behind the stigma need further unpacking, bound up as they are with social class, education, religion and social connectedness (individualist or collectivist cultures), all of which may play a determining role in pathways into care and the degree of engagement with services.

Religion

Religion and supernatural beliefs may be salient to the individual's conceptualisation of suffering and distress, prompting a help-seeking pathway that involves some form of spiritual or religious resolution or amelioration. Again, although not unique to minority ethnic communities, supernatural beliefs concerning spiritual disturbance and spirit possession have much stronger currency among non-Western cultures. For example, Pentecostalism, a strongly experiential religion with a literal attachment to biblical text on witchcraft and demonic possession, has grown rapidly among many African communities in Western settings. Pentecostal beliefs and practices seldom sit well with secular health systems and in the UK have provoked considerable alarm, as in the Victoria Climbié[i] case (Laming 2003). Similarly, among Muslim communities, beliefs in black magic and jinn possession as explanations for mental illness or emotional distress remain powerful and problematic for individuals and for services (Leavey et al. 2007). How psychiatry should engage and accommodate supernatural beliefs and healing practices is still unresolved (Leavey and King 2007). Nevertheless, given the central importance of faith-based organisations and religious leaders in many migrant communities, it is essential that mental health services and religious groups establish a two-way dialogue in which mental health literacy and cultural beliefs about disorders are exchanged (Leavey et al. 2007).

Somatic illness

The somatisation of mental illness in which bodily symptoms can be understood as a manifestation of mental distress has been much explored and described. While somatisation is certainly not restricted to BME communities, it may be more prevalent among such communities, again, for reasons associated with stigma (Keyes and Ryff 2003, Kleinman 1977, Ohaeri and Odejide 1994). For others, however, symptoms are connected to social situations, past experiences and adjustment or settlement issues rather than a mental disorder (Patel 1995). Franks et al. found that some mental health difficulties, for example depression, were not recognised as an issue to be addressed by a mental health professional but rather as part of a normal process of adjustment (Franks et al. 2007).

The differing and somewhat conflicting ideologies between people from BME groups and mental health professionals may have a significant impact on the mental health care experiences of BME groups. Many ethnic minorities recognise this disparity and consequently believe that their opinions and beliefs may not be fully taken into account or considered when attending mental health services. Ethnic minority groups fear that health care providers will not comprehend what they are trying to say and that their beliefs may be disregarded, disrespected or misunderstood by health care providers, with the consequence that ineffective treatment may be provided (Reitmanova and Gustafson 2009).

Language

The existence, efficiency and quality of interpreting services for ethnic minorities significantly influence BME groups' satisfaction with mental health services. The infrequency of encountering a clinician with the same language (Saechao et al. 2012) means that using interpreters is the most feasible way to communicate. Finding an interpreter of rare languages and/or interpreters who are culturally and/or politically appropriate are also key factors, either due to gender or political differences (Asgary and Segar 2011). The lack of professional interpreters means that BME individuals may not appropriately access services or understand care providers. There is significant fear amongst some about the use of interpreters due to sensitivity of the discussion and the risk that the interpreter will disclose information revealed in the clinical encounter to others in their community (Reitmanova and Gustafson 2009). However, a lack of or unwillingness to use professional interpreters may necessitate the use of family members, resulting in potentially damaging miscommunication, breaches of confidentiality, vicarious traumatisation and an erosion of traditional family roles (Sadavoy et al. 2004).

ETHNIC MINORITIES' INEQUITABLE MENTAL HEALTH CARE EXPERIENCES

People from BME communities appear to have worse experiences than their white counterparts while in contact with mental health services, including delays in seeking professional help, less chance of a medical referral, greater involvement of the police and emergency services and higher proportions of compulsory and secure-unit admissions (Bhui et al. 2003, Linehan et al. 2002). When attending services, they may be less likely to be offered 'talking therapies', more likely to receive higher drug dosages, to be diagnosed with schizophrenia and to endure coercive and restraining practices than their white counterparts (Bhui et al. 2003, Lawlor et al. 2012, McLean et al. 2003, Morgan et al. 2005,

Morgan et al. 2004). However, two recent reviews have highlighted a number of methodological problems that characterise much of the previous research in this area (Bhui et al. 2003, Morgan et al. 2004) including the use of crude ethnic categories; small and heterogeneous sample sizes; limited adjustment for potentially confounding factors; and an over-emphasis on inpatient samples with little focus on community-based populations, and even less on qualitative evidence (Weich et al. 2012). Moreover, there has been a gradual recognition of the complex interplay of numerous contributory factors: social, cultural and institutional. In particular, two studies that have considered pathways to care in patients with a first episode of psychosis have both found no association between ethnicity and compulsory admission (Burnett et al. 1999, Cole et al. 1995). The factors significantly associated with compulsory admission in Cole et al.'s (1995) sample were living alone, living in public housing, the absence of a GP or family's/friends' involvement in the pathway to care and living away from family. After other factors were controlled for, only the absence of a GP and the involvement of family/friends remained statistically significant. Burnett et al. (1999) similarly found that socio-demographic and service-related factors were the most important in pathways to care at first contact.

Thus, it is often the distribution of economic and social resources that explains health and other outcomes in the vast majority of studies. Perhaps for this reason, levels of mental distress need to be understood less in terms of individual pathology and more as a response to relative deprivation and social injustice, which can erode the emotional, spiritual and intellectual resources essential to psychological wellbeing. Resettling in new host countries can bring hope and optimism to some; for others it brings often unexpected stressors. An extensive body of research suggests that post-migration stressors can include social and economic strain, social alienation, discrimination and status loss (Pumariega et al. 2005). In particular, ethnic minorities from cultures that are extremely different from Western cultures face distinct challenges in terms of individual identity and family life (Bhugra 2004, Bhugra and Becker 2005).

In light of this evidence, there is growing recognition that while developing cultural understanding is essential for providing good care for BME groups, it is also important to recognise that a number of socio-structural issues can also affect health and access to health services.

BME MENTAL HEALTH SERVICE PROVISION

Internationally, culturally and racially diverse societies increasingly acknowledge and recommend that all mental health professionals and services be 'culturally competent'. The concept of 'cultural competence' essentially aims to make health care services more accessible, acceptable and effective for people from BME communities. While the drive for cultural competency among services is generally considered well-intentioned (Whitley 2007), there is no consensus as to the definition of cultural competency, what the essential components are, or how cultural competency actually plays out in practice. In fact, not only is there no consensus, but it has been described as outright 'confusion' (Bhui et al. 2007).

Cultural competence has been defined numerous times, each time with different emphases and foci on particular aspects; Cross et al. define it as 'a set of congruent behaviours, attitudes, and policies that come together in a system, agency, or among professionals and enable that system, agency, or those professionals to work effectively in cross-cultural situations' (Cross et al. 1989:iv), whilst Betancourt et al. state that it is 'the ability of systems to provide care to patients with diverse values, beliefs and behaviours, including tailoring delivery to meet patients' social, cultural, and linguistic needs' (Betancourt et al. 2003:v). It is argued that these definitions provide little guidance as to *how* to achieve a gold standard of cultural competency.

In an effort to unpack these definitions, some have tried to identify the key components of successful cultural competency. However, there is equally as much confusion in this regard, with many citing long lists and multiple configurations of alleged 'optimal' cultural competency models. Neither does the identification of these components necessarily guarantee any success in putting them to use. Cultural competence in operation can look and feel very different (Bhui et al. 2007, Fernando 2005, Ganesan and Janze 2005, Kirmayer et al. 2003, Lo and Chung 2005) depending on the situation; different countries have approached the mental health care concerns of ethnic minorities within their own unique frameworks with corresponding foci, reflecting their specific histories of immigration, national attitudes towards migrants, citizenship, and racial and cultural integration policies (Hernandez et al. 2009). This diversity of approach makes it extremely difficult to efficiently compare and assess results across and between countries.

One of the principal concerns about how to achieve cultural competence is the question of whether specialist mental health services should be developed for BME communities. The advantages of such specialist services are considerable. They often involve health professionals with comprehensive knowledge of cultural factors. Thus, though there is little evidence of the effectiveness of specialist services, it is theorised that there would be less of a cultural gulf between the service users and the professionals in such a system, which would then lead to better engagement and outcomes. In regards to ethnically matched specialist services, in which the ethnicity of the health professionals is matched to that of the service user, BME service users are thought to be more likely to be 'understood' by the professional, thus reducing the need for interpreters, 'culture brokers' and the time required to conduct a competent assessment (Sue 1998).

In Ireland, such specialist services are few, and all are located in central Dublin, each with a specific focus on subsets of the BME community. SPIRASI and the HSE Psychology Service for Refugees and Asylum Seekers (PSRAS) accept referrals country-wide for refugees and asylum seekers only. Similarly, The Travelling Counselling Service offers services to the Irish Traveller community. The former Cultural Psychiatry Clinic (CPC) at the Mater Hospital was the only specialist service offering care to all migrants in the Mater catchment area but it is no longer operating (Kelly et al. 2008). Such services, whether located in Ireland or internationally, do not evaluate process and outcome (Beach et al. 2005, Bhui et al. 2007, Lim et al. 2008, Price et al. 2005), which somewhat limits the potential for transferability to other countries and contexts. Furthermore, in other countries, such specialist services are usually restricted to the voluntary sector and have time-limited budgets, which negates any opportunities for service development, evaluation, teaching or training (Bhui et al. 2000). Although ethnically matched specialist services have their benefits, they also have their difficulties, principally that the resources to fully develop dedicated services for every ethnic group are not available (Bhui et al. 2000). Problems may arise when the service, albeit for pragmatic reasons, is based on race, ignoring differences in culture, religion, place of origin and social class (Sue 2006). In addition, the development of dedicated specialist services often lets the mainstream service 'off the hook'. Therefore, dedicated services can be counter-productive in working towards integration and particularly so for Irish national mental health policies, which call for improvements in the quality of mental health services for all populations (Kelly 2009).

Ireland must be cognisant of the lessons learned in other countries in this regard. Whilst both ethno-specific services and cultural competency have their advantages and disadvantages when applied broadly to mainstream services, if they are initiated in isolation they are often 'tokenistic' or piecemeal strategies. The advantage of specialist services is that they have the confidence and trust of BME communities and are perceived as places of comfort and care and not coercion, but they often lack sufficient funding and thus are not sustainable for the future (Bhui et al. 2000). The overarching advantage of implementing cultural competency in generic mainstream services is that responsibility for delivering equitable services is placed on all and not just the token few; yet its generic approach has been criticised for 'essentializing, commodifying and appropriating culture, leading to stereotyping and further disempowerment of patients' (Kirmayer 2012:160). Thus the necessity to collaborate between specialist and generic mental health services is potentially the way forward (Bhui et al. 2000). This would necessitate the commitment of national health bodies to adequately fund and invest in high-quality specialist services which would work in partnership with mainstream services with shared accountability and clear detailed operational agreements. Successful and effective cultural competency strategies must have an efficient interpreting service. However, interpreting services in Ireland are under no regulatory or professional body. There is a need to implement such a regulation system, perhaps like the Australian system of accreditation and specialisation.

In addition, the majority of the described approaches concentrates entirely on the treatment and rehabilitation of individuals with existing mental health problems with little focus on prevention and mental health promotion. However, in order to address the mental health inequalities of BME groups, we must also pursue and prioritise promotion and prevention (European Commission 2005). Promotion of mental health and prevention of mental ill health addresses individual, family, community and social determinants of mental health by strengthening protective factors (e.g., resilience) and reducing risk factors (poor housing, unemployment, low income and status) (European Commission 2005). Initiatives include early years and home visiting programmes for families at risk, parenting programmes, pre-school and school-based programmes for young people, comprehensive interventions in the workplace, and community and health service programmes (Barry 2007). Ireland is keeping pace with our European neighbours in this regard (Llopis and Anderson 2006) despite no explicit or co-ordinated national policy framework (Llopis and Anderson 2006). A number of opportunities to strengthen existing mental health promotion efforts have been identified (Llopis and Anderson 2006) yet they do not cite the necessity for initiatives which specifically target BME communities. Generic mental health promotion programmes, which tend to 'speak' to a white, middle-class population, cannot simply be applied across populations but need to recognise the diversity of Ireland's national profile and begin to develop strategies in collaboration with the communities it seeks to target (Department of Health 2004).

FUTURE POLICY AND ACTION

Early intervention is a well-established concept in health care and social policy which has obvious relevance to safeguarding the well-being of migrant communities and the Traveller Community in Ireland, pre-empting the costs attached to mental health difficulties. However, the lessons from the UK and other Western countries indicate the need for a number of actions. First, national data on health service use by people from BME communities in Ireland is limited. In order to develop appropriate, accessible services, there is an urgent need to initiate a more comprehensive strategy on ethnic monitoring of services with regard to access, process and outcomes. Moreover, ethnic monitoring should be extended to all areas that have a direct impact on health and well-being – housing, employment, education and the criminal justice system.

Second, it is important to develop a better understanding of how cultural competency can be understood and developed within services. As we noted previously, this is no simple task. Rather, it demands an acknowledgement of cultural heterogeneity between and within minority ethnic groups and certainly must reach further than simple recognition of religious festivals or dietary regulations. We also need honest recognition of the delineation between culturally determined behaviours, mental health difficulties and the role of structural factors like poverty and discrimination. In connection with this, there is an obvious need to gain an understanding of the lives of migrant and ethnic minority communities in Ireland, and this will require a much stronger engagement with the BME communities by both academic institutions and health services.

*

REFLECTIVE QUESTIONS FOR DISCUSSION AND DEBATE: PRACTICE

- Do you have friends, relatives or acquaintances who are members of BME/Traveller communities? How much do you understand about their lives and beliefs?
- Can you identify elements of health services that may exclude or deter members of BME/Traveller communities?
- Have you attended any training on ethnicity and culture? If so, what did you find useful?
- If you could design a culturally competent mental health service, what elements do you think would be crucial to it?

REFLECTIVE QUESTIONS FOR DISCUSSION AND DEBATE: RESEARCH

- There is a dearth of evidence about the mental health of BME/Traveller communities in Ireland. Which areas of research do you think should be prioritised, and why?
- What lessons can we learn from other countries' research before Ireland conducts its own?

REFERENCES

Asgary R, Segar N (2011) Barriers to health care access among refugee asylum seekers. Journal of Health Care for the Poor and Underserved 22 (2) 506-22

Barry M M (2007) Generic principles of effective mental health promotion. International Journal of Mental Health Promotion 9 (2) 4-16

Beach M C, Price E G, Gary T L, Robinson K A, Gozu A, Palacio A, Smarth C, Jenckes M W, Feuerstein C, Bass E B (2005) Cultural competency: a systematic review of health care provider educational interventions. Medical Care 43 (4) 356-373

Betancourt J R, Green A R, Carrillo J E, Ananeh-Firempong O (2003) Defining cultural competence: a practical framework for addressing racial/ethnic disparities in health and health care. Public health reports 118 (4) 293-302

Bhugra D (2004) Migration and mental health. Acta Psychiatrica Scandinavica 109 (4) 243-258

Bhugra D (2004) Migration distress and cultural identity. British Medical Bulletin 69 (1) 129-141

Bhugra D, Becker M A (2005) Migration cultural bereavement and cultural identity. World Psychiatry 4 (1) 18-24

Bhui K, Bhugra D, McKenzie K (2000) Specialist services for minority ethnic groups? Maudsley discussion paper no. 8. London: Institute of Psychiatry

Bhui K, Stansfeld S, Hull S, Priebe S, Mole F, Feder G (2003) Ethnic variations in pathways to and use of specialist mental health services in the UK Systematic review. The British Journal of Psychiatry 182 (2) 105-116

Bhui K, Warfa N, Edonya P, McKenzie K, Bhugra D (2007) Cultural competence in mental health care: a review of model evaluations. BMC Health Service Research 7:15

Boydell J, van Os J, McKenzie K, Allardyce J, Goel R, McCreadie R G, Murray R M (2001) Incidence of schizophrenia in ethnic minorities in London: ecological study into interactions with environment. British Medical Journal 323 (7325) 1336-1338

Burnett R, Mallett R, Bhugra D, Hutchinson G, Der G, Leff J (1999) The first contact of patients with schizophrenia with psychiatric services: social factors and pathways to care in a multi-ethnic population Psychological Medicine 29(2) 475-83

Central Statistics Office (2012) Profile 6; Migration and Diversity. Dublin: Stationery Office

Clare A (2002) Immigration: new challenges for psychiatry and mental health services in Ireland. Irish Journal of Psychiatric Medicine 19(1) 3

Cole E, Leavey G, King M, Johnson-Sabine E, Hoar A (1995) Pathways to care for patients with a first episode of psychosis: A comparison of ethnic groups. The British Journal of Psychiatry 167(6) 770-776

Cross T L, Bazron B J, Dennis K W, Isaacs M R (1989) Towards a Culturally Competent System of Care: A Monograph on Effective Services for Minority Children Who Are Severely Emotionally Disturbed. Washington, DC: Georgetown University

Daly A, Walsh D (2012) Activities of Irish Psychiatric Units and Hospitals 2011 Main Findings. HRB Statistics Series 18. Dublin: Health Research Board

Das-Munshi J, Leavey G, Stansfeld S, Prince M (2012) Migration social mobility and common mental disorders: critical review of the literature and meta-analysis. Ethnicity & Health 17 (1-2) 17-53

Department of Health (2004) Celebrating our Cultures: Guidelines for Mental Health Promotion with Black and Minority Ethnic Communities. London: Department of Health Publications

Department of Health and Children (2006) A Vision for Change; report of the Expert Group on Mental Health Policy. Dublin: Stationery Office

European Commission (2005) Green Paper: Improving the Mental Health of the Population: Towards a Strategy on Mental Health in the European Union COM (2005) 484. Brussels: Green Paper Health and Consumer Protections Directorate, European Commissions

Fazel M, Wheeler J, Danesh J (2005) Prevalence of serious mental disorder in 7000 refugees resettled in western countries: a systematic review. Lancet 365 (9467) 1309-1314

Feeney L, Kelly B, Whitty P, O'Callaghan E (2002) Mental illness in migrants: diagnostic and therapeutic challenges. Irish Journal of Psychiatric Medicine 19 (1) 29-31

Fernando S (2005) Multicultural mental health services: projects for minority ethnic communities in England. Transcultural Psychiatry 42 (3) 420-36

Foley-Nolan C, Sheahan A, Cahill D (2002) A better world – healthwise: a health needs assessment of immigrants in Cork and Kerry. Cork: Southern Health Board

Franks W, Gawn N, Bowden G (2007) Barriers to access to mental health services for migrant workers refugees and asylum seekers. Journal of Public Mental Health 6 (1) 33-41

Ganesan S, Janze T (2005) Overview of culturally-based mental health care. Vancouver Transcultural Psychiatry 42 (3) 478-90

Ghane S, Kolk A M, Emmelkamp P M G (2012) Direct and indirect assessment of explanatory models of illness. Transcultural Psychiatry 49(1) 3-25

Goater N, King M, Cole E, Leavey G, Johnson-Sabine E, Blizard R, Hoar A (1999) Ethnicity and outcome of psychosis. The British Journal of Psychiatry 175 (1) 34-42

Harrison G, Owens D, Holton A, Neilson D, Boot D (1988) A prospective study of severe mental disorder in Afro-Caribbean patients. Psychological Medicine 18 (3) 643-657

Health Service Executive (2008) National Intercultural Health Strategy 2007-2012. Naas, Co. Kildare: HSE

Health Service Executive (2012) National Service Plan 2012. Dublin: HSE

Hernandez M, Nesman T, Mowery D, Acevedo-Polakovich I, Callejas L (2009) Cultural competence: a literature review and conceptual model for mental health services. Psychiatric Services 60 (8) 1046-1050

Kelleher C, Staines A, Daly L, Moore R (2010) All Ireland Traveller Health Study: Our Geels. Dublin: University College Dublin

Kelly B D (2009) Health services psychiatry and citizenship in a globalizing world: a perspective from Ireland. Health Policy 93 (1) 48-54

Kelly F, Kelly B, Ryan D (2008) Assessment of Psychiatric and Psychological Needs Among Help-Seeking Migrants in Dublin: Final Report. Dublin: National Disability Authority

Kennedy N, Jerrard-Dunne P, Gill M, Webb M (2002) Characteristics and treatment of asylum seekers reviewed by psychiatrists in an Irish inner city area. Irish Journal of Psychiatric Medicine 19 (1) 4-7

Keyes C L, Ryff C D (2003) Somatization and mental health: a comparative study of the idiom of distress hypothesis. Social Science Medicine 57 (10) 1833-45

King M, Coker E, Leavey G, Hoare A, Johnson-Sabine E (1994) Incidence of psychotic illness in London: comparison of ethnic groups. British Medical Journal 309 (6962) 1115-1119

Kirmayer L (2012) Rethinking cultural competence. Transcultural Psychiatry 49 (2) 149-164

Kirmayer L J, Groleau D, Guzder J, Blake C, Jarvis E (2003) Cultural consultation: a model of mental health service for multicultural societies. Canadian Journal of Psychiatry 48 (3) 145-53

Kirmayer L J, Narasiah L, Munoz M, Rashid M, Ryder A G, Guzder J, Hassan G, Rousseau C, Pottie K (2011) Common mental health problems in immigrants and refugees: general approach in primary care. Canadian Medical Association Journal 183 (12) E959-E967

Kleinman A (1977) Depression, somatization and the new cross cultural psychiatry. Social Science and Medicine 11 (1) 3-10

Kleinman A (1987) Anthropology and Psychiatry: The role of culture in cross cultural research on illness. British Journal of Psychiatry 151:447-454

Knifton L (2012) Understanding and addressing the stigma of mental illness with ethnic minority communities. Health Sociology Review 21 (3) 287-298

Lakeman R, Matthews A, Munck R, Redmond M, Sanders T, Walsh J (2008) New Communities and Mental Health in Ireland: A Needs Analysis. Cairde: Dublin City University

Laming H (2003) The Victoria Climbié Inquiry: Report of an Inquiry Presented by the Secretary of State for Health and the Secretary of State for the Home Department by Command of Her Majesty, January 2003. Norwich: Stationery Office

Lawlor C, Johnson S, Cole L, Howard L M (2012) Ethnic variations in pathways to acute care and compulsory detention for women experiencing a mental health crisis. International Journal of Social Psychiatry 58 (1) 3-15

Leavey G, Guvenir T, Haase S, Dein S (2007) Finding help: Turkish speaking refugees and migrants with a history of psychosis. Transcultural Psychiatry 44 (2) 258-274

Leavey G, King M (2007) The devil is in the detail: partnerships between psychiatry and faith-based organisations. British Journal of Psychiatry 191: 97-98

Leavey G, Loewenthal K, King M (2007) Challenges to Sanctuary: the clergy as a resource for mental health care in the community. Social Science and Medicine 65:548-559

Leavey G, Rozmovits L, Ryan L, King M (2007) Explanations of depression among Irish migrants in Britain. Social Science and Medicine 65:231-244

Lim R, Luo J, Suo S, Hales R (2008) Diversity initiatives in academic psychiatry: applying cultural competence. Academic Psychiatry 32 (4) 283-290

Linehan S, Duffy D O, Neill H O, Neill C, Kennedy H G (2002) Irish Travellers and forensic mental health. Irish Journal of Psychological Medicine 19 (3) 76-79

Littlewood R, Lipsedge M (1997) Aliens and alienists: ethnic minorities and psychiatry. New York: Routledge

Llopis E J, Anderson P (2006) Mental health promotion and mental disorder prevention across European Member States: a collection of country stories. Luxembourg: European Commission

Lo H T, Chung R C (2005) The Hong Fook experience: working with ethnocultural communities in Toronto 1982-2002. Transcultural Psychiatry 42 (3) 457-77

McCabe R, Priebe S (2004) Explanatory models of illness in schizophrenia: comparison of four ethnic groups. The British Journal of Psychiatry 185 (1) 25-30

McGinnity F, O'Connell P, Quinn E, Williams J (2006) Migrants experience of racism and discrimination in Ireland. Dublin: Economic and Social Research Institute

McLean C, Campbell C, Cornish F (2003) African-Caribbean interactions with mental health services: experiences and expectations of exclusion as (re) productive of health inequalities. Social Science and Medicine 56 (3) 657-669

Morgan C, Mallett R, Hutchinson G, Bagalkote H, Morgan K, Fearon P, Dazzan P, Boydell J, McKenzie K, Harrison G, Murray R, Jones P, Craig T, Leff J (2005) Pathways to care and ethnicity 2: Source of referral and help-seeking Report from the AESOP study. British Journal of Psychiatry 186:290-6

Morgan C, Mallett R, Hutchinson G, Leff J (2004) Negative pathways to psychiatric care and ethnicity: the bridge between social science and psychiatry. Social Science and Medicine (1982) 58 (4) 739

Nurse D (2009) Development and Implementation of the HSE National Intercultural Health Strategy: Lessons learned along the way. Translocations, Migration and Social Change

Nwachukwu I, Browne D, Tobin J (2009) The Mental Health Requirements for Asylum Seekers and Refugees in Ireland – Position Paper. Dublin: College of Psychiatry in Ireland

Odegaard O (1932) Emigration and insanity: a study of mental disease among the Norwegian-born population of Minnesota. Acta Psychiatrica Scandinavica 7 (suppl 4) 1-206

Ohaeri J U, Odejide O A (1994) Somatization symptoms among patients using primary health care facilities in a rural community in Nigeria. American Journal of Psychiatry 151 (5) 728-31

Patel V (1995) Explanatory models of mental illness in sub-Saharan Africa. Social Science and Medicine 40 (9) 1291-1298

Price E G, Beach M C, Gary T L, Robinson K A, Gozu A, Palacio A, Smarth C, Jenckes M, Feuerstein C, Bass E B (2005) A systematic review of the methodological rigor of studies evaluating cultural competence training of health professionals. Academic Medicine 80 (6) 578-586

Pumariega A J, Rothe E, Pumariega J B (2005) Mental health of immigrants and refugees Community. Mental Health Journal 41 (5) 581-97

Reitmanova S, Gustafson D L (2009) Primary mental health care information and services for St John's visible minority immigrants: gaps and opportunities. Issues in Mental Health Nursing 30 (10) 615-23

Sadavoy J, Meier R, Ong A Y (2004) Barriers to access to mental health services for ethnic seniors: the Toronto study. Canadian Journal of Psychiatry 49 (3) 192-9

Saechao F, Sharrock S, Reicherter D, Livingston J D, Aylward A, Whisnant J, Koopman C, Kohli S (2012) Stressors and barriers to using mental health services among diverse groups of first-generation immigrants to the United States. Community Mental Health Journal 48 (1) 98-106

Sanders T, Whyte S (2006) Assessing the Health and Related Needs of Minority Ethnic Groups in Dublin's North Inner City A case study of a Community Development Approach to Health Needs Assessment. Dublin: Cairde Community Development and Health Programme

Sue S (1998) In search of cultural competence in psychotherapy and counselling. American Psychologist 53 (4) 440

Sue S (2006) Cultural competency: From philosophy to research and practice. Journal of Community Psychology 34 (2) 237-245

United Nations (2000) United Nations Economic and Social Council Substantive issue arising in the implementation of the international covenant on economic social and cultural rights general comment no. 14

Weich S, Griffith L, Commander M, Bradby H, Sashidharan S P, Pemberton S, Jasani R, Bhui K S (2012) Experiences of acute mental health care in an ethnically diverse inner city: qualitative interview study. Social Psychiatry and Psychiatric Epidemiology 47(1) 119-28

Weich S, Nazroo J, Sproston K, McManus S, Blanchard M, Erens B, Karlsen S, King M, Lloyd K, Stansfeld S (2004) Common mental disorders and ethnicity in England: the EMPIRIC study. Psychological Medicine 34 (08) 1543-1551

Whitley R (2007) Cultural competence evidence-based medicine and evidence-based practices. Psychiatric Services 58 (12) 1588-1590

Wilson C J, Deane F P, Marshall K L, Dalley A (2010) Adolescents' suicidal thinking and reluctance to consult general medical practitioners. Journal of Youth and Adolescence 39 (4) 343-356

NOTES

[i] Victoria Climbié, a child from Côte d'Ivoire, suffered extreme abuse and died while living with her aunt and her aunt's partner. Social and clinical services in London failed to intervene in this highly publicised case. It emerged during the hearings and criminal trial that her aunt considered Victoria to be demonically possessed and these beliefs were significant in the abuse.

10

'A state of semi-lunacy'? The marginal status of drinking problems within the Irish mental health system

Shane Butler

INTRODUCTION

In the field of mental health, which is generally characterised by conflict and controversy as to the nature – if not indeed the very existence – of mental illness, the specific status of alcohol-related problems is by no means less contentious. The aim of this chapter, therefore, against a background of major change in policy and provision in the decades following the enactment of the Mental Treatment Act, 1945, is to look critically at changing approaches to the management of drinking problems within the Irish mental health system over this time period.

The dominant theoretical perspective which will be applied here is sociological: one which will challenge rationalistic views that changes in policy and practice in relation to the management of alcohol problems are primarily based on scientific research. Instead, sociological approaches (e.g. Gusfield 1996, Room 2003, Reinarman 2005) suggest that changes in the way in which drinking problems are conceptualised may be understood as social constructions which occur under certain historical and cultural conditions, and which are reflective of political and economic interest group activity – rather than indicative of progress based upon value-free science. Particular use will be made of Gusfield's (1981) concept of 'ownership' of social problems, which refers to the way in which certain institutions – such as the medical profession, the criminal justice system or even the Church – claim that they uniquely understand certain problems and should be granted primacy in, if not a monopoly on, the societal management of such problems. Also, by way of contrast with the view that changes to funding arrangements for alcohol treatment systems follow and are largely determined by advances in scientific understanding of 'what works', this chapter draws specifically on the notion that treatment ideology may in fact be the dependent variable which is subject to change when financing systems are altered. For instance, Weisner and Room's (1984) study of the impact of new funding systems on alcohol treatment in California concluded that as a result of enhanced funding arrangements, treatment ideology changed dramatically to justify practices which enlarged the total pool of potential clients.

However, prior to looking in detail at Irish mental health service developments in relation to drinking problems between 1945 and 2013, there will be a brief historical review of public policy developments in this sphere during the 19th century and early part of the 20th century.

INSTITUTIONAL MANAGEMENT OF DRINKING PROBLEMS IN 19TH- AND EARLY-20TH-CENTURY IRELAND

During the Victorian era, a network of district lunatic asylums was developed across Ireland on foot of recommendations made in 1817 by a parliamentary committee which was concerned with the 'relief of the lunatic poor' (Finnane 1981). As in England, the medical profession claimed and was granted exclusive rights to govern the Irish public lunatic asylums, with 'resident medical superintendents' replacing lay managers within a few decades of the establishment of these institutions. Given the vagueness of the concepts of insanity and lunacy, it is not surprising that the Irish lunatic asylums became the 'most obvious, even the only place where irritating, noisy, disturbing people could be sent' (Finnane 1981:146), even if this was not always to the satisfaction of the medical directors of these institutions. Historical accounts of these early asylums make it clear that there was a constant flow of admissions which was related to alcohol consumption: these consisted of people whose alcohol-related behaviour posed a risk to themselves and/or was socially disruptive. They could, in present-day parlance, be regarded as people suffering from 'dual diagnosis' in the sense that their mental state was obviously impaired by their consumption of alcohol – although in most cases they did not appear to be insane once they became alcohol-free; alternatively, from a criminal justice perspective they could be categorised as offenders who were involved in 'domestic violence' or prone to the commission of 'public order offences'. Their admission to the medically managed lunatic asylums reflected a belief that they did not engage in such drinking as an act of will for which they could be held responsible, but rather that problematic drinking of this kind was indicative of an underlying and somewhat mysterious disease state. Although asylum administrators were ambivalent about these alcohol-related admissions, they accepted them stoically and Finnane has estimated that by 1901 more than 10% of asylum admissions were attributed to 'intemperance in drink' (p146).

Quite apart from the lunatic asylums, and reflecting ongoing debate during the 19th century as to whether drinking problems should be regarded as health issues or moral failings (Kilcommins 2003), the Irish prison system was also heavily burdened with inmates commonly referred to as 'chronic inebriates' or 'habitual drunkards'. Ireland's first experiment with specialist treatment for problem drinkers occurred following the enactment by the Westminster Parliament of the Inebriates Act of 1898, when a state inebriate reformatory was established by the General Prisons Board at Ennis in County Clare and two state-licensed inebriate reformatories were established by voluntary bodies at Wexford and Waterford. As in other countries, these inebriate reformatories saw themselves as catering for people who had 'diseases of the will' (Valverde 1998) and their regimes owed more to ideas of religious or moral suasion than to medical science. As was also the case in other countries, the Irish inebriate reformatories never worked effectively (Bretherton 1987, Smith 1989), and by 1925, when the newly-established Irish Free State created an Intoxicating Liquor Commission to review various aspects of alcohol policy, the inebriate reformatories had ceased to function and the commission saw no merit in re-opening them (Butler 2010:25-28). The minutes of the evidence submitted to the commission make it clear that, in terms of Gusfield's concept of 'ownership' of social problems, neither the healthcare system nor the criminal justice system was laying claim to problem drinking and that each would happily have ceded ownership to the other. The marginal status of problem drinkers and the practical difficulties associated with their management was expressed colourfully by an Assistant Commissioner of An Garda Síochána who gave evidence to the 1925 Commission that:

> [Inebriates] get into a state of semi-lunacy and a doctor has got to certify them. They are put into an asylum, but they can get out soon again. They cannot be kept under the lunacy jurisdiction once they get sober. They get out, start off again, and the whole thing goes on in a vicious circle. (Intoxicating Liquor Commission Report, Minutes of Evidence, 5 May 1925)

In its final report, the commission was unequivocally tough in its views as to how Irish society should deal with inebriates ('We think the only effective home for such people is a gaol, and the only suitable occupation plenty of hard labour', p.19), but these views had no policy impact and the tendency to regard mental hospitals as the appropriate site for the management of drinking problems persisted for the next 20 years. This practice continued, not particularly because

Irish psychiatrists were actively claiming 'ownership' of problem drinking but rather as a continuation of a pragmatic arrangement, which, for want of anything better, had evolved since the early 19th century.

CONSTRUCTING AND DECONSTRUCTING ALCOHOLISM AS DISEASE: 1945–2013

The disease concept of alcoholism

In attempting to trace analytically the various changes that have occurred in the way in which Irish mental health systems deal with drinking problems, it is useful to focus chronologically on the changing fortunes of what is commonly referred to as the 'disease concept of alcoholism'. This concept, as it is generally understood nowadays, had its origins during the 1930s and 1940s in post-Prohibition America, when an array of institutions and interest groups combined to promote an understanding of alcohol-related problems which was self-consciously modern, scientific and as far removed as possible from what were now considered to be the moralistic and outmoded views of those temperance campaigners whose lobbying had resulted in the United States' Prohibition experience between 1920 and 1933 (Beauchamp 1980, Jellinek 1960, Room 1978). At the heart of the disease concept was the proposition that in any given society the total population of drinkers could be validly divided into two subpopulations: a majority (perhaps as high as 90%) of 'social drinkers' who drank pleasurably and in a style that was non-problematic; and a minority who drank in a way that was uncontrolled or compulsive, and which was invariably linked to a range of health and social problems. This latter group, it was asserted, suffered from the disease of alcoholism, a disease thought to be causally attributable to individual predispositions of a biological and/or psychological nature, rather than to any negative properties inherent in alcohol per se. Proponents of this individualistic perspective on alcohol-related problems argued firstly that alcoholism was a discrete disease for which its sufferers could not be held responsible, and secondly that healthcare providers should adopt a more wholehearted and less moralistic approach to the provision of effective treatment – usually within mental health services – for the condition. Given the cultural hegemony of the US during the mid-20th century, it was inevitable that the disease concept would be diffused globally. However, the process of diffusion was given a significant boost in 1950 when E. M. Jellinek, one of the concept's US-based promoters, was given a five-year contract as consultant on alcoholism to the newly established World Health Organisation (WHO). While his views on the scientific validity of the disease concept altered somewhat over this period, Jellinek used his time at WHO headquarters in Geneva to promote the disease concept globally, particularly arguing the case for the development of specialist alcoholism treatment systems within existing mental health services (Booth-Page 1997).

The 1945 Mental Treatment Act and the coming of Alcoholics Anonymous

If one looks at events during the 1940s which might be seen as evidence of the diffusion of the disease concept to Ireland, there are two in particular that suggest themselves: the inclusion of addiction within the country's new mental health legislation, and the advent of Alcoholics Anonymous (AA) – not just Ireland's, but the world's first mutual help association in the sphere of mental health.

The 1945 Mental Treatment Act, the first mental health legislation to be enacted in independent Ireland, listed 'addiction' as one of the conditions that could be treated, either on a voluntary or involuntary basis, within the country's mental health system. Given the virtual non-existence of illicit drug use in Ireland at this time, it seems clear that this primarily referred to alcohol dependence. It might be thought, therefore, that the inclusion of addiction within this new legislation reflected an early and unequivocal policy shift towards the disease concept of alcoholism, or a new determination on the part of Irish psychiatrists to claim ownership of drinking problems. However, study of the legislative process (Butler 2002:22-25) reveals that this was not the case. The addiction provisions were not contained in the 1944 Mental Treatment Bill but, in response to criticism by the Irish Medical Association, were introduced as an amendment at the committee stage of the legislative process. Referring to this amendment, in the Dáil debate on the new mental health legislation, Dr F. C. Ward, the Parliamentary Secretary (the title by which Junior Ministers were previously known), made it clear that problem drinkers were still a marginal client group within the mental health system. The amendment was seen as offering a legal basis for specialist alcoholism treatment facilities that might be established at some future time, rather than as a mandate for routine management of alcoholism within the mainstream mental health services:

> I should tell the House that, at this stage, we can only provide the necessary [legal] machinery, and that until such time as suitable institutions are available we cannot deal adequately with the problem that this amendment is intended to deal with. It will only be in case of urgency, or particular emergency, that addicts will be received in the ordinary institutions. In the course of time it is hoped that we may be able to provide special institutions. (Dáil Debates, 1945)

Similarly, to view the establishment of AA in Ireland at the end of 1946 as evidence of a deliberate strategy by its American founders to promote the disease concept within Irish society is to misunderstand the unique nature of this institution that chooses to describe itself as a 'fellowship'. AA had been founded in Akron, Ohio, in 1935 (Kurtz 1991) and had evolved slowly in the decade or so prior to its establishment in Ireland. By the time it reached Ireland, AA had not only formalised its programme of recovery, the '12 Steps of AA', but it had also – and perhaps even more significantly – drafted its administrative philosophy, the '12 Traditions of AA', which guided its introduction to and general conduct within Ireland and other societies to which it was diffused. AA's 12 Steps were commonly referred to as a 'suggested programme of recovery' and, insofar as they were based on mutual support rather than expert-led treatment, could be seen as having features in common with present-day concepts of recovery within mental health policy documents (e.g. *A Vision for Change* 2006) or in the wider arena of service-user involvement (e.g. Weinstein 2010). As laid down in its 12 Traditions, however, AA was absolutely clear that it would not become involved in the policy process or in service planning. It saw itself as existing solely to provide a support for people who wished to stop drinking; and lest it be diverted from this purpose by being drawn into debate on scientific or policy issues, it chose to regard these as 'outside issues' on which it had no opinion. While individual AA members may have personally believed in the disease of alcoholism, and while such beliefs may have seeped gradually into the wider culture, AA did not see itself as a stakeholder in the alcohol policy process; it did not seek or accept representation on policy bodies, did not make written submissions to statutory authorities and did not use the media to promote the disease concept of alcoholism at a policy level (Butler 2010).

Commission of Inquiry on Mental Illness 1966

It was not, in fact, until 1966 that Irish mental health policy committed itself unequivocally to the disease concept, and Table 10.1 presents in summary form the ideological shifts which have occurred on this issue as manifest in successive mental health policy documents.

Table 10.1: Changing constructions of alcohol problems and their ownership by the Irish mental health system – as reflected across major policy documents

Policy Document	Year	Perspective on role of mental health system in managing alcohol problems
Report of the Commission of Inquiry on Mental Illness	1966	Alcoholism is a disease appropriately treated within the psychiatric services
The Psychiatric Services: Planning for the Future	1984	Alcohol contributes to a range of social and health problems (the concept of alcoholism as a discrete disease is scientifically discredited); the mental health system cannot be expected to cure problems whose prevalence is primarily a function of population drinking habits, and mental health service management of alcohol problems should continue, but mainly through community-based service provision
A Vision for Change: Report of the Expert Group on Mental Health Policy	2006	Responsibility for care of addiction lies outside of the mental health system – except for people with psychiatric co-morbidity

The *Report of the Commission of Inquiry on Mental Illness* (1966) was the first policy document to present a detailed rationale for the replacement of traditional psychiatric hospitals by what was popularly referred to as 'community care'. It was also the first policy document to wholeheartedly endorse the disease concept of alcoholism. On this latter subject, the Commission began with the simple assertion that: 'Alcoholism is a disease and is regarded by the World Health Organisation as a major health problem' (Commission of Inquiry on Mental Illness 1966:77). The remainder of the discussion, while acknowledging that primary healthcare could play a role in its treatment, largely reflected the belief that alcoholism was a disease best managed within the psychiatric service – optimally through the provision of specialist inpatient care:

> The Commission recommends that the residential facilities should be provided in conjunction with short-term psychiatric units. It also

recommends that all alcoholic patients in any one hospital should be concentrated in a particular, self-contained section, and should not be dispersed through a number of sections, mixed with other categories of patients. The establishment of alcoholic units on these lines would facilitate the group psychotherapy which is such an important feature of the treatment process. (bold in original) (p.81)

This discussion of alcoholism by the Commission of Inquiry on Mental Illness was explicitly predicated on the belief that the disease concept of alcoholism was by now a non-contentious and scientifically based development, which had invalidated moralistic approaches to the societal management of drinking problems; and generally the Commission's views on this matter reflected all of the main tenets of the American disease concept. These beliefs were reinforced by the establishment, also in 1966, of a voluntary body, the Irish National Council on Alcoholism (INCA), modelled on the National Council on Alcoholism in the US and effectively operating as a lobby group for the disease concept (Butler 2002, 33-36).

The Commission noted in passing that in Ireland at this time 'most alcoholics are treated in private hospitals – in particular in St. John of God Psychiatric Hospital, Dublin, which has a special unit for alcoholics, and in St. Patrick's Hospital, Dublin' (p.79). This comment was almost certainly read contemporaneously as a rebuke to the public sector for its lack of commitment to alcoholism treatment but, with the wisdom of hindsight, the Commission could be faulted for its failure to explore the differing responses of the public and private psychiatric sectors on this issue: differences which seem largely explicable in terms of changed funding arrangements. In 1957, Ireland's first private health insurance scheme – the Voluntary Health Insurance (VHI) Board – had been established as a semi-state body to provide middle- and upper-income groups with the option of being treated in private hospital settings (Barrington 1987). The popularity of this initiative led to an expansion of private hospital care – including private psychiatric hospital care. One unanticipated consequence of VHI's establishment was that middle-class problem drinkers, who might have baulked at the prospect of admission to the squalid environment of the public mental health system, could now access the more salubrious private sector. This meant that, from the late-1950s onwards, specialist alcoholism treatment began to emerge as a niche market for the private sector, delivering a steady flow of relatively uncomplicated patients whose bills were always paid and whose care provided a financial cushion for institutions which might otherwise have struggled financially. One can argue, therefore, that the ideological enthusiasm of the private psychiatric system for the disease concept of alcoholism (and it is worth noting that the establishment of INCA was primarily driven by the private sector) was heavily influenced by the advent of private health insurance.

Similarly, one can argue that the reluctance of the public psychiatric system to accept ownership of drinking problems was influenced by a suspicion that to admit and constantly readmit people with this 'relapsing illness' was to squander scarce resources which might otherwise be used for patients not considered to be the authors of their own misfortunes.

Paradoxically, it would seem that acceptance of the disease concept at public policy level occurred in Ireland at a relatively late period, when international critics were already beginning to point out that this was a social construction rather than a scientific discovery. For instance, as early as 1962 Seeley, an American sociologist, had written that 'the bare statement that "alcoholism is a disease" is most misleading, since (a) it links up with a much-too-narrow concept of disease in the public mind, and (b) it conceals what is essential – that is that a step in public policy is being *recommended*, not a scientific discovery announced' (Seeley 1962:593). The Commission report of 1966, however, had no such caveats and appeared satisfied that psychiatry could legitimately be given ownership of this previously contentious issue.

The Psychiatric Services: Planning for the Future 1984

Ireland's next mental health policy document (commonly referred to as *Planning for the Future*) was concerned with accelerating the pace of change to community care and, as such, differed from the Commission's 1966 report primarily through its focus on organisational strategies – particularly the introduction of 'sectorised' service systems – designed to achieve this aim. On the specific topic of alcoholism, however, *Planning for the Future* effectively contradicted all of the main ideas and recommendations of its 1966 predecessor, beginning with a summary dismissal of the scientific validity of the disease concept:

> Until recently, the generic term 'alcoholism' has been used to refer to a variety of problems resulting from alcohol abuse. However, because the word is difficult to define satisfactorily and because it suggests a particular type of alcohol problem to the exclusion of others, it is limited in what it covers. The term 'alcohol-related problems', although more cumbersome, is more accurate. This term acknowledges that alcohol can cause or, or at least contribute to, an assortment of social and physical problems which include public drunkenness, family violence, absenteeism, road traffic accidents, liver and heart disease and disorders of the central nervous system. (Department of Health 1984:104)

This tendency to 'disaggregate' alcohol-related problems rather than to speak of a single, discrete disease entity reflected changed World Health Organisation (WHO) thinking on the topic (Edwards et al. 1977). In line with this perspective,

Planning for the Future went on to argue that the prevalence of problems was demonstrably linked to population drinking habits, and that it was unrealistic to expect the mental health system to provide a technical solution for what was essentially a lifestyle issue – since Irish alcohol consumption had been steadily increasing over the previous 30 years.

Again in line with revised WHO ideas, the authors of *Planning for the Future* recommended that the state should set in place an integrated national alcohol strategy which would use alcohol control measures (such as increased price and reduced availability) as a means of changing population drinking habits (Bruun et al. 1975). In a very practical sense, however, *Planning for the Future* thinking on alcohol problems and their management reflected the 'heavy demand on the psychiatric services' (p.104) which these problems were now making. Furthermore, the Study Group that had drawn up the report (and which on this occasion had no representation from the private psychiatric sector) was of the view that increased demand for inpatient alcohol treatment was not simply indicative of an increased prevalence of alcohol-related problems, but that it was also a measure of the success of the rhetoric of alcoholism as a treatable psychiatric disorder: 'It is likely that at least some of the increased demand is due to greater acceptance of the psychiatric hospital as a treatment centre for such problems' (p.105).

Table 10.2: Irish psychiatric hospitals and units, all and alcohol-related admissions for selected years

Year	All Admissions	Alcohol Admissions	Alcohol Admissions as Percentage of All Admissions
1966	16,526	1,757	11%
1976	26,434	6,101	23%
1986	29,392	7,132	24%
1996	26,656	5,435	20%
2006	20,288	2,767	14%

Source: Annual 'Activities' reports for Irish psychiatric hospitals and units, Medico-Social Research Board / Health Research Board

Table 10.2 presents data on alcohol admissions to inpatient psychiatric care, indicating how alcohol admissions relative to all admissions had increased in the years between the 1966 Commission report and the publication of *Planning for the Future*, by which time alcohol admissions were accounting for approximately one in every four admissions into the country's mental health beds. It might be inferred from the overall tone of their discussion of alcohol problems that the authors of *Planning for the Future* had flirted with the idea of completely disowning these problems, such was the burden which they imposed on an already over-stretched and under-resourced public mental health system. Rather than do this, however, they recommended that mental health service management of alcohol problems should customarily take place in community-based services, justifying this by reference to the evaluative literature:

> The effectiveness of specialised alcohol treatment programmes has been seriously questioned. There is no evidence that intensive, high-cost in-patient treatment is in any way superior to simple, inexpensive community-based intervention ... The over-specialised approach to alcohol problems is also a separatist approach. It draws the problem away from the community and family and tends to exclude the contribution of primary care and community medical and social services from the management of the problem ... (Department of Health 1984:107)

In line with this view, the major recommendation of the 1984 report was for the continuing management of alcohol problems by the psychiatric system, albeit within community-based services, which would now include alcohol counsellors in addition to traditional mental health professionals. In summary, Irish psychiatry, while considerably less enthusiastic about accepting responsibility for the management of drinking problems, was not yet inclined to disown this problem.

A Vision for Change 2006

In late 2006 the Mental Health Act, 2001, a statute that was largely concerned with safeguarding the rights of patients involuntarily detained in Irish psychiatric hospitals, came into full effect. For those interested in mental health service involvement with alcohol issues, what was most significant in the new legislation was that it ended the practice of involuntary admission of patients with a primary diagnosis of addiction. The decision to exclude addiction as a condition which might warrant involuntary admission to a psychiatric unit had been flagged briefly in the White Paper: A New Mental Health Act (Department of Health 1995:23): 'There is widespread agreement that addiction to drugs, intoxicants or perverted conduct should not, **in itself**, be considered as evidence of a mental disorder ... **the Government proposes to exclude addiction from the scope of the definition mental disorder in new legislation**' (bold in original). What this cryptic comment conceals is the fact that addiction – or more precisely a range of substance-related problems – featured in both DSM and ICD (the two diagnostic systems most commonly used internationally) as disorders in their own right.

Earlier in 2006, a new mental health policy document, A Vision for Change, was published. The discussion of 'substance abuse' and 'addiction' contained in this policy document was as notable for its brevity as its content. In contrast with the fuller discussion of alcohol problems presented in the two earlier documents, the 2006 discussion consisted of just a single page, and no attempt was made to offer a detailed rationale for its pronouncement that responsibility for the management of addiction (except in cases of serious psychiatric co-morbidity) lay outside of the mental health system. The argument put forward by the authors of *A Vision for Change* that Irish addiction services have their own funding structures outside of the mental health service was somewhat disingenuous, suggesting that they had not taken the trouble to differentiate between the free-standing addiction service for users of illicit drugs (largely based in the greater Dublin area) which did employ a number of psychiatrists and the continuing management of alcohol problems by the adult mental health system.

Not surprisingly, there was some controversy about this attempt to exclude addiction from the ambit of mental health, particularly when a sub-group (including several psychiatrists) that had advised the main *Vision for Change* group on addiction issues wrote to the *Irish Times* to dissociate itself from this recommendation:

> This means that the services required by people with substance abuse problems will not now be developed as part of the new comprehensive model of mental health services ... Despite receiving an interim report from our sub-group, the expert group never indicated that it was considering the dramatic step of excluding addiction treatment from mental health services. We have serious concerns about the effect on clients with drug or alcohol addiction. No evidence is presented to back up its recommendations and, as practitioners in the field, we are certainly not aware of where such evidence could have been obtained. We are unaware of any member of the expert group who has any specific expertise in treating addiction. Consequently, we are confused as to how the group could ignore our advice so completely. (Barry et al. 2006)

It is also noteworthy that within two months of the publication of the *Vision for Change* document, Dr Conor Farren, a consultant psychiatrist at St Patrick's Hospital (a private hospital) and one of the signatories of the *Irish Times* letter just cited, addressed a joint parliamentary committee on drug issues. Dr Farren, who introduced himself as chairperson of the Addiction Faculty of the Irish College of Psychiatry, presented a traditional view of the value and importance of treating 'alcoholism' within inpatient psychiatric facilities such as his own hospital, giving no hint of how this view diverged from that contained in the newly published mental health report (Parliamentary Debates 2006).

In the absence of any explanation of its decision, one can only speculate on the dynamics and motivations within the Expert Group which led to this 'dramatic step', but there are some plausible 'push/pull' factors which will be considered here. In a general sense, the move to 'push' alcohol problems out of psychiatry may have been influenced by a sense of frustration with the delays experienced in implementing the 1984 recommendation on managing alcohol problems primarily within community-based services.

Table 10.3: Irish psychiatric hospitals and units, all and alcohol-related admissions by hospital type for the year 2006

Hospital Type	All Admissions	Alcohol Admissions	Alcohol Admissions as Percentage of Admissions
Psychiatric Hospitals	6,400	895	14%
General Hospital Psychiatric Units	10,111	1,099	11%
Private Psychiatric Hospitals	3,777	773	20%
All Hospitals	20,288	2,767	14%

The category *Psychiatric Hospitals* refers to traditional, public psychiatric hospitals which are being gradually phased out; the category *General Hospital Psychiatric Units* refers to acute mental health admission units, publicly funded and based within general hospitals, which are replacing the old psychiatric hospitals; the category *Private Psychiatric Hospitals* refers to private psychiatric hospitals which within Ireland's mixed healthcare system are mainly used by patients with private health insurance – in 2006, for example, 19% of all inpatient psychiatric admissions were into such private facilities.

Source: Activities of Irish Psychiatric Hospitals and Units 2006

As Table 10.3 indicates, inpatient admission data for the year 2006 (a year that is no way atypical) revealed substantial numbers of alcohol admissions more than 20 years after *Planning for the Future* had advocated that such patients be managed within community-based services. The breakdown by hospital type also gives a clear sense of the difficulties associated with the implementation of national policy directives within a complex and evolving psychiatric system. It is important to note that the private psychiatric hospitals – significant players in a mixed healthcare system where in 2008 just over half of the population had private health insurance (Health Insurance Authority 2009) – operated with a considerable degree of autonomy, as well as with financial incentives for retaining alcohol admissions as a major part of their workloads. As long as health insurance continued to offer cover for inpatient treatment of alcohol problems (which it did albeit with restrictions on the amount of such cover), private psychiatric hospitals could be expected to admit problem drinkers, regardless of national policy guidelines on this issue. Tensions between public and private psychiatry on the value of inpatient treatment of alcoholism had been evident for several decades (Butler 2002:62-72), contributing inter alia to the demise of the Irish National Council on Alcoholism in 1987. Perhaps then, this exclusion of addiction in the *Vision for Change* report may be seen as representing a determination by the public system that, whatever the private sector chose to do, public psychiatry was no longer prepared to indulge in a practice deemed to have no evidence base and to be wasteful of scarce public resources. The fact that the psychiatric hospitals (the last vestiges of the Victorian lunatic asylums) had a higher proportion of alcohol admissions would appear to be largely explicable with reference to the extra availability of beds in these old institutions, while the newer acute units within general hospitals operated with much smaller numbers of beds and could be expected to be circumspect about 'wasting' beds on unnecessary alcohol admissions.

The disowning of responsibility for managing addictions within psychiatry may also be viewed as reflecting the failure of health system managers to integrate the role of community-based alcohol counsellors into the overall workings of the sectorised mental health teams, as envisaged in *Planning for the Future*. Although no systematic evaluation was carried out at national level on the implementation of these *Planning for the Future* recommendations, there is some evidence to suggest that alcohol counselling was not consistently integrated into sectorised mental health teams but instead functioned as an alternative treatment system. Keenan's (2005) view that many of the new alcohol counselling services had become unhitched from the parent mental health system is broadly supported by the findings of an external evaluation of addiction counselling in the Dublin area in 2001 (Velleman et al. 2001). Thus, while alcohol-related admissions declined gradually over the years, it cannot be assumed that they did so solely or primarily because of the availability of a community-based alternative. From this perspective, then, the *Vision for Change* rejection of addiction treatment may simply be seen as formal confirmation of what effectively was the status quo: specifically that alcohol counselling services had detached from the parent mental health service.

On the 'pull' side of the equation, it may be speculated that the growth of alcohol counselling had led to the emergence of a cadre of professionals happy to challenge the 'medical model', and to argue that addiction treatment did not necessarily involve mental health specialists. This was particularly true of the development, from the late-1970s onwards, of the so-called 'Minnesota Model' residential treatment agencies, which were run by voluntary bodies and which were staffed largely by alcohol counsellors. These agencies challenged the monopoly previously enjoyed by private psychiatric hospitals and despite any demonstrable evidence of effectiveness, have remained popular, continuing to function through a combination of client fees, private health insurance cover, voluntary fundraising and some statutory support. Perhaps within the Expert Group there were forces happy to cede ownership of addiction – including alcohol dependence – to such professionals outside of mainstream psychiatry.

DISCUSSION

In seeking to understand how Irish mental health policy has flip-flopped over its conceptualisation of drinking problems and its approach to their practical management since 1945, perhaps the most fundamental point to be made is that this is an area that remains contested. It is not merely that public health experts differ from mental health experts in their overall response to the question, but that *within* the specialism of psychiatry there are differences of opinion. Psychiatrists working in private hospitals tend to favour the retention of alcohol problems within mental health treatment systems, as perhaps do some public sector psychiatrists working in specialist addiction services. However, some psychiatrists, at least in the public mental health system, would happily disown these problems. Private psychiatry in Ireland still has strong financial incentives to maintain its long-standing commitment to residential treatment programmes for problem drinkers, while the public sector – in the face of constant concern about the proportion of the total healthcare spend allocated to mental health (Independent Monitoring Group, 2010) – continues to be ambivalent about accepting responsibility for alcohol problems.

Although the word 'alcoholism' has virtually disappeared from official policy discourse in Ireland, it survives in popular language and culture, being implicitly maintained by the continuing support of private psychiatric hospitals for inpatient rehabilitation and explicitly supported by non-medical services based upon the so-called Minnesota Model. Generally, it would be foolish to assume that policy rejection of the disease concept in 1984 means that it is no longer a force to be reckoned with in Irish society. It is not surprising that Irish problem drinkers, either of their own volition or impelled by their families, the police or primary care professionals, should continue to seek help from mental health services, since this is what has been happening for almost 200 years.

It should be pointed out in conclusion that no systematic effort has, to date at least, been made to implement the addiction recommendation of A *Vision for*

Change, in the sense of introducing an absolute ban on alcohol admissions to publicly funded mental health beds. There are, in any event, practical difficulties associated with this recommendation that the mental health services should retain responsibility for people with addiction and psychiatric co-morbidity (that is, people who have both a substance misuse diagnosis and a mental health diagnosis) while handing over responsibility for uncomplicated addiction to a parallel addiction service. Psychiatric co-morbidity (Raistrick et al. 2006, Mills et al. 2010) would appear to be the norm rather than the exception for treatment-seeking patients with alcohol dependence, and it is not easy for clinicians to determine the severity or chronicity of psychiatric disorders until their patients have been detoxified. The development of a parallel service system could result in service users being constantly shuttled across services, a difficulty which would be obviated in a single, integrated service. One could predict that as the total stock of mental health beds decreases (in line with the closure of old psychiatric hospitals), clinicians in Ireland's public sector will admit fewer patients whose primary diagnosis relates to alcohol use, and that (as annual 'Activities' reports consistently show) length of hospital stay for such admissions will be short. However, it is unlikely to be the case that such alcohol admissions will totally disappear. The practice of managing problem drinking through Ireland's mental health system may ultimately be considered a pragmatic mode of problem management, based neither on scientific precision nor on any claim to its ownership by the public psychiatric system. While he had no pretensions to professional or scientific competence, the words of the Assistant Garda Commissioner from 1925 still have a certain resonance in an arena where science has not resolved the question of ownership of drinking problems and where meanings are still obviously contested: Ireland's mental health system seems likely to continue to play a major role in the management of problem drinkers who, as in the past, present in 'a state of semi-lunacy'.

*

REFLECTIVE QUESTIONS FOR DISCUSSION AND DEBATE: PRACTICE

* To what extent do changes in the way in which Irish mental health policy has approached the management of alcohol problems reflect scientific progress and research evidence?
* Under what circumstances should problem drinkers be admitted to inpatient care in the Irish mental health system?
* What role should alcohol counsellors play in the management of problem drinkers as part of multi-disciplinary mental health teams?

REFLECTIVE STATEMENTS FOR DISCUSSION AND DEBATE: RESEARCH

* Explore the attitudes of community psychiatric nurses towards problem drinkers.
* Compare length of inpatient stay for patients with a primary alcohol diagnosis with lengths of stay for other patients.

REFERENCES

Barrington R (1987) Health, Medicine and Politics in Ireland 1900-1970. Dublin: Institute of Public Administration

Barry J, Farren C, Keenan E et al. (2006) Excluding addiction from mental health services. Irish Times 15 December 2006

Beauchamp D (1980) Beyond Alcoholism: Alcohol and Public Health Policy. Philadelphia, PA: Temple University Press

Booth-Page P (1997) EM Jellinek and the evolution of alcohol studies: a critical essay. Addiction 92:1619-1637

Bretherton G (1987) Irish Inebriate Reformatories, 1889-1920. Contemporary Drug Problems 13:473-502

Bruun K, Edwards G, Lumio M et al. (1975) Alcohol Control Policies in Public Health Perspective. Helsinki: Finnish Foundation for Alcohol Studies

Butler S (2002) Alcohol, Drugs and Health Promotion in Modern Ireland. Dublin: Institute of Public Administration

Butler S (2010) Benign Anarchy: Alcoholics Anonymous in Ireland. Dublin: Irish Academic Press

Commission of Inquiry on Mental Illness (1966) Report of the Commission of Inquiry on Mental Illness. Dublin: Stationery Office

Dáil Debates (1945). Volume 96: column 1009

Department of Health (1984) The Psychiatric Services: Planning for the Future: Report of a Study Group on the Development of the Psychiatric Services. Dublin: Stationery Office

Department of Health (1995) White Paper: A New Mental Health Act. Dublin: Stationery Office

Department of Health and Children (2006) A Vision for Change: Report of the Expert Group on Mental Health Policy. Dublin: Stationery Office

Edwards G, Gross M, Keller M, Moser J and Room R (eds.) (1977) Alcohol-related disabilities. Geneva: World Health Organisation

Finnane M (1981) Insanity and the Insane in Post-Famine Ireland. London: Croom Helm

Gusfield J (1981) The Culture of Public Problems: Drinking-Driving and the Symbolic Order. London: University of Chicago Press

Gusfield J (1996) Contested Meanings: The Construction of Alcohol Problems. Madison, WI: The University of Wisconsin Press

Health Insurance Authority Annual Report and Accounts 2008 (Appendix A) (2009). Dublin: Health Insurance Authority

Independent Monitoring Group (2010) Fourth Annual Report on Implementation 2009 – A Vision for Change: the Report of the Expert Group on Mental Health Policy. Dublin: Department of Health and Children http://www.dohc.ie/publications

Intoxicating Liquor Commission Report (1925) Minutes of Evidence 5 May 1925. Dublin: Stationery Office

Jellinek E (1960) The Disease Concept of Alcoholism. New Brunswick, NJ: Hillhouse Press

Keenan E (2005) Irish addiction services – past, present and future. Irish Journal of Psychological Medicine 22:118-120

Kilcommins S (2003) Reconstructing the Image of the 'Habitual Drunkard' in Kilcommins S, O'Donnell I (eds.) Alcohol, Society and the Law. Chichester: Barry Rose Law Publishers 60-103

Kurtz E (1991) Not-God: A History of Alcoholics Anonymous (expanded edition). Center City, MN: Hazelden

Mills K, Deady M, Proudfoot H et al. (2010) Guidelines on the management of co-occurring alcohol and other drug and mental health conditions in alcohol and other drug treatment settings. Sydney: National Drug and Alcohol Research Centre

Parliamentary Debates: Minutes of the Joint Committee on Arts, Sport, Tourism, Community, Rural and Gaeltacht Affairs 1 March 2006

Raistrick D, Heather N, Godfrey, C (2006) Review of the effectiveness of treatment for alcohol problems. London: National Treatment Agency for Substance Misuse

Reinarman C (2005) Addiction as Accomplishment: The Discursive Construction of Disease. Addiction Research and Theory 13:307-320

Room R (1978) Governing Images of Alcohol and Drug Problems. PhD Dissertation: University of California, Berkeley

Room R (2003) The Cultural Framing of Addiction. Janus Head 6:221-234

Seeley J (1962) Alcoholism as a Disease: Implications for Public Policy in Pittman D, Snyder C (eds.) Society, Culture and Drinking Patterns. New York: Wiley 592-599

Smith B (1989) Ireland's Ennis Inebriates Reformatory: A 19th Century Example of Failed Institutional Reform. Federal Probation 53:53-64

Valverde M (1998) Diseases of the Will: Alcohol and the Dilemmas of Freedom. Cambridge: Cambridge University Press

Velleman R, Davidson R, Mistral W, Howse, I (2001) The Role of Counselling in the Drug and Alcohol Services: External Review of Eastern Health Authority Addiction Counselling Services. Dublin: Eastern Regional Health Authority

Weinstein J (ed.) (2010) Mental Health Service User Involvement and Recovery. London: Jessica Kingsley

Weisner C, Room R (1984) Financing and Ideology in Alcohol Treatment Social Problems 32:167-184

11

The interface between mental health and the criminal justice system: legal and policy perspectives

Darius Whelan and Michael Brennan

The various steps of the criminal justice system, whether at arrest, trial or sentencing stage, affect thousands of people each year, including people with mental health conditions. There is a vast literature on the relationship between mental health and the criminal justice system (see for example Peay 2010; Laing 1999). The criminal justice system is primarily geared towards the punishment of offenders (with elements of rehabilitation as well), and it is difficult to reconcile the goal of punishment with provision of treatment for a person's mental health condition. Matters are further complicated by the fact that criminal justice and health are the responsibilities of two different government departments – the Department of Justice and Equality (DOJE) and the Department of Health, respectively. While there is an increasing focus on human rights in discussion of policy regarding civil mental health, there is far less discussion of human rights in the context of mental health in criminal justice. Internationally, a key policy goal is diversion of those with mental health conditions from the criminal justice system (Freeman and Pathare 2005:75) but the word 'diversion; rarely appears in Irish government policies (one notable exception being *A Vision for Change*, Department for Health and Children 2006:138-143). An Interdepartmental Group is currently examining the issue of people with mental health problems coming into contact with the criminal justice system (DOJE 2012).

In this chapter, we outline aspects of current law and policy on the interface between mental health and criminal justice in Ireland. We begin by considering the meaning of 'mentally disordered offenders', the criminal law defences of insanity and diminished responsibility, fitness for trial and the relationship between human rights law and the Criminal Law (Insanity) Act 2006. We then discuss sentencing, forensic mental health services, prisoners and mental health law, and the role of Gardaí in civil detention.

THE MEANING OF 'MENTALLY DISORDERED OFFENDERS'

'Mentally disordered offenders' are defined as individuals who have, or are alleged to have, broken the law and to have a diagnosed mental disorder. It may also include those exhibiting challenging behaviour or those deemed difficult to place (Mental Health Commission (MHC) 2011) (though interestingly, the latter is a non-offending group). Webb and Harris (1999:2) allude to a sense of confusion with regard to mentally disordered offenders, stating that 'they are not exclusively ill or uncomplicatedly bad'. James et al. (2002:88-89) suggested that this group may be more aptly described as 'offending mentally disordered'. This may be due to the fact that many of these people are known to psychiatric services prior to their involvement with the criminal justice system (O'Neill 2006, WHO 2007). This factor is of major significance according to Peay (2003) because it has implications for how and by whom this group of people should be treated and cared for. These are particularly pertinent questions with regard to mentally disordered offenders, especially considering the relatively recent changes in Irish civil and criminal law and in its mental health policy (Mental Health Act 2001, Criminal Law (Insanity) Acts 2006, 2010, Department of Health and Children 2006). While these changes have fundamentally improved mental health service provision, challenges remain with regard to the appropriate mental health care provision for this group because it involves an interface between the criminal justice and mental health systems.

CRIMINAL LAW DEFENCES: INSANITY AND DIMINISHED RESPONSIBILITY

Prior to 2006, the insanity defence was based on a combination of common law and 1883 legislation on 'lunatics', and resulted in a verdict of 'guilty but insane' (Whelan 2009:444). The 2006 Criminal Law (Insanity) Act introduced the verdict of 'Not Guilty by Reason of Insanity' (NGRI). According to s.5(1) of the Act, a person can be found Not Guilty by Reason of Insanity if:

(a)   The accused person was suffering at the time from a mental disorder, and
(b)   The mental disorder was such that the accused person ought not to be held responsible for the act alleged by reason of the fact that he or she
    (i)   did not know the nature and quality of the act, or
    (ii)   did not know that what he or she was doing was wrong, or
    (iii)   was unable to refrain from committing the act.

Under s. 1 of the 2006 Act, 'mental disorder' is defined as including mental illness, mental disability, dementia or any disease of the mind, but not including intoxication. While many mental health conditions are included in the definition of mental disorder, defendants rarely raise the insanity defence as they must show that they either did not know what they were doing, did not know it was wrong or were unable to refrain from committing the act (see generally Campbell et al. 2010:993-1003). The first two limbs of this part of the defence are derived from the M'Naghten rules, which were developed in England in 1843. The third limb ('unable to refrain from committing the act') is also sometimes referred to as volitional insanity or irresistible impulse and is based on the Irish case of *Doyle v Wicklow County Council* (1974). The court must hear evidence of a consultant psychiatrist before the NGRI verdict can be returned.

If the person is found NGRI, this is a special verdict and does not lead to automatic release, although in a small number of cases, the court might release the person if he or she no longer has a mental disorder requiring detention for treatment. In most cases, the court will move on to order the person's detention in the Central Mental Hospital (CMH) in Dundrum in Dublin for treatment. The court will order such detention if the person has a mental disorder within the meaning of the Mental Health Act 2001 (for discussion of the definition of mental disorder under the 2001 Act, see Whelan 2009:75-91). Essentially, a civil test of the need for detention is applied to a person who has just been through a criminal process. While at first glance this may seem anomalous, the reasoning is that the need for detention at the end of the trial is an entirely different question from that of criminal responsibility for the act, which may have occurred some years previously.

When a court orders a person's detention in the CMH, it does not place a time limit on the person's detention. Instead, the person's case is reviewed regularly by the Mental Health (Criminal Law) Review Board, normally at six-monthly intervals. This board has the power to discharge the person, either with conditions attached or unconditionally.[i]

Perhaps due to the uncertainty about the length of detention under the 2006 Act – a person could end up detained longer than would have been the maximum sentence for the crime committed – some defendants choose not to raise an insanity defence at trial and prefer to take the risk of a determinate prison sentence.

The partial defence of Diminished Responsibility is governed by s.6 of the Criminal Law (Insanity) Act 2006. It only applies if a person is charged with murder, and if the defence is successfully raised, the person is convicted of manslaughter rather than murder. The jury must find that the person

(a)   committed the act alleged,

(b)   was at the time suffering from a mental disorder, and

(c)   the mental disorder was not such as to justify finding him or her not guilty by reason of insanity, but was such as to diminish substantially his or her responsibility for the act.

In effect, the jury is finding that the person had a mental disorder which did not remove their culpability for the act, but diminished it substantially. It recognises that the relationship between mental health conditions and criminal acts can be complex, and in some cases the person with a mental disorder is partially responsible for a killing.

The definition of mental disorder here is the same as it is for the insanity defence. If a person is found guilty of manslaughter on grounds of diminished responsibility, the normal rules for manslaughter verdicts apply, so he or she may receive a custodial sentence of any duration up to life imprisonment, or indeed may even receive a suspended sentence (Burke case 2010). The court does not have the statutory power to sentence a person to hospital, although he or she may be transferred to hospital from prison. The Mental Health (Criminal Law) Review Board does not review the cases of those found guilty of manslaughter on grounds of diminished responsibility if they are serving a sentence in prison.

FITNESS FOR TRIAL

At an early stage of criminal proceedings, a court may find that the accused person has a mental disorder so severe that he or she is 'unfit for trial'. This applies under s.4 of the Criminal Law (Insanity) Act 2006, which states that an accused person shall be deemed unfit to be tried if he or she is unable by reason of mental disorder to understand the nature or course of the proceedings so as to

(a) plead to the charge,
(b) instruct a legal representative,
(c) in the case of an indictable offence which may be tried summarily, elect for a trial by jury,
(d) make a proper defence,
(e) in the case of a trial by jury, challenge a juror to whom he or she might wish to object, or
(f) understand the evidence.

As with all of the 2006 Act, 'mental disorder' is defined as including mental illness, mental disability, dementia or any disease of the mind, but does not include intoxication. The test of unfitness for trial is a narrow one, and once a person has a basic understanding and knowledge of what is going on during the trial, the court may find him or her fit for trial.

Following a finding of unfitness for trial, the procedures in the Act are complex, but in essence the person may be detained in the Central Mental Hospital (CMH) for treatment or treated on an outpatient basis.[ii] While they are being detained in the CMH, the person's case will be reviewed regularly by the Mental Health (Criminal Law) Review Board. Once their treatment is complete and they are fit for trial, they can then be returned to court for a trial of the charge. In cases where treatment and detention are lengthy, there may never be a trial on the charge as it may be impractical.

A further unusual aspect of fitness for trial is that after a person is found unfit for trial, the court may hold an optional 'trial of the facts' to determine whether the accused committed the act alleged. If the court is satisfied that there is a reasonable doubt as to whether the accused committed the act alleged, it orders the accused to be discharged. This gives the person the opportunity to be released if the prosecution's case is very thin, even though they are not fit to make a proper defence. If the court does not find that there is reasonable doubt as to whether the accused committed the act alleged, the normal consequences of a finding of unfitness for trial follow.

CRIMINAL JUSTICE, MENTAL HEALTH AND HUMAN RIGHTS LAW

Generally, constitutional rights and human rights litigation regarding the insanity defence and related topics has concerned procedural rights. For example, a person cannot be deprived of their personal liberty 'save in accordance with law' under Article 40.4.1 of the Constitution. If proper procedures are not followed, this is a breach of the person's constitutional right to personal liberty and the court may order the person's release. This occurred in F.X. v Clinical Director of the Central Mental Hospital (2012), where the accused had been found unfit for trial but the trial judge had inadvertently not followed the correct procedure regarding his psychiatric assessment. Interestingly, the court in this case did not order Mr X's immediate release and instead put a two-day stay on the order to allow steps to be taken to render the detention lawful. In B.G. v Murphy (No.2) (2011), the court emphasised that a person with a mental disability has a right to equal treatment under Article 40.1 of the Constitution, and found that in cases of possible unfitness for trial, the procedures in the Criminal Law (Insanity) Act 2006 must be applied in such a manner that the person with mental disability is not discriminated against without objective justification.

There has been some litigation where prisoners have claimed breaches of their constitutional or human rights due to lack of access to appropriate psychiatric treatment. In Aerts v Belgium (2000) Mr Aerts had allegedly committed a serious assault and, as he had a borderline personality disorder and was found not to be criminally responsible, was detained under social protection legislation. He was not convicted of the offence but was detained in a prison and not given appropriate treatment. He successfully claimed that the conditions of his confinement breached Article 5(1) of the European Convention on Human Rights (ECHR) on the right to personal liberty.

The Irish Penal Reform Trust (IPRT) and two named prisoners commenced an action seeking various declaratory reliefs upon the basis that the defendants had failed in their constitutional obligation to provide adequate psychiatric treatment and/or facilities and/or services for prisoners in Mountjoy Men's Prison and Mountjoy Women's Prison, and further a declaration that the treatment of the named prisoners in Mountjoy Prison was a breach of their constitutional rights. One of the prisoners was placed in a padded cell in Mountjoy Prison for two weeks pending the availability of a bed in the Central Mental Hospital. The IPRT was found to have *locus standi* to bring the claim in 2005 (*IPRT v Governor of Mountjoy Prison* 2005) but the full claim has not yet come to trial.[iii] In 2011, the High Court found that a prisoner's constitutional rights were breached by his detention in a padded cell in Mountjoy but did not order that he be released (*Kinsella v Governor of Mountjoy Prison* 2011). Instead, the court stated that the authorities must have an opportunity to rectify the situation and eventually the prisoner was transferred to Cloverhill Prison.

One unusual aspect of the insanity and diminished responsibility defences is that, if the defendant raises such a defence, he or she must prove on the balance of probabilities that the defence applies. This is known as placing the burden of proof on the defendant, making it harder for the defence to succeed, which might appear to conflict with the normal principle that the prosecution must prove all elements of the case beyond a reasonable doubt. There are important policy reasons why this approach has been adopted, e.g. because the prosecution cannot force the defendant to undergo a psychiatric examination and thus might not be able to prove that the accused was not 'insane'. Article 6(2) of the European Convention on Human Rights (ECHR) states that a person shall be presumed innocent until proven guilty. In *H. v UK* (1990), it was held that it was not a breach of Article 6(2) for English law to place the burden of proof on the defendant as regards the insanity defence. Similarly, in *Robinson v UK* (1993) the placing of the burden of proof on the defendant in diminished responsibility cases was also upheld.

In *Rocha v Portugal* (2001), the Strasbourg court stated in applying Article 5 of the ECHR that an initial court order detaining a person found not guilty by reason of insanity lasts only for a period of time that is proportional to the gravity of the offence. After that, the person must be able to apply for reviews of their detention, as happens in Ireland with reviews by the Mental Health (Criminal Law) Review Board. *Johnson v UK* (1997) considers conditional discharge of persons with mental disorders who have committed criminal offences. The court held that if a person's discharge is deferred while a suitable placement is being found, discharge must not be unreasonably delayed as to do so will lead to a breach of Article 5.[iv]

There is very little room for substantive arguments based on the ECHR about the definition of 'mental disorder' in criminal matters, as the Convention has been interpreted as mainly dealing with procedural matters. Bartlett and Sandland comment that the European Court of Human Rights is strong on ensuring appropriate due process protections, but weak on substantive issues (Bartlett and Sandland 2007:29).

The UN Convention on the Rights of Persons with Disabilities (CRPD) was adopted in 2006 and applies to people with mental health disabilities; Ireland has signed and proposes to ratify it at some stage in the future. The Convention represents a move away from a medical model of disability to a social one, and requires a paradigm shift in the rights of those with mental health conditions. Kennedy (2011) draws attention to the fact that the CRPD will address the cultural differences between the legal and medical professions in regard to one's best interest by placing an emphasis on everybody's right to liberty and security (Art 14), right to live within one's own community (Art 19) and right to legal capacity (by providing varying levels of assisted decision-making) (Art 12). However, as stated, the CRPD has yet to be ratified by Ireland. One of the main reasons for this is that the Government has not yet, as of writing, replaced its outdated capacity laws such as the Lunacy Regulation (Ireland) Act 1871. The Government published the Assisted Decision-Making (Capacity) Bill in July 2013, and issues of legal capacity will be the focus of intense discussion as the Bill goes through the legislative process.

The potential implications for mental health law of the Convention are unclear at present, and a substantial literature is already building up on these issues, mainly focusing on issues of legal capacity (e.g. McSherry and Weller 2010). Less attention has been paid to the relationship between the CRPD and criminal law. Article 12 of the CRPD states that countries must recognise that persons with disabilities enjoy legal capacity on an equal basis with others in all aspects of life. This has been interpreted by the High Commissioner for Human Rights to mean that defences based on the negation of criminal responsibility because of the existence of a mental or intellectual disability must be abolished (UN High Commissioner for Human Rights 2009, para 47). This interpretation would have far-reaching and challenging consequences that have not necessarily been adequately considered. Bartlett (2012) has pointed out that if criminal defences based on mental disorders were abolished, more people with mental disorders would end up in prison, which is contrary to policies of community integration in the CRPD. In addition, disability-neutral laws, whether on civil or criminal matters, would still indirectly discriminate against people with mental disabilities, as disability-neutral laws on topics previously governed by disability-specific laws would have more pronounced effects on people with disabilities than those without disabilities (Bartlett 2012).

SENTENCING

If a person is found guilty of a criminal offence (or has pleaded guilty), and if the Irish courts propose to order that he or she be detained, the courts only have power to send the person to prison; they do not have the power to send them to a mental health centre for treatment. There has been no progress on the proposal from a 1995 White Paper to enable courts at sentencing stage to refer a person to a psychiatric centre for treatment (Department of Health 1995, Chapter 7). However, the courts have acknowledged that if a person's mental disorder reduces their culpability for the crime, this will be a mitigating factor in sentencing (e.g. *People (DPP) v Redmond* 2006). In diminished responsibility cases, a person's mental disorder may even mean that they receive a suspended sentence for manslaughter (Burke case 2010).

INTERFACE BETWEEN THE FORENSIC MENTAL HEALTH SERVICE AND THE CRIMINAL JUSTICE SYSTEM

The word 'forensic' implies an association with the courts of law. The Faculty of Forensic Psychiatry of the Royal College of Psychiatry defines forensic psychiatry as a 'speciality in psychiatry concerned with helping people who have a mental disorder and who present a significant risk to the public' (cited by MHC 2011:7). However, Gordon and Lindqvist (2007) provide a much broader perspective. According to them, the composition of forensic mental health services includes the interface between mental health and the law, affording expert evidence in civil and criminal courts, and the assessment and treatment of mentally disordered offenders and similar service users who have not committed any offences.

The National Forensic Mental Health Service (NFMHS) provides care and treatment for people with mental health problems who have come into contact with the criminal justice system, i.e. via the Courts and the Prison Service. The NFMHS also provides consultation services to generic mental health services on the assessment and management of people with mental/emotional distress who have a propensity for violence and challenging behaviour (O'Neill 2011). It provides inpatient services, community services, day centre clinics, outpatient clinics, community hostels, prison in-reach services and a Court Liaison Service at Cloverhill District Court, Dublin.

The responsibility for prison mental health is that of the Department of Justice and Equality. This is clarified in the Irish Prison Service Annual Report (2009) which states that the provision of healthcare is a statutory obligation of the Irish Prison service, as defined in the Prison Rules 2007. Notwithstanding this, prisons are often considered grossly inappropriate environments for prisoners with mental health problems (Irish Penal Reform Trust 2001, WHO 2001, Coyle 2005, O'Neill 2006, Corston 2007, WHO 2007, Durcan 2008, Knight and Stephens 2009). Indeed, Knight and Stephens (2009) contend that the prison ethos conflicts with the principles of healthcare provision, which emphasise self-determination underpinned by a philosophy of recovery. In fact, Durcan (2008) found that the prison itself is a risk factor for emotional distress, as well as having a disproportionate population composed of people from disadvantaged backgrounds with a history of trauma, loss and low resilience to distress.

The European Committee for the Prevention of Torture Report (2007) reiterated its serious concerns about how Ireland's criminal justice system provides for the needs of prisoners with mental health problems. The MHC (2011) expanded further by emphasising the need to develop a multi-agency approach to healthcare within the prison system (MHC 2011:21). In 2009 the Irish Prison Service (IPS) set as its objective for healthcare provision within prisons that it should be based on the principle of providing care that is equivalent to that available in the community (IPS 2009). This is to be achieved by applying a primary care approach (IPS 2009). Indeed such an approach to healthcare is imperative in order to adhere to Article 3 of the ECHR, which outlaws torture and inhuman or degrading treatment. The principle of equivalence as enunciated in the United Nations Mental Illness Principles (1991) must underpin the provision of mental health services to prisoners. To that end, the European Committee for the Prevention of Torture Report (2011) did note improvements in how prisoners' mental health needs are addressed. This is further emphasised in a recent PhD study conducted in the Irish Prison System, which observed several developments that have improved the quality of the mental health care provided in Irish prisons (Brennan 2012). For example, in March 1999, the first cohort of Nurse Officers was recruited to the Irish Prison Service (IPS 1999-2000:14). In December 2010 a Vulnerable Persons Unit (VPU), which is a nine-bed facility, opened in the Medical Unit in Mountjoy Prison. Indeed this unit has won several awards both nationally and internationally to date. This unit provides expert, supportive, short-term care for prisoners who are in an 'acutely disturbed phase of a mental illness'. The VPU provides a more controlled and supportive environment for a vulnerable prisoner as a short-term intervention (IPS 2010:31). However, as yet, this model has not been replicated throughout the Irish prison system. The IPS also provides a psychology service that comprises 21 psychologists, the primary functions of which are to provide mental health services to prisoners and to help offenders address factors that put them at risk of re-offending (ibid. p.25).

Currently the majority of prison mental health services are provided by the NFMHS. This service provides 20 consultant-led in-reach sessions weekly at all Dublin prisons, Portlaoise Prison and the Midlands Prison. Specialist in-reach services are in place for consultant-led mental health sessions in the remaining prisons (IPS 2010:30). However, this means that some prisons situated around Ireland have limited input from the NFMHS, and this is a matter of concern for the European Committee for the Prevention of Torture (2011). The NFMHS also established Ireland's first Psychiatric In-Reach and Court Liaison Service (PICLS) operating from Cloverhill Remand Prison in Dublin in 2005. In fact, between 2006 and 2011 at least 3,195 remand prisoners received a comprehensive psychiatric assessment as a result of this initiative (McInerney et al. 2013). Nevertheless, despite such positive developments, Dressing and Salize (2009) note that in Ireland, as in many other European countries, it is general practitioners who screen all new prisoners on committal, even though many GPs do not necessarily have training in specialist areas such as mental health. This may result in poor recognition of mental health problems at an early and often vital point (Brooker et al. 2009). Therefore the need for training on mental health issues for all prison personnel involved with this group remains vital (Brennan 2012).

Such developments are important, as prisons are increasingly becoming a pathway to accessing mental health care (Brennan 2012). Yet this fact leads to a very pertinent question: should prisons become the mental health facilities of the 21st century? This is worthy of note considering that Brennan (2012) found that mentally disordered offenders within Irish prisons are gradually becoming re-institutionalised. Indeed Kelly (2007) showed a strong link between the closure of large psychiatric hospitals and the growth in the number of people with mental health problems within the Irish prison system. These findings suggest that the WHO's prediction within the Trencín statement that prisons 'will' become 21st-century asylums (WHO 2007:5) has in fact already been fulfilled (Brennan 2012).

Recent Irish studies (Duffy et al. 2003, Linehan et al. 2005, Wright et al. 2006) have shown a significant increase in the prevalence of mental illness among prisoners, particularly since the process of deinstitutionalisation that began in Ireland in the late 1970s. Also common among this group is co-morbidity with conditions such as personality disorder, alcoholism and drug dependence (Duffy et al. 2003, Linehan et al. 2005, Wright et al. 2006). Duffy et al. (2003) found that drugs and alcohol dependence and their harmful use were by far the most common problems, present in between 61% and 79% of prisoners.

The rate of psychosis among remand prisoners stands at 7.6% (Linehan et al. 2005), more than double the rate found in comparable samples in other jurisdictions (O'Neill 2006). The UN Mental Illness Principles (1991) state that every person should be treated the same as any other citizen regardless of their disability. However, O'Neill (2011) draws attention to the fact that this may not always be the case, particularly if a person appears in court and has a mental illness. This is because people in this category will find it more difficult to fulfil requirements for bail such as presenting a sum of money, being able to give an address and having a person to vouch for them. A Vision for Change (2006) recommended that the 'NFMHS should be expanded and reconfigured so as to provide court diversion services and legislation should be devised to allow this to take place' (Department of Health and Children 2006 Recommendation 15.1.2). As noted previously, in 2005 Ireland's first Psychiatric In-Reach and Court Liaison Service (PICLS) was established, operating from Cloverhill Remand Prison in Dublin. Of the 3,195 remand prisoners who received comprehensive psychiatric assessments between 2006 and 2011, 572 were diverted from the criminal justice system to mental health services (89 to a secure forensic hospital, 164 to community mental health hospitals and 319 to other community mental health services).

Furthermore, when a person is sentenced to a prison term, if he or she has a severe mental disorder, a transfer can be arranged from prison to the Central Mental Hospital (Whelan 2009:534-536). Demand for places in the CMH often exceeds supply and many prisoners with severe mental health problems cannot access the services they require (e.g. see Inspector of Prisons 2005:18-24). A transfer to the NFMHS may not always be in the best interest of the prisoner, as they do not always require the level of security provided by this service. Such practice is at odds with the principles of Ireland's national mental health policy. By way of contrast, in countries such as Cyprus, Denmark, Norway, Iceland and Slovenia the referral of prisoners experiencing psychosis to psychiatric hospitals in the national health system is the most frequently used option (Dressing and Salize 2009).

As advocated in A Vision for Change, 'Every person with serious mental health problems coming into contact with the forensic system should be afforded the right of mental healthcare in non-forensic mental health services unless there are cogent and legal reasons why this should not be done' (Department of Health and Children 2006:136). Kennedy (2006) advocates a 'flat hub and spoke' model to ensure a better and more accessible service. This model is designed to provide local, low-security resources which will reduce the strain on medium- and high-security resources (O'Grady 1990). However, in order for this model to be effective, it must be supported by an adequately resourced multidisciplinary primary care infrastructure (McDaid et al. 2009). This model is in line with the principles set out by the Expert Group on Mental Health Policy (Department of Health and Children 2006) for a contemporary forensic mental health service.

INTERFACE BETWEEN AN GARDA SÍOCHÁNA AND MENTAL HEALTH SERVICES WHEN DEALING WITH ISSUES OF CIVIL DETENTION

The MHC's annual report states that in 2012 22% of all applications for civil detentions were made by Gardaí by invoking s.12(1) of the Mental Health Act

2001 (MHC 2013). This represents an increase of 6% in such applications for civil detentions made since 2007 by members of An Garda Síochána (MHC 2013:35), a noteworthy point, considering the low rate (8%) of use of the authorised officers facility under s. 9 of the MHA 2001 in cases of civil detentions. A continuance of this trend would further exacerbate the distress and stigma experienced for both family members and the individual involved in such circumstances. Furthermore it is remarkable that such a steady increase in applications by Gardaí has taken place since the launch of Ireland's national policy guidelines in 2006. This would seem at odds with its philosophical position on the provision of mental health services, which purports to have the service user at its centre and to be recovery focused. Given An Garda Síochána's role in civil detention, it is clear that they need support, knowledge and resources to manage such circumstances. For example, as recommended by the Expert Group (Department of Health and Children 2006), the NFMHS should be available (and are in many cases) to provide support in order to assist law enforcement agents to make decisions in such circumstances. The Expert Group strongly pushed for mental health training issues for Gardaí (Department of Health and Children 2006:141, 196), which was followed by a report of a Working Group (MHC and AGS 2009) and a Memorandum of Understanding between the HSE and An Garda Síochána to clarify roles and responsibilities (AGS and HSE 2010). While training is provided for new recruits, such training has not always been provided for the existing Garda workforce.

CONCLUSION

In this chapter, we have reviewed aspects of the interface between mental health and the criminal justice system. The overall impression is one of fragmented services and unimplemented policies. While there have been various positive developments, such as the enactment of the Criminal Law (Insanity) Act in 2006 and the setting up of the Cloverhill diversion scheme, there is an urgent need for improvement of law and policy concerning the rights of people with mental health difficulties who come into contact with the criminal justice system. This is partly due to a need for increased resources, but it also requires joined-up thinking between the multitude of agencies involved. In addition, serious questions arise about the implications of the CRPD for the interface between mental health and the criminal justice system that will need to be answered in the future.

*

REFLECTIVE QUESTIONS FOR DISCUSSION AND DEBATE: PRACTICE

* How can the policy goals of treatment for persons with mental health difficulties and punishment for criminal acts be reconciled?
* Why are psychiatric services for prisoners inadequate? Is it due to lack of resources, or is it related to society's attitudes to prisoners with mental health problems?
* Have the courts dealt appropriately with issues concerning criminal justice and mental health?

REFLECTIVE STATEMENTS FOR DISCUSSION AND DEBATE: RESEARCH

* How can joined-up thinking between the various agencies involved in the interface between criminal justice and mental health be improved?
* Is it possible to enact criminal laws which are disability-neutral in order to comply fully with the policies in the CRPD?
* Would increased training in mental health issues for policymakers, NGOs, lawyers, judges, Gardaí, prison officers and probation officers be an effective means of improving mental health services for those who come into contact with the criminal justice system?

REFERENCES

Aerts v Belgium (2000) European Human Rights Reports, 29, 50

An Garda Síochána and HSE (2010) Memorandum of Understanding on Removal to or Return of a person to an Approved Centre in accordance with Section 13 & Section 27, and the Removal of a person to an Approved Centre in accordance with Section 12, of the Mental Health Act 2001

B.G. v Murphy (No.2) [2011] IEHC 445 High Court Hogan J, 8 December 2011

Bartlett P (2012) The United Nations Convention on the Rights of Persons with Disabilities and Mental Health Law. Modern Law Review 75:752

Bartlett P, Sandland R (2007) Mental Health Law: Policy and Practice 3rd ed. Oxford: Oxford University Press

Brennan M (2012) Pathways to Mental Health Care of People with Mental Health Problems within the Irish Criminal Justice System. Unpublished PhD thesis: Trinity College Dublin

Brooker C, Ullmann B, Lockhart G (2009) Inside Out: solutions for mental health in the criminal justice system. London: Policy Exchange

Burke case (2010) reported in Irish Times 24 March 2010

Campbell L, Kilcommins S, O'Sullivan C (2010) Criminal Law in Ireland: Cases and Commentary. Dublin: Clarus Press

Corston J (2007) The Corston Report: a review of women with particular vulnerabilities in the criminal justice system. London: Home Office

Council of Europe (1950) European Convention on Human Rights

Coyle A (2005) Understanding Prisons: Key Issues in Policy and Practice. Maidenhead: Open University Press

Department of Health (1995) A New Mental Health Act: White Paper. Dublin: Stationery Office

Department of Health and Children (2006) A Vision for Change: Report of the Expert Group on Mental Health Policy. Dublin: Stationery Office

Department of Justice and Equality (2012) Press release: Interdepartmental Group to examine the issue of people with mental illness coming into contact with the criminal justice system. Dublin

Doyle v Wicklow County Council [1974] Irish Reports 55

Dressing H, Salize H J (2009) Pathways to psychiatric care in European prison systems. Behavioral Sciences & the Law 27:801-810

Duffy D, Linehan S, Kennedy H (2003) Screening prisoners for mental disorders. Psychiatric Bulletin, 27:241-242

Durcan G (2008) From the inside: experiences of prison mental health care. London: Sainsbury Centre for Mental Health

European Committee for the Prevention of Torture and Inhuman or Degrading Treatment or Punishment (CPT) (2007) Report to the Government of Ireland on the visit to Ireland from 2 to 13 October 2006. Strasbourg: Council of Europe Inf (2007) 40

European Committee for the Prevention of Torture and Inhuman or Degrading Treatment or Punishment (CPT) (2011) Report to the Government of Ireland on the visit to Ireland carried out from 25 January to 5 February 2010. Strasbourg: Council of Europe, Inf (2011) 3

F. X. v Clinical Director of the Central Mental Hospital [2012] IEHC 272, High Court, Hogan J, 8 July 2012

Freeman M and Pathare S (2005) WHO Resource Book on Mental Health, Human Rights and Legislation. Geneva: World Health Organization

Government of Ireland (2006) Amendment (2010) Criminal Law (Insanity) Act. Dublin: Stationery Office

Government of Ireland (2001) Mental Health Act. Dublin: Stationery Office

Government of Ireland (2006) Criminal Law (Insanity) Act. Dublin: Stationery Office

Gordon H, Lindqvist P (2007) Forensic Psychiatry in Europe. Psychiatric Bulletin 31:421-424

H. v United Kingdom (1990) Application No. 15023/89, European Commission on Human Rights

Inspector of Prisons (2005) Annual Report of the Inspector of Prisons 2004–2005

Irish Penal Reform Trust (2001) Out of Sight, Out of Mind: Solitary Confinement of Mentally Ill Prisoners. Dublin: Irish Penal Reform Trust retrieved from www.iprt.ie on 10 September 2013

Irish Penal Reform Trust v Governor of Mountjoy Prison [2005] IEHC 305, High Court, Gilligan J, 2 September 2005

Irish Prison Service Report (1999 and 2000). Dublin: Stationery Office

Irish Prison Service (2009) Annual Report. Retrieved from http://www.irishprisons.ie on 5 September 2013

Irish Prison Service (2010) Annual Report. Retrieved from http://www.irishprisons.ie/documents/2010_Annual_Report.pdf on 7 October 2013

James D, Farnham F, Moorey H, Lloyd H, Blizard R and Barnes T (2002) Outcomes of psychiatric admissions through the courts. London: Home Office, RDS Occasional paper No 79

Johnson v United Kingdom (1997) Application No.22520/93, European Human Rights Reports 27, 296

Kelly B D (2007) Penrose's Law in Ireland: An ecological analysis of psychiatric inpatients and prisoners. Irish Medical Journal 100 (2) 373-4

Kennedy H G (2006) The future of forensic mental health services in Ireland Irish Journal of Psychological Medicine 23 (2) 45-46

Kennedy H G (2011) Severe Mental Illness, Vision for Change and the Criminal Justice System in Association for Criminal Justice, Research and Development, Mental Health in the Criminal Justice System – The deliverables of the Government's 'Vision for Change'. Retrieved from http://www.acjrd.ie on 20 August 2013

Kinsella v Governor of Mountjoy Prison [2011] IEHC 235, High Court, Hogan J, 12 June 2011

Knight L, Stephens M (2009) Mentally Disordered Offenders in Prison: A Tale of Neglect? Internet Journal of Criminology 1-16

Laing J (1999) Care or Custody?: Mentally Disordered Offenders in the Criminal Justice System. Oxford: Oxford University Press

Linehan S, Duffy D, Wright B, Curtin K, Monks S, Kennedy H G (2005) Psychiatric morbidity in a cross-sectional sample of male remanded prisoners. Irish Journal of Psychological Medicine 22 (4) 128–132

McDaid D, Wiley M, Maresso A, Mossialos E (2009) Ireland: Health system review. Health Systems in Transition 11 (4) 1–268

McSherry B, Weller P (eds.) (2010) Rethinking Rights-Based Mental Health Laws. Oxford: Hart

Mental Health Commission (2006) Discussion Paper – Forensic Mental Health Services for Adults in Ireland. Dublin: Mental Health Commission

Mental Health Commission (2011) Forensic Mental Health Services Adults in Ireland – Position paper. Dublin: Mental Health Commission

Mental Health Commission (2013) Annual Report 2012. Dublin: Mental Health Commission

Mental Health Commission and An Garda Síochána (2009) Report of Joint Working Group on Mental Health Services and the Police. Dublin: MHC

McInerney C, Davoren M, Flynn G, Mullins D, Fitzpatrick M, Caddow M, Caddow F, Quigley S, Black F, Kennedy H G, O Neill C (2013) Implementing a court diversion and liaison scheme in a remand prison by systematic screening of new receptions: a 6 year participatory action research study of 20,084 consecutive male remands. International Journal of Mental Health Systems June 25 7 (1) 18

O'Grady J (1990) The complimentary role of regional and local secure provision for psychiatric patients. Health Trends 22:14-16

O'Neill C (2006) Liaison between criminal justice and psychiatric systems: Diversion services. Irish Journal of Psychological Medicine 23 (3) 87

O'Neill C (2011) Workshop Three: Prison In-reach and Court Liaison Services in Ireland in: Association for Criminal Justice, Research and Development, Mental Health in the Criminal Justice System – The deliverables of the Government's 'Vision for Change'. Retrieved from http://www.acjrd.ie on 20 August 2013

Peay J (2003) Decisions and Dilemmas: Working with Mental Health Law. Oxford: Hart

Peay J (2010) Mental Health and Crime. New York: Routledge

People (DPP) v Redmond [2006] 3 Irish Reports 188

Prior P (2007) Mentally disordered offenders and the European Court of Human Rights. International Journal of Law and Psychiatry 30:546

Robinson v United Kingdom (1993) App No. 20858/92, European Commission on Human Rights, 5 May 1993

Rocha v Portugal (2001) European Human Rights Reports 32:16

United Nations General Assembly (1991) The protection of persons with mental illness and the improvement of mental health care (widely known as the Mental Illness Principles). A/RES/46/119 75th plenary meeting

United Nations (2006) Convention on the Rights of Persons with Disabilities and Optional Protocol

United Nations High Commissioner for Human Rights (2009) Thematic Study on enhancing awareness and understanding of the Convention on the Rights of Persons with Disabilities. A/HRC/10/48

Webb D, Harris R (1999) Managing People Nobody Owns. London: Routledge

Whelan D (2009) Mental Health Law and Practice: Civil and Criminal Aspects. Dublin: Round Hall

Whelan D (2012) Annotation of the Criminal Law (Insanity) Act 2010. Irish Current Law Statutes Annotated R.137:40-01–40-18

World Health Organization (2001) Mental Health: New Understanding New Hope. Geneva: World Health Organization

World Health Organization (2007) WHO Health in Prisons Project in collaboration with its Collaborating Centre, UK Department of Health and the Sainsbury Centre for Mental Health. Trencín, Slovakia. Geneva: World Health Organization

Wright B, Duffy D, Curtin K, Linehan S, Monks S, Kennedy H G (2006) Psychiatric morbidity among women prisoners newly committed and amongst remanded and sentenced women in the Irish prison system. Irish Journal of Psychological Medicine 23 (2) 47-53

NOTES

[i] Note also the amendments made to the 2006 Act by the Criminal Law (Insanity) Act 2010; see generally Whelan 2012.

[ii] See Whelan 2009:492-500; Whelan 2012.

[iii] In a brief judgment on 2 April 2008, the Supreme Court decided that the question of *locus standi* could not, in the circumstances of the case, be wholly separated from the issues of the justiciability of all or at least some of the matters in issue and referred the case back to the High Court.

[iv] For further discussion of ECHR case-law on these issues, see Prior 2007.

SECTION 3: EMERGING ISSUES AND IMPLICATIONS FOR THE FUTURE

12

Current trends in the economics of mental health care in Ireland

Brendan Kennelly

INTRODUCTION

This chapter outlines the economic aspects of key issues in Irish mental health policy. The chapter begins with an overview of economics in general with particular focus on issues in health economics. I then examine the contribution of economic analysis to answering four questions:

- What is the economic impact of mental distress in Ireland?
- Does mental health receive an appropriate share of the Irish public health budget?
- Are Irish mental health care resources allocated fairly and efficiently?
- What treatments and strategies are potential priorities for new investment?

In discussing these issues, I will address the implications of some of the distinctive features of mental health and mental health care and identify a number of important data deficits and challenges in the policymaking environment in Ireland that currently constrain the application of economic analysis in mental healthcare. The chapter will conclude with suggesting a number of measures that, if implemented, could result in Irish mental health policy being informed by improved health economic evidence.

WHAT IS THE ROLE OF ECONOMICS IN MENTAL HEALTH POLICY?

In a very broad sense, economics is concerned with two important issues – the efficient allocation of resources and the distribution of opportunities and outcomes. In the case of mental healthcare, economists are interested in whether the available resources (facilities, health professionals, pharmaceuticals etc.) are being combined to help the largest number of people, and whether the services produced are being used by those people whose need or demand for them is greatest. There are in turn another set of resource allocation choices that address the issue of how the available resources are themselves produced.

The primary attention paid by economists to efficiency is typically attributed to the fundamental problem of scarcity – if the demand for mental healthcare exceeds supply, then choices must be made as to how the available scarce mental healthcare resources should be allocated to achieve the best possible outcome. Furthermore, any resources devoted to producing mental healthcare have an 'opportunity cost' in that they could be used instead to produce other valuable services.

The first requirement of efficiency, which is relatively uncontroversial, is that the available resources should be used in the most productive way so that the maximum level of output (in this case, mental healthcare) is produced. The second efficiency requirement, allocative efficiency, specifies that mental healthcare resources should be allocated to those people who place the highest value on those resources.

The allocative efficiency requirement strikes many people as reasonable when we are thinking about ordinary private goods. Assuming that individuals are in the best position to know how they value particular goods leads to the conclusion that the allocation of such goods is most efficiently allocated in markets. However, economists have long argued that healthcare is not an ordinary private good and that it is unlikely that private markets will lead to an efficient allocation of healthcare. A very influential paper by Kenneth Arrow published in 1963 is generally taken as the first paper on health economics. One of its main arguments was that the peculiar nature of healthcare meant that the standard efficiency arguments for private markets may not necessarily apply. There are a number of reasons why healthcare is different including the external effects associated with some health problems such as contagious diseases, and agency issues where the standard economic assumption that an individual generally knows what is best may not apply, leading to problems such as supplier induced demand. Furthermore, uncertainty about the timing and size of healthcare expenditures leads to a demand for insurance services. Arrow suggested two problems that are likely to make private health insurance markets inefficient: adverse selection (people who think they are at higher risk of needing healthcare will be more likely to purchase health insurance) and moral hazard (people will behave in riskier ways after they buy health insurance).

Health economic analysis also addresses a second broad issue: distribution and equity. Mental healthcare is demanded not because individuals like it in itself, but because they want or need it to treat an underlying mental health problem. Thus one aspect of mental health economics asks whether mental health problems are uniformly distributed over the population. The evidence from Ireland and all over the world is that this is generally not the case. Instead, epidemiologists have found substantial socio-economic differences in the incidence and prevalence of almost every major illness, including mental disorders. This phenomenon is one part of the socio-economic gradient of health. Another equity issue concerns how healthcare is accessed and utilised by different individuals in a society – for example, whether available treatments are delivered disproportionately to different income groups. Some, but by no means all, philosophical theories have argued that healthcare is a special good that should be distributed as equally as possible to individuals regardless of their income. For example, Norman Daniels and others have argued that health is a primary social good (in the Rawlsian sense) that is necessary for an individual to be able to pursue the life he or she wants to pursue (Daniels 1985).

For these and other reasons, the majority of healthcare, including mental healthcare, is provided by the state in most market-oriented economies such as Ireland. The efficiency and equity with which governments allocate healthcare resources is therefore a core concern of mental health economists.

The issues outlined above are generally the main issues of concern to mental health economists. On the efficiency side, research has focused on whether particular interventions (drugs, therapies, different methods for delivering services, public health campaigns) are worth their cost from an economic perspective, while on the distribution side, research has focused on the incidence of mental health problems across socio-economic groups and on the equity of access to appropriate care for people with mental health problems. At the same time the relatively poor standing of mental health in the policy decision-making process has been taken on board by many mental health economists and their work might be better described as political economy than 'simply' economics.

QUANTIFYING THE NEED FOR MENTAL HEALTHCARE

The first step with any analysis of the system of care for people with mental/ emotional distress in any country is to estimate the needs of the population. Estimating the incidence of mental distress at any point in time is not a straightforward issue. Ideally, the starting point should be a psychiatric morbidity survey that surveys a representative sample of the population and administers a standardised test that will allow a deduction to be made as to whether a respondent meets some established criteria for a mental disorder. The respondents in the survey who satisfy such criteria are then resurveyed with additional questions about their health and social conditions in order to come up with a more precise estimate of the number of people with particular mental health problems in that country. These surveys are expensive because a large number of people need to be surveyed so that enough people with underlying mental health problems can be identified. Unfortunately such a study has not yet been conducted in Ireland. This is a severe limitation, most importantly for health planners trying to decide what services to supply, but also for researchers trying to analyse the overall effectiveness of the system of mental healthcare in Ireland. As we will see throughout this chapter, data limitations continue to plague researchers on mental health policy in Ireland.

Instead, researchers in Ireland have to rely on much smaller surveys to estimate the likely prevalence of mental health problems. The Health Research Board has conducted two valuable population-level surveys of psychological wellbeing and distress in Ireland (Tedstone Doherty et al. 2007, Tedstone Doherty and Moran 2009). In both cases, about 1,000 people aged 18 or over were surveyed. Questions regarding use of mental health services in the previous year as well as self-reported mental health were included. In addition the General Health Questionnaire (GHQ) was completed by respondents. A score of 4 or more on this index indicates a moderate or severe level of mental distress.

Fieldwork for the most recent survey was conducted in November and December of 2007 (Tedstone Doherty and Moran 2009). 12% of the respondents reported that they had experienced less-than-good mental health in the previous year. In another question, almost 15% of respondents said that they had had a mental health problem in the previous year. The mental health problem was described as having severe limitations on people's physical health by 1.2% and on their social activities by 1.4%. 12% of respondents also received a score of 4 or higher on the General Health Questionnaire. 6% of people said they were taking psychotropic medication at the time of the survey. Almost 10% of the respondents had visited their GP about a mental health problem in the previous year. Many of the people who had visited their GP about a mental health problem in the previous year reported that their mental health was good. Whether this is due to stigma or whether the people in question felt that their mental health problem had been resolved is not clear.

At least 5% of the respondents had been in contact with at least one of a range of secondary mental health services. 2.2% said they had been in contact with inpatient psychiatric services. This is a surprising result as the number of people admitted to a psychiatric hospital or unit in Ireland in 2007 was 20,769, which is a much lower proportion of the population than 2.2%.

A second useful source of information on mental health is the Slán survey, the most recent of which was also carried out in 2007 (Barry et al. 2009). This included face-to-face interviews with 10,364 adults in Ireland. Respondents were asked a series of questions about their mental health as part of a longer survey about health and wellbeing. One question referred to non-specific psychological distress. This was measured using the five-item Mental Health Index-5 (MHI-5). A respondent is considered to have a probable mental health problem if they have a score of 52 or lower on this scale. Approximately 7% of the sample (6.3% of men and 7.5% of women) was identified as having probable mental health problems. This figure is considerably lower than other population level surveys on mental health in Ireland in the past ten years such as the HRB survey referred to earlier. Barry et al. (2009:77) suggest that respondents may be less inclined to disclose their true level of psychological distress in face-to-face interviews.

The Slán survey also provided information that would lead to a probable diagnosis of (a) a major depressive disorder and (b) a generalised anxiety disorder. A diagnosis of a major depressive disorder means that the respondent fulfils the criteria for an episode of depression for at least two weeks of the previous 12 months. Respondents were also asked whether they had depression in the previous 12 months and, if so, whether it had been diagnosed by a doctor. A diagnosis of generalised anxiety disorders (GAD) means that the respondent fulfils the criteria for GAD for at least 6 months of the previous 12 months.

Overall, 6% of the respondents were assessed as having a probable major depressive disorder in the past year (8% of women, 5% of men). About 6% of the sample reported that they had had depression in the previous 12 months with over three quarters of this group reporting that the depression had been diagnosed by a doctor. Interestingly, less than half of the group that reported they had been depressed were diagnosed as having a probable major depressive disorder as measured by the CIDI-SF instrument. This might be the result of them having received appropriate treatment or because they were depressed for a relatively short period. Overall, over 3% of the respondents were diagnosed as having had generalised anxiety disorder in the previous year. The rates for depressive disorder and generalised anxiety disorder were similar to what had been found in other surveys in Ireland.

One interesting development towards the kind of psychiatric morbidity study that is needed in Ireland is the research being done by the Psychiatric Epidemiology Research group at the RCSI (Cannon et al. 2013). They are conducting research on two epidemiological cohorts of young people. In one study, Cannon et al. surveyed the extent of mental health problems in over 1,000 adolescents from Dublin County and Kildare aged between 11 and 13 using the Strengths and Difficulties Questionnaire. A sub-sample of over 200 adolescents and their families was interviewed by psychologists and psychiatrists between 2007 and 2010. The interview schedule used was the Schedule for Affective Disorders and Schizophrenia for School-Aged Children, Present and Life-time Version (K-SADS-PL) and the interviews took between 2 and 4 hours.

The results indicate that about 1 in 6 of the young adolescents was experiencing a mental disorder at the time of interview. Furthermore the interviews revealed that over 30% of the sample had experienced a mental disorder at some point in their life. The most common disorders were anxiety and mood disorders. The current rate of disorder among the Irish cohort was over 50% higher than the corresponding figure found in a cohort of 11- to 12-year-olds in the UK.

The second cohort study being analysed by Cannon et al. is a group of 169 young people aged between 19 and 24 from North Dublin City. Study participants were assessed for mental disorders using the Structured Clinical Interview for DSM-IV Psychiatric Diagnoses I instrument. The assessments were conducted between 2008 and 2010. Cannon et al. (2013:29) found that almost 1 in 5 young adults were experiencing a mental disorder at the time the study was conducted and that over half the sample had experienced a mental disorder at some point in their lives. Mood and anxiety disorders were the most common problems. The lifetime rates for mental disorders in Dublin were similar to rates found in the United States but higher than rates found in Northern Ireland and Germany. About one third of the people who met the criteria for a lifetime disorder had never received any professional help for a mental health problem. While the sample sizes are relatively small in both of these studies, they represent an important development in our understanding of the extent of mental disorders among young people in Ireland.

In addition to identifying the need for mental health care, an analysis of the economic impacts of mental disorders must also estimate the cost of these disorders. There is a two-way relationship between ill-health and the economy, which means that economists are interested in both how resources are or should be allocated to treat ill-health and how ill-health in turn affects economic activity. The economic effects of mental health problems are associated with the ability to work, other productive contributions to society, personal income, and the utilisation of health care and other support services. For example, when we think of the economic costs of poor mental health we must consider the indirect costs such as the lost output that is not produced both by the people with mental health problems and by people who are providing informal care to them as well as the direct costs that fall on service users, their families, and the health system.

While these general health economic concepts are all relevant for mental healthcare, there are sound reasons to expect that from an economic perspective there are likely to be particularly challenging questions regarding mental health. The chronic nature of some mental health difficulties means that indirect costs are particularly difficult to estimate. The question of stigma means that returning to employment after a period of ill health is often a much more complicated and difficult issue in the case of mental health. Mental health problems are frequently associated with poor physical health as well. There is a good deal of evidence that mental health problems are in part caused by economic factors as illustrated, for example, by the relationship between economic conditions and suicide rates.

Estimates of the impacts of mental ill-health in Ireland and elsewhere have generally found them to be large. For example O'Shea and Kennelly (2008) calculated that the total direct and indirect costs associated with poor mental health in Ireland in 2002 was approximately €3 billion. About two-thirds of this cost was represented by the value of output that was not produced by people with poor mental health or by people who were providing informal care to them. The exact cost of such a wide ranging and heterogeneous set of conditions cannot be precisely estimated. The main point of cost of illness studies is to indicate the rough size of the economic burden associated with a particular disease and in that respect there is no surprise that the number found by O'Shea and Kennelly is as large as it is.

Behan et al. (2008) calculated the economic cost associated with schizophrenia in Ireland. They estimated that the overall cost was over €460 million in 2006. About a quarter of these costs were direct healthcare costs with most of the remainder being due to lost output due to illness or premature mortality. While the data on the prevalence of schizophrenia underlying the study is likely to be more reliable than the prevalence data in the O'Shea and Kennelly study (which covered all mental disorders), data problems were still a major problem for Behan et al. who noted the lack of comprehensive data on community-based services as well as reliable unit cost data. There remains a pressing need in Ireland for reliable data on the quantity and cost of different services that are provided to people with poor mental health care.

We also need to keep the economic impacts of poor mental health in perspective. They stand alongside the often huge personal costs of mental health problems – symptoms that are usually very painful and distressing for the individual concerned, including psychological pain and distress, medication side-effects, co-morbid physical disorders, limitations on social functioning, stigmatisation by the rest of society, social isolation, lack of self-esteem, and so on. These costs are often difficult to measure and value, but are equally important.

QUANTIFYING EXPENDITURE ON MENTAL HEALTHCARE

There is considerable confusion about the level of expenditure on mental health in Ireland. In 2005, O'Keane et al. used the phrase 'Black Hole' in the title of a paper on the funding allocated to adult mental health services in Ireland and, as we shall see, there are still significant gaps in what is known about how much is spent on mental health services by the government in Ireland. Even less is known about how what is spent is allocated to different services within the overall budget. To compound matters further little or nothing is known about how much is spent by individuals on privately purchased mental health services.

One of the peculiar aspects of the mental healthcare system in Ireland is the significant role played by private hospitals in providing inpatient care.

Nevertheless some progress has been made in collecting consistent financial data and I hope this section will help us understand some important financial facts about the mental health system while also pointing out the significant gaps that hinder systematic analysis of the economics of mental health in Ireland. The 2012 budget included a special allocation to improve the collection of mental health expenditure data and hopefully that allocation will bear fruit in the not too distant future.

The most basic indicator of the State's commitment to mental healthcare is how much is spent on it in any particular year. Yet as we will see even this fundamental number is subject to omissions and confusion. Different official sources give different numbers and it is difficult to know which source is best. I have decided to rely on various issues of the useful publication 'Health in Ireland: Key Trends' to produce the following table.

Table 12.1: Current Expenditure (€million) on the Mental Health (MH) programme in Ireland, 1997-2010; total and percentage of total current public expenditure on health (HE)

Year	Mental Health Expenditure	Health Expenditure	MH/HE
1997	327	3,648	9.0
1998	347	4,040	8.6
1999	395	4,807	8.2
2000	434	5,610	7.7
2001	497	7,010	7.1
2002	564	8,167	6.9
2003	619	9,117	6.8
2004	661	9,923	6.7
2005	775	11,029	7.0
2006	984	11,888	8.3
2007	1042	13,432	7.8
2008	1044	14,352	7.3
2009	1007	14,698	6.9
2010	963	14,165	6.8

Sources: Health in Ireland: Key Trends 2007, 2009-2012

A few points should be noted about these figures. One is the steady large increase in expenditure on mental health between 1997 and 2007. During this period, expenditure increased by about 300%. However, during the same time, total public expenditure on healthcare in Ireland increased more rapidly so the share of total health expenditure accounted for by mental health declined from 9.0% in 1997 to 6.7% in 2004 before increasing to 7.8% in 2007. One can conclude that, during the largest economic boom ever experienced in Ireland, public expenditure on mental health grew rapidly, but did not increase as rapidly as total public health expenditure. A second point is that large changes in particular years seem to be in part the result of administrative changes in how expenditures are reported rather than due to changes in services. In particular the 27% increase in expenditure in 2006 vastly overstates the actual change in expenditure that occurred in that year. A third point is that there has been a considerable reduction in pay costs in recent years because of pay cuts so that a reduction in expenditure does not necessarily imply fewer employees or fewer services.

The publications that these figures are extracted from note that the sources of these figures are the Revised Estimates for Public Services for various years. One might be forgiven for thinking that these were reliable sources. Yet the most recent edition of 'Health in Ireland: Key Trends' (Department of Health 2012) states that the figures for 2011 cannot be compared with figures for earlier years because central costs such as pension costs that had been formerly apportioned to care programmes were instead apportioned to a corporate heading. The following table contains estimates of mental health expenditure and total health expenditure based on the last 5 editions of the HSE National Service Plan. Overall, the picture is of mental health expenditure representing a little over 5% of the total expenditure on services by the HSE in recent years.

Table 12.2: Current Expenditure (€million) on the Mental Health (MH) programme in Ireland, 2009-2013

Year	Mental Health Expenditure	Total Health Expenditure	% MHE/THE
2009	787	14,794	5.3
2010	721	14,349	5.0
2011	712	13,565	5.2
2012	711	13,332	5.3
2013	733	13,404	5.5

Sources: HSE, National Service Plans, 2010-2013

The situation is exacerbated by the fact that the amount listed as the total expenditure on mental health excludes large amounts of money that are in fact spent by the Government on mental health care. Two examples are prescription charges for medication for 'mental illness' and medical services provided to people with mental health problems by GPs. I have estimated how much is spent by the state on medication for mental health problems (Kennelly 2014). The annual reports of the Primary Care Reimbursement Scheme contain data on how much is spent on different drug types. I assigned two sub categories – psychoanaleptics and psycholeptics – to mental illnesses and assigned one third of another sub category (anti-epileptics) to mental illnesses as these drugs are often prescribed for problems such as schizophrenia and bipolar disorder. The following table contains estimates of the amount spent by the state under three schemes (the GMS scheme, the Drug Payment scheme, and the Long Term Illness scheme) on drugs for mental health problems since 1998. The increase in expenditure on these drugs has been broadly in line with the increase in expenditure on all drugs prescribed under these schemes during this period.

Table 12.3: Estimates of the amount spent by the government on medications for mental illnesses (€million)

1998	45.6
1999	56.4
2000	74.8
2001	95.9
2002	116.4
2003	113.8
2004	151.3
2005	170.3
2006	190.6
2007	207.9
2008	222.1
2009	225.8
2010	204.0

Source: Kennelly (2014).

Another significant item is the amount spent by the State on services provided by GPs for people with mental illnesses. It is difficult to find recent studies that estimate the proportion of GP consultations that are concerned with mental health issues. I took a conservative approach and estimated that 15% of GP visits under the General Medical Scheme could be attributed to mental illnesses. In 2010 the total amount paid to doctors in the GMS was €493.83 million and 15% of this is €74.1 million.

The challenge in coming up with an accurate figure for total mental health expenditure for a single country means that we should be cautious about making cross country comparisons. Yet much attention in policy debates is given to the proportion of the public health budget that is spent on mental health programmes. The World Health Organisation has published a series of country briefs that include data on the proportion of the health budget spent on mental health for 2011. Ireland is one of several countries for which the proportion is listed as 'not available'. For countries that do report this data the proportion varies from between 10 and 13 per cent in Netherlands, Germany and France to less than 6 per cent in Portugal, Spain and Finland (where it is only 3.9 per cent). As noted earlier a peculiar feature of the Irish mental health system is the role played by private psychiatric hospitals which accounted for 11% of inpatient days in Ireland in 2012. We don't have any estimates on expenditure on private mental health services but a conservative estimate would suggest that the total spent on mental health in Ireland is likely to be around 6% of total health expenditure.

The OECD has some cross country data on various inputs of the mental healthcare system. For example, the Health at a Glance Report published in 2013 contained data on the number of psychiatrists and mental health nurses per 100,000 (OECD 2013). Ireland ranked high on both of these indicators; indeed the number of psychiatric nurses was second only to the Netherlands. These figures need to be interpreted with caution as different countries might classify psychiatric nurses in different ways, including the issue of whether formal specialised training is needed or not before one is classified as a psychiatric nurse (Faedo and Normand 2013:22). The OECD is currently conducting a major project on mental health and this may produce a larger set of comparable, reliable figures.

There remains some debate as to whether a combination of stigma and historic patterns of resource distribution have resulted in mental healthcare receiving a lower share of the public health budget than is appropriate. In addition to citing cross country comparisons, some point to mental health's budget share being significantly less than its share of national illness burden. However, determining how much of the overall health budget should be allocated to mental health is more complex than referencing such simple benchmarks. There is no objectively correct proportion as such decisions involve values based trade-offs between efficiency (how much health gain is generated from investing a euro in mental healthcare compared to other types of healthcare) and equity (ensuring individuals from different illness categories can access some minimum level of healthcare, even if treatments in their illness category are relatively non-cost-effective).

ASSESSING EQUITY AND EFFICIENCY

The spatial distribution of resources for mental health care is another topic that has been analysed in recent years. A *Vision for Change* recommended that extra funding be provided for areas that exhibit social and economic disadvantage with associated high prevalence of mental health problems. A systematic attempt to examine how the allocation of health care resources across geographic areas would be affected in a new resource allocation model was carried out by Staines and colleagues in a 2010 report commissioned by the HRB and the HSE (Staines et al. 2010). The authors note at the beginning of their work that 'at present, it is difficult to ascertain exactly how resources are allocated between care groups at LHO [local health office] level. Budgets do not reflect service provision to the population at LHO level and there is no truly systematic approach to resource allocation' (Staines et al. 2010:vi). They proposed a resource allocation model in which resource allocation in Primary, Continuing and Community Care (which includes mental health) would be driven by LHO population and weighted by age and gender-specific estimated need. These allocations should be further refined using LHO data on deprivation and healthcare utilisation (Staines et al. 2010). The difference between the current allocations and the proposed allocations are very large for some LHOs as is illustrated in the following table.

Table 12.4: Mental Health Care Per Capita Allocation, 2007 (€)

Local Health Office	Actual Expenditure	Expenditure under proposed model	Variation
Dublin North Central	420.1	188.2	-231.9
Galway	271.1	70.1	-100
Longford/Westmeath	285	182	-103
Meath	31.7	148	116
North Cork	285.4	183.9	-101.5
North Tipperary/East Limerick	28.7	166	137.3
Sligo/Leitrim/West Cavan	304.3	192.7	-111.6
West Cork	54.8	193.4	138.6

Source: Brick et al. (2010) based on Staines (2010)

It is clear from these examples that levels of funding were not necessarily related to need or demand and that some areas with high funding maintained high levels of institutional care with less than fully developed community-based alternatives. A Vision for Change also argued that catchment boundaries should be realigned in order to reflect the current social and demographic composition of the population. There is some evidence that this is underway in a recent report that obtained information from the HSE on how the mental health budget was allocated to what are called 'super catchment areas' in 2010 (Faedo and Normand 2013).

Table 12.5: HSE Mental Health Budget by Super Catchment Area

Super Catchment Area	Per Capita Budget, 2010 (€)	Per Capita Budget, 2011 (€)
Limerick, Clare, North Tipperary	166	162
Donegal, Sligo, Leitrim, West Cavan	218	204
Galway, Mayo, Roscommon	300	215
North Lee, North Cork	221	220
South Lee, West Cork, Kerry	133	116
Wexford, Waterford	145	138
Carlow, Kilkenny, South Tipperary	268	249
North Dublin	140	137
Louth, Meath, Cavan, Monaghan	127	119
North West Dublin, Dublin North Central	225	219
Dun Laoghaire, Dublin South East, Wicklow	147	150
Dublin West, Dublin South West, Dublin South City	130	179
Laois, Offaly, Longford, Westmeath, Kildare, West Wicklow	133	131

Source: Faedo and Normand 2013

Even though these areas are much larger in terms of population than the Local Health Office areas used in the Staines et al. analysis, there is still a large difference of over 100 per cent between the lowest and highest per capita allocation. Caution should be exercised in interpreting these figures as the HSE has eleven separate accounting systems that encompass approximately 12,000 individual cost centres and the accounting systems are not always consistent with each other.

Official mental health policy in Ireland for many years has favoured community-based interventions over inpatient care and there has been a dramatic reduction in the number of inpatient days in psychiatric hospitals and units as outlined in a previous chapter in this book (see Brennan Chapter 2). This trend has continued in recent years with the closure of more large psychiatric hospitals and a reduction in the number of inpatient days from over 513,000 in 2009 to just over 453,000 in 2012 (these numbers exclude stays of over one year). Yet over the same period the proportion of the mental health budget accounted by inpatient care remained constant at 58% while the proportion represented by community services remained constant at 27% (Faedo and Normand 2013:40). The question of transferring resources to the services that most urgently need them remains a continuing challenge for the mental health service in Ireland.

So far we have seen the difficulty of obtaining accurate national data about expenditure on mental healthcare. This severely hinders economic research on mental healthcare particularly with respect to economic evaluation. Sound economic evaluation depends on accurate unit cost data as well as accurate measures of health outcomes. The latter need not necessarily be limited to measures of various symptoms associated with particular mental health problems; they could also include broader measures of quality of life and beyond that they could include measures of the process of care as well as its outcome. The two methods of evaluation that are most often used in health economics are cost effectiveness analysis and cost utility analysis.

Cost-effectiveness analysis (CEA) involves the systematic comparison of the costs and outcomes of alternative interventions in which the outcomes are measured in terms of health units. Outcomes may be assessed in terms of the number of lives saved, the number of life-years gained or the change in some other 'natural' unit associated with the health problem in question (for example in the case of depression a natural unit could be the number of symptom-free days.) The cost-effectiveness of a programme or intervention is then expressed as a ratio in which the costs are divided by the relevant health outcomes. In general, an incremental cost-effectiveness ratio (ICER) is utilised to compare alternatives. This involves calculating the difference in costs and outcomes of two interventions and expressing this as a ratio. A limitation of CEA is that it only facilitates comparison between programmes that produce the same health outcome.

Cost-utility analysis (CUA) is a subset of cost-effectiveness analysis in which health outcomes are measured in terms of quality adjusted life-years (QALYs). Therefore, cost-utility analysis takes into account the changes in the quality of life as well as prolongation of life achieved by a programme or intervention. The quality of a programme is determined by a set of values or weights called utilities, one for each possible health state, that reflect the relative desirability of the health state (Drummond et al. 2005). Programmes are then assessed according to the cost per QALY gained.

One major difficulty with economic evaluation in Ireland is the absence of consistent data on costs. In order to do a cost effectiveness study of a particular intervention for a mental health problem we need accurate estimates of the unit costs of all the types of resources that are used in the intervention. These could include hospital care, community health facilities, drug and talk therapies, and consultations with various health professionals. Unfortunately there is no reliable source for these data in Ireland and, instead, researchers have to rely on data generated elsewhere and/or the cooperation of individuals involved in delivering particular services. Furthermore, the challenges in diagnosing mental health problems correctly and in deciding on the correct treatment means that analysing the cost effectiveness of treatments can be particularly difficult. This is exacerbated by the relatively low levels of treatment adherence for many of the medications and rehabilitation programmes recommended for mental health problems (Faedo and Normand 2013:26).

There are only very limited examples of applying economic evaluation to mental health care in Ireland. However, two examples of economic evaluation of mental health interventions in Ireland were published in 2012. Gibbons et al. (2012) examined whether changing to a more community-based model of service delivery in the Kildare/West Wicklow catchment area would be more or less cost effective than the traditional model which was oriented towards inpatient care. The catchment area is divided into five sub areas each with its own mental health team. Two of the areas that were thought to rely on different models of care were selected for comparison. The North East sector follows a comprehensive community model with access to a day centre, a day hospital and a homecare team as well as access to a full range of relevant professional disciplines. The Mid East sector at the time of the study (2008) relied far more on a traditional service model that placed a strong reliance on inpatient care. Data on clinical activity levels and costs were collected for both areas as well as some evidence on the satisfaction of service users and family members with the services in the respective areas.

Gibbons et al. (2012) found that the quality of care provided in the comprehensive community model was superior to the traditional model based on a number of indicators. For example waiting times for assessments were considerably lower in the community model and the admission rate and length of stay in inpatient care was much lower in the community model. In addition, service users and their families expressed higher levels of satisfaction with care in the community model. On the cost side, the cost of the traditional model was 27% higher on a per capita basis than the community model.

The second recent example is a report that evaluated an intervention called a Suicide Crisis Awareness Nurse (SCAN) that was introduced in two catchment areas – Cluain Mhuire in Dublin and Wexford in the past ten years (Bradley et al. 2012). The SCAN service is a community based referral service, which provides General Practitioners with an additional option of specialised nurse-led care when a person presents to the GP clinic exhibiting behaviour symptomatic of suicidal risk. While those deemed at immediate high risk are typically referred directly to inpatient psychiatric hospital services as well as to SCAN, those deemed at lower risk are typically referred initially to the SCAN service. This process involves a referral for an immediate consultation with a specialised nurse, who then determines the next stage of the patient's treatment process. This may involve referral for further care in primary care, community care, hospital outpatient care, or inpatient hospital care. The SCAN nurse facilitates the patient's adherence to their assigned method of care.

In the evaluation, the economic analysis focused on comparing the healthcare costs associated with the SCAN service with an estimate of what these costs would have been had the SCAN service not been in place. The key variable in the analysis was the effect that the SCAN service had on reducing the number of people admitted to inpatient psychiatric care. Bradley et al. (2012) found plausible evidence in both Wexford and Cluain Mhuire that the decline in inpatient admissions since 2008 was related to the introduction of the SCAN service. The proportion of the reduction in inpatient admissions that can be ascribed to the SCAN service was harder to determine. Under reasonable assumptions about the size of effect Bradley et al. found that the SCAN service resulted in a reduction of healthcare costs. Given that survey evidence indicated a high level of satisfaction among service users and providers with the service there was a high probability that the service was cost effective.

In addition to cost comparisons and simulations economists also like to have an estimate of the value of an intervention. Many health services are generally provided by the state so in the absence of having a market price, economists have turned to non-market techniques to estimate the value of interventions. One of these techniques is contingent valuation and O'Shea et al. (2008) used this technique to elicit preferences for mental health care in Ireland. This is one of a small number of papers that have used the contingent valuation technique to discover how much individuals would be willing to pay for a specific intervention in mental health.

The study asked people about their willingness to pay for and ranking of similar interventions in mental healthcare, care of the elderly and cancer care and found that the cancer care programme was generally ranked as more important than the elderly care programme, which was in turn regarded as more important than the mental healthcare programme. This was true for people who had personal or close family experience of mental health and for people who considered themselves at higher risk of needing mental health care services.

One potential explanation for these rankings is that individuals may have been sceptical that the proposed intervention in mental health would work as outlined in the survey. While health professionals are keen to stress that recovery is possible for mental distress and that effective treatments are available, the general public in Ireland may be more circumspect in their views of the effectiveness of mental healthcare programmes (although over half the people in a 2012 survey thought that the majority of people could recover from a mental health problem (Millward Brown Lansdowne 2012). It should also be noted that the contingent valuation technique continues to be the subject of lively debate about its methodological validity and that respondents accustomed to dealing with health care provision in a non-market environment in Ireland may not be able to think about changes to specific health care programmes in a very direct financial way.

CONCLUSION

Well-conducted health economic analysis can make significant contributions to our understanding of almost every aspect of policy and practice development in the mental health field. Economics can support decisions relating to the funding and provision of services and can help to improve the efficiency with which scarce mental health resources are allocated.

However, despite the positive role that economic analysis can play in mental health policy, it is hard to find evidence that decision-makers in Ireland take a systematic approach to utilising economic evaluations in the development or implementation of mental health policy. Furthermore, structural data deficits make conducting high quality economic analysis relevant to the Irish context more difficult. Addressing these culture and data issues will make a significant contribution to developing a more evidence-based framework for mental health policy in Ireland.

*

REFLECTIVE QUESTIONS FOR DISCUSSION AND DEBATE: PRACTICE

* How can a discipline such as economics contribute to the development of better policies in the area of mental health?
* Can the standard approach of health economics be reconciled with the Recovery Model of mental health?
* Are cost of illness studies relevant for policymakers?

REFLECTIVE QUESTIONS FOR DISCUSSION AND DEBATE: RESEARCH

- What practical steps can be taken to improve the quality of data on costs and outcomes in Ireland and how could such data be made available to people who wish to conduct research in the economic analysis of mental health in Ireland?
- How does mental health policy and practice vary across different catchment areas in Ireland?
- When might a psychiatric morbidity survey be conducted in Ireland?

REFERENCES

Arrow K J (1963) Uncertainty and the welfare economics of medical care American Economic Review 53:941-973

Barry M, Van Lente E, Moicho M, Morgan K et al. (2009) SLÁN 2007: Survey of Lifestyle Attitudes and Nutrition in Ireland: Mental Health and Social Well-Being Report. Dublin: Department of Health and Children

Behan C, Kennelly B, O'Callaghan E (2008) The economic cost of schizophrenia in Ireland: A cost-of-illness study Irish Journal of Psychological Medicine 25 (3) 80-87

Bradley S, Murphy K, Devane D, Kennelly M et al. (2012) Research Evaluation of the Suicide Crisis Assessment Nurse (SCAN) Service. Dublin: HSE

Brick A, Nolan A, O'Reilly J, Smith S (2010) Resource Allocation, Financing and Sustainability in Health Care. Dublin: Economic and Social Research Institute

Cannon M, Coughlan H, Clarke M, Harley M, Kelleher I (2013) The Mental Health of Young People in Ireland: a report of the Psychiatric Epidemiology Research across the Lifespan (PERL) Group. Dublin: Royal College of Surgeons in Ireland

Daniels N (1985) Just health care. Cambridge: Cambridge University Press

Department of Health and Children (2006) A Vision for Change: Report of the Expert Group on Mental Health Policy. Dublin: Stationery Office

Department of Health and Children (2007) Health in Ireland: Key Trends 2007. Dublin: Stationery Office

Department of Health and Children (2009) Health in Ireland: Key Trends 2009. Dublin: Stationery Office

Department of Health (2011) Health in Ireland: Key Trends 2011. Dublin: Stationery Office

Department of Health (2012) Health in Ireland: Key Trends 2012. Dublin: Stationery Office

Drummond M et al. (2005) Methods for the Economic Evaluation of Health Care Programmes, 3rd edition. Oxford: Oxford University Press

Faedo G, Normand C (2013) Implementation of 'A Vision for Change' for Mental Health Services Report to Amnesty International Ireland. Dublin: Stationery Office

Gibbons P, Lee A, Parkes J, Meaney E (2012) Value for Money: A comparison of costs and quality in two models of Adult Mental Health Service provision. Dublin: HSE

Health Service Executive (2012) National Service Plan. Dublin: HSE

Kennelly B (2014) The Economics of Mental Health Services in Cullinan J, Lyons S, Nolan B (Eds.) The Economics of Disability: Insights from Irish Research. Manchester: Manchester University Press (forthcoming)

Millward Brown Lansdowne (2012) Research 2012: Irish attitudes towards mental health problems available at http://seechange.ie/wp-content/themes/seechange/images/stories/pdf/See_Change_Research_2012_Irish_attitudes_towards_mental_health_problems.pdf

OECD (2013) Health at a Glance 2013: OECD Indicators. OECD Publishing O'Keane V et al. (2005) The Black Hole. Dublin: Irish Psychiatric Association

O'Shea E, Kennelly B (2008) The Economics of Mental Health Care in Ireland Dublin: Mental Health Commission

O'Shea E, Gannon B, Kennelly B (2008) Eliciting Preferences for Resource Allocation in Mental Health Care in Ireland. Health Policy 88:359-370

Staines A et al. (2010) Towards the Development of a Resource Allocation Model for Primary, Continuing and Community Care in the Health Services – Volume 2: Technical Report. Dublin: Dublin City University

Tedstone Doherty D, Moran R, Kartalova-O'Doherty Y (2007) Psychological distress, mental health problems and use of health services in Ireland, HRB Research Series 5. Dublin: HRB

Tedstone Doherty D, Moran R (2009) Mental health and associated health service use on the island of Ireland. HRB Research Series 7. Dublin: Health Research Board

World Health Organisation (2011) Mental Health Atlas. Geneva: World Health Organisation

13

Emerging issues in the law within a changing human rights framework

Mary Keys

INTRODUCTION

Mental health law serves a wide variety of purposes and interests, although its main focus tends to be on situations in which admission and treatment can take place without consent. The law places limitations on such interventions by providing safeguards for persons subject to intervention and regulating the activities of those involved. The societal justification for such laws is the belief that persons with mental/emotional distress need to be treated for their own good or that of others, even without their consent. The conflict between the welfare approach, which permits intervention on the basis of the person's best interests, and the mandate of human rights law, which requires recognition of the person's autonomy, gives rise to significant tension.

Obligations under human rights law have exposed deficiencies in the Irish system and have been influential in driving law reform. The Mental Treatment Act 1945 underpinned a medical discretion model by delegating extensive power to the psychiatrist, resulting in a medically orientated approach to framing mental health problems. The Mental Treatment Act was replaced in 2006 by the Mental Health Act 2001 (2001 Act), which was intended to meet the evolving human rights standards laid down in the European Convention on Human Rights (ECHR). Reform is again required to bring Ireland into line with changing human rights obligations. One example involves legal capacity, where a decision of the European Court of Human Rights (European Court) has ruled in *Shtukaturov v Russia* (Application no 44009/05 27 March 2008) that mental disorder cannot be the sole reason for denial of legal capacity. The innovative UN Convention on the Rights of Persons with Disabilities (CRPD) places mental health law within the area of disability law and requires a shift from a medical model to a social and human rights model of disability.

This chapter discusses Ireland's human rights obligations under the CRPD and the ECHR. Key elements of Irish law are examined for compliance with human rights standards and explored with reference to commentary and recommendations for change from key stakeholders. The focus on the future includes reference to the Department of Health (2012) proposals in the *Interim Report on the Review of the Mental Health Act* 2012 (IR).

HUMAN RIGHTS LAW

United Nations Convention on the Rights of Persons with Disabilities

The core purpose of the CRPD is 'to promote, protect and ensure the full and equal enjoyment of all human rights by all persons with disabilities, and to promote respect for their inherent dignity' (CRPD Article 1). Equality is the dominant value underpinning the CRPD. Disability is regarded as an evolving concept resulting from the interaction between persons with impairments and barriers that hinder their full participation in society on an equal basis with others. The focus of the guiding principles of the CRPD (Article 3) is the inherent dignity and autonomy of the person and the freedom to make one's own choices and participate fully in society without discrimination due to disability. A core element of disability equality is the duty of reasonable accommodation. Lawson describes it as a 'duty to "accommodate" the specific circumstances of a particular disabled person by adjusting the physical and organizational structures and practices' (Lawson 2012:846)

There is no definition of disability; instead, an illustrative description states that, 'persons with disabilities include those who have long-term physical, mental, intellectual or sensory impairments which in interaction with various barriers may hinder their full and effective participation in society on an equal basis with others' (CRPD Article 1). It is important to acknowledge that not everyone who has a mental health difficulty wants to be thought of as having a disability. However, in acknowledging 'long-term mental impairment' as a disability, the CRPD specifically provides a framework for the full recognition by the law of the human rights of persons with experience of mental/emotional distress. The focus therefore, is not on a person's inability to participate in all aspects of life, but on the difficulties created by the various barriers in society to full participation. This is a fundamental shift away from the traditional medical model to a social and human rights model. Dhanda maintains that '[t]he paradigm of the CRPD is up against the barrier of the mind' requiring significant changes in attitude and practice (Dhanda 2012:181).

Barriers come in all shapes and can include single restrictions or a combination of many others described as follows:

disabled people experience disability as a social restriction, whether those restrictions occur as a consequence of inaccessibly built environments, questionable notions of intelligence and social competence, the inability of the general population to use sign language, the lack of reading material in Braille or hostile public attitudes to people with non-visual disabilities. (Scotch 2000:12)

Hostile public attitudes and inaccurate presumptions around intelligence and social competence are prevalent experiences for persons with experience of mental/emotional distress (National Disability Authority 2011, Thornicroft 2006, Mac Gabhann et al. 2010).

CRPD and legal capacity

Article 12 states that 'persons with disabilities have the right to recognition everywhere as persons before the law ... [and] enjoy legal capacity on an equal basis with others in all aspects of life'. Access to support to exercise legal capacity must be provided and decisions must respect the 'rights, will and preferences' of the person (Article 12(3)(4)). Dhanda comments that disability and the 'reality of difference can be accommodated in this new paradigm of universal legal capacity' (Dhanda 2012:179). The denial of legal capacity affects a disproportionate number of people who are excluded from making decisions, resulting in a cycle of disempowerment and invisibility (Hammamberg 2011, Lewis 2012). Reform of capacity law and policy presents one of the urgent challenges facing policymakers and legislators (Keys 2009).

It is important to understand the difference between legal and mental capacity. Legal capacity is the law's recognition of a person's ability to exercise rights and duties; being an adult enables persons to engage in particular legal activities, e.g., making a contract to buy a house, making a will, voting or marrying. It is the key to accessing legally recognised participation in society. Mental capacity on the other hand focuses on the person's decision-making skills or abilities, which may vary from time to time, from one decision to another and vary between persons. Mental capacity is influenced by a wide variety of factors including social, emotional and environmental factors.

Current law in Ireland, the Lunacy Regulation (Ir.) Act, 1871, does not differentiate legal capacity from mental capacity, so if a person is deemed not to have the skills required for a particular decision, such as managing property or money, she will be deemed not to have legal capacity and will be admitted to wardship. She will then be virtually invisible to the law and prevented from making any other legal decisions. In contrast, Article 12 (4) requires that the person retain her legal capacity and have support to make a particular decision in order that her 'will and preferences' are recognised. The legal and policy reform required is to move from a substitute decision-making regime, as is the case with wardship, to one based on supported decision-making.

Substitute decision-making occurs when someone makes a decision for another based on the fact that a person has a disability (status approach), or that the person's decision disagrees with what is proposed (outcome approach), e.g. regarding treatment by staff in an approved centre (Emmett 2013, Williams 2012). The law facilitates this approach by delegating power to others to make decisions for persons subject to guardianship or wardship legislation. Some Australian jurisdictions recognise involuntary admission as a form of clinical guardianship where the power to make decisions rests with a consultant psychiatrist (Victorian Law Reform Commission 2011, O'Mahony 2012:893).

In order to fulfil the requirements of the CRPD, supported decision-making is explicitly required to replace substitute decision-making in legal capacity laws (Article 12(3)). When a person who experiences mental/emotional distress has difficulty with decision-making she must be supported in a way that respects her will and preferences. Bach and Kerzner (2010:74) refer to decision-making supports as including: life-planning; independent advocacy; communicational, interpretive and representational assistance; and relationship-building. Ireland has some elements of such a support system with its peer advocates in the mental health care system (Davison 1999:165). Similarly, the successful Personal Ombuds (PO) user-controlled service in Sweden, funded by the state, is a system of support whereby POs work independently with persons who no longer use or trust services, build relationships with them and work only at their direction (Jesperson 2012). These successful approaches are examples of supported decision-making which could ensure that involuntary admission is genuinely a last resort measure as proposed in the IR.

Impact of legal capacity denial

The impact of the deprivation of legal capacity is significant, resulting in a profound loss of control and self-esteem. Bach and Kerzner (2010:7) refer to the 'social and legal harm' arising from a judgment of incapacity. The self-defeating nature of a finding of incapacity is likely to ensure the person will not learn the skills required for future decision-making. The EU Agency for Fundamental Rights (FRA), carried out a study of the experience of persons following the loss of their legal capacity and other restrictions on their ability to make decisions (EU FRA 2013). Participants who lost their legal capacity 'shared a sense of powerlessness and described experiences often characterised by a lack of explanation or an opportunity to challenge the process' (EU FRA 2013:50-71). Of note is that informal restrictions on freedom to take decisions, whether in institutions or the community, compounded legal measures to limit or remove their legal capacity. This is a significant issue that needs to be addressed in Ireland.

In contrast, the study participants were positive about the support to take decisions, underlining how freely chosen and personalised support can empower and promote self-esteem. Research indicates that feelings of control are crucial to one's outlook in life. Fox (2012:90), a neuroscientist, suggests that 'if we have a real sense that we control our destiny, this not only helps us bounce back from setbacks but also maximizes our enjoyment of life.'

While the right to physical and mental integrity on an equal basis with others is protected in Article 17, it is not yet clear what is required in domestic law in order to fulfil this right (Bartlett 2013:431). This is a loss identified by one commentator as 'one of the most critical areas of human rights violations for persons with disability – the use of coercive state power for the purpose of 'treatment' – remains without any specific regulation' (Kayess and French 2008:30).

CRPD and the right to liberty

Article 14 of the CRPD protects the right to liberty on an equal basis with others. It states that 'the existence of a disability shall in no case justify a deprivation of liberty' (Article 14(1)). The UN High Commissioner for Human Rights (2009:48) stated that 'legislation authorising the institutionalisation of persons with disabilities on the grounds of their disability without free and informed consent must be abolished.' This might seem to require the end of mental health detention based on diagnostic criteria. The High Commissioner goes on to clarify that:

> this should not be interpreted to mean that persons with disabilities cannot be lawfully subject to detention for care and treatment or to preventive detention, but that the legal grounds upon which restriction of liberty is determined must be de-linked from the disability and neutrally defined so as to apply to all persons on an equal basis. (2009:48)

This provision has been interpreted as requiring disability-neutral criteria for involuntary admission to mental health care in order to solve the problem of discrimination. A leading commentator, Bartlett refers to these neutral grounds 'like risk or dangerousness which would also apply to the general population subject to detention', and questions how practical this might be, as it seems also to permit preventive detention (Bartlett 2013:276).

CRPD and the right to independent living

Article 19 of the CRPD recognises the equal right to live in and be included in one's community, with choices equal to others about where to live and with whom, and the right not to be obliged to live in a particular living arrangement (Article 19(a)). Physical change of location alone is not adequate to ensure inclusion and participation. Adults with 'long-term mental impairment' may be pressured to move into particular community residential settings in the absence of alternatives. Some are institutional, in remote places and/or allow little choice about any aspect of life. An institution is defined by the European Coalition for Community Living as:

> any place in which people who have been labelled as having a disability are isolated, segregated and/or compelled to live together. An institution is also any place in which people do not have, or are not allowed to exercise control over their lives and their day to day decisions. An institution is not defined merely by its size. (2012)

Importantly, this definition focuses on the impact of the environment on the person. As described in Chapters 2 and 3, many efforts at deinstitutionalisation have resulted in extending the institutional mindset to the community. *Stanev v Bulgaria* (below) highlights the obligations on the state to examine life in community facilities. This is further reinforced by Article 19. The subtleties of control and lack of personal choice are potentially more difficult to identify in community situations requiring instead, a rigorous approach to the recognition of legal capacity and ensuring a truly supportive environment.

CRPD *and the right to participation*

The CRPD requires that the views of people with disabilities, including children, must be sought and must influence the most appropriate kinds of law and policy reforms. Clifford (2011:14) comments that without direct consultation progress will not be made:

> persons with disabilities will inevitably be burdened with laws and procedures that do not account for their individual experiences and that reproduce the paternalistic approach that has sustained historic disadvantage.

The UN Special Rapporteur on the Right to the Highest Standard of Physical and Mental Health (Hunt 2005:para 60) stated that 'the right of persons with mental disabilities to participate in decision-making processes that affect their health and development, as well as in every aspect of service delivery, is an integral part of the right to health.' A report on choice and control carried out in nine EU Member States found that providing 'a platform to those individuals whose voices are seldom heard ... provides invaluable information on how the lives of individuals are affected by laws and policies, or by the lack of them' (EU FRA 2012b:7). This direct consultation method is an important measure in influencing policymakers and legislators.

MENTAL HEALTH POLICY

The national mental health policy, *A Vision for Change* (DOHC 2006) (AVFC) outlines a comprehensive community model of mental health services. AVFC is consistent with the requirements of Article 19 of the CRPD. Based on principles of person-centredness, participation and the recovery ethos, it underpins partnership in its development and in its proposals. That it was published five years after the enactment of the 2001 Act means that the Act was not directed towards its implementation, although there are fundamental elements that are directly compatible with AVFC such as the individual care planning requirement in s66, which is included in the Regulations and elaborated on in the NHC document *Quality Framework in Mental Health Services* (MHC 2007). The IR recommended that recovery would be one of the guiding principles in the revised Act in keeping with the emphasis in AVFC (2012:13). Mental Health Reform (MHR) proposed that there should be a coherent legal and policy framework so that mental health legislation is consistent with the principles of AVFC (2011:2). An Independent Monitoring Group (IMG) set up in 2006 for six years to monitor the implementation of AFVC was highly critical of the pace of implementation, as were others (IMG 2007-2012, Irish Mental Health Coalition 2008, 2009; Mental Health Commission (MHC) 2012b). The European Committee for the Prevention of Torture Report (CPT) commented that the proposals 'could have an immediate positive impact on the quality and cost-effectiveness of psychiatric care in Ireland' (2010:59).

Participation is vitally important for sustainable transformation of attitudes in policymaking and delivery of mental health services. Brosnan highlights issues concerning the involvement of the key stakeholders and states:

> service-user involvement is a new development in the Irish context, resisted fiercely by some interests, and welcomed as a potential source of reform by others. Like Recovery, it is being incorporated into the official discourses without sufficient attention being paid to the complexities of the social justice issues inherent in the user-perspective and failing to problematize the power dynamics service-users must engage with if they choose to enter the new spaces into which they are being invited. (Brosnan 2012:62)

A Health Research Board study of personal experiences of service users concluded that, '[p]erson centred care requires a paradigm shift towards refocusing on the aspirations and goals of those recovering, and the vital importance of their input in care' (Kartalova-O'Doherty and Tedstone Doherty 2010:46).

Participation in one's own individual care plan is a key element of the recovery ethos and is mandated by the Act and in the regulations (2001 s66(2)(g);

Regs. 2006, Article 15). The Office of Inspector of Mental Health Services (IMH) highlighted the poor response of services with comments such as, 'weak conceptual grasp of individual care planning ... inadequate understanding of the values underpinning mental health legislation and policy' (MHC 2012a:54). Referring to service compliance in 2012, the Inspector's report describes progress as 'fair with no significant improvement on previous years' and stated, '[w]e were dismayed to discover several examples of inadequate and absent individual care plans...' (ibid.).

In relation to the development of multi-disciplinary mental health teams in line with AVFC, the IMH report (MHC 2012a:53) refers to the fact that management 'had become even more centralized and less open to disciplines other than psychiatry and nursing.' Such response effectively prevents the implementation of the agreed community-based approach (AVFC) and social model advocated in the CRPD.

MENTAL HEALTH ACT 2001

The Mental Health Act 2001 (2001 Act) was fully implemented in November 2006 with the aim of meeting the requirements of the European Convention on Human Rights (ECHR). Compared with the Mental Treatment Act 1945, changes included the narrowing of criteria for involuntary admission, independent review of detention, (the mental health tribunals) and safeguards around consent to treatment. A key feature was the creation of an independent statutory body, the Mental Health Commission (MHC), with responsibility for the promotion of high standards and good practice in the delivery of mental health services and protection of the interests of those who are detained in approved centres. The Act also provides a statutory basis for the role of Inspector of Mental Health Services (IMH).

The Act underpins the important work of the MHC in the promotion of standards and quality improvements including the licencing of 'approved centres' (registered for inpatient care), based on formal inspections, mainly unannounced (MHC 2007). Inspections are carried out by the IMH, which includes multidisciplinary inspectors. The primary focus for the IMH under the Act is on inpatient services, although in practice the role has extended to inspection of community mental health services. The MHC publishes annual reports incorporating the Inspector's reports.

Principles

The 'best-interests' principle is given precedence in the Act although it is not defined (UNICEF 1996). There is a widespread belief that the Courts have taken an overly paternalistic interpretation of the Act (see *MR v Cathy Byrne* [2007] 3 IR

211, *T. O'D v Kennedy* [2007] 3 IR 689) rather than giving greater consideration to the wishes of the person, and that the Act is in need of reform based on human rights standards.

The requirement to notify the person before decisions concerning admission and treatment are made along with the right of a response as far as practicable, is potentially an important participation principle (MHA s4(2)). This means the views of the person, her right to autonomy and self-determination, must be weighed in the balance. This requirement has significant untapped potential to support both a focus on the will and preferences of the person and engage in dialogue with him/her. There is also a requirement to respect the right to dignity, bodily integrity, privacy and autonomy (s4(3)). There is no information on how this aspect is monitored.

The IR (Department of Health 2012:10) recommends the adoption of a rights-based approach as well as a presumption of capacity. It states:

> a human rights based approach would underscore the fundamental rights of a person to participate in care and treatment decision-making processes which affect them. Paternalism is incompatible with such a rights-based approach and accordingly the Act should be refocused away from 'best interests' in order to enhance patient autonomy.

Involuntary admission

The right to liberty is protected by the ECHR Article 5(1)(e) so that persons with mental/emotional distress cannot be deprived of their liberty except in accordance with law (*Herczegfalvy v Austria* (1993) 15 EHRR 437, *Winterwerp v. Netherlands* (1979) 2 EHRR 387). Under the ECHR the aim of involuntary admission is considered to be therapeutic, and so it must be clearly established that the person has a 'mental disorder' (the legal term used in Irish law and by the ECHR) before liberty is removed. The European Court listed the requirements for involuntary admission except in emergencies: there must be reliable evidence of a mental disorder based on medical expertise, it must be serious enough to require detention and the continuing detention must be justified as necessary (referred to as the 'Winterwerp criteria').

The seriousness of loss of liberty is only justified where other less severe measures have been looked at and found to be inadequate to safeguard the person or others, so that 'the deprivation of liberty must be shown to have been necessary in the circumstances' (*Litwa v Poland* (2001) 33 EHRR 53 para 78). Many of the other ECHR rights are somewhat based on Article 5 because of the impact of involuntary admission. Along with the loss of liberty, restrictions can impact on other fundamental rights, such as the right to privacy, autonomy, self-determination, freedom of expression and association. Safeguards in the form of rights to information concerning the detention, the regular review of continuing detention as well as safeguards for consent to treatment are usually provided. However, one report indicated that more than half of the people involuntarily admitted were not given any written information about their rights despite the statutory obligations to do so (IMH 2011a).

Involuntary admission criteria

Under the Mental Health Act 2001, a person can be involuntarily admitted if she has a 'mental disorder', a legal term which includes a range of factors. It means a mental illness, a significant intellectual disability or a severe dementia (MHA s3). It also requires that there be a serious likelihood of immediate and serious harm to the person or others. Additional factors include: the severity of the illness, impaired judgement, a risk of serious deterioration and prevention of appropriate treatment if the admission is not made. The likelihood of benefit from the admission must be included, although little information is available on this aspect.

One recommendation for reform of the criteria included in the IR is to exclude significant intellectual disability as a ground for detention (MHC 2011b Department of Health 2012). Other aspects of involuntary admission include that the consultant psychiatrist make the admission order with periods of detention for up to 21 days in the first instance, followed by periods up to three months, similarly six months and 12 months. The IR recommends that renewal orders of 12 months be reduced to 9 months (Department of Health 2012:27). A mental health tribunal review takes place at each period of detention. Detention orders revoked before the tribunal hearing took place totalled 1,530 in 2012 or 46.8% of the total admission and renewal orders that year (MHC 2012a:35).

Involuntary admission procedure

Involuntary admission to an approved centre is underpinned by two procedures: one community-based and the other inpatient-based. The community-based procedure is the most common one involving three stages starting with the applicant, commonly a family member, who makes an application to a doctor. The second stage is the recommendation from the GP following an examination, and the third stage is when the consultant psychiatrist makes an admission order following an examination. There were 1,574 such admissions in 2012 (MHC 2012a, 32), the highest number of involuntary admissions since the Act commenced. There were 18,173 admissions of which 11% were involuntary (Daly and Walsh 2013:2-3). A study in a community mental health service in Dublin found that approximately 30% of individuals referred for involuntary admission did not have their orders completed, indicating a need for further research (Ramsay 2013:86).

Different categories of persons, including an Authorised Officer (AO), are permitted to make applications to a doctor for a recommendation for involuntary admission (s9(8)). While the role of the AO was introduced to allow for an alternative to the application being made by a member of the family, this potentially useful role is underused. Most applications are undertaken by family members, 901 (57%) in 2012, (68% in 2007), followed by Garda applicants at 336 (22%), up from 16%, a steady increase since 2007; the category of 'any other person' had a total of 13% or 210 in 2012. In contrast, the AO was involved in 127 (8%) in 2012 compared with 7% in 2007, the lowest of all applicants (MHC 2012a:35).

Research indicates that both the person concerned and their family members experience pressure as well as an emotional burden in carrying out the applicant role (Western Alliance 2005). Persons who were involuntarily admitted experienced a negative impact on the relationships with their family as a result of the involuntary admission (O'Donoghue 2009). Evidence indicates that experiences are more positive when admission is voluntary and 'conducted in a way that granted ... individual choice and control over the treatment'(EU, FRA 2012:7). The IR refers to the considerable benefits of the AO 'to provide specific advice and mobilise support for the service user and family' (Department of Health 2012:31). The AO should be a member of the community mental health team with a specific remit regarding mental health crisis at the pre-admission stage.

The second procedure leading to involuntary admission arises while the person is in an approved centre as a voluntary patient. The person must 'indicate a wish to leave' triggering a second psychiatrist's opinion who may affirm the 'mental disorder' and regrade the individual to involuntary status (ss23, 24). There were 567 such re-gradings in 2012 (MHC 2012a:33). This second opinion is not required to be independent, contrary to the European Court decision in X v Finland (2012 Application No. 34806/0, 3rd July 2012, para 126). The 24-hour holding power can prevent a voluntary patient from leaving in these circumstances (s 23).

Clarification as to whether the ordinary powers available in the community can be used to regrade a voluntary patient to involuntary status was provided for the first time by the High Court in a recent case, KC v Clinical Director of St Loman's Hospital & HSE 4th July 2013. The case concerned a challenge to the legality of this procedure by a voluntary patient who refused all treatment, and 'who never expressed a wish to leave the hospital', so that the trigger for involuntary admission in sections 23 and 24 did not arise. The person was assessed as 'urgently in need of treatment' and the community admission procedure was used instead in order to provide treatment without consent as provided for in the 2001 Act. Holding the detention lawful, the Court stated that the location of the patient is not relevant, since admission under section 14 is concerned with the status of the patient as involuntary rather than his physical location at the time of the admission. It seems that voluntary patients are even more susceptible now to the shadow of compulsion following this decision. Informed consent must be voluntary to be valid, but where there is a threat of detention it potentially invalidates that voluntariness (Donnelly 2005:225).

Voluntary patients

Persons admitted voluntarily include: those who have capacity and consent to admission and those who have impaired capacity, but are compliant and not objecting to the admission. Like all voluntary patients, the compliant incapacitated group are treated on the basis of the common law doctrine of necessity and are sometimes referred to as de facto detained. Voluntary patients should, theoretically, be able to leave hospital and refuse treatment, but these choices are not open to compliant incapacitated persons who are voluntary admissions, nor do they have the safeguards available to detained patients. The 2001 Act, however, effectively legalises this situation by defining a voluntary patient as 'a person receiving care and treatment in an approved centre who is not the subject of an admission order or a renewal order' (s2; *EH v St Vincent's Hospital* (2009) 2 ILRM 149) so that under the Act, a voluntary patient includes someone who lacks capacity to consent to admission.

The issue of voluntary or informal detention arose in the landmark case *HL v. United Kingdom* (2005) 40 EHRR 32 5th October 2004 (Bournewood case), involving a man with autism who was informally admitted for mental health care from his day centre. His foster family were not permitted to see him for months and challenged the legality of his status. The European Court believed that, 'the health care professionals exercised complete control over his movements and care from the outset including his assessment, treatment, contacts and his residence' (*HL*, para 91). He had been sedated and his foster family was unable to meet him or take him home. The actual situation was that *HL* was under continuous supervision and control and was not free to leave. The European Court concluded that he was deprived of his liberty in breach of Article 5 without any safeguards (*HL*, para 120).

This is the current situation in Ireland. There is no requirement to have safeguards, which, as the European Court stated, are of equal importance for patients who have impaired capacity and have, as in *HL*, extremely limited communication abilities. Fennell argues that, if strong treatment like neuroleptics or ECT is used without consent, then the level of control involved in giving this treatment may tip the balance towards a deprivation of liberty (2005:166).

The term 'voluntary' is misleading as it indicates a person with capacity to consent who volunteers to go to hospital. A 24-hour holding power can apply to a voluntary patient, and is a power about which the person is not informed in advance, contrary to human rights law. The lack of safeguards for persons, like *HL*, who are effectively deprived of their liberty, points to a potential breach of Article 5 of the ECHR. Many recommendations have been made for an amendment to the definition of 'voluntary patient' to refer to a person with capacity to consent (for example, MHR 2011:5; Amnesty International Ireland (AI) 2011:1). The IR recommends that 'voluntary' be defined as a person 'who consents on his own behalf or with the support of others or on whose behalf a personal guardian appointed under capacity legislation consents to admission' (Department of Health 2012:21).

The issue was highlighted in the case of *EH v St Vincent's Hospital* (2009 2 ILRM 149), challenging the lawfulness of the person's admission as a voluntary patient though she lacked the capacity to make decisions. The Supreme Court rejected the claim of illegality and held that the meaning of 'voluntary' in section 2 of the Act 'does not describe such a person as one who freely and voluntarily gives consent to an admission order' and the Court unquestioningly accepted the definition in the Act (2009 2 ILRM 149) leading to significant criticism and concern (Murray 2010, Whelan 2009:165, AI 2011:12, IHRC 2010:7).

The CPT expressed concern that voluntary patients could be detained for assessment if they attempted to leave and recommended that 'acceptance of a need for treatment would be implicit in voluntary admission' at the outset; if a patient refuses, then admission should not proceed, and if later they refuse all treatment, they should be discharged (2010, para 117).

The IR recommends that sections 23 and 24 be amended so that a voluntary patient wishing to leave should be allowed to do so. Where risk arises the person could be detained for up to 12 hours and the AO called to consider alternatives, offer advice and support for the service-user and the family (Department of Health 2012:24). Concern has been expressed also that voluntary patients do not have any statutory entitlement to information apart from common law requirements. At the point of admission they should be told of the possibility of detention were they to 'indicate a wish to leave' or refuse treatment (2001 Act s23, KC v Clinical Director of St Loman's Hospital & HSE 2013). This is also important for voluntary patients who have impaired capacity or their representatives.

The concern too for voluntary patients is that there are no treatment safeguards in the Act. The IR states that the revised 2001 Act must dovetail with the Assisted Decision-Making (Capacity) Bill 2013 (ADM Bill) and recommends that the Act must extend to voluntary patients (Department of Health 2012:20). There should be a presumption of capacity regarding admission and treatment. The provisions of the ADM Bill on support to make decisions should apply in this context. The IR recommends that substitute decision-making be the last resort and must be based on the known will and preferences of the person. The success of this recommendation would necessitate greater support to avoid admission as well as meaningful alternatives.

The link between the loss of legal capacity and loss of liberty in a mental health social care home was established in *Stanev v Bulgaria*, Application No 36760/06, 17th April 2012. Mr Stanev was placed in guardianship, excluded from any participation and deemed incapable of expressing his wishes. Forced to live in appalling conditions in a social care institution for eight years, he alleged he was deprived of liberty with no means of challenging it or leaving due to his extreme isolation, lack of money and retention of his identity papers. The European Court found there had been a breach of Article 5, as he was subject to constant supervision with a strict daily routine which led to a deterioration in his health and the onset of institutionalisation, resulting in a potential loss of ability to reintegrate in his community (*Stanev v Bulgaria*, Application No 36760/06, 17th April 2012, paras 130, 135).

The European Court emphasised that if he had not been deprived of his legal capacity due to his mental disorder he would not have been deprived of his liberty. The Court found he was subject to inhuman and degrading treatment contrary to Article 3 of the ECHR, due to appalling living conditions which had been highlighted in a number of independent reports (CPT 2004; Amnesty International, Bulgaria 2002). One stated that, 'in most cases, placement of people with mental disabilities in a specialised institution led to a de facto deprivation of liberty' (CPT 2004, para 11.7). The Stanev decision highlights the need to address obligations under Articles 12 and 19 of the CRPD and the supports needed to make community living a reality in Ireland.

Consent to treatment

The legality of any intervention to treat a person depends on informed consent, or where the individual has impaired capacity, some other lawful authority. The right to autonomy was expressed as a fundamental human right and is recognised by Article 8 of the ECHR in *Pretty v United Kingdom* (2002) (35 EHRR 1, para 65). It protects the individual's right to physical and psychological integrity, the right to mental stability and privacy rights that include self-determination in relation to medical treatment. The right to dignity as an aspect of private life is regarded as fundamental under the ECHR. This dignity right has been interpreted as including the preservation of mental stability (*Bensaid v. United Kingdom* (2001) 33 EHRR 205, para 49).

Rights to privacy, autonomy and bodily integrity are also recognised as rights under the Irish Constitution (*Ryan v Attorney General* [1965] IR 294). In a case involving withdrawal of nutrition and hydration, *Re a Ward (Withdrawal of Medical Treatment* ([1995] 2 ILRM 401 p404), the Supreme Court stated that the constitutional rights of every person include the right to privacy, autonomy and self-determination. These rights were held to apply to persons without capacity to consent equally with those who could consent but are administered in a different way.

The test in the 2001 Act for capacity to consent is similar to that required for informed consent to medical treatment: that the person understand the nature, purpose and likely effects of the treatment (s56). It places responsibility on the doctor regarding the communication of information. Mental health laws are different in that refusal of treatment by involuntary persons can be overridden regardless of capacity. The CPT Irish visit received complaints that the consent provisions (s57) allow too much discretion. The government responded that the capacity legislation may fill the gap (CPT Gov. Response 2011, 69). The Act has specific requirements in relation to psychosurgery, electroconvulsive therapy (ECT) and medicine (ss59 (1)(b) (ii).

The issue of the meaning of 'treatment' arose in *MX v HSE* [2012] IEHC 491 involving an involuntary patient with impaired capacity and the legality of her having blood taken without her consent. Referring to consent, the Court said, '[a] finding of incapacity can have substantial legal and social consequences, and involves a serious curtailment of rights' (para 5). The Court allowed the procedure to take place on a best-interests basis as ancillary to treatment necessary to improve her mental illness.

The UN Special Rapporteur on Torture and other cruel, inhuman or degrading treatment or punishment, Juan E. Méndez has stated that persons with disabilities are particularly affected by forced medical interventions, and continue to be exposed to non-consensual medical practices (UN Special Rapporteur 2013, para 80).

The CPT says that as a matter of principle, patients should be in a position to give their free and informed consent to treatment and that the involuntary admission of a person should not be construed as authorising treatment without consent (CPT 1998, para 12; CPT 2003 Visit to Finland). This point was reaffirmed by the European Court in *X v Finland* Application No. 34806/04: 3rd July 2012 para 214, finding a breach of Article 8:

> that the forced administration of medication represents a serious interference with a person's physical integrity, and must accordingly be based on a 'law' that guarantees proper safeguards ...

Involuntary admission in Irish law effectively authorises medicine to be given without consent for up to three months after which the entitlement to a second opinion arises if the person refuses. The decision of the European Court in *X v Finland* 2012 Application No. 34806/04, 3rd July 2012, requires substantive safeguards to be applied between compulsory admission and treatment in order to comply with Article 8. In this case also the lack of an independent second opinion was held to breach Article 8 (*X v Finland* 2012, para 169). These omissions are significant in relation to treatment against the will of a mentally competent adult but also persons with impaired capacity.

The 2001 Act does not differentiate between adults who have impaired capacity and those who do not in relation to ECT and medicine. Where the patient is either 'unable or unwilling' to consent to treatment, the outcome is the same (sections 59 and 60). Refusal of capable persons can be overridden by the provision of a second opinion and treatment can be imposed. The CPT recommended that these two sections be amended to ensure the second opinion is independent (2010, para 126). The government's response to the CPT referred to the proposed capacity legislation as a possible solution to this gap. The Report mistakenly referred to the second opinion as if it were independent, contrary to the legal reality (Gov. Response 2011, 65).

Recommendations for reform of this provision in relation to ECT followed intensive lobbying which resulted in a commitment from government to delete the 'unwilling' category and provide increased safeguards for those 'unable' to consent to ECT (AI 2011:28; MHR 2011:10). Although there are MHC Rules governing ECT, the Act does not impose any offence for a contravention thereof, in contrast with the Rules on seclusion and restraint (MHC 2009c; MHC 2009d). In view of the proposed ADM Bill and Article 12 of the CRPD access to the kinds of appropriate supports must be considered. The IR recommends support to make informed decisions about care and treatment:

> in no circumstances should a patient who is capable of giving informed consent in relation to a particular decision at a given time be forced to take treatment against their will – accordingly 'unwilling' should be removed from sections 59 and 60 in relation to medicine and ECT. (Department of Health 2012:25)

In the case of medicine, the failure to get the person's consent or to provide a second opinion prior to the three-month period is difficult to justify. Regardless of capacity, persons can be forcibly treated against their wishes without any oversight. There appears to be unquestioned acceptance of the three-month 'stabilising period' despite the severe effects of some medications for mental/emotional distress. The need for oversight is supported by Non-governmental Organisations (NGOs) having regard to the IMH report highlighting the over-prescription of benzodiazepines and overuse of polypharmacy (IMH 2011b, MHR 2011:9; AI:29).

ASSISTED DECISION-MAKING (CAPACITY) BILL 2013

In keeping with the obligations under Article 12, the proposed Assisted Decision-Making (Capacity) Bill 2013 (ADM Bill) will replace wardship legislation. The presumption of capacity will apply to everyone, s8(2), and decisions must be made on the basis of the person's 'rights, will and preferences ... in so far as is practicable' (58(7)). There is no reference to 'best interests' in the Bill although the term 'interest' is used in some places. The Bill provides for a functional approach to the assessment of capacity which will be time- and issue-specific, but great care will be required to avoid the pitfalls of such an approach (Dhanda 2012, Emmett 2013, Williams 2012). Provisions for supported decision-making will be introduced, including: decision-making assistance (s10), co-decision-making (s16) and advance directives (to be introduced at Committee Stage). Where it is believed that the person has impaired capacity, a decision-making representative can be appointed to make the decision but must abide by the principles in s8 of the Bill, including the will and preferences of the person. It is hoped that all persons who use inpatient services will benefit fully from the provisions of the ADM Bill so that these proposals stand to make an important contribution to meeting Ireland's human rights obligations.

ADVANCE DIRECTIVES

Advance directives are regarded as particularly appropriate mechanisms to support the will and preferences of persons receiving mental health care. The focus is on advance planning in anticipation of a future mental health crisis when a person's decision-making capacity may be impaired. Advance directives can have a significant therapeutic value in their preparation where a collaborative approach is adopted. Morrissey states that they 'provide the opportunity to realise the social model of disability and embed values such as equality, participation, autonomy and inclusion...' (2012:436).

Where persons make advance directives, it also leads to a greater sense of control as well as longer periods of wellness. They are not limited to treatment issues, and can include life-planning issues. The IR recommends a legislative basis for advance directives as part of the legal tools proposed to enhance decision-making and that they should apply equally for physical and mental health care (Department of Health 2012:13; see also MHR Appendix 2011:16). The tendency in some countries has been to exclude the application of advance directives to persons who are involuntarily admitted. However, if progress is to be made, advance directives should only be departed from in clearly specified, life-threatening emergency situations to ensure equality and avoid accusations of discrimination (CRPD Article 12, Committee on CRPD 2013).

SECLUSION AND RESTRAINT

Persons who have been subject to seclusion or restraint have described very negative feelings about their experience, including feelings of humiliation and loss of dignity. The CPT standards reflect this impact:

> As a matter of principle, hospitals should be safe places for both patients and staff. Psychiatric patients should be treated with respect and dignity, and in

a safe, humane manner that respects their choices and self-determination. ... it is essential that staff be provided with the appropriate training and leadership to be capable of meeting in an ethically appropriate manner the challenge posed by an agitated and/or violent patient. (CPT 2006:35)

The European Court in *Bures v The Czech Republic*, Application No 37679/08, 18th January 2013, involving mechanical restraints, said Article 3 of the ECHR prohibits in absolute terms torture or inhuman or degrading treatment or punishment, irrespective of the circumstances or the victim's behaviour (2013 para 83). It stated that physical restraints can be used only exceptionally, as a matter of last resort and when their application is the only means available to prevent immediate or imminent harm to the person or others (Bures 2013:89-90, 95). The UN Special Rapporteur on Torture addressed restraint in healthcare settings, saying that even for a short time, any restraint on people with mental disabilities may constitute torture and ill-treatment (2013).

Neither seclusion nor restraint is defined in the Act, but both are in the relevant codes of practice (MHC 2009c). These management interventions apply not only to involuntary patients but also to voluntary patients and children, without triggering specific limitations or safeguards. The only stipulation is that this intervention must be necessary for the purposes of treatment, or to prevent the patient from injuring himself or others, and it must comply with the MHC Rules. In the MHC Rules, coercion is perceived as incompatible with the recovery approach. The IMH commented that seclusion and restraint practices are 'an even higher order of deprivation of liberty. In order to justify this, the rationale must be thoughtfully calculated and documented accordingly' (MHC 2012a:57).

Neither physical nor chemical restraint is considered in the Act although these are the most commonly used restrictive interventions. The MHC published a code of practice to highlight best-practice guidelines on physical restraint in the absence of statutory support (MHC 2009b). Chemical restraint is not the subject of any specific MHC rules. On their Irish visit, the CPT met patients who had been given medication for behaviour control rather than for improving symptoms of disease, especially after a violent incident. Their Report noted that chemical restraint does not qualify as a means of restraint in the 2001 Act, and recommended that clear rules govern the use of chemical restraint with robust oversight (CPT 2010, para 132). The MHC is currently developing a seclusion- and restraint-reduction strategy and following extensive consultation have a draft strategy that will include proposals dealing with chemical restraint (MHC 2013).

CHILDREN

Both the UN Convention on the Rights of the Child (CRC (Article 12) and the CRPD (Article 7)) state that children have a right to express their views, to be consulted and to participate in all matters affecting them, and the CRPD refers to respect for the evolving capacities of children with disabilities (Article 3). Information and advocacy should be priorities although there is no statutory requirement to provide either in the 2001 Act. Human rights law requires us to look at children as individual rights holders. In *Glass v United Kingdom*, (Application No 6187/00 9th March 2004), the European Court affirmed the child's independent right to respect for his private and family life in the context of medical treatment. The CRPD refers to the 'best interests' of the child as paramount in relation to respect for home and family (Article 23). The Law Reform Commission (LRC) suggests that the 'best interests' principle is more than just a paternalistic test of 'parents know best' or 'doctor knows best' and can be viewed with a rights-based approach and it 'has an objective aspect that ensures an appropriate level of protection against outcomes that would be inconsistent with the rights of children' (LRC 2011, para 1.34).

The issue of family and proxy decision-making arose in *Glass v. United Kingdom*, where the mother of a minor with severe mental and physical disabilities acted as her son's legal proxy, which is perfectly legal for a parent. The Court held that the decision to impose treatment in defiance of the mother's objections gave rise to an interference with the son's right to respect for his private life and, in particular, his right to physical integrity. The failure to obtain court authorisation for the treatment resulted in a breach of Article 8, as there was no emergency to justify the intervention.

In its consultation process for the report on children and medical treatment, the Law Reform Commission received submissions from young people which, 'emphasised that relevant legislation ought to look at the issue of mental health from a young person's perspective...' (2011, para 3.03). There is no sense of this in the 2001 Act, which is blunt when dealing with children. It defines children as those up to 18 years, with no reference to the capacity of the child.

Children are admitted for inpatient care mainly with the consent of their parents. In 2012, the MHC was notified of 428 admissions of 357 children to approved centres, including adult wards. Admission of children to adult wards is a source of major concern. As a result of this concern, in 2011 the MHC issued an *Addendum* to the *Code of Practice on Children* providing that no child under 18 years could be admitted to an approved centre for adults from the 1st of December 2011 and any exceptions must be explained to the MHC. (MHC Code Addendum 2009a, S 2.4.1) Despite the increase in the number of approved centres for children, in 2012 there were 106 children admitted to adult units, accounting for one quarter of all child admissions. The main reason given for the 'exceptional' admission was that 'no age appropriate bed was available' (MHC 2012a:28).

Where necessary, an order from the District Court, under section 25 will be made for admission and extension periods for broadly similar periods as adults. District Court orders permit 'detention for treatment'. In 2012 there were 18 such orders (involving 15 children) compared to 21 in 2011. Four of these involuntary admissions were to adult units and 14 were to child units. Children are de facto detained or formally detained at all times and effective and appropriate safeguards must be provided to meet human rights standards. Admission orders could continue to be made by the District Court, with follow-up reviews of detention carried out instead by an appropriate mental health tribunal system.

The approach to children in the Act is minimalist and urgently needs reform, although the *Code of Practice for Children* attempts to fill some gaps (MHC 2009a). Contrary to the LRC Report (2011 ch.3) and all recent commentary on the issue (Children's Mental Health Coalition (CMHC) 2011), the view that the Act provides a lower standard of safeguards for children than for adults was disputed by the High Court. In *XY v HSE* (2013 No. 4413 P) November 2013), involving a 16-year-old refusing treatment, the Court held that, 'the regime to which XY is subject serves her 'best interests' (para 40) and 'when read in conjunction with the ... Child Care Act 1991, as it ought to be, provides significant safeguards' (para 15). Interestingly, the Court stated, 'the judges in the District Court ... will be very aware of the importance attached both domestically and internationally to hearing the voice of the child' (para 21).

Although XY had a guardian ad litem to represent her voice and support her, there is no automatic right to representation. Neither is there a right to have the specialist services of a child psychiatrist or even an independent psychiatrist for court hearings, court reports or while receiving treatment in adult centres. There is no right to information on admission or treatment in the Act for the child other than 'the less tangible rights' (Whelan, para 4.86) contained in s4 (2) but the *Code of Practice* and the *Headspace Young Persons' Toolkit* compensate somewhat (MHC 2009a; MHC 2011a).

The LRC states that '[i]t is of the utmost importance to involve children in the management of their health care plans, to facilitate their participation and allow them to develop the skills to make decisions and assume responsibility for aspects of their health care' (2011, para 3.112). Treatment issues do not require any safeguards over and above that applying to adults (s61) except that ECT for detained children must have court approval. Safeguards should include regular and effective review and include specialist independent second opinions. Clarity is needed on the relationship between the 2001 Act and the Non-Fatal Offences against the Person Act 1997 (which permits consent to medical treatment at 16 years) and how this will be addressed in the ADM Bill 2013. Particular concern arises about 16- to 18-year-olds and their difficulties accessing appropriate services. The recommendation to reduce the age of a child to 16 years will not necessarily result in greater access without significant commitment by Government and the HSE.

The IR recommends a dedicated part of the Act for children to include specific guiding principles from the CRC recognising the evolving capacity of a child to participate in all matters affecting him or her. It recommends a specialist child advocacy service and a mechanism to review their detention (2012:16, 17). The lack of clarity around Child and Adolescent Mental Health Services (CAMHS), and the inadequacy of provision for 16- and 17-year-olds, 106 of whom were admitted to adult units in 2012, was raised by the IMH (MHC 2012a:55). The LRC and the CMHC recommended that 16- and 17-year-olds would be presumed to have capacity to consent or refuse treatment, including mental health treatment in line with Article 12 of the CRC (LRC 2011, para 3.86, CMHC 2011:7). The proposal by the IR to reduce the age of consent to 16 years must be accompanied by a commitment to the provision of appropriate services for young people. Acknowledging developments in the CAMHS services, the LRC (2011, para 3.17) poses a challenge with its proviso:

> if a completely holistic approach to service provision is applied, it must also be asked whether hospital admission, even to an age-appropriate ward, is actually 'appropriate' in its widest sense.

CONCLUSION

The IMH has referred to the opportunity to focus on reframing mental health services from two perspectives: good governance and the protection of human rights. Good governance requires 'clear administrative structures' while the human rights approach would require 'advocacy, education in human rights theory, a change of philosophical focus and a commitment to maintain beneficial change' (MHC 2012a:57).

Human rights law was influential in the reforms that led to the 2001 Act, and the CRPD now stands to make a significant impact by requiring equality and outlawing discrimination in the response to people with mental/emotional distress. Despite progress in the law, policy and reducing numbers in institutions, Ireland has failed to move towards providing a sustainable community care system and reducing dependency on inpatient care. Coercion and force remain substantial features of Irish mental health law. Dhanda queries the influence of the availability of coercion and compulsion, which may have 'impeded the capability development of the mental health profession, who, due to the easy presence of force, have not felt the need to develop skills of dialogue, persuasion and understanding' (Dhanda 2012:187).

Concern has been expressed as to the impact and widespread use of coercion and physical restraint and how much they detract from recovery and the therapeutic purpose of care and treatment. Instead of coercion, the focus should be on providing a wide range of accessible supports, including advance planning.

The proposed ADM Bill should have a positive influence on the revision of the 2001 Act although it poses significant challenges for the Department of Health Expert Review Group (appointed in 2012 to review the Act), for legislators and policymakers. Working to overcome these challenges is worthwhile and should lead to a genuinely more person-centred law by ensuring greater support for participation in care and treatment decisions.

*

REFLECTIVE QUESTIONS FOR DISCUSSION AND DEBATE: PRACTICE

• The Mental Health Act 2001 was intended to meet human rights standards and now evolving standards require further changes to the Act. Having read this chapter, what changes do you think will have the most positive impact on the experiences of adults and children who use inpatient services?

• The law on legal capacity is to be reformed with the introduction of the Assisted Decision-Making (Capacity) Bill 2013. This proposed law presumes that all adults have legal capacity and will include a supported decision-making system with emphasis on the will and preferences of the person. How do you think this will be useful to persons who use mental health services, including voluntary and involuntary inpatients?

• The law permits force in the form of various restraints, including chemical restraint, to be used in particular contexts in mental health services. Do you think enough time is given to avoiding coercion by discussion, persuasion and developing excellent skills in responding to challenging situations?

• Advance care directives are expected to be introduced in the near future. How do you think you could assist someone with advance planning in anticipation of a future mental health crisis in their life? What might be the role for peer advocates in the planning process?

REFLECTIVE STATEMENTS FOR DISCUSSION AND DEBATE: RESEARCH

• The views of persons who use services on the level of participation in admission and treatment decisions and recommendations for improvement.

• Based on the content of individual care plans, an examination of actual outcomes centred on the views of the person concerned.

• What is 'quality of life' in terms of human rights in community mental health residences?

REFERENCES

Amnesty International Ireland (2011) Mental Health Act 2001: A Review: Summary Paper. Dublin: Amnesty International Ireland

Bach M, Kerzner L (2010) A New Paradigm for Protecting Autonomy and the Right to Legal Capacity. Law Commission of Ontario 1:9

Bartlett P, Sandland R (2007) Mental Health Law: Policy and Practice 3rd ed. Oxford: Oxford University Press

Brosnan L (2005) What part of the Picture? Perspectives of Service Users and Carers on Partnerships within Mental Health Services. Galway: Western Alliance for Mental Health

Brosnan L (2012) Power and Participation: An Examination of the Dynamics of Mental Health Service-User Involvement in Ireland. Studies in Social Justice 6 (1) 45-66

Children's Mental Health Coalition (2011) Submission to the Department of Health on the Review of the Mental Health Act 2001. Dublin: Children's Mental Health Coalition

Clifford J (2011) The UN Disability Convention and its Impact on European Equality Law. Equal Rights Review 6:12

Daly A, Walsh D (2013) Activities of Irish Psychiatric Units and Hospitals 2012 Main Findings. Dublin: Health Research Board. Available at www.hrb.ie

Davidson L, Chinman M, Kloos B, Weingarten R, Stayner Kraemer Tebes (1999) Peer Support Among Individuals with Severe Mental Illness: A Review of the Evidence. Clinical Psychology: Science and Practice 6 (2) Summer 165

Dhanda A (2012) Universal Legal Capacity as a Universal Human Right in Dudley M, Silove D, Gale F (eds.), Mental Health and Human Rights: Vision, praxis, and courage. Oxford: Oxford University Press 179

Department of Health (2012) Interim Review of the Steering Group on the Review of the Mental Health Act 2001. Dublin: Department of Health

Department of Health and Children (2006) [2008-2012] A Vision for Change: Report of the Expert Group on Mental Health Policy. Dublin: Stationery Office

Donnelly M (2005) Treatment for Mental Disorder: The Mental Health Act 2001, Consent and the Role of Rights. Irish Jurist 40:220

Emmett C, Poole M, Bond J, Hughes J (2013) Homeward bound or bound for a home? Assessing the capacity of dementia patients to make decisions about hospital discharge; Comparing practice with legal standards. International Journal of Law and Psychiatry 36:73-82

European Union Agency for Fundamental Rights (FRA) (2013) Legal Capacity of persons with intellectual disabilities and persons with mental health problems. Vienna: FRA 50-71. Available at www.fra.europa.eu

European Union Agency for Fundamental Rights (FRA) (2012a) Involuntary Placement and involuntary treatment of persons with mental health problems. Available at www.fra.europa.eu

European Union Agency for Fundamental Rights (FRA) (2012b) Choice and control: the right to independent living – Experiences of persons with intellectual disabilities and persons with mental health problems in nine EU Member States 2012. Available at www.fra.europa.eu

European Committee for the Prevention of Torture, Report to the Bulgarian Government on the visit to Bulgaria carried out by the European Committee for the prevention of torture and inhuman and Degrading Treatment or Punishment (CPT) CPT/Inf (2004); Amnesty International, Bulgaria, Far from the Eyes of Society: Systematic Discrimination against people with mental disabilities (2002) EUR 15/005/2002

European Committee for the Prevention of Torture and Inhuman or Degrading Treatment of Punishment (CPT), (2010), Report to the Government of Ireland. Strasbourg: Council of Europe

European Committee for the Prevention of Torture and Inhuman or Degrading Treatment or Punishment (CPT) (2011) Report to the Government of Ireland on the visit to Ireland carried out from 25 January to 5 February 2010. Strasbourg: Council of Europe, Inf (2011) 3

European Committee for the Prevention of Torture and Inhuman or Degrading Treatment or Punishment (CPT) CPT Standards ((CPT/Inf/E/2002)1 – Rev 2010)). Strasbourg: Council of Europe

European Committee for the Prevention of Torture and Inhuman or Degrading Treatment or Punishment (CPT) (2006) Standards: Means of restraint in psychiatric establishments for adults. Extract from the 16th General Report [CPT/Inf (2006) 35]. Strasbourg: Council of Europe

European Committee for the Prevention of Torture and Inhuman or Degrading

Treatment or Punishment (CPT) (2003)(8th General Report [CPT/Inf (98) 12]). Strasbourg: Council of Europe

European Coalition for Community Living (2012) at www.community-livinginfo/

Fennell P (2005) The Mental Capacity Act 2005, the Mental Health Act 1983, and the Common Law. Journal of Mental Health Law 163-168

Fox E (2012) Rainy Brain Sunny Brain. London: Heinemann

Government of Ireland (2001) Mental Health Act. Dublin: Stationery Office

Government of Ireland (2013) Assisted Decision-Making (Capacity) Bill. Available at www.oireachtas.ie

Hammerberg T (2011) Human Rights for persons with disabilities, keynote speech at Disability Rights: From Charity to Equality. Open Society Foundations, Law Program Coordinators Meeting, Dublin, 1-3 June 2011

Hunt P (2005) Annual Report to the Human Rights Commission by the UN Special Rapporteur on the right of everyone to the enjoyment of the highest attainable standard of physical and mental health E/CN.42005/51 11 February 2005 in Lewis O, Munro N, The Right to Participation of People with Mental Disabilities in Legal and Policy Reforms 589 in Dudley M, Silove D, Gale F (eds.) (2012) Mental Health and Human Rights: Vision, Praxis and Courage. Oxford: Oxford University Press 585-598

Independent Monitoring Group (2007-2012) Annual Reports of the Independent Monitoring Group for A Vision for Change. Dublin: Department of Health

Inspectorate of Mental Health Services (2011a) National Overview of Service User Representatives, Carers/Family Representatives and Advocacy Groups 2010. Dublin: Mental Health Commission

Inspector of Mental Health Services (2011b) Mental Health Services 2010: Medication report. Dublin: Mental Health Commission

Irish Human Rights Commission (IHRC) (2010) Policy Paper concerning the Definition of a 'voluntary patient' under s.2 of the Mental Health Act 2001. Dublin: Irish Human Rights Commission

Irish Mental Health Coalition (2009) [2008] Third Anniversary of A Vision for Change: Late for a Very Important Date. Available at www.imhc.ie

Jesperson M (2012) PO-Skåne: a concrete example of supported decision-making. Paper delivered at the International Conference on Good Policies for Persons with Disabilities. Vienna 23 January 2012

Jesperson M (2007) Personal Ombudsman in Skåne: A User-controlled Service with Personal Agents in Lehmann P, Stastny P (ed.) Alternatives Beyond Psychiatry. Berlin: Peter Lehmann Publishing 299-304

Kartalova-O'Doherty Y, Tedstone Doherty D (2010) Reconnecting with life: personal experiences of recovering from mental health problems in Ireland HRB Series 8. Dublin: Health Research Board

Kayess R, French P (2008) Out of Darkness into Light? Introducing the Convention on the Rights of Persons with Disabilities. Human Rights Law Review 8:1. Available at www.lawreform.ie

Keys M (2009) Legal Capacity Law Reform in Europe: an urgent challenge, in Quinn G and Waddington L (eds.) European Yearbook of Disability Law 1:59-87

Law Reform Commission (2011) Report: Children and the Law: Medical Treatment [LRC 103-2011]. Dublin: Law Reform Commission

Lawson A (2012) Disability equality, reasonable accommodation and the avoidance of ill-treatment in places of detention: the role of supranational monitoring and inspection bodies. The International Journal of Human Rights 16(6) 845-864

Lewis O (2012) Stanev v Bulgaria: On the Pathway to Freedom 19 Human Rights Brief Issue 2, 7

Lunacy Regulation (Ir) Act 1871 to be replaced by the Assisted Decision-Making Bill 2013

Mac Gabhann L, Lakeman R, McGowan P, (2010) Hear My Voice: The Experience of Discrimination by People with Mental Health Problems. Dublin: Amnesty International Ireland

Mental Health Act (Approved Centre) Regulations 2006. S.I. No. 551

Mental Health Commission (MHC) (2013) Draft Seclusion and Restraint Reduction Strategy, July 2013. Unavailable until finalised

Mental Health Commission (2012a) Annual Report Including Report of the Inspector of Mental Health Services. Dublin: MHC

Mental Health Commission (2012b) Assessment of Progress on A Vision for Change. Dublin: MHC

Mental Health Commission (2011a) Headspace Young Persons Toolkit. Dublin: MHC

Mental Health Commission (2011b) Mental Health Commission Submission on the Review of the Mental Health Act 2001. Dublin: MHC

Mental Health Commission (2011c) Addendum to the Rules Governing the Use of Seclusion and Mechanical Means of Bodily Restraint. Dublin: MHC

Mental Health Commission (2009a) Addendum to the Code of Practice Relating to the Admission of Children under the Mental Health Act 2001. Dublin: MHC

Mental Health Commission (2009b) Code of Practice on the Use of Physical Restraint in Approved Centres. Dublin: MHC

Mental Health Commission (2009c) Rules Governing the Use of Seclusion and Mechanical Means of Bodily Restraint. Dublin: MHC

Mental Health Commission (2009d) Rules Governing the Use of ECT. Dublin: MHC

Mental Health Commission (2006a) Code of Practice Relating to the Admission of Children under the Mental Health Act 2001. Dublin: MHC

Mental Health Commission (2007) Quality Framework: Mental Health Services in Ireland. Dublin: MHC

Mental Health Reform (2011) Submission to the Department of Health on the Review of the Mental Health Act, 2001. Available at www.mentalhealthreform.ie

Morrissey F (2012) The United Nations Convention on the Rights of Persons with Disabilities: A New Approach to Decision-Making in Mental Health Law. European Journal of Health Law 19:423-440

Murray C (2010) Reinforcing paternalism within Irish mental health law-Contrasting the decisions in EH v St Vincent's Hospital and others and SM v The Mental Health Commission and others 32 DULJ 273

National Disability Authority (2011) A National Survey of Public Attitudes to Disability in Ireland. Dublin: National Disability Authority

O'Donoghue B, Lyne J, Hill M, Larkin C, O'Callaghan E (2009) Involuntary admission from the patient's perspective. Social Psychiatry and Psychiatric Epidemiology 45 (6) 631-638

O'Mahony C (2012) Legal capacity and detention: Implications of the UN disability convention for inspection standards of human rights monitoring bodies, International Journal of Human Rights 16 (6) 883-901

Ramsay H, Roche E, O'Donoghue B (2013) Five years after implementation: A review of the Irish Mental Health Act 2001. International Journal of Law and Psychiatry 36:83-91

Scotch R (2000) Models of Disability and the Americans with Disabilities Act 21 (1) Berkeley Journal of Employment and Labor Law 21(1) in Clifford J (2011) The UN Disability Convention and its Impact on European Equality Law. Equal Rights Review 6:12

Thornicroft G (2006) Shunned: Discrimination Against People with Mental Illness. Oxford: Oxford University Press.

UNICEF, Innocenti Studies (1996) The Best Interests of the Child: Towards a Synthesis of Children's Rights and Cultural Values [Florence:, 1996]. Available at http://www.unicefirc.org/publications/pdf/is_best_interest_low_eng.pdf. For a discussion in the origin of the best interests principle.

United Nations Committee on the Rights of Persons with Disabilities (2013) Draft General comment on Article 12 of the Convention – Equal Recognition before the Law* www.un.org/disabilities/

United Nations (2006) Convention on the Rights of Persons with Disabilities and Optional Protocol

United Nations High Commissioner for Human Rights (2009) United Nations High Commissioner for Human Rights and Reports of the Office of the High Commissioner and the Secretary General, Thematic Study by the Office of the United Nations High Commissioner for Human Rights on enhancing awareness and understanding of the Convention on the Rights of Persons with Disabilities (A/HRC/10/48 26 January 2009).

United Nations Special Rapporteur on Torture, 2013 Report of the Special Rapporteur on torture, and other inhuman or degrading treatment or punishment, Juan E. Mendez, General Assembly (A/HRC/22/53 1 February 2013)

Victorian Law Reform Commission (2011) Guardianship: Reference Consultation Paper. State of Victoria: Victorian Law Reform Commission

Whelan D (2009) Mental Health Law and Practice. Dublin: Round Hall

Williams V, Boyle G, Jepson M, Swift P, Williamson T, Heslop P (2012) Making Best Interests Decisions: People and Processes. Available at http://mentalhealth.org.uk/content/assets/PDF/publications/best_interests_report_FINAL1.pdf

14

Risk and the risk society: the impact on the mental health services

Michael Nash, Jo Murphy-Lawless and Marina Bowe

INTRODUCTION

Like every other branch of medicine and indeed, the social services in general, mental health care services has permitted itself to be absorbed in recent decades by the growing imperative to order its work in relation to perceived risk. In this chapter, we want to explore whence this imperative has arisen and the stark issues that lie behind it. We explore the source of the pressure to generate formal risk assessment schemes and ask what distinguishes top-down risk schedules from the risks borne by individuals differentially subjected to and made vulnerable by the vicissitudes of neoliberal health systems.

We review the recognised risk assessment tools and critique the current HSE risk management policy toolkit. Staff members feel that they are working within a management culture of blame and must also manage the expectations of carers. Yet they need to feel free to take risks, to respond fully with the 'heightened awareness' of a skilled clinician (Berger and Mohr 1981:146).

In the concluding sections of the chapter, we explore the concept of recovery and how this relates to accepted definitions of risk. The recovery movement, a grass roots movement begun by those who have been subjugated, has contested the rationales of 'managerial and prescriptive regimes (Liebenberg et al. 2013), posing instead the steps to achieving a transformation of conditions for the individual.

We begin with a discussion of the 'risk society'.

THE 'RISK SOCIETY'

In the midst of ordinary everyday activities, we are beset in the most unexpected ways with formal reminders about risk operates a set of meanings to which we must respond if we are to be seen as responsible. You reach up and open the cupboard to look for some tuna fish to make the children's school lunches and you suddenly realise that staring you in the face on the tin from the supermarket is the warning: 'Allergy advice: contains **fish**' [their emphasis]. Indeed the tin does contain tuna fish. That is why you bought the tin, which says on it in quite big letters, 'TUNA FISH'. You also know which of your children has allergy problems, because you live with them and care for them.

At the weekend, you take the children to their friends' house for the afternoon. They are playing in the back garden on a very large, completely fenced-in trampoline. You bend over to help your youngest child, now three, up into the centre of the trampoline to join the fun. That is when you see the following exclusion clauses sewn into the rim of the trampoline:

Do not use during pregnancy

Do not use when suffering from high blood pressure

Only one person on the trampoline

No somersaults

Use only bare feet

No smoking

Remove sharp objects

Use trampoline only with mature knowledgeable supervision

Not suitable for children under the age of six

Secure against unauthorised use

Do not use in wet and windy conditions

This strange assemblage of exclusion clauses is a crude form of risk schedule, that is, an attempt to categorise activities, purporting to deal methodically with uncertain, unexpected events so to make life more certain, more manageable by eliminating danger. As Gerd Gigerenzer writes, 'Certainty has become a consumer product. It is marketed the world over – by insurance companies, investment advisors, election campaigns and the medical industry' (2002:14).

The peculiar list about the trampoline suggests concerns about liabilities that are the bread and butter – and very good profit-making – of the insurance industry. It does not really suggest that the group from the manufacturers or their insurance company who met to draw up the list had an intimate understanding of how children play or how teenagers interact. To cover all the imagined possibilities of those two groups, the list would be far more lengthy than it is. However, just as with the tin of tuna fish, one of the things the list does is to take from an individual a sense of personal skill and the capacity to respond quickly and appropriately to untoward events in our everyday lives if any danger does arise. Were we to conform to such lists, it would induce a kind of paralysis in our social interactions because of all the prohibitions, yet it is from those very social interactions that we learn: we watch how other parents reassure and encourage their children to be skilful in how they move, and to stretch the limits of how far they can go just a bit further. We know how to do this with our own children and that learning makes them more competent and confident.

This kind of common sense is profoundly relational. As Zgymunt Bauman argues, 'to live in the company of other people, we need a lot of knowledge; and common sense is the name of that knowledge' (1997:10). By contrast, the operations of the risk society within late modernity seek to subvert relational knowledge and to replace it with the knowledge of experts with this consequence: 'we the non-experts, the ordinary people cannot form opinions about such matters unless aided – indeed instructed – by the scientists' (p.9).

The scientific expert is central to the 'risk society'. Ulrich Beck coined the term in 1986, observing that the first phase of modernity when the rationalities achieved with simple industrialisation, bringing about the rapid expansion of capitalism, had been overtaken by a more complex phase, late modernity, in which technologies were now producing unanticipated consequences and manmade risks, requiring yet more scientific expertise to interpret and advise and overcome (at least as a temporary fix until this accommodation also broke down) the risks these new technologies generated. Think of the nuclear plant explosion at Chernobyl in the Ukraine, a world-changing event that coincidentally occurred in 1986 when Beck first published his book in German. The traditional sense of 'fate' that had shaped human understanding from time immemorial was tossed aside by the risks these new technologies entailed. Two potent aspects of late modernity collided in the Chernobyl nuclear accident:

- the expansion of science and technology driven by the belief that everything is solvable by these twin engines of development
- and the increasing production of risks related to that very blanket use of science and technology

This was a twin genie that could not go back into the bottle. Chernobyl had been built to provide nuclear power to support industrial growth. Beck writes of this, 'in developed civilisation which had set out ... to free people from the constraints of nature and tradition, there is emerging a new global ascription of risk, against which individual decisions hardly exist for the simple reason that the toxins and pollutants are interwoven with the natural basis and the elementary life processes of the industrial world' (Beck 1992:41).

Moreover it created new inequalities in our world related to how the technologies impact on poorer, more marginal, more vulnerable populations: 'these arise especially where risk positions and class positions overlap – on an international scale' (ibid.). In relation to Chernobyl, for example, the immediate population was the most horribly afflicted with the impact of massive acute radiation, and of course the former USSR had to carry the cost of the clean-up at vast expense. Further away, however, the spreading radiation affected adversely the pastoral way of life of the reindeer-herding population of the Sámi in Norway and Sweden who had never sought to benefit from or participate in the way of life that accompanied advanced industrial societies.

In these contexts, the notion of risk has taken on new meanings: 'Risk may be defined as a systematic way of dealing with hazards and insecurities induced and introduced by modernization itself' (Beck 1992:21). However these cannot be identified by ordinary people 'the prospective victims of such dangers' (Bauman 1993:200). To be systematic, risk measurement must be scientific. A systematic calculability (or how many times a child under six gets injured on a trampoline) suggests the need for the expert. This opens up a new seam of power and possibilities as science comments on and works to resolve its past failures with yet more science. 'Science promotes progress through revealing and criticising the unwholesome nature of its past accomplishments ... science is busy producing, or encouraging production, of the objects of its future indignation' (Bauman 1993:200). As risks 'enter the stage' of the risk society, they have already been 'appropriated and managed by science and technology' (ibid.).

Moreover, even as living within the 'risk society' appears to promise certainty as a result of the streams of 'theories, experiments, measuring instruments ' required by science to calculate specific risks 'in order to become visible or interpretable as hazards at all' (Beck 1992:27), certainty fractures under the weight of probability statistics, which can at best bring 'a degree of psychical comfort through the illusion of control over destiny' (Bauman 1993:201).

A BRIEF HISTORY OF RISK AND PROBABILITY

Whoever drew up the list of exclusions on trampolines with safety netting is more likely to rely on invented horrors, as indicated by the haphazard nature of that list, and rather less likely to rely on probability statistics. Nonetheless, the trampoline manufacturers have to straddle the line between pointing out risk, so that they cannot later be held liable for not having issued warnings, and actually selling their product.

In this way they are distant cousins to the original purveyors of risk schedules. Dangers had always been named and comprehended in human history, and of course people tried to protect themselves from terrible perils like the plague. They did so by invoking fate, by praying, and by relying on superstitions. The concept of 'risk' was different to that of danger, however, in that it began to be developed as a technical component of a new arm of early international trade. Insurance companies played a strong role in the Dutch commercial empire in the seventeenth century, calculating the probabilities of ships and their cargo going down at sea. As part of what was seen as the 'science of insurance' (Ewald 1991:199), this treatment of risk shifted meanings away from danger as understood in everyday life and towards a technical meaning, a kind of technology in itself, 'a mode of treatment of certain events capable of happening to a group of individuals' (ibid.) In this frame of understanding 'nothing is a risk in itself; there is no risk in reality ... but anything *can* be a risk' (ibid.).

Risk increasingly came to be seen as something that could be 'measured objectively ... by computing the statistical probability that disaster will strike' (Bauman 1993:201). These statistics, calculations and schedules of risk assessment comprised a technology that considered the potential of certain life events occurring for specific groups of people. For example, money-making for the Dutch maritime insurance industry was found in its schedules of risk assessment: if say, in any given year, of 100 insured ships, only 10 ships sank, the insurance company paid out for them, making a profit from the insurance paid by the other 90 which had not gone down. There would be no money to be made in insurance if all 'risks' translated into actual events and everyone, say all 100 ship owners, claimed for damages. Sinking at sea was not so much an objective threat as one that became subject to objective measurement. The skill and hence the profits for the maritime insurance industry were in how they defined, calculated and prioritised risks, not as actual events but as probabilities. Risk calculation had arrived as an important technology in its own right.

By the 19th century, the emerging 'bureaucratic power' that was to become such a feature of modernity was beginning to draw on an explosion of numbers, measurements and statistics (Hacking 1991). These units were used to order how society was viewed: 'Many of the modern categories by which we think about people and their activities were put in place by an attempt to collect numerical data' (ibid.:182-183). Understanding statistics and statistical intervals was thought to be key in helping to move from a world of random chance to a more predictable order where the laws governing chance could be clearly laid out. At the beginning of the 19th century, probability was argued as being 'subjective' in nature (Hacking 1991:185), but by the end of the 19th century probabilistic calculations were viewed quite differently.

These technologies and changing perceptions of how groups in society were defined by statistics, of having regular predictable statistical laws whereby a greater degree of control could be exercised to bring about social order, of risk calculation and of probability became knitted into and influenced the history of psychiatry as well. Castel (1991:283) sees a major shift once risk can be seen as a mode of definition standing independently of danger: whereas psychiatry had to rely on classifying someone as dangerous only after the fact, thereby encouraging confinement in advance of any 'threatened action' occurring, risk cast matters in a different light: '[Risk] is the effect of a combination of abstract factors which renders more or less probable the occurrence of undesirable modes of behaviour' (Castel 1991:287). Psychiatry was set to become the assessor-administrator of these undesirable modes, their diagnoses opening up a particular 'career' for an individual.

RISK AND UNDESIRABLE BEHAVIOUR IN A NEOLIBERAL ERA

Nikolas Rose (1996) takes up this theme of psychiatry as administration within late modern society, the 'risk society'. We have already explored how risks are unequally distributed within this risk society in relation to Chernobyl. Vulnerable individuals are rendered more vulnerable by the withdrawal of a state no longer committed to the common good of widespread social protection. The fragmenting and privatising of core health and social services that neoliberalism brings with it result in the privatising of risk with those least able to deal with their cumulative and complex needs carrying the greatest burden. A psychiatric diagnosis plunges an individual into a maze of abstract risk assessment schedules by numbers of agencies with the bare minimum of actual social support. Rose traces how this tragedy played out in relation to a fatal stabbing in London in 1992 by a man named Christopher Clunis, who had a lengthy history as both an inpatient and outpatient. Diagnosed with schizophrenia, his so-called treatment was a maze of countless professionals over a number of years, including over 20 consultant psychiatrists, social workers, housing officers, police officers, prison officers, people gone on leave, moved to another job, lost records, misplaced notes, and so on, leading to zero stability for Clunis. The inquiry in 1994 into how Clunis' treatment had broken down and left a man dead could only conclude, as Rose does, that Clunis 'was as much a victim of the mental health system as the man he killed.' (1996:2).

Rose (1996) goes on to analyse how psychiatrists participate with other social and healthcare professionals in an 'administration of risk' across the community. In other words, without an asylum in which to confine people, and without a commitment to genuine resources for mental health, risk assessment becomes the only feasible technology. Within this frame of reference, professionals cope with absurdly large caseloads and measure their clients' progress in their ability to adapt to and cope with (ibid.:12) the meandering pathways of community care. The 'language of risk' and 'risk management' are used to make sense of this non-sense of care, with the individual having been assessed through its categories and 'increasingly held responsible for the management of their own fate' (p.13). Thus patients must be compliant with the care being doled out to them or, given the shortage of resources, it will be withdrawn. Risk management and risk protocols become all, occluding what is clinical and relational skill.

As Rose phrases it 'risk management and risk reduction, as logics for professional action, have come to supplement or replace other forms of professional actions and judgements' (ibid.). In other words, be very careful how you use that trampoline.

Mental health professionals working under this regime face a deep crisis. They simply are not permitted to care. It raises the terrible dilemma that John Berger explored in his account of John Sassall's GP practice in a rural community in England: 'How far should one help a patient to accept conditions which are at least as unjust as the person is sick?' (Berger and Mohr 1981:141).

The use of risk assessment tools, which now form a core component for clinical services, prevent us from being honest about this late modern society which, in Wendy Browne's summary, is 'overregulated and under-resourced' (2001:12). Placed in this light, how much weight can be given by clinicians to such tools, given the pre-existing pressures to conform to increasing constraints on policies and funding (Liebenberg et al, 2013)? Do clinicians not need to reconnect instead with this insight: 'Vulnerability may have its private causes, but it often reveals concisely what is wounding and damaging on a much larger scale?' (Berger and Mohr 1981:141).

RISK PRACTICE IN MENTAL HEALTHCARE

We now turn to exploring how risk practices operate for mental health professionals. In many cases, risk in mental health is successfully managed on a daily basis, even though it is recognised that psychiatry is practised in many settings where risk is difficult to manage (Buchanan and Grounds 2011). However, we need to ask, 'at what cost,' to professional notions of care and social concepts of liberty and personal autonomy?

Risk assessment is now a routine part of mental health services work (Hawley et al. 2010). The practice of risk assessment and management has been adopted by mental health professional groups, such as psychiatrists and nurses. In Ireland, the College of Psychiatrists of Ireland (CPI) (2012) has twelve specific learning outcomes for risk assessment and management in its curriculum for training in psychiatry. The Psychiatric Nurses Association (PNA) (2008) recognises the role and potential contribution of mental health nurses in risk in areas such as liaison psychiatry, crisis nursing for deliberate self-harm and forensic mental healthcare. Social workers work with risk in the areas of youth justice (see Young 2009) and domestic violence (see Murphy and McDonnell 2008).

While risk assessment and management have been absorbed into training and practice, one could argue that the practice of risk prediction has not been so readily accepted. As far back as 1976, Cocozza and Steadman (1976:1089-99) suggested that there was little empirical evidence that psychiatrists or anyone else had the ability to predict dangerousness accurately, just as we have described above in relation to Chernobyl. Indeed in the UK, the Royal College of Psychiatrists (2008) reported concern that '... a culture preoccupied with risk to others has emerged within the UK, particularly in England, and most recently in Northern Ireland. This has been influenced by homicide and other inquiries that have suggested failings in risk assessment and management by mental health professionals.' Feeney (2003) suggests that there is an unrealistic expectation that psychiatrists should be able to predict violent and sexual crime in those they assess and that they should therefore be able to protect society.

DETERMINING RISK IN MENTAL HEALTH

Nevertheless, in mental healthcare there are risk assessment tools that have been validated for a range of risk events. Examples of these include: violence and aggression, Historical Clinical Risk Management -20 (HCR-20) (Webster et al. 1997) scale and for suicide, the Suicidal Intent Scale (Beck et al. 1979). Risk assessment tools are, in some respects, actuarial instruments which assess the presence of risks factors that have been 'proven' in research studies to be associated with risk events; e.g. alcohol and substance use is an actuarial risk factor for self-harm, suicide and violence. On the other hand, the ubiquity of such tools has led Hawley et al. (2010:89) to suggest that 'there is a wide variability in design and measurement which highlights important concerns about validity'.

Validity in this regard refers to the risk factors that are inherently service-user-centred, i.e. those usually negative circumstances arising out of the service-user's condition, 'deviant' behaviour, or an adverse mental state, physical environment or support network – as if the risk is endogenous and comes only from within the person. Yet mental health services expose service users and their families to risk in a number of ways, but the balance of risk in these tools is weighted in favour of individual service-user risk characteristics, when organisational shortcomings in risk practices may be more pertinent.

In their review of homicides by service users in the community, Parker and McCulloch (1999) found the most critical factors to be: poor risk management, communication problems, inadequate care planning, lack of inter-agency working, procedural failures in administration and legal factors, lack of suitable accommodation, lack of resources, substance misuse and non-compliance with medication. Out of these nine critical factors only two can be directly attributed to the service user in the actuarial risk nomenclature – substance misuse and non-compliance.

Therefore, while warnings about exposure to risk for the individual – no matter how remote (e.g. the trampoline example) or intentional (the tins of tuna) – are a standard practice in consumer society, the same cannot be said for healthcare services in general or mental health services in particular. While it is acceptable to warn consumers that 'smoking can damage your health', a warning that 'being in this mental health service may damage your health' may be a step too far in risk identification. This is why, in risk assessment tools, we will not find a tick-box menu assessing organisational risks. Warnings relating to the iatrogenic risks associated with exposure to mental health services or professionals are seldom provided.

IATROGENIC HARM FROM RISK PRACTICES

The risk posed to mental health service users by being in mental health services is a neglected part of the risk discourse. Ivan Illich (1972) refers to iatrogenesis as the preventable harm from medical treatment of patients. Pilgrim and Rogers (1996:184) use the term 'iatrogenic risk' in a mental health context to denote 'being damaged by what is provided by treatment', e.g. the side effects of medication or detrimental effects of abusive therapists. While largely illustrated through the physical nature of harm, iatrogenic harm in mental health can transcend the physical and harm service-users' fundamental rights in respect of liberty, personal agency and recovery. The risk assessment and management procedures in psychiatry are emerging as key contributors to this harm.

To help illustrate the potential iatrogenic effects we will focus on the risk of violence and the potential for homicide. This is because violence (and homicide) by service users in the community engenders what Szmukler and Rose (2013:125) term 'moral outrage', which is 'associated with an implied culpability when certain types of tragedy occur.'

In mental health, preoccupation with risk to others is an emotive aspect of practice. No one wants to be involved in an incident in which the outcome is a grievous injury or fatality. The dilemma with this in mental health is that the extreme events that we are trying to risk-manage, such as homicide, are so rare that it makes prediction difficult. However, while rare, homicide has an intensely devastating impact on the victim's loved ones, their professional support, the perpetrator, mental health services, professional reputations and societies feeling in need of protection.

Risk management of violence and aggression, in the absence of accurate prediction and certainty, is based on the utilitarian principle of the greatest good for the greatest number; locking someone up protects the general public from harm. The liberal *modus operandi* for this is that interference with personal liberty in the prevention of harm to others – a therapeutic pre-emptive strike – is justifiable. However, in order to achieve the greatest good while impinging on personal liberty, risk practices require an underpinning legal framework, a psychiatric bureaucracy and new mental illness diagnoses.

Busfield (1996:134) suggests that mental health services and psychiatric ideas and practices are also moulded and fashioned by the policies and activities of the state and its attendant bureaucratic structures. This entails devolving powers for risk to professional groups and developing and implementing new legal frameworks.

LEGAL FRAMEWORKS

Civil and legal proceedings are devised by policymakers and lawyers and enforced by mental health professionals and the police. These proceedings are not specifically forensic ones but risk-management strategies applied to adult service-users in general mental health settings.

Detention under mental health law is a form of psychiatric committal in many jurisdictions. However, people cannot be locked up without just cause, so risk assessment and management give the clinical rationale for the deprivation and loss of liberty: a person assessed as being at high risk of violence is most likely to be detained for their and the public's protection. However, risk in mental health is not an exact science. Risk tools have poor predictive value, which exposes service users to the risk of a false positive prediction for violence, e.g. the identification of a risk that does not exist, such as a person being assessed as a risk of violence when the risk is not there. Monahan (1981), states that professional predictions of violence are wrong twice as often as they are right.

Conversely, a false negative fails to identify a risk of violence when it is actually present. Errors in risk prediction can result in iatrogenic harms for both services and service users – if a risk is not identified and a member of the public is injured or killed, then there is the usual government and managerial opprobrium, professional hand-wringing, media frenzy and reputational loss for psychiatry and mental health services. On the other hand, a false positive risk assessment can result in the deprivation of liberty through the detention, possibly with enforced treatment, of a service user who has been incorrectly identified as being at risk. However, this does not attract the same opprobrium.

MANAGING RISK AFTER DISCHARGE

Unlike the common criminal who is released (probably with remission) once their sentence is served, the service user assessed as being at a high risk of violence is unlikely to escape the clutches of 'community confinement'. This is the type of confinement based on a psychiatric bureaucracy and modelled on criminal justice measures that makes future, or continuing, liberty contingent on the adherence to a community care plan. These care plans are highly proscriptive and usually come under a section of mental health law. At present Ireland does not have specific laws for 'community confinement', however, examples include

- Supervised Community Treatment and supervised aftercare under Section 117 in the UK
- Community Treatment Orders (compulsory community treatment) in jurisdictions such as the UK (Burns et al. 2012), the US, Australia and Canada.
- Electronic tagging of service users (Department of Health UK 2010)[i]
- Civil commitment (preventative detention) in the US[ii]

Hatfield and Antcliff (2001) suggest that mental health law needs to strike a balance between, 'public protection and protection of the individual themselves and adequate protection against unnecessary deprivation of liberty or restrictions on autonomy.' These risk management strategies are used in general adult psychiatric populations and we must rigorously question whether service users who are not guilty of any crime deserve to be 'cared' for with conditions on their liberty comparable to those found in the criminal justice system.

NEW MENTAL ILLNESS DIAGNOSES

Diagnosis is controversial in psychiatry and the relevant arguments are well established and will not be repeated here (see Mac Gabhann, Chapter 3). When errors are possible, a political dimension is often introduced to emphasise the need for risk management. The controversial diagnosis of Dangerous and Severe Personality Disorder (DSPD) is a politically constructed diagnosis not mentioned in either the ICD-10 or the DMS IV when it was developed. Corbett and Westwood (2005) offer an excellent analysis of this concept best summed up as a psychiatric manifestation of the risk society.

THE CONCEPT OF RECOVERY: A CHALLENGE TO THE RISK AGENDA?

Recovery has emerged as an alternative philosophy to traditional paternalistic mental healthcare and service delivery (see Higgins and McGowan, Chapter 5). Recovery principles are the cornerstones of mental health care policy, service development and delivery in different jurisdictions. In Ireland, A Vision for Change (Department of Health and Children 2006) illustrates this. As recovery challenges traditional and institutional ideas about power and care in mental health, it is also challenging ideas around the notion of risk as applied to service users by professionals.

Roychowdhury (2011) is mindful of the approaches to risk assessment, management and values-based recovery practice being seen as at odds with each other, due to the values that underlie recovery and risk assessment and management. The complexity of this value clash can be examined using one controversial example: medication. In terms of clinical risk, non-compliance with medication is considered a key risk factor in a range of risk events: from violence and aggression (Swartz et al. 1998), mental health crisis (Gray 1999) and relapse (Ayuso-Gutierrez and del Rio Vega 1997). However, in recovery-oriented care, being medication free may be a goal. Slade (2009) suggests staff can support the use of medication as a recovery tool by supporting people who want to come off medication, e.g. by giving information about advantages and disadvantages, and McDaid (2013) suggests that people seeking support should be able to choose between medication and talking therapies as a first option.

Medication is only one aspect of the risk and recovery debate, but it is a significant one regarding recovery goals and risk aims. Only time will tell if these two divergent views on medication can be reconciled. Yet, if this one point can be amicably resolved, others would soon follow and it would represent a departure from paternalistic practices.

CONCLUSION

In this chapter, we have stripped back the arguments and rationales about risk in the late modern 'risk society' to expose the many contradictory aspects of care in a system that relies on risk assessment and risk management. We have considered how outcomes for recipients of care and for mental health care practitioners are uneven, to say the least, when having to rely on such schematisations. Staff members feel that they are working within a management culture of blame and are not free to respond as they might and yet they must manage the expectations of individuals and their family members and carers. Mental health professionals need not to be bound by preconceived schedules of risks, but to feel free to take risks, to respond fully with the 'heightened awareness' of a skilled clinician who recognises all that an individual is facing. We argue that the recovery movement is a crucial counterweight to this risk culture, underpinned by values that match those of the responsive clinician. These values that can be supported only if we shift our understandings away from risk management as a goal in itself and towards a more creative use of our resources, enabling clinicians to adapt more freely to the needs and conditions of each individual.

*

REFLECTIVE QUESTIONS FOR DISCUSSION AND DEBATE: PRACTICE

- How can we balance the demands of clinical risk management with service user autonomy?
- How can we reconcile recovery principles with risk assessment and risk management?
- How can service users be involved in organisational risk assessment?

REFLECTIVE STATEMENTS FOR DISCUSSION AND DEBATE: RESEARCH

- Examine the role of protective factors in making risk assessment more recovery-oriented.
- Critically explore service user involvement in the risk process.
- Examine the impact of risk assessment and management on service-user recovery.

REFERENCES

Ayuso-Gutiérrez J L, del Rio Vega J M (1997): Factors influencing relapse in the long-term course of schizophrenia. Schizophrenia Research 28:199-206

Bauman Z (1993) Postmodern Ethics. Oxford: Blackwell

Bauman Z (1997) Thinking Sociologically. Oxford: Blackwell

Beck A T, Kovacs M, Weissman A (1979) Assessment of suicidal intention: The Scale for Suicide Ideation. Journal of Consulting and Clinical Psychology 47 (2) 343-352

Beck Ulrich (1992) The Risk Society: towards a new modernity. London: Sage

Berger J, Mohr J (1981) A Fortunate Man. London: Writers and Readers Publishing Cooperative

Brown, W (2001) Politics Out of History. Princeton, NJ: Princeton University Press

Buchanan A, Grounds A (2011): Forensic psychiatry and public protection. British Journal of Psychiatry 198:420-423

Burns T, Rugkåsa J, Molodynski A et al. (2013) Community treatment orders for patients with psychosis (OCTET): a randomised controlled trial. The Lancet 381 (9878):1627-1633

Busfield J (1996) Professionals, the state and development of mental health policy in Mental Health Matters, Heller et al. (eds.) Hampshire: Palgrave Press

Castel, R (1991) From dangerousness to risk in G Burchell et al. (eds.) The Foucault Effect: Studies in Governmentality. Brighton: Harvester Wheatsheaf

Cocozza J J, Steadman H J (1976) The Failure of Psychiatric Predictions of Dangerousness: Clear and Convincing Evidence. Rutgers Law Review 29 (5) 1099

College of Psychiatrists of Ireland (CPI) (2012) Curriculum for Basic and Higher Specialist Training in Psychiatry. Dublin: Irish College of Psychiatry

Corbett K, Westwood T (2005): 'Dangerous and severe personality disorder': A psychiatric manifestation of the risk society. Critical Public Health 15 (2) 121-133

Department of Health and Children (2006) A Vision for Change: Report of the Expert Group on Mental Health Policy. Dublin: Stationery Office

Department of Health UK (2010): Electronic tagging of mental health patients. Available at http://webarchive.nationalarchives.gov.uk/+/www.dh.gov.uk/en/MediaCentre/Statements/DH_118964?PageOperation=email accessed 12 December 2013

Ewald F (1991) Insurance and risk in G Burchell et al. (eds.) The Foucault Effect: Studies in Governmentality. Brighton: Harvester Wheatsheaf

Feeney A (2003): Dangerous severe personality disorder. Advances in Psychiatric Treatment 9:349-358

Foucault M (1975) 'Panopticism' in Discipline and Punish: The Birth of the Prison. Penguin Social Sciences April 1991

Gigerenzer G (2002) Reckoning with Risk: Learning to Live with Uncertainty. London: Penguin

Gray R (1999) The role of psychopharmacology in managing crisis and risk in Ryan T (ed.) Managing Crisis and Risk in Mental Health Nursing 2nd Ed. Cheltenham: Nelson Thornes

Hacking I (1991) How should we do the history of statistics? in G Burchell et al. (eds.) The Foucault Effect: Studies in Governmentality. Brighton: Harvester Wheatsheaf

Hare R (2003) Manual for the Hare Psychopathy Checklist – Revised, Version 2. Toronto: Multi-Health Systems

Hatfield B and Antcliff V (2001) Detention under the Mental Health Act: balancing rights, risks and needs for services. Journal of Social Welfare and Family Law 23 (2) 135-153

Hawley C J, Gale T M, Sivakumaran T, Littlechild B (2010) Risk assessment in mental health: staff attitudes and an estimate of time cost. Journal of Mental Health 19 (1) 88-98

Illich I (1975) Medical Nemesis: The Expropriation of Health. London: Calder and Boyars

Liebenberg L et al. (2013) Neo-Liberalism and Responsibilisation in the Discourse of Social Service Workers. British Journal of Social Work: 2013 *doi: 10.1093/bjsw/bct172*

McDaid S (2013) Recovery ... what you should expect from a good quality mental health service. Dublin: Mental Health Reform

Monahan J (1981) Predicting violent behaviour. Beverly Hills, CA: Sage

Murphy C, McDonnell N (2008): Escalating Violence: How to Assess and Respond to Risk – A Review of International Experience. Dublin: Aoibhneas Women and Children's Refuge Coolock

Parker C, McCulloch A (1999): Key issues from homicide inquiries: An analysis carried out by MIND. London: MIND

Pilgrim D, Rogers A (1996) Two notions of risk in mental health debates in Mental Health Matters, Heller et al. (eds.). Hampshire: Palgrave Press

Psychiatric Nurses Association (2008) Public Consultation commission on nursing hours PNA Submission to the Commission on Nursing Hours. Available at http://www.pna.ie/uploads/Final%20Doc%20Commisson%20on%20 %20Nursing%20Hours%20Submission%20PNA%2015%20Sept%2008.pdf accessed 15 December 2013

Raghunathan A (2012) 'Nothing Else but Mad': The Hidden Costs of Preventive Detention available at http://georgetownlawjournal.org/files/2012/03/ Raghunathan.pdf Accessed 12 December 2013

Rose N (1996) Psychiatry as a political science: advanced liberalism and the administration of risk. History of the Human Sciences 9 (2) 1-23

Roychowdhury A (2011) Bridging the gap between risk and recovery: a human needs approach The Psychiatrist 35:68-73

Slade M (2009): 100 ways to support recovery: A guide for mental health professionals Rethink recovery series: volume 1. London: Rethink

Swartz M S, Swanson J W, Hiday V A et al. (1998) Violence and severe mental illness: the effects of substance abuse and nonadherence to medication. American Journal of Psychiatry 155:226-231

Szmukler G (2001) Violence risk prediction in practice. British Journal of Psychiatry 178:84-85

Szmukler G and Rose N (2013) Risk Assessment in Mental Health Care: Values and Costs. Behavioral Sciences and the Law 31:125-140

Royal College of Psychiatrists (2008) College Report CR150 Rethinking risk to others in mental health services. Final report of a scoping group Royal College of Psychiatrists London June 2008. Available at http://www.rcpsych.ac.uk/files/pdfversion/cr150.pdf accessed 15 December 2013

Webster C D, Douglas K S, Eaves D, Hart S D (1997) Historical-Clinical-Risk Management-20 (HCR-20): Assessing Risk for Violence (Version 2). Simon Fraser University

Young S (2009) Literature Review Risk Assessment Tools for Children in Conflict with the Law. Irish Youth Justice Service May 2009. Available at http://www.iyjs.ie/en/IYJS/Literature%20Review%20-%20Risk%20 Assessment.pdf/Files/Literature%20Review%20-%20Risk%20Assessment.pdf accessed 15 December 2013

NOTES

[i] In 2010 South London and Maudsley Hospital trialled the tracking of mental health patients by fitting them with a steel ankle strap linked to a GPS tracking system that helped to monitor their location.

[ii] Raghunathan (2012) defines civil commitment as 'a form of preventive detention, which is often defined as the state's confinement of an individual without a criminal conviction because it fears he may hurt himself or others.'

15

Challenging the dominance of the pharmaceutical industry in psychiatry

David Healy

As I write this, some Irish newspapers are carrying articles claiming that the EU is seeking to rein in the price of drugs in Ireland (McEnroe 2013). A favourable tax regime has resulted in Ireland being a European base for many pharmaceutical companies, even for companies who do no marketing in Europe. As a result, over 50% of the value of Irish exports lies in pharmaceuticals.

It would be very unusual if this strong industrial presence did not have an effect on the practice of medicine in Ireland, and not just on the price of drugs. Worldwide, pharmaceutical companies are putting pressure on governments to speed up access to medicines and to make health services company friendly. Doctors are encouraged to 'partner' with industry.

In the US, the only thing both sides of the most divided Congress in history can agree on is a Bill to speed up access and get the Food and Drug Administration (FDA) to consider not just the efficacy and safety of drugs but also the fact that drug manufacturing creates jobs (Scott 2012). The availability of better and more efficacious drugs seems like a not unreasonable solution to the healthcare crisis.

In the UK, everything from Marxist publications through to brochures for pharmaceutical companies suggest that 15–20% of us are mentally ill and in need of access to treatment (Godrej 2012). All 50 shades of the political left and right agree we are awash in a sea of unmet need.

THE THERAPEUTIC PARADOX

But the more we meet these unmet needs, the worse our health gets. Life expectancy in countries that consume the greatest amount of recently developed medicines is falling relative to other countries. This suggests that the market in healthcare is not working.

The usual social democratic response to market failure is to call for more regulation, but the current situation has developed in the context of a comprehensive regulatory system. The conservative response is to call for a freeing of the market, but in this case, those most likely to object to a freeing of the market are private enterprises.

THE ORIGINS OF A UNIQUE MARKET

In the face of widespread and dangerous exploitation of patients around the 1900, with mark-ups on drugs of 500%, an advertising industry that sold beauty rather than health, product labelling that was grossly fraudulent, and a lack of effective treatments, there was a push to regulate the pharmaceutical industry.

The first regulations were adopted in the US in 1906 and other countries quickly followed suit. It is now clear that a consequence of regulation is the growth of pharmaceutical companies as they create the apparatus to manage their regulatory requirements, which is in turn built into the cost of drugs. This much is a simple story about a predictable consequence of regulation, and is not unique to the market in drugs. Since then, a unique market that was not predicted and had not been discussed in detail elsewhere has developed.

The initial thrust behind the regulation of drugs was patient safety. The first call was for accurate labelling of products. During the 20th century there was a push towards some specification of the effectiveness of drugs. This interest in effectiveness was originally a safety issue; if a drug wasn't effective it couldn't be safe.

The emergence of the randomised controlled trial (RCT) bolstered the argument for demonstrating effectiveness and a requirement for controlled trials was built into the 1962 Food and Drugs Act in the US (Healy 2012a). But, as will be shown, far from improving safety this development led to a comparative efficacy market that has had adverse consequences for safety.

The 1962 crisis with the sleeping pill thalidomide (Healy 2012a) produced other changes, including a decision about the patent status of pharmaceuticals, and a requirement to make new medications available on prescription only.

These distinct regulatory elements have shaped the pharmaceutical market, the practice of medicine and global consciousness to this day. They have produced the perfect raw material, perfect product and perfect consumer. But if the desired outcome was an increase in personal good health and national wealth, the market is now producing unimaginably bad outcomes.

THE PERFECT RAW MATERIAL

Every product is built from a raw material. This puts constraints on the developer, as there may be difficulties fashioning the product from the material, or the material may be costly or scarce. There is the delicate matter of the mark-up from raw ingredient to product, for the market will only bear so much.

In the late 20th century, bottling water produced a perfect product. A few years earlier no one could have imagined that something as ubiquitous and inexpensive as water could be sold at such a mark-up in places where tap water quality was good. Except in cases of water shortage, almost all the value of bottled water comes from its marketing, and thus lies in the eye of the beholder.

Around the year 1900 patent medicines, which often contained little more than water, came as close as bottled water to being a perfect product. The mark-up on these proprietary products was, however, greater than for bottled water now. The marketing process for bottled water and almost everything else developed first in the patent medicines market.

Compared with patent medicines and bottled water, prescription-only drugs are complex products that require both chemicals and information that transforms the chemicals into a medical product. This information specifies the conditions under which the chemical is best used, and its likely effects at particular doses and in particular circumstances.

The costs of chemicals today are little more than the costs of bottling water. The information, at least superficially, seems not so readily manufactured. It took companies a while to realise that they are all but able to invent this information.

The information adds apparent value that supports mark-ups of a 1000% – not seen in any other market. Were the value real rather than apparent, these mark-ups might be justifiable, but far from being real, what appears to be added value in many cases increases rather than reduces the risk from the chemical. Problems with the informational component of medicines lie at the heart of the therapeutic paradox and are the reason why the more we access medicines, the more problems we have.

At the centre of this information lies the randomised controlled trial (RCT). RCTs made it tantalisingly possible to insert an efficacy requirement into the system. Controlled trials were introduced after it was demonstrated that their application could weed out unwarranted claims for treatment efficacy. This appeared to raise the bar to entry into the market. The idea was that RCTs would keep the purveyors of patent nostrums out of healthcare and force the financial camels of the pharmaceutical industry to get through the eye of a scientific needle if they were going to make money out of sick people.

If the use of trials had been restricted to keeping drugs that didn't work off the market, trials could have made a major contribution to drug safety. For better or worse, a number of drugs we currently have would not be available. More to the point, RCTs would not have become vehicles to sell drugs, hide side effects and drive clinical practice, as they have done. Instead, as evidence-based medicine has developed we have entered a stranger and stranger world.

THROUGH THE LOOKING GLASS

First, the use of RCTs to disprove claims of efficacy has been largely subverted. Even if a preponderance of the RCTs undertaken fail to show a drug is of benefit, if any trials show hints of a positive outcome the treatment is likely to be permitted onto the market. Worse again, the treatments supported by independent reviewers for the purposes of developing regulations – reviewers who take an evidence-based medicine approach – are in many instances treatments that have the least successful trials. This happens because guidelines must be based on published trials and can neither take into account the negative trials that remain unpublished nor the negative trials published as positive for the drug.

An example is the case of Tamiflu, a drug marketed to treat influenza. Peter Doshi and colleagues, who recently reviewed the evidence on Tamiflu, offered the view that it is not possible to assess the efficacy of a drug without full access to all the studies that have been done (Jefferson et al. 2011). The fuller the datasets they acquired, the less effective Tamiflu appeared to be. Yet on the basis of the original published data, governments throughout the world spent several billion dollars stocking Tamiflu in 2007 and 2008.

Second, if a study has huge numbers of participants, it makes it likely that some irrelevant benefit will be shown for a given drug, simply because the larger the pool of participants, the more likely that someone will show a benefit of some kind. At the most extreme, snake oil could be demonstrated to be of benefit in large studies. Far from seeing this, doctors seem to be more impressed by a study that contains thousands of patients than by one that needs a handful of patients to demonstrate a benefit. The most prestigious journals are also more likely to take a multicentre study with thousands of patients showing a trivial clinical benefit, than to take a small study showing a clear-cut clinical effect.

Third, the only data from a trial that can ordinarily be generalised are the estimates of the reliability of a trial's primary outcome measure. But in practice, almost anything that turns up in the course of a trial – anything of use to a drug company – is taken as having been established simply by virtue of it having happened in the course of an RCT.

Few trials include the right instruments to measure outcomes other than the primary outcome. This is particularly true for adverse events in which, in addition, the data are commonly creatively coded or relocated or otherwise massaged to make problems vanish (see Healy 2004).

Fourth, trials are usually run by pharmaceutical companies. From the start, these trials aim to produce information to serve a commercial purpose rather than producing information for its own sake. Any inconvenient information that turns up in studies is likely to be discounted.

RCTs are indeed a gold-standard method as is claimed by the adherents of evidence-based medicine. However, for the reasons just outlined, they are in practice a gold-standard method for hiding adverse events rather than for demonstrating efficacy. They might have made a significant contribution to safety if their use had been restricted to weeding out ineffective agents, but in practice they have been used to conceal adverse events and as such they have been detrimental to the development of a comparative safety market.

There is little recognition in the world of medicine that the mantras of the gold standard – statistical significance and evidence-based medicine – are essentially rhetorical tropes that need dismantling.

TRANSFORMING BASE METALS INTO GOLD

A new default has been created. Until about 1960, drugs were viewed as poisons with the art of medicine lying in the ability to find the right dose in order to balance the risks and benefits of treatment. Now supposed proof that drugs 'work' has transformed these chemicals into fertilisers or vaccines to be administered as widely as possible. Where once the greatest art in medicine lay in knowing when not to treat, it now seemingly lies in knowing how to get people on as many drugs as possible for as long as possible.

This all stems from the use of controlled trials. Extraordinarily, a technique that was introduced to contain company claims has become the means by which companies create knowledge within health care and drive the sales of drugs.

But it is the actual conduct of trials that makes them into the alembus in which pharmaceutical company alchemists can transform base metal into gold.

First, an initial set of trials is conducted on healthy volunteers. These trials uniquely reveal the hazards of drugs in a way that clinical trials on patients do not, but the data from these trials are impossible to access. There is no register of healthy volunteer trials and publications from these studies are commonly deeply misleading (see Healy 2012b).

The trials that doctors and others hear about are undertaken on patients. In these, patients volunteer to take the risk of ingesting chemicals that may prove too toxic to market. They do so without being informed of all of the risks. As the exercise is billed as scientific, most participants likely believe that the data from their participation will be made available to experts to contribute to a knowledge base that is incrementally driving medicine forward. In fact, while clinical trial registers now offer some evidence that the trial took place, in close to 100% of cases the actual data is sequestered by companies.

When it comes to transforming the data into information that will shape clinical practice, companies can select which trials they wish to publish; they can select the data from these trials that suit their purpose. In some areas of medicine, a third of trials may remain unpublished, and of those published up to one third are portrayed as positive when regulators or others who have seen the data deem them to be negative.

The data are written up to produce a 'publication', which is the primary marketing tool of companies. Owing to a supreme sleight of hand, these marketing aids are designated as scientific articles, although they fall at the first scientific hurdle by not making the data on which claims are based publicly available.

Once the publication is complete, in order to add value to the marketing copy, ghost writers may add the names of distinguished medical academics. Academics provide this service in return for modest amounts of money. The publication is then sent to a journal. Unlike quality newspapers, which check the integrity of the primary sources on which a story is based, academic journals never do. Furthermore, even after claims in an article have been shown to be fraudulent, journals refuse to retract the publications (Newman 2010).

The publications are then incorporated into national guidelines that de facto require doctors to use the latest on-patent and more expensive drugs rather than older, less expensive and more effective drugs. The guidelines process is one that enables pharmaceutical companies to co-opt even the most independent and company-hostile academics into endorsing their products.

Efforts to constrain commerce by way of clinical trials have infected therapeutics even more radically. In 1962 the hope was to demonstrate that a drug worked before it was let on the market. As a result, studies were conducted in disease states. In practice this means that if the trial is not negative, companies are licensed to advertise the fact that drug Y works for condition X. But the drug may work better for other conditions. Imipramine, for instance, is a more effective treatment for panic disorder than any of the drugs that have been licensed for this purpose. SSRIs are more effective for premature ejaculation than they are for depression (Healy 2004).

If a company promotes its drug for some purpose without undertaking a study in that condition, this is called 'off-label promotion'. There is concern about off-label promotion, as a result of which the majority of doctors think that they cannot prescribe imipramine for panic or SSRIs for premature ejaculation. Furthermore, guidelines only endorse the licensed indications of a drug. This effectively hands medicine over to pharmaceutical companies. Business executives rather than doctors now decide for what a drug is given.

Having a resource like this that can be moulded into virtually anything that the company wants might be expected to cost a lot of money, but it costs little. The trial patients are paid nothing. In the 1960s, their participation did liberate us from scourges that had plagued humanity for millennia; the same effort today is inflicting harm on people that will take decades to eliminate.

Doctors also come cheap. In many jurisdictions, doctors are told it is government policy that they 'partner' with industry, and one way to do this is to participate in clinical trial networks to make the testing of new drugs quicker and easier. Policies like this stem from government efforts to keep pharmaceutical business 'in-country' even though it is difficult to see any related economic return. The doctors running the trials for companies are paid by the state. Any notional fees they get are a fraction of the true costs of the exercise.

Meanwhile, for economic reasons companies are relocating most clinical trials to countries such as India, where the oversight and costs are less. The publications that come out of Indian trials still have Western academics listed as their authors.

There is a perfect symbol of how the field has developed. As of 1962, the only drug that had been demonstrated to be effective and safe in a placebo-controlled trial before being brought to the market was thalidomide. In 2012, antidepressants have become the most commonly used drugs in pregnancy, despite increasing evidence they double the rate of birth defects and miscarriages and cause significant cognitive delay in children (Healy et al. 2010). The increase in prescriptions for antidepressants is happening on the basis that these drugs have supposedly been shown to be efficacious, and withholding something that is efficacious is portrayed by public relations companies as being unsafe and unconscionable.

In terms of policy, the one indisputable fact for both conservatives and liberals is that this market is not free. Companies are able to sequester data so that it is impossible for doctors or patients to know the risks and benefits of a treatment. The consequent labelling of most drugs is deeply misleading, has in some cases been accused of being fraudulent, and is in all cases in breach of the norms of science.

These norms include access to the data and a commitment to empiricism. They make science democratic and make for the ultimate free market; the freedom of this market has worked to enrich and liberate us all. Within healthcare, however, companies have been able to create the appearance of science to generate mark-ups on branded drugs not seen since the days of patent medicines. As healthcare costs escalate dramatically, while actual health deteriorates, these mark-ups pose an increasing threat to the economies of developed countries.

THE PERFECT PRODUCT

A further step taken in 1962 made it possible to shape the raw material from clinical trials into the perfect product. This development hinged on the strategy chosen to reward pharmaceutical companies. In 1962, the options were to offer either product or process patents for drugs or some other form of reward.

With process patents, if another pharmaceutical company can find a different way to make a drug, they too can put that drug on the market. Process patents had been the norm in Europe prior to 1960. On reviewing the differences between countries with process and product patents in 1962, US Senator Kefauver's staff, charged with looking at the regulation of the pharmaceutical industry, discovered that process patent countries were more innovative than product patent countries and produced cheaper drugs.

The US had consistently adopted product patents more than any other country. Despite the data on innovation and cost, in 1962 Congress opted to maintain a product patent system. Other countries followed.

In the 1960s holding a product patent meant having a patent that applied to a national territory. The development of TRIPs (Trade Related Aspects of Intellectual Property Rights) in the 1980s meant that product patents now had a global reach. This laid the basis for the emergence of blockbuster drugs – drugs worth a billion dollars a year or more for pharmaceutical companies due to the potential for global sales.

There have been two important consequences of the emergence of blockbuster drugs. One was that the ability to make so much money put a premium on drugs that could be marketed to the widest number of people, rather than a premium on drugs that were effective for diseases that needed cures. This reward system also put a premium on transforming short-term acute illnesses into chronic conditions that would require long-term use of medication.

The second feature was that as company survival came to depend on the fortunes of a single drug, companies have had an incentive to conceal any hazards that might be linked to that drug. In contrast, if several different companies can produce drugs that come with a hazard, the benefits of innovation will lie with the company that can find a way to manage rather than conceal the hazard.

The 1962 regulations were ostensibly about enhancing safety, as the 1906 and 1938 regulations had been. But in fact, the motivational market incentives pointed the opposite way. One of the important consequences of this is that in practice, safety is more neglected now than it was in the 1950s. It appears to be assumed that if a drug is efficacious it cannot pose a safety risk. It is highly likely that if a new thalidomide were to come on the market that it might remain on the market for a decade or more, as today the risks of prescription-only drugs take over a decade to travel from convincing description to wider recognition.

There is another aspect to the patent system that developed after 1962. In a free market, the patent system is recognised as a perversion whereby the citizenry of a country give a third party rewards for a limited period beyond what the market would ordinarily support, in return for some originality or utility that will benefit the country.

Before 1962 patent officers were a force to be reckoned with, but over the past 20 years this has changed. Companies have applied for and been granted patents on isomers or metabolites of already patented compounds. They can, for instance, get patents by modifying the salt composition of an already existing compound. They are able to take patents out on compounds that their own scientists describe as being as like already marketed compounds as two drops of water. The requirement for originality has de facto been abandoned.

The requirement for utility has also been abandoned. If the second drop of water currently being patented were patented for a novel and necessary indication, this might be acceptable, but second drops of water are typically patented for the same conditions for which the first drop of water is already available. Indeed, in a number of cases, once a new compound is patented, companies seem to be able to find safety issues with their initial compound sufficient to withdraw it from the market.

In the face of such laxity in the application of patent law, what happens next depends on the consumers of the product. If consumers cannot be easily fooled into buying a much more expensive on-patent version of an identical, cheaper, off-patent product, patent laxity might not matter. But as we shall see, the 1962 amendments have also created the perfect consumer, one who can be fooled into buying the most expensive bottled water in the shop.

The 1962 regulations created the perfect product. They made it possible to take out product patents on water. Reflecting this laxity, pharmaceutical companies, which once had scientific divisions and engaged in research, have outsourced most of these functions and become close to the kind of pure marketing operation expected from a bottled water or patent medicines company, where the brand is everything.

THE PERFECT CONSUMER

Central to building the perfect market is a set of arrangements that create the perfect consumer. Prescription-only status for all new drugs does just this.

Prescription-only status was a police function introduced in 1914 to control the abuse of heroin and cocaine. It was extended slowly to all new drugs after the Second World War because these were thought likely to come with significant risks, and it was considered that doctors as a body would be sceptical of their claimed benefits and would be cautious about using them. It was also thought doctors would be able to quarry the appropriate information out of drug companies about medicines, or generate the appropriate information to make these unavoidably risky drugs as safe as possible.

Up to 1962, the idea of making new drugs available on prescription only was hotly contested – was it appropriate to treat the citizens of a free country as though they were potential addicts? The thrust of regulation up to 1962: had been focused on the accuracy of the labelling of over-the-counter drugs. Regulating prescription-only compounds broke new ground in 1962: nowhere else have regulators attempted to constrain the use of products so that they are sold to a professional group only.

It is clear that in 1962, Congress had no wish to regulate the practice of medicine, but the intrusion of 'government' into clinical practice has extended from the thin end of this wedge. It is now common to find civil servants who know nothing about medical practice dictating to doctors what the content of clinical encounters must be.

Regulators claim that all they are doing is regulating the wording used by pharmaceutical companies to prevent it from misleading to consumers, just as they have done since 1906. But in this case the consumers are doctors and the regulator guarantees wording that originates with pharmaceutical companies. Doctors who are looking at what is in essence advertising view it as authoritative scientific statements, whose use is endorsed by regulators.

Before the 1962 regulations were passed, US Senator Kefauver, the person responsible for the Act, noted that prescription-only status created a unique market: 'He who buys does not order and he who orders does not buy', meaning that in the case of medicines, prescription-only status makes doctors into the ones who order medicines while not being the ones who buy them (Healy 2012a). The fact that thalidomide had been available over the counter in Germany where its hazards came to light may have influenced the decision-making process and allayed concerns about prescription-only arrangements. No one considered the possibility that the risks of thalidomide had come to light precisely because the drug had been sold over the counter, and as doctors do not make a living out of over-the-counter drugs, they have no incentive to hide their risks.

Linked to the prescription-only status of drugs, the regulations also encouraged companies to develop medicines for disease indications. The idea behind this was to restrict the use of medicines to conditions that posed a greater risk than the risk stemming from the chemicals used to treat them, so that there would be a favourable risk/benefit ratio.

What was not anticipated was that if companies were restricted to selling medicines for diseases only, they would have an incentive to widen the net of what counted as a disease and convert what had been a series of vicissitudes of everyday life and normal variation in terms of beauty and functionality into a set of diseases. The consequence has been an increase in diagnosis, so that many more people are told they have disorders such as depression, osteoporosis, hyperlipidemia (hypercholesterolemia), etc., where they might previously have been seen as having burn-out, aging bones that could be managed by exercise and a diet-related issue that is only significant against a background of more important cardiac risk factors.

For companies, an unexpected benefit of this restriction was that they had to learn to speak the language of doctors: diseases. They have learnt to do this to an extent that medicine fails to appreciate. A range of vicissitudes have been transformed into illnesses, acute illnesses have become chronic and the moral imperative to treat brought to conditions like tuberculosis has been co-opted to the sales of almost any pharmaceutical product for indications no matter how trivial. Where patients might be wary of taking chemicals, they are increasingly faced with doctors attempting to persuade them that a certain chemical will correct some abnormality and that they are almost duty-bound to take it.

Kefauver recognised the risks inherent in third-party buying arrangements. These are well recognised and form a major part of conservative arguments against government involvement in healthcare. The market simply will not work efficiently if the person ordering doesn't also buy and benefit from or suffer the consequences of their purchase. If this is not the case, at the very least those doing the buying should be trained in the hazards of what they are doing.

In 1962, the third party was seen as an independent professional who most people thought would be working on behalf of their patient, almost to the extent that a pilot flying a plane works on behalf of those entrusted to her care. Unfortunately, since 1962, professional discretion has been all but outlawed to the extent that doctors' prescribing choices are now largely dictated to them not by market pressure, but by health systems that mandate the use of the latest and most expensive on-patent medicines, the medicines on which there is the least data as regards safety.

Doctors may be the only significant group of buyers who are not trained in the pitfalls of buying for a third party. They do not even realise that they are not trained in an area of huge consequence for them and their patients.

Recent estimates suggest that companies spend over US$50,000 per annum per doctor marketing to doctors. Doctors, in other words are subject to a greater concentration of marketing power than any other group of people on earth. But, just as they know nothing about buying for a third party, neither are doctors trained to recognise the way companies market to them. This will soon apply to nurses and other non-medical prescribers also.

Those involved in healthcare largely fail to spot that prescribers are the consumers of medicines and that they 'consume' by putting pills in patients' mouths. In so doing they consume without consequences or side effects. Companies fully appreciate this and exploit it. If the patient has a problem, company marketing ensures that the prescribers have available a great deal of evidence suggesting that any problems are part of the patient's illness rather than a consequence of treatment. Clinical trials are used to argue that any reports of difficulties from doctors or patients are simply anecdotes.

Prescribers are also often unaware of the way that companies use psychology to market their products. Companies categorise doctors in terms of whether they are likely to innovate with medicines, want to adhere to guidelines or merge with the crowd. Prescribers rarely know how they are profiled, and rarely realise how marketing programmes are designed to take account of their differing profiles.

Finally, many prescribers appear to be more susceptible to the effects of branding even than teenagers faced with choice of designer outfits. This happens because the development of branding feeds into the most powerful bias in medicine. Unlike drugs, brands come free of side effects. The temptation for a doctor is to go with the brand, because no one wants to give a patient something that might injure them. Quite aside from transforming prescribers into the perfect consumer in this sense, in 1962 it was not appreciated how much a mechanism designed to improve safety might, in fact, do just the opposite by transforming clinical encounters into captive situations. Making drugs available on prescription only means that patients have nowhere else to go to get a medicine they need, or think they need. They effectively become a captive rather than a patient and risk the development of something akin to Stockholm syndrome.

In 1962 the term 'Stockholm syndrome' had not yet been coined. It is now known that people whose lives are at risk and who are isolated, when held hostage by kind captors concerned about their welfare (as doctors are increasingly trained to be) are highly likely to identify with their captors and want to keep them happy. Similarly, in clinical circumstances, especially when the patient finds their condition worsening, it may become very difficult to raise the possibility that what the doctor has done in good faith to help might in fact be causing problems.

It is not inconceivable that the safety consequences of turning patients into captives far outweigh the risks inherent in the drugs that doctors prescribe. Such an outcome would be consistent with the fact that treatment induced adverse events have now become a leading source of death and disability. Meanwhile, no doctors are trained to recognise their capacity to induce Stockholm syndrome.

A THOUGHT EXPERIMENT

The regulatory hoops through which a company has to jump are now so few that it would be as easy to get alcohol, nicotine or opiates on the market as anti-depressants.

Alcohol with all its risks is a good example, because we are happy to have it be available over the counter. Prescription-only drugs are available on prescription only precisely because we have every reason to think they will be as risky as or riskier than alcohol.

A key factor that prevents companies bringing alcohol on the market as an antidepressant is consumer familiarity. This provides a source of competing information that companies cannot control. In contrast, SSRIs, statins or bisphosphonates are unknown quantities, which makes it possible to manage the views of doctors and patients more readily.

Getting on the market

In our case, the regulatory requirements regarding clinical trials allow us multiple opportunities to get a positive result for alcohol. For some antidepressants only one third of trials have been positive.

In these trials, we can use as our yardstick of success not lives saved, or people returning to work, or people objectively performing better, or people performing better in their own estimation – but rather a change in score on rating scales. These rating scales are sensitive to the side effects of the drug so that simply taking the drug may produce a benefit on the scale whether or not there is a benefit for the underlying condition. The anxiolytic or sedative effects of alcohol would produce substantial benefits on scales like the Hamilton rating scale for depression or scales for anxiety.

We can compare alcohol to placebo in a set of mild problems rather than against a treatment known to work or in a set of severe disorders. We can improve the profile of alcohol by screening out anyone showing a good response to placebo or a bad reaction to alcohol during the first week of the study.

Only some of the studies we undertake have to show a benefit for alcohol over placebo. If there are a lot of studies, perhaps even a preponderance of studies, in which alcohol fails to beat placebo, these can be discounted. Regulators can conceal the fact that they have seen studies where alcohol has failed to beat placebo. As a result, patients and doctors need not be aware of negative studies.

In the cases of alcohol and nicotine, placebo effects might well account for 80–90% of any rating scale benefit found. Nevertheless, the studies could be deemed a successful demonstration that alcohol and nicotine 'work'. Regulators and academics could happily give doctors and the public the impression that 100% of the apparent benefits of alcohol for depression stem from the alcohol and none from placebo factors.

In a proportion of our alcohol studies, investigators may find out later that not all the patients actually existed. Conveniently, non-existent patients do not have troublesome side effects. The trend towards non-existent patients is likely to increase as clinical trials of more recently developed alcohols become outsourced to Mexico, Eastern Europe, India and elsewhere. But even if this comes to light, it will make no difference. Once on the market, our license to sell alcohol as an antidepressant will likely not be revoked.

In one study of aripiprazole as a mood-stabiliser, it proved no better than placebo in a trial with 30 American and Canadian study centres, but was dramatically better than placebo in two Mexican centres. When the US and Mexican centres were added together, the overall results for aripiprazole were marginally superior to placebo. The US FDA approved this study. The published account of the study gave no indications that alcohol only 'worked' in Mexico (Rosenlicht et al. 2012). With this kind of license for an alcohol study, there is little way we can fail to prove alcohol that is an antidepressant.

We can therefore do studies in which more people die on alcohol than the placebo, fail to get back to work on alcohol compared to placebo, prove better than placebo in perhaps no more than 33% of cases on our chosen rating scale, and in these 33% of cases prove better in only 3% of centres, and we will still be able to market alcohol as an 'antidepressant'.

After approval, in order to make our market, we need only publish the trials in which there were positive findings. But we can publish these multiple times, giving the impression that there were far more positive trials than in fact there were. We can aim at having up to 50 publications for each trial. Our ghostwriters can also take a negative study and polish the results to make it look positive. Ghostwriters never mention studies that have failed to show efficacy.

In due course when it comes to shaping the marketing campaign for alcohol, the data generated by these studies will be almost free-floating content that can be moulded into almost any shape we might wish. For instance, if an opportunity arises in the painkiller market because another compound like Vioxx has run into trouble, some minimal benefits that may have been registered in the trial (in terms of feeling slightly better in painful situations) can be polished by ghostwriters into a series of articles that trumpet the analgesic qualities of alcohol in order to take advantage of any opportunity that has opened up.

Based on the published trials, guidelines will have to endorse alcohol for use in nervous disorders and perhaps have it as a first-line therapy based on its excellent safety profile. Endorsement by a guideline makes it almost mandatory for doctors to prescribe alcohol. Furthermore we can likely engineer it so that – while a guideline recommending alcohol first may only do so for a three-month period – in line with the evidence the involvement of our consultants and marketing efforts mean that later iterations will successively extend the recommended treatment period so that an increasing number of patients being treated by doctors who adhere to guidelines are likely to have alcohol for life.

Staying on the market

When it comes to the side-effects of alcohol, ghostwriters can hide these under terms such as 'failure of response' or perhaps list an initial side effect such as nausea, when in fact the individual had nausea, vomiting, followed by an epileptic convulsion. They can also simply fail to mention problems by saying they have only included those problems that appeared at a 10% rate or more.

When patients have suffered an adverse effect of alcohol, such as a convulsion, we can dismiss this as anecdotal – 'not evidence-based'. In contrast, we can write up any dramatic improvement on alcohol during its early period on the market in both the academic and mainstream media, even featuring it on television and radio, under headings like 'alcohol saved my life'.

The trials we have to undertake to bring alcohol to market only have to last for six to eight weeks. This is particularly helpful in terms of adverse events, in that few of the problems that might be expected from alcohol (or nicotine) emerge in a six- to eight-week period. In the case of any problems that emerge outside this time frame, we can argue that no placebo-controlled data support the claimed adverse event, and both we and doctors have to operate only on the basis of the scientific evidence.

If there is an increase in epileptic convulsions on alcohol compared to the placebo in the course of our clinical trials, but it is not statistically significant, we can rely on journals, regulators and academics to say there is no evidence for any increase in the rate of convulsions.

We have yet another defence. Should there be any hints of liver problems on alcohol in the course of our trials, which is unlikely because of the short duration of the trials, we can attribute this to the depression for which the person is being treated. Even though the medical literature might not have a scrap of evidence that depression causes liver dysfunction, and there may be a substantial amount of other evidence that alcohol causes liver dysfunction, within an astonishingly brief period of time (weeks) we have the ability to get a significant proportion of the medical profession to agree that it is well known that depression causes liver dysfunction.

The bias of doctors, as helped by us, means that a culture will emerge early on in the use of alcohol that will attribute any of the difficulties people may have in stopping using alcohol to the nervous problem that was being treated in the first place rather than to dependence and withdrawal. We can be sure that 20 years after alcohol is first marketed that a majority of doctors will fail to recognise that it causes dependence. They will instead be likely to explain to patients that it's just like insulin – their bodies are not producing enough alcohol and they need to continue treatment for life.

In the case of pregnancy, this bias and our marketing means that we should be able to make alcohol one of the most commonly prescribed drugs in pregnancy within a few years. And indeed, compared with other antidepressants, a glass or two of wine per day is positively harmless. Doctors will tell women who avoid coffee, soft cheeses, etc., that leaving their nerves untreated will harm their babies.

Finally, we know from past experience with other drugs that in a few years' time alcohol is likely to be linked to suicide and perhaps violence. We have a number of academics whom we can enlist to produce graphs to show that as alcohol consumption has gone up, suicide and violence rates have fallen in countries like the Netherlands or in parts of the US. We can depend on the editors of leading journals to refuse to publish any correspondence that might be critical of studies like this.

We can organise for cost utility analyses as thick as telephone books to demonstrate that the cost of alcohol is minimal compared to the quality of life gained. Provided the analysts stick to the published data, we can show that if governments pay for widespread access to alcohol that there will be a net benefit to society.

A key difference between prescription and over-the-counter drugs lies in an inversion of the stranger/neighbour phenomenon. We are in general wary of strangers and comfortable with neighbours. We neglect the fact that we are most likely to be abused or harmed by neighbours or relatives. Neighbours and relatives are familiar and we think we can manage the risks associated with them.

In this scenario alcohol in drinks or nicotine in cigarettes are familiar (neighbours) while alcohol and nicotine as antidepressants are unfamiliar (strangers). We have a feel for the traditional risks of alcohol and nicotine, but far from treating therapeutic alcohol or other new drugs as strangers and regarding them as dangerous and risky, when mediated through our local risk-laundering service (doctors), we will treat these prescription-only drugs as safer than traditional alcohol or nicotine, even though prescription-only drugs are sold as such precisely because we have every reason to think they will be riskier than drugs like alcohol.

For instance, we regard prescribed amphetamines as safe to give to children, even toddlers, while the authorities jail others for possession of street amphetamines on the basis of the risks they pose. We do the same for prescribed as opposed to proscribed opiates.

Doctors provide us with other services. Getting treatment from a doctor suspends the natural caution that our consumers might feel about taking our new chemical. Even though prescribed alcohol has now been tested in protocols in which it looks safer than and as effective as SSRIs, and doctors know what the risks of traditional alcohol are, they are, it seems, prepared to act as though prescribed on-patent alcohol comes risk free. This is partly because unlike traditional alcohol, doctors would never get a hangover from prescribed alcohol and never crash because of it.

In fact it is now clear that making alcohol or nicotine available through doctors is a way to hide hazards such as liver failure or lung cancer on average for 10 to 15 years from the time that people in the street have begun to claim that their liver failure or lung cancer stems from our drug. Not only can the medical profession be depended on to deny such a link while patients are reporting a link but even after regulators put black-box warnings on alcohol about their risks, even if those risks are lethal, most doctors will still deny that these risks exist.

Finally, doctors provide us with significant insurance against product liability. In the event that a doctor testifies that he would have given alcohol no matter what the warning on it, we are legally immune to any product liability actions stemming from its use.

Freeing the market

With many treatments in mental health care and across medicine, we are doing the equivalent of ensuring that as many people take prescription alcohol as possible, and take it indefinitely, and we are reaping the economic consequences that would likely ensue from such a course of action.

Expenditure that makes a population more economically productive by getting people off sick leave and back to work is an investment. Expenditure that gives people illnesses they were not complaining of in the first place, puts them on treatments that make them less economically competent and causes death and disability comes close to being a tax on us and our jobs, but a tax paid to corporations rather than government.

There is a cost in alienation besides the economic costs. The marketing of drugs is changing the fabric of what it means to be human. The struggles over female sexual dysfunction exemplify this. Where once women just fell in love, scientists now try to tease apart the components of female desire so that it can be turned into a commodity. It appears that Viagra has the same effects on women as men, but the women are not as motivated by these effects as men. The answer apparently is to coat Viagra with testosterone to mimic oestrous when women are more likely to respond to the effects of Viagra. If marketed, any benefits that may accrue to some women are unlikely to outweigh the alienation inflicted on all by marketing that will reduce love to physiology pure and simple.

Doctors are also alienated. Where medicine was once a vocation, for a growing number it has become an industrialised enterprise that makes them increasingly likely to be sacked if they try to practice good medical care. It is difficult to envisage doctors rising up to put things right. They are more likely to act if they realise that they are being replaced by nurses and other non-medical prescribers, provided they realise in time.

But unlike climate change or mass starvation in Africa, where the complexity of the problems induce an inability to act, these problems are ones that we can solve. There are several key changes which would transform the picture.

The leading problem is that the market is not free. Unless the data on treatments can be accessed and are as comprehensive as possible, no other part of the market can be free. Science by definition is based on accessible data. In contrast, a great deal of what passes for evidence-based medicine as promoted by pharmaceutical companies can perhaps be described as fraudulent. However it is described, it is costing us money in return for which we get on balance more disability and premature death than benefit.

The problems that stem from data sequestration are aggravated by product patents. Having a lax patent system combined with lack of access to the data is the worst of all systems. It is a system that could not be better designed for the purpose of transforming pharmaceutical companies with as little concern for health as tobacco companies.

The sticking plasters we apply to attempt to stop the haemorrhage of money only aggravate the problem. The latest is comparative effectiveness research. This rests on misguided notions of what randomised controlled trials can do, and fails to understand healthcare. It assumes that people have a greater desire to get from Washington, D.C. to Seattle 15 minutes faster than to get there alive. It is easy to see that a slightly more effective but less safe airline will go out of business. Somehow getting to the healthcare equivalent of Seattle quicker is supposed to solve all our problems.

Effectiveness was originally a component of safety. One of the key conceptual problems at the heart of our current difficulties is the failure to realise that the market will work if it is a comparative safety but not a comparative effectiveness market. This is not a precautionary principle argument. It encourages innovation and will reward it out of the wealth created by making people healthier.

But it does require a shift in perspective. We need guidelines for people rather than guidelines for diseases. Increasingly, doctors are killing people very effectively by following faultlessly an ever-increasing number of disease guidelines, the results of which are to multiply exponentially the possible interactions between treatments and create a series of prescribing cascades. Extirpating diseases is not the goal; keeping people safe is.

Congress in the US likely thought it was creating a comparative safety market when it made new medicines available on prescription only in 1962. Instead, it gave doctors a guaranteed income. It is more difficult than ever to take malpractice actions against doctors even as evidence accumulates that people are likely to be injured unnecessarily for a decade or more by new treatment induced problems that doctors fail to detect. We need to find a way to re-educate doctors, or reward them for keeping people safe, or consider re-engineering the prescription-only system.

The market that Congress envisaged in 1962 is at odds with the realities of health today; they viewed citizens essentially as dupes in need of protection. The advent of the Internet has meant that many of us know more about our treatments than our doctors do. We need new collaborative models of care that recognise this and harness the drive and energy of patients to make medicines safer.

*

REFLECTIVE QUESTIONS FOR DISCUSSION AND DEBATE: PRACTICE

- Only 1% of adverse events on medicines are reported. Why?
- The drugs introduced to the market in the 1950s before RCTs were more potent than those introduced since. Should we remove the RCT requirement for drug approval?
- Could adjustments be made to prescription-only arrangements so that only the most toxic drugs were prescription-only?

REFLECTIVE STATEMENTS FOR DISCUSSION AND DEBATE: RESEARCH

- Research needs to be done on taking adverse events to prescribers – doctors and nurses – and cataloguing the range of reactions.
- We know that treatment-induced death is the third leading cause of death in hospital. We need studies to find out where treatment-induced deaths rank in community settings.

REFERENCES

Godrej D (2012) Mental Illness – The Facts. New Internationalist 452 (May): 18-19

Healy D (2004) Let Them Eat Prozac. New York: New York University Press

Healy D (2012a) Pharmageddon. Berkeley, CA: University of California Press

Healy D (2012b) Mystery in Leeds. Davidhealy.org 26 February

Healy D, Mangin D, Mintzes B (2010) The ethics of randomized placebo controlled trials of antidepressants with pregnant women. International Journal of Risk and Safety in Medicine 22:7-16

Jefferson T, Doshi P, Thompson M, Heneghan C (2011) Ensuring safe and effective drugs: who can do what it takes? British Medical Journal 342:148-151

McEnroe J (2013). Troika chief: Pharmaceutical drug costs cannot be justified. Irish Examiner 1 November

Newman M (2010) The Rules of Retraction. British Medical Journal 341:1246-148.

Rosenlicht N, Tsai AC, Parry P I, Spielmans G, Jureidini J, Healy D (2012) Aripiprazole in the maintenance treatment of bipolar disorder: A critical review of the evidence and its dissemination into the scientific literature. PLoS Medicine 8: e10000434

Scott P J (2012) The consumer advocate. Minneapolis Star Tribune Opinion Page 3 June www.startribune.com/opinion/commentaries/156486195.html

16

Into the future: promoting mental health and democratising support for people with mental/emotional distress

Agnes Higgins, Shari McDaid and Paddy McGowan

INTRODUCTION

Ireland's mental health system is in a process of major transition. Peppered throughout are pockets of innovation that exemplify a future characterised by a more democratic and humanistic response to people experiencing mental distress. At the same time others hold on to last-century practices, clinging to a discursive framework in crisis, while others adopt the language of reform without ever challenging or changing their way of being or responding.

Predicting social change is a fool's game, but this volume has highlighted a number of issues that cannot be avoided and are bound to effect policy and practice into the future. In the final chapter we look forward and discuss a range of factors that will undoubtedly affect the way mental health services are delivered in the future, including: policy on mental health and wellbeing, the organisation, funding and supply of mental health services, the technologies of support, the legal framework within which services are provided, the arrangements for involving those affected, and the methodologies for research and evaluation of effectiveness. All of these structures, systems and arrangements will be framed within a language not yet agreed and an understanding not yet accepted. In this sense, the next phase in mental health support and practice will undoubtedly represent a new 'discourse' in the Foucauldian meaning of a system of arrangements and power relations reflecting a way of talking about a phenomenon.

PROMOTING A MENTALLY HEALTHY IRELAND

There is increasing recognition internationally that the health and well-being of an individual is not just a personal issue but a societal asset and public good that is central to the social and economic prosperity of a country (WHO 2005, European Commission 2005). Alongside this, there is a greater appreciation that an integral part of improving individual health and well-being rests on improving mental health – in other words no health without mental health. The recent publication *Healthy Ireland: A Framework for improving health and wellbeing 2013-2025* sets out a vision for the country were 'everyone can enjoy physical and mental health and wellbeing to their full potential, where wellbeing is valued and supported at every level of society and is everyone's responsibility' (Department of Health 2013:6). In relation to mental health, achieving the vision and goals set out in *Healthy Ireland* will require a conceptual shift away from illness and treatment to what is increasingly being called a 'wellness trend', where the focus is on positive mental health. Moving towards a healthier Ireland will also require a shift in mindset from one that equates the absence of 'mental illness' with the presence of mental health, as if mental health resides on one end of a single health–illness continuum to viewing mental health in a more dynamic manner. Given the complex challenges of creating a truly mentally healthy population, the agenda for mental health and wellbeing will only be achieved through a broad, inclusive approach that takes a population-based or society-wide lens, and moves beyond the mental health services to incorporate all sectors of society. There will also be a need for models of mental health promotion that strengthen individuals' and communities' resilience, participation, cohesion and integration, as well as providing each individual and community with a platform from which to contribute to the mental health agenda in a meaningful way.

Increasing the number of people who are mentally healthy at all stages of life will require more than strengthening individuals and communities. Unless the social and economic barriers to mental health and the health inequalities created by these barriers are addressed, the vision outlined in *Healthy Ireland* will, like so many previous policy documents, remain mere aspiration and political rhetoric. The need to address 'the causes of the causes' is not new, with the World Health Organization's *Mental Health Declaration and Action Plan* (WHO 2005) for Europe, the European Commission's Green Paper on *Towards a strategy on mental health for the European Union* (European Commission 2005), and the *Vision for Change* document (Department of Health and Children 2006) all highlighting the need to reduce the health inequalities that contribute to mental health problems. All these documents have consistently stressed the critical need to tackle issues such as poverty, unemployment, poor education and social isolation. Addressing social and economic deprivation continues to be a priority, and doing so is becoming increasingly urgent, as the current economic crisis will no doubt contribute to widening existing inequalities as more people experience unemployment and reduced incomes. In tandem with addressing social and economic determinants of 'mental ill health' and distress, there is also a need to recognise the bidirectional relationship between mental distress and deprivation, and address the social and health inequalities that people who experience mental distress encounter, such as social exclusion, stigma and discrimination and the barriers to staying in education, work and housing. However, as it is beyond the capability of any one government department to address health inequalities, real impact in the area of mental health and well-being will only come about if mental health is prioritised as an area for action across government and a whole-government approach is taken. Without a mental health framework for interdepartmental co-operation and intersectoral approaches towards policy and practice, economic and social inequalities will remain and the cycle of social exclusion will continue to be perpetuated.

PROMOTING MENTAL HEALTH AND RECOVERY WITHIN THE HEALTH SYSTEM

The last few years have seen major change in the organisation of the health service, with the creation of new governance structures and six directorates organised along service lines to include: primary care, mental health, social care, hospitals, child and family services, and health and well-being. Central to the new structures is a model of care based on a system of primary care centres. From a mental health perspective, primary care is an essential component of a well functioning mental health system. However, to be effective, the primary care system requires sufficient numbers of professionals with the skills and knowledge required to provide a comprehensive range of interventions to people who do not require referral to secondary mental health services. Co-ordination between mental health and primary care will also be a major challenge into the future. There needs to be a real commitment to developing a standardised, collaborative and shared care model of service delivery between primary care and secondary mental health services. This will require the development of services within secondary care so that primary care workers can be assured that when they turn to secondary services for referrals, support and supervision that they will receive the most appropriate, effective and timely service.

The challenges to service demand and the nature of resources required arising from societal level changes in demographics also require priority consideration. Since 2006, the population of the Republic of Ireland has increased by 8.2% and now stands at 4.6 million (CSO 2013). The number of people aged 65 years and over has grown by 14.4% since 2006, with a 37% projected increase by 2020, compared to 19% for the EU (CSO 2013). This presents new challenges in terms of ensuring that people age healthily, maintaining both their physical and mental health. In addition, as the population ages, not only will we see an increase in chronic physical diseases like arthritis and diabetes, but also an increase in diseases of aging such as the dementias. The recent increase in birth rates evident in the 0 to 4 age group (CSO 2013) has implications for planning child and adolescent mental health services. Similarly there are projected increases in other mental health issues among the population. Depression, for example, currently ranks 4th among the 10 leading causes of the global burden of disease; however, it is predicted that by the year 2030 it will be the leading cause of chronic disease (WHO 2008). The economic crisis is also expected to take its toll on the human spirit, producing mental health issues that are predicted to increase suicide- and alcohol-related deaths (WHO 2011). If these figures are even vaguely correct, significantly different roles, practices, services and resources are going to be needed to manage this burden of 'illness' and emotional distress in homes, communities, primary care centres and hospitals.

In addition to demands on services as a result of changing age and distress profiles, as Murphy and Leavey have flagged in Chapter 9, the increasing diversity of Irish population will also require services to embrace different perspectives on mental/emotional distress and develop intercultural competencies. Currently people from over 199 different nations reside in Ireland, with the proportion of 'non-nationals' having doubled from 5.8% of the population in 2006 to 12% of the population in 2011 (Government of Ireland 2012).

FUNDING AND COMMISSIONING OF SERVICES

The mental health services are currently facing significant uncertainty in relation to funding. In the 20th century, the major part of specialist mental health care in Ireland was funded on an ongoing basis by legacy arrangements arising from the old psychiatric hospitals and organised around catchment areas. The current government is planning to move to a commissioning model of funding in which providers will compete to win contracts to provide a set basket of services will fit alongside the plans for Universal Health Insurance (UHI). Universal Health Insurance (UHI) is about creating a single-tiered service in which access to health care is based on need and not the ability to pay. Under the UHI model, everyone will be insured for a standard package of primary care and hospital services, including mental health services. There is no doubt that universal access to GP/primary care services, free at the point of delivery, holds the potential to facilitate earlier access to support and thereby enhance an early intervention agenda. However, what will be included in the standard basket of mental health services provided to service users requires careful thought and consideration. If the only treatment that individuals are offered or receive in the GP/primary care centre is a prescription, this will not reflect the type of holistic, individual response that mental health service users have said they want or need.

With UHI, the principle of 'the money follows the patient' can be put into practice. Currently the principle of 'the money follows the patient' that is being planned in hospital-based medicine and disability services will, in theory, give patients and disability service users more control over their own treatment. Even though this budgeting system is not imminent for mental health services, the process of shifting towards a commissioning model where service providers will tender to provide a set scope and level of service in exchange for funding is on the horizon and is likely to bring with it disruption to the normal flow of resources and integration of service delivery. A commissioning approach brings opportunities: the commissioner (in the form of the lead government agency) can set targets for service inputs, outputs, scope and quality that could provide an important leaver to ensure delivery aligns with the government's policy goals. A commissioning agent that is attentive to service-user and family supporter feedback could ensure more responsive services than are in place currently. However, there is also concern that the neoliberal policies that have opened the doors to outsourcing and a 'creeping privatisation' (Pillinger 2012) will enable private providers to flourish while the public health system deteriorates in a commissioning system. Also there is concern that rather than bringing equality, value for money, quality and universal access, a commercial model will lead to an inequitable and inefficient system of service provision. While such a system may increase the power of users of services as individual consumers, it may reduce their ability to influence the system as citizens. In the context of mental health, there is a growing concern that unless human rights and the recovery ethos underpin the commissioning arrangements, the individual service user who should be at the centre of provision, and the principles outlined in *A Vision for Change* will potentially become sacrificed to economic demands. Given the lack of information about the economics of mental health in Ireland, including basic information about resource allocation (as discussed by Kennelly in Chapter 12), it is difficult to see how managers can effectively plan a commissioning process.

E-HEALTH AND TECHNOLOGIES OF CARE

Another issue that requires consideration is the impact of technology on health and health care delivery. The potential for the Internet to empower service users and family members cannot be underestimated. Increasingly, we will have a more educated and engaged public, as individuals can readily access diverse sources of information online. The speed with which information can be obtained on the Internet, both in preparation for and following on from a clinical encounter, means that the meeting that was once closed between a 'patient' and professional is now wide open; suddenly the conversation becomes a discussion between the individual concerned, their professional, family supporter and every online contact or information source they access. Such easy access is, of course, a double-edged sword. While Internet access can empower individuals to engage with medical expertise, on the other hand people in mental and emotional distress and their family supporters may be ill-equipped to sift through the information, or to distinguish between disinterested and interested sources, and evaluate the evidence presented.

The Internet also holds the potential to provide a powerful competitor to traditional psychiatric services through the provision of synchronised and asynchronised online psychoeducation, therapy and support. As a growing body of evidence supports the effectiveness of this mode of service provision for certain people, and practitioners' concerns about the ethical and legal perils are addressed, there is no doubt that this form of intervention will become part of the menu of service provision. No longer will geographic location, working hours or local availability determine the care and choice provided, as around-the-clock virtual consultation systems become the norm for those who have Internet access (Kraus et al. 2010). While Healy (Chapter 15) has critically analysed the historical developments that gave rise to the current predominance of pharmacological treatments, the Internet also provides those prescribed medication with a means of direct involvement in debates about drug efficacy and a means of reporting adverse drug effects. They no longer must depend on the professional to record and return this data, but can now report adverse drug effects directly to the Irish Medicines Board and to alternative websites such as RxISK.org.

While the Internet and other computer-mediated technologies are increasingly becoming a source of information and therapy for individuals in distress and family members, their use is also changing the social context of people's lives and giving rise to a whole new set of mental health challenges. Technology has exacerbated the problem of bullying or cyber-bullying (bullying via electronic methods) by allowing it to be accomplished easily and anonymously. In addition we are witnessing the emergence of new channels for criminal behaviour such as Internet grooming, easy access to spaces for addictive behaviour in the form of online gaming addictions, sexual addictions, and online gambling, and unregulated arenas encouraging self-harm in the form of websites and Facebook pages that promote eating disorders, suicide, and other self-harming behaviours. In this uncontrolled virtual environment, many people, and particularly the young, will be exposed to hurtful material that may damage their mental health.

The world wide web also reiterates divides already presented within society, as the opportunities it offers for new information and new modes of therapy/ education are not universally accessible. Almost one in five Irish adults have never used the Internet, and these 'non-liners' are likely to be from the very groups most at risk of mental/emotional distress, e.g. the unemployed, elderly or disadvantaged (Department of Communications, Energy and Natural Resources 2013). There is a danger that those most in need of mental health support will be excluded from the information to make informed choices about treatment and from innovative modes of service delivery, while a twin-track system of empowering, digital support for the 'haves' and old-fashioned, face-to-face public mental health services for the 'have nots' emerges.

DEMOCRATISING SERVICE AND DISRUPTING CURRENT POWER RELATIONS

Discussion on power relationships within the mental health system is not new, with numerous writers having described and theorised unequal positions between the different players within the mental health services. While the shape of future power relations around mental health is still unclear, there are a number of factors that are unsettling the traditional order of thinking and action. Brosnan (see Chapter 6) has shown that the service-user/survivor movement in Ireland can be discussed as a health social movement in so far as it seeks not only to influence health service delivery, but to challenge the language of debate. By developing a national peer advocacy service, the movement has already begun the process of disrupting power relations within 'inpatient units', and this disruptive influence will continue to grow into the future. At the level of the individual clinical encounter, while there is some change afoot in term of recovery planning and advance directives, there is little evidence to suggest a widespread move away from the focus on maintenance and symptom reduction towards recovery-orientated prescribing practices, or a move away from a risk-adverse culture to one that embraces the notion of positive risk and the idea that risk is a normal part of autonomous life and a condition of citizenship. Similarly, so far, user involvement in planning, delivering and evaluating services at a local level has been ad hoc and dependent on the good intentions of motivated individual practitioners. Current plans for appointing a service user to every area management team may bring more consistency, and hopefully, if the service-user/survivor movement develops into a powerful, organised and strategic voice in the public sphere, their involvement in services will no longer depend on the good intentions of individuals. However, the service-user/survivor movement is facing into the headwinds of well-established political organisations that speak for psychiatric practitioners and the pharmaceutical industry, and need to resist colonisation in order to maintain independence. They are also going to experience other challenges, such as the force of governance imperatives that lean towards cost-saving, and wider public attitudes that are at best ambivalent towards and at worst prejudiced against those with long-term mental health disabilities. The existence of national, organised voices for reform of the mental health services that involve a range of stakeholders including NGOs, professionals and people with self-experience of mental/emotional distress may help mediate some of these challenges. Amnesty International Ireland was the first to run a national campaign seeking stronger protection of human rights for people using mental health services and this has been followed by the development of the national NGO coalition Mental Health Reform that engages in public and political advocacy on an ongoing basis.

If the position and influence of users of services is uncertain, that of family members is even more so. As McDaid and Higgins highlighted in Chapter 8, from the beginnings of deinstitutionalisation a fear existed that the move into the community would fall heavily on family supporters. The extent to which 'community care' has become 'family care' in Ireland is still unknown due to the lack of an evidence base. What is clear, however, is that family members have been made invisible under Irish mental health law and excluded in practice due to the strictures of professional ethical codes; NGOs such as Mental Health Reform and Shine are beginning to advocate for this to change. Mental Health Reform has recommended changes to the Mental Health Act to impose duties on mental health services both to provide information to family members and to assess family members' support needs (Mental Health Reform 2011). So too, Shine has recently developed a 'family friendly services' initiative that seeks to improve practice around family member involvement in supporting recovery (see http://www.shineonline.ie/index.php/realising-family-friendly-mental-health-services). One way that family members are entering the conversation is through the development of trialogue approaches that involve the three perspectives of service user, professional and family supporter. Although embryonic there is a sense that this idea of a trialogue is beginning to penetrate the system through the initiative of local individuals and the support of senior HSE management. However, achieving a balance between increasing the role of family members while respecting and protecting the individual's human rights will be one of the challenges to be addressed in future law, policy and practice.

The law also has the potential to strengthen the power of those in receipt of treatment. As shown by Keys in Chapter 13, at the level of the law, the implications of the UN Convention on the Rights of Persons with Disabilities are likely to play themselves out over many years to come. One need only think of the length of time between the European Convention on Human Rights (passed in 1948) and the Irish Mental Health Act (passed in 2001) to see that it can take decades to fulfil human rights in the law. Nevertheless, ideas of equality, autonomy, self-determination and independence are currently to the fore in the legal sphere, reflected in the review of the Mental Health Act, 2001 and are likely to be a strong influence in mental health law in the near future.

The pending Assisted Decision-Making legislation and the introduction of advance directives, if applied to acute mental health services, could enable individuals to ensure that their own will and preferences are followed when they are in severe mental or emotional distress, and act as a powerful counter-discourse to the dominant paternalism and risk adverse culture that prevails currently.

Of course, power differentials exist not only between professionals and users of services, but also between professionals themselves. Irish mental health law underpins the unilateral authority of psychiatrists over 'patients' in the context of involuntary detention and treatment. Under current law, only a psychiatrist can determine if a person is to be involuntarily detained, or whether they lack capacity and require treatment. Psychiatrists also currently have ultimate clinical authority over the services, as set out under Section 71 of the Mental Health Act 2001. This legal authority serves to perpetuate the administrative leadership of the profession of psychiatry within mental health services and hinders true multidisciplinary responsibility for service decision-making. There is some prospect that the review of the Mental Health Act 2001 may begin to equalise this authority if it allows other professionals to be involved in decisions about involuntary detention, while the Assisted Decision-Making legislation could also spread responsibility for assessing capacity more widely than is currently the case. So too, the sheer weight of numbers may help to re-balance power relations within mental health teams as more professionals from non-medical disciplines are now being appointed. As Mac Gabhann has highlighted (Chapter 3), the future position of nurses within teams is uncertain – they have traditionally benefited from aligning themselves to psychiatric authority but are increasingly demanding their own, autonomous power to influence service delivery. There is a risk that in the current context of expanding professional disciplines within teams there will be a wave of professional territorial battles, and the voice of individuals in distress and family supporters will be overwhelmed or marginalised.

The pharmaceutical industry also represents a powerful hand in the landscape of the mental health field – strongly influencing what happens on a day-to-day basis, but at a distance and often unseen. However, already the dominance of this industry is being disrupted. The pharmaceutical industry is itself in flux, needing to respond to demands for greater transparency and a more robust regulatory framework while at the same time defending its right to make a profit. Some of the issues that Healy identifies in Chapter 15, such as the inaccessibility of randomised control trial data and its impact on regulatory decision-making, are already, albeit slowly, beginning to be addressed, with some companies voluntarily providing more transparent access to their study results while the European Union is currently considering how to make this the norm. Whether pharmaceutical companies will continue to find psychotropic medication a profitable field is also open to question; with the advent of generic medicines the industry itself could decide to withdraw somewhat from the market.

RECOVERY BEYOND THE HEALTH SERVICES

Importantly, and as flagged even as far back as 1984 in *Planning for the Future* (Department of Health 1984), real deinstitutionalisation widens the net of responsibility for mental health and recovery beyond professionals and secondary mental health services to include the varied institutions, agencies, non-governmental organisations, groups and individuals in the community. The spheres of education, work, housing and leisure all become sites for mental health practice, be it raising mental health literacy, promoting well-being, strengthening resilience, supporting recovery or preventing discrimination. Watts in his chapter highlighted the positive role that peer support plays in people's recovery journeys and the importance of people reconnecting with every day services within the community. Responding to this type of thinking will require practitioners in primary and secondary services to generate new relationships with, and appreciate the value of, peer support and other voluntary services. Ultimately in this new primary-community-based mental health universe, everyone will have a role to play in supporting recovery: family member, peer and friend, teacher, GP, workmate, teammate, employer, etc. The National Disability Strategy has the potential to be a vehicle for action on this front, as it is a cross-departmental strategy for action on social inclusion of people with disabilities including mental health disability (see http://www.justice.ie/en/JELR/Pages/PB13000321).

There is also the issue of how to provide timely, good-quality help to those who cross departmental and directorate boundaries. In Chapter 10, Butler showed that the Irish mental health services currently provide uneven access for those with problematic alcohol use. As he points out, the current policy of trying to separate out services for problematic alcohol use from those for mental distress may be impractical given the frequent overlap between these two situations. Similar challenges remain with regard to those involved in the criminal justice system (see Whelan and Brennan, Chapter 11), though this time the individual is caught between two powerful government departments with very different orientations and remits. Structural boundaries will also be a potential issue for people with other disabilities, older people, and children and adolescents, as older people and people with other disabilities will fall under the directorate on social care, and children and adolescents fall within the remit of the new Child and Family Agency outside the health service. Human beings and human distress does not neatly conform to departmental, directorate or institutional boundaries and there is a persistent risk that the 'shuttling back and forth' of service users between the services that occurs today, with one or the other professional denying an individual help on the basis that they have a diagnosis outside that professional's remit, will continue. Not alone is this frustrating for the individual concerned and financially costly to the person, family and the taxpayer; it has the potential to increase service user and family distress and exacerbate risks to service user safety as individuals fall between the stools of service provision.

RECONCEPTUALISING MENTAL DISTRESS AND CELEBRATING DIVERSITY

Framing all of the factors just discussed, the manner in which mental distress is conceptualised and the ways new information is 'discovered' about it, are likely to have the most profound influence on policy, practice and law into the future. Some claim that the recovery ethos represents a new paradigm for mental health and a challenge to traditional 'biopsychiatric' constructions of mental/emotional distress. Whether recovery represents a paradigm shift depends not only on the extent of its impact, but on the content of its interpretation. In terms of the extent of its impact, the recovery ethos is certainly making itself felt, although slowly, throughout the system, in the configuration of management teams to include a 'service-user representative', in HSE guidance documents, in Mental Health Commission policy and standards that promote the recovery ethos, in curricula for mental health practitioners, in the College of Psychiatry's 'Refocus' user involvement group, and in research practice that increasingly presumes people with personal experience of mental/emotional distress should be involved in planning and leading research.

In terms of the permanence of its impact, it would be tempting to say that recovery has permeated the system to such an extent that there is no going back. However, we believe this is naïve as there are many services and practitioners who are continuing to work within their traditional structures, thinking and methods, while proclaiming to be recovery orientated. There are others who simply re-label rehabilitation services as recovery, as happens when practitioners speak of 'personal recovery plans', when they mean treatment plans designed by practitioners, or when they claim that a 'recovery college' is about teaching 'self-management' within an 'illness' framework, or when practitioners talk about recovery-oriented medication practices, when they are simply negotiating medication dosage within an ethos that does not subscribe to the right to forego medication.

If recovery is to represent a new paradigm for the mental health services in Kuhn's (1962) sense of paradigm, where new ideas are not commensurate with previous thinking, it needs to incorporate a new way of conceptualising mental distress, and this new way of thinking cannot simply be accommodated within traditional explanations and practices. Hence, there is an urgent need to open up discussion and to debate the ontology and epistemology of mental distress. If recovery is to be a transformational ideology that challenges ideas and beliefs about the nature, cause and treatment of 'mental illness', as well as enabling people experiencing mental distress to take ownership of their experience and the meaning of that experience, this type of discussion, is a necessity and not, as some might suggest, an academic luxury of little relevance to the practitioner. Real collaboration, partnership and recovery orientation will only happen when the institution of psychiatry is ready to recognise the damaging effect of current models of care on service users, family supporters, and indeed practitioners. Without this realisation, the true meaning of a recovery approach, 'multiple truths', and the idea of co-producing understandings and solutions, will be marginalised and subverted by practitioners who continue to assert themselves as an authority on the cause and meaning of the person's mental/emotional distress. Furthermore, without this type of debate the recovery ideal can easily be co-opted by tradition and the human rights and social inclusion agenda marginalised.

The idea of diversity goes even further than recovery. The suggestion that individuals should be able to be 'proud' of being mad, as espoused by the Mad Pride movement, challenges even the notion of needing to recover from an unwanted state of distress. Mental health in a diversity framework comes closer to the idea of the social model of disability that locates injustice not in the individual's difference, but in society's reaction to that difference. The 2006 UN Convention on the Rights of Persons with Disabilities (CRPD) recognises the diversity of individuals with disabilities and:

> the valued existing and potential contributions made by persons with disabilities to the overall well-being and diversity of their communities, and that the promotion of the full enjoyment by persons with disabilities of their human rights and fundamental freedoms and of full participation by persons with disabilities will result in their enhanced sense of belonging and in significant advances in the human, social and economic development of society and the eradication of poverty. (CRPD Preamble, para (m))

Respect for diversity will pose a huge challenge for practitioners and services that continue to be geared towards ameliorating symptoms and producing some type of observable improvement in those whom they see as 'objects' of care. In the context of diversity it is appropriate, we think, to conclude with some questions resonating in our minds. Questions for the future include: will and, if so, how will the mental health system acknowledge value and respect each individual's unique mental and emotional experiences? How will each person's explanatory framework be fully respected, acknowledged and supported? Can valuing diversity extend as far as those who hear voices, or those who offer non-traditional explanatory models? How can 'positive risk-taking' that supports recovery take hold in the context of a society that is risk averse?

One idea that has yet to feature prominently in the mental health system is that of 'interdependency', the recognition that we are all potentially vulnerable to mental/emotional distress, all potentially in need of support, and simultaneously, all potentially both the 'wounded' and the 'healer'. In this context, some questions for the future include: how can the mental health system take account of and reflect this interdependency alongside autonomy? How can each person's insights as a 'wounded healer' be incorporated into professional practice?

CONCLUSION

While much has been covered in this volume, there are also many significant issues that have not been addressed. Gender is a topic that was ignored in the 2006 mental health policy *A Vision for Change*, though it undoubtedly impacts on both the experience of mental/emotional distress and appropriate support. Policymakers and service providers need to engage in a process to develop gender-sensitive mental health services. So too, we have not addressed the influence of sexual orientation and the need to address the particular vulnerability of people from the LGBTQ community to mental/emotional distress and to respect their diversity. The overlap between other disabilities and mental health has been little discussed in this volume, though few individuals will go through life without experiencing both. At a wider level, we have not yet considered the issue of trauma in the context of mental/emotional distress and how services need to ensure that they are providing 'trauma-informed' care that recognises experiences of trauma and abuse and responds. These issues are all equally worthy of consideration as those that ended up between the pages of this text and, we hope, will feature in a future edition.

In the meantime, we must consider both the inheritance of the past and the possibilities for the future. Deinstitutionalisation has been the narrative of the latter 20th and early 21st centuries. In Ireland this process was slower than in other English-speaking and western European countries, with the last few psychiatric hospitals still open at the time of writing. Since then much of what passed for progress in mental health service delivery turned out to be re-institutionalisation in the community (see McDaid, Chapter 4), while some who could not make it on the 'outside' ended up in the parallel institution of the prison. The frustration that people have endured and survived with is a heavy burden, a struggle that unfortunately some have not been able carry. This narrative of re-institutionalisation and segregation and the concomitant scourges of prejudice, discrimination and social exclusion will undoubtedly be one of the major challenges in the near future. For the first phase of deinstitutionalisation it was mental health professionals who were the target of transformation, but now and into the future 'mental health' must be everyone's business.

The turn of the 21st century has provided an opportunity to shake off Ireland's asylum legacy. The current generation of young people can grow up without the spectre of the psychiatric hospital in their consciousness. Already we can see in young people's strong interest in promoting positive mental health a more accepting and understanding attitude. With so many changing influences at play, there is reason to expect that discourse and knowledge will be opened up to new language, conceptualisations and perspectives and that the configuration of service delivery will be radically different in the future, while the empowering effects of the internet and the law could equalise control over decision-making. We who have long watched the sluggish move into the community may yet live to see mental health a welcomed guest in Irish society among a people that understands itself to be interconnected, emotional, creative and universally wounded. We can only marvel at the exciting role that the professionals of the future may play in such an Ireland.

REFERENCES

Central Statistics Office (2013) Census Statistics: Population by Age 2011. Dublin: Central Statistics Office

Department of Health (1984) Psychiatric Services – Planning for the Future: Report of a Study Group on the Development of the Psychiatric Services. Dublin: Stationery Office

Department of Health (2013) Healthy Ireland: A framework for improving health and wellbeing 1013-1015. Dublin: Stationery Office

Department of Health and Children (2006) A Vision for Change: Report of the Expert Group on Mental Health Policy. Dublin: Stationery Office

Department of Communications, Energy and Natural Resources (2013) National Digital Strategy available from http://www.dcenr.gov.ie/NR/rdonlyres/54AF1E6E-1A0D-413F-8CEB-2442C03E09BD/0/NationalDigitalStrategyforIreland.pdf

European Commission (2005) Improving the mental health of the population: Towards a strategy on mental health for the European Union. Brussels: Green Paper Health and Consumer Protections Directorate, European Commissions

Government of Ireland (2012) Profile 6; Migration and Diversity. Dublin: Stationery Office

Kraus, R Stricker, G Speyer C (eds.) (2010) Online counselling a handbook for mental health professionals. London: Academic Press Publications

Kuhn T (1962) The Structure of Scientific Revolutions. Chicago: University of Chicago Press

Mental Health Reform (2011) Submission to the Department of Health on the Review of the Mental Health Act, 2001 available from http://mentalhealthreform.ie

Pillinger J (2012) The future of healthcare in Ireland. Position paper on the health crisis and the government's plans for health care. Prepared for IMPACT www.impact.ie accessed 23/11/2013

United Nations (2006) Convention on the rights of Persons with Disabilities and Optional Protocol

World Health Organisation (2005) Mental Health Action Plan for Europe. Facing the challenges, building solutions. Geneva: World Health Organisation

World Health Organisation (2008) The global burden of disease: 2004, update 2008. Geneva: World Health Organisation

World Health Organisation (2011) Impact of the economic crisis on mental health. Geneva: World Health Organisation

Index